MIRANDA J. GREEN

Dictionary of Celtic Myth and Legend

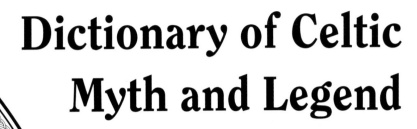

243 illustrations

THAMES AND HUDSON

For Eunice, Stephen and Ann

Frontispiece
The Keltic Mandala, an original design by
Jen Delyth. This is a symbolic illustration
of the Celtic year, with its seasonal cycle,
in the form of a wheel. The mandala
incorporates many motifs found in Celtic
art and mythology, such as the stag, the
bull, birds, the solar wheel, oak leaves and
the Tree of Life.

© 1992 Thames and Hudson Ltd, London

First paperback edition 1997

British Library Cataloguing-in-Publication Data
A catalogue record for this book is available from
the British Library
ISBN 0-500-27975-6

Printed and bound in Singapore

Dictionary of Celtic Myth and Legend

Contents

'Events which can be dated and analysed, and placed at a proper distance from the present, can also at some stage begin to appear far away; can fade. Myths are fresh; they never lose their force.'

V.S. Naipaul

Acknowledgments

I should like to express my gratitude to the following people, who have helped me on this project in many ways: Wynne Lloyd, for teaching me Welsh; Brian Ramsden, for helping to get me computerized; Paul Barrett; Dr Sioned Davies; Frank Delaney; Professor Geraint Gruffydd; Dr Brynley Roberts; Dr Terry Thomas; Dr Graham Webster. Finally, I want to say a special word of thanks to Stephen, whose encouragement acted as my Cauldron of Regeneration!

Reader's Guide

The *Dictionary of Celtic Myth and Legend* is organized alphabetically, each entry being introduced by a 'headword', which consists of the name of a god, mythological character, type of sacred animal, site, object or symbol, natural phenomenon or concept. There is a list of headwords, grouped by subject, in the Subject Index at the beginning of the book. Bibliographical references are placed at the end of each entry; these relate to a full bibliography at the back of the volume. In some instances, an individual entry provides a cross-reference in SMALL CAPITALS to another, closely related one. Cross-references also direct the reader to other entries which provide further information on the subject at hand. Occasionally, in order to avoid repetition, a headword does not precede an entry but instead refers the reader directly to another headword and entry which cover the same subject. An example of this is: 'afterlife *see* OTHERWORLD'.

The *Dictionary* is preceded by an Introduction, which provides a short description of the world of the pagan Celts, a resumé of the nature of the evidence for religion and mythology, and a brief overview of Celtic religion and belief. The geographical scope of the work consists of Ireland, Britain, Gaul, the Rhineland, Iberia, North Italy, Yugoslavia, Central and Eastern Europe. Thus the whole area of maximum Celtic expansion during the last few centuries BC is embraced. The exception is Galatia (part of modern Turkey) about whose religion and mythology virtually nothing is known. The chronological scope is essentially the pagan Celtic period, circa 700 BC – AD 400, with due acknowledgment of the fact that the vernacular literature is late in its existing form (*see* Introduction). In terms of thematic content, the *Dictionary* embraces all aspects of pagan Celtic, pre-Christian religion and myth which are evidenced by archaeology and literature. Categories of subject-matter include divinities and heroes (like Taranis and Cú Chulainn), the supernatural forces perceived in natural phenomena (such as thunder and fire) or natural features of the landscape (for example, trees, mountains and springs), ritual (such as sacrifice, divination and head-hunting), abstract concepts (like healing, the sanctity of number and what happens after death), and sacred places (including built shrines, groves and sacred wells).

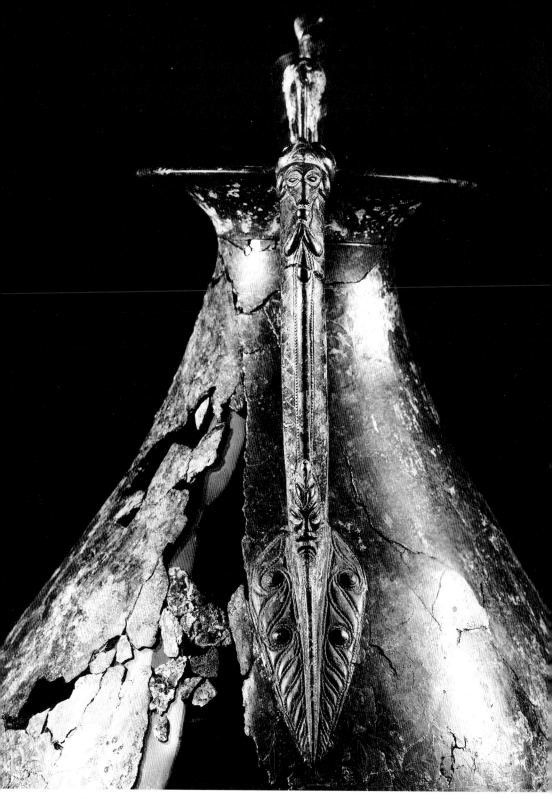

Detail of a gilded bronze wine flagon, showing the handle decorated with floreate La Tène designs and a human head. On the lid of the vessel is a human-headed horse. From a mid-4th c. BC princess' grave at Reinheim, Germany.

Introduction

Who were the Celts?

What do we mean by the term 'the Celts'? The problem is that 'Celts' and 'Celtic' are widely used terms which can mean different things to different people. The Celts who are the subject of this book are the ancient peoples of pagan Celtic Europe, from about 700 BC to AD 400. So in the present context, the words 'Celt' and 'Celtic' are used to describe and identify the huge group of pre-Christian communities living in much of Europe north of the Alps. At the time of their maximum geographical expansion (4th to 3rd c. BC), the Celts occupied a vast area which stretched from Ireland and Spain in the west to Eastern Europe. These pagan Celtic communities are identified by the evidence of Classical literature, linguistics and archaeology. The scope of the *Dictionary* does not embrace the broader sense of the term 'Celtic'. Thus, such subjects as the Celtic saints, illuminated manuscripts and Arthurian Romance are not included. Modern Celtic culture, as found in present-day Wales, Scotland and Ireland, is likewise outside the scope of this book.

There are many difficulties to be faced in endeavouring to define the ancient Celts. These are mostly concerned with the different kinds of evidence which are employed to identify these people. We first hear of Celtic people in the writings of such Greek historians as Hecataeus of Miletus, who alluded to *Keltoi* in about 500 BC, and Herodotus, who mentioned the Celts in his *Histories* (for example II, 35; IV, 48). We have to ask the question of what those Greek and Roman authors who described the Celts actually meant when they used the term. We need also to pose the question of whether the Celts recognized themselves as such. Since pagan Celts did not write about themselves, we have no means of knowing if they thought of themselves as 'Celtic'. Was there, then, a Celtic ethnic consciousness in antiquity? For the Classical authors, the term 'Celtic' referred to a broad geographical description. In some manner or other, there must have been sufficient unity, in material culture and perhaps also in language, in the great group of peoples living in much of non-Mediterranean Europe, for them to be identified as a homogeneous entity, with a common name, by their Classical neighbours. Whilst there was considerable diversification within this group of communities, there must equally have been broad cultural and/or linguistic features which were shared. It is interesting that these Mediterranean chroniclers of the Celts made no allusion to Britain or Ireland as being inhabited by Celts. We have also to remember that the Classical literary references to the Celts are relatively scanty for the 'free Celtic' period, that is, until the Roman occupation of these areas.

Apart from their identification by Classical commentators, there exist two other means of defining the ancient Celts. One is archaeological, the study of the material culture (the tangible, physical remains of man's past) of the peoples of 'barbarian' Europe during the later 1st millennium BC. The other method of definition is based on linguistics. In seeking the origins of the ancient Celts, both archaeological and linguistic evidence need to be considered.

The early linguistic evidence for the Celts consists of inscriptions, coin legends and the names given to people and places in the Classical literary sources. All these sources date from the last few centuries BC and, together, they demonstrate that by the time of the Roman occupation at the end of the 1st millennium BC Celtic languages were spoken in Britain, Gaul, North Italy, Spain, Central and Eastern Europe (Renfrew 1987, 211–50; Mallory 1989, 95–107). For Wales and Ireland, the linguistic evidence is later. The earliest major source for Ireland occurs in Ptolemy's *Geography*, dating from the 2nd c. AD. Celtic inscriptions in Ireland are no earlier than the 4th c. AD and are in the linear script known as ogham. The first inscription in Welsh appears on the early Christian monument known as St Cadfan's stone from Towyn, Merionethshire, which dates from the 7th–9th c. AD (Nash-Williams 1950, 26, no. 287), though Goidelic written in ogham occurs on several of the earlier 5th–7th c. AD monuments in Wales (Nash-Williams 1950, 2–4). Written Irish (as opposed to inscriptions) appears in glosses applied to Latin manuscripts of the 8th–9th c. AD, but the first manuscripts written entirely in Irish date no earlier than the 12th c. AD. Written Welsh appears first in notes and glosses of Latin texts in the 8th c. AD (Roberts 1988, 61–87).

The foregoing survey of Celtic language demonstrates that, whilst some data refer to the last few centuries BC, most of the evidence is rather later. But we have already seen that Classical writers refer to the 'Celts' from about 500 BC. It is the archaeological evidence which appears to corroborate these literary references to an identifiable series of culturally related communities living north of the Alps by the second half of the 1st millennium BC, the so-called 'La Tène' period (see below). However, the material culture of much of non-Mediterranean Europe indicates that the origins of the European Celts may be sought somewhat earlier than the 5th c. BC.

A study of the archaeological remains of later Continental prehistory suggests that the historical Celts (those known from written sources) had their roots within the later Bronze Age cultures of non-Mediterranean Europe. Indeed, the Celts were the lineal descendants of generations who can be traced as far back as the first Neolithic farmers, c. 4000 BC (Burgess 1974, 196–7; 1980, 277–8). In archaeological terms, the Celts did not suddenly appear in Europe, but rather became 'Celtic' by accretion, through process of time. No one culture should be sought as the immediate source of Celtic beginnings. Celticization was a gradual process, which must have been long-established by the time that Classical writers began to mention Celts.

The later Bronze Age of the mid-late 2nd millennium BC in Central Europe saw the appearance of a new material culture which archaeologists call the 'Urnfield tradition'. This name is due to a distinct burial rite, observable in the archaeological record, consisting of cremation in pots in flat cemeteries. Technologically, the Urnfield tradition is characterized by the new ability of smiths to manipulate bronze into thin sheets for the manufacture of such commodities as large vessels, body armour and shields. This Urnfield tradition occurred widely in regions occupied by later Celts, and it is possible that they may be regarded as proto-Celts (Coles & Harding 1979, 367; Harding 1974, 86; Cunliffe 1979, 15). Moreover, certain motifs decorating Urnfield bronzework, particularly the sun-wheel and bird-ship, recur in the iconography of the subsequent 'Hallstatt' culture.

By the 8th c. BC new cultural elements, recognizable archaeologically, began to appear in Central Europe. At about this time, the horse was adopted on a large

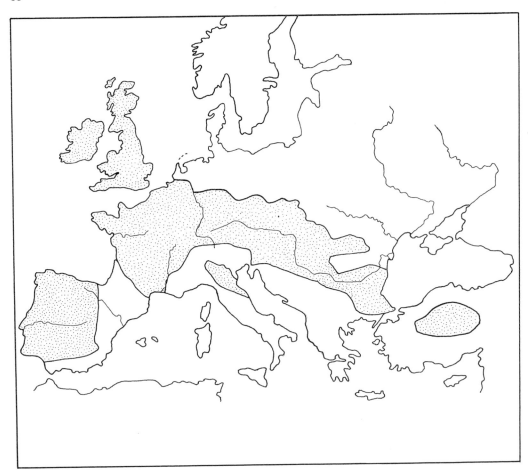

Map of the Celtic world. The stippled areas indicate the geographical spread of the Celtic peoples at the period of maximum expansion, in the 4th–3rd c. BC.

scale as a riding animal (rather than merely for traction), and new metal types related to harness and horse gear indicate the existence of equestrian warriors, precursors of the Celtic knights. Long swords were used for cavalry fighting. This new material culture is called 'Hallstatt' after the type-site, a great cemetery in the 'Salzkammergut' (salt route) of the Hallein region in Austria. By 700 BC ironworking was widespread in non-Mediterranean Europe; and the metal was used in Britain and Ireland from about 600 BC (Champion et al. 1984, 270–3; Megaw 1970, 13). The Hallstatt tradition is distinctive through its wealth and its trading links with the Classical world. It was characterized by rich inhumation-burials, like those at Vix in Burgundy and Hochdorf in Germany (Megaw & Megaw 1989, 25–49), the dead often being interred on four-wheeled wagons within a wooden mortuary house, beneath a great earthen mound. These burials introduce us to an élite class of men and women, princes and princesses, who imported luxury goods, especially drinking equipment, from the Mediterranean world and, perhaps, traded salt to that world in return. These Hallstatt communities had princely strongholds, such as Mont Lassois near the site of the Vix burial, which imported Attic pottery in the 6th c. BC. Another such fortified palace was the Heuneberg, near the tomb of Höhmichele in Germany, whose fortifications were constructed by a man familiar with Greek building techniques. Most scholars are agreed that these Hallstatt peoples were the first Celts (Cunliffe 1979, 36; Mallory 1989, 95–107; Green 1991c).

By the early 5th c. BC, the centres of power had shifted north and west to the Rhineland and the Marne, possibly because of the reorientation of trade routes, at a time when Etruria was becoming more powerful and began to trade directly with the Celts. The new material culture which is recognized archaeologically is called 'La Tène' after the metalwork types found at the lake-edge settlement of La Tène on Lake Neuchâtel in Switzerland. Warrior accoutrements are plentiful; vehicle-burial continued to occur, but the heavy four-wheeled wagon was replaced by a light, two-wheeled cart or chariot. The La Tène period is characterized by fine art, essentially an aristocratic art, used particularly for metalwork decoration. Celtic artists were influenced by previous Hallstatt traditions, and they borrowed and adapted themes from the Classical and Oriental worlds (Megaw & Megaw 1986). This art consisted mainly of abstract designs, but incorporated as integral parts of those designs were such motifs from the natural world as animals, foliage and human faces, all of which were subjected to a unique Celtic stylization of flowing forms and interwoven images. Much of this art was symbolic and perhaps religious.

The La Tène period marks the full flowering of the Celtic civilization. It is now possible to recognize the heroic, war-oriented, feasting, hierarchical Celtic society of which Classical writers speak and which many of the early vernacular sources (see below) describe.

Before looking in a little more detail at Celtic society, we should briefly summarize the later history of the 'free' Celts. The 5th–3rd centuries BC saw a great series of rapid migrations from the Celtic homelands north of the Alps. Land pressures and an expansionist outlook took the Celts south into the Po Valley of North Italy, west through Gaul and Iberia, east along the Danube into Hungary, Greece, Turkey and across the North Sea into Yorkshire. By 400 BC the Celts were in Italy, and in 390 or 387 they sacked Rome. In 279 a group of Celts entered Greece and plundered the sanctuary of Delphi; in 278 a splinter group established itself in Asia Minor (Galatia). South-east Britain had long been in contact with the Continental Gauls, and here 'Celticization' was probably the result of continued cross-channel trade, gift exchange and perhaps limited travel. But in the 4th c. BC some Marnian Celts appear to have established themselves in East Yorkshire, bringing with them their distinctive burial rite of inhumation with a two-wheeled chariot or cart (Stead 1979). Certainly by the 4th c. BC the Celts were looked upon by their Mediterranean neighbours as one of the four great peripheral nations of the known world (Duval 1977, 7–45; Cunliffe 1979; Green 1984a, 12–14). But the later 3rd c. BC saw a reversal of Celtic fortunes: in 225 the Celts were heavily defeated by the Romans in Italy at the Battle of Telamon. In 191 the North Italian Celts were subdued, and the Romans took over Gallia Cisalpina (Gaul on the Italian side of the Alps). The Galatians of Asia Minor were defeated by the Pergamene kings. From the 2nd c. BC the Celts were under severe pressure from the Germans across the Rhine. In the later 2nd c. the Romans conquered southern Gaul and turned it into The Province (modern Provence). In the mid 1st c. BC the Romans turned their attention to the heartlands of Gaul which was finally subjugated by Julius Caesar in 50 BC. Under the emperors Augustus and Tiberius, the remainder of Celtic Europe was subdued. Claudius initiated the conquest of Britain in AD 43; by 84, the armies of the Roman governor Agricola reached northern Scotland, marking the end of most of the 'free' Celtic world. Only Ireland remained virtually untouched by the presence of Rome. Nevertheless, in such Celtic lands as Britain and Gaul, the indigenous culture was not submerged, but rather flourished within a new, hybrid milieu, that of the Romano-Celtic world.

Celtic Society and Life-style

Archaeology and the literary sources paint a picture of a powerful, warlike, élitist people. From the later Bronze Age the presence of hillforts in Europe indicates aggression and tension between communities. Weapons abound in the archaeological record, and Classical writers speak of the Celts as formidable adversaries in war. In Britain and Gaul, hillfort construction and refurbishment continued until the end of the first millennium BC. Sometimes these hillforts, like Bibracte in Gaul, were very large, bigger than later towns; and they were frequently sites of permanent occupation. The hillfort of Danebury in Hampshire has all the signs of dense settlement, with numerous houses. In addition to hillforts, in the later free Celtic period there were large, sprawling, plains 'towns', like Manching in Bavaria. Centres like these suggest a more stable society and a kind of 'city living' which was probably influenced by Mediterranean civilization. These early Celtic towns not only had permanent houses but also an organized trading system based on a money economy.

Celtic society possessed a deeply stratified socio-political system, based on a rigid hierarchy. At the top were kings, who were gradually replaced by magistrates and a ruling oligarchy closer to the governmental system of Rome. Immediately beneath were the warrior-aristocracy, the knights, the cream of the army. Relatively close to the top were the craftsmen and the religious leaders, whom Caesar called 'druids'. There were poets and storytellers too, the bards. The free landowners made up the bulk of the true Celtic citizenry; below them were the landless men who had no rights and were virtual serfs. Extended families made up the 'tuath' or tribe. Groups of people were tied by oaths of allegiance, which were crucial in relationships. Clientdom and vassalage played important roles in society, and the custom of fostering between noble families bound communities tightly together. An important feature of Celtic society was that, economically, it was capable of supporting non-food-producers: the knights, priests and craftsmen (Cunliffe 1983; Jackson 1964; Ross 1986).

The use of iron enabled the Celts to clear areas of dense woodland, to dominate and farm large tracts of land. The basic unit of rural settlement was the single farm or small hamlet. Houses were generally circular, large enough for an extended family. A typical smallholding would consist of one or more houses, with farm buildings, granaries, storage pits and stock enclosures. The local raw material would be used for building: stone in highland areas; timber, thatch and wicker in the lowlands (Green 1991c; Reynolds 1979).

Classical writers tell us something of the Celts' appearance (Ross 1986, 31–9). Some Graeco-Roman commentators describe the Gauls as tall and fair, with loud voices and piercing eyes (for example Diodorus Siculus V, 28, 31; Ammianus

Marcellinus XV, 12.1). Tacitus (*Agricola* 11) distinguishes several different Celtic types in Britain: the Scots or Caledonii had reddish hair and large, loose limbs; the Silurians of South Wales were, by contrast, swarthy with dark curly hair. Diodorus (V, 32) comments that Gaulish women were nearly as big and strong as their husbands. Dio Cassius describes the Icenian queen Boudica as being large and frightening with bright red hair (LXII, 2, 1–4). The vernacular sources of Ireland and Wales allude to the ideal of Celtic beauty as having a fair skin and (usually) fair hair: Queen Medb had yellow hair, but Cú Chulainn and Naoise had dark locks. The Celts were careful of their appearance; according to some contemporary observers, men thought it shameful to be overweight. They were also noteworthy for their cleanliness and fastidiousness. Certainly the Celtic bog-body, Lindow Man, was found to have a neatly trimmed moustache and well manicured finger-nails. Everyday dress consisted of trousers for men and heavy cloaks; but some Celts fought naked. Women wore long tunics and cloaks. These outdoor garments were sometimes multicoloured or plaid. Evidence for appearance and clothing comes not only from literary sources but also from archaeological evidence, especially from iconography. Strabo (IV, 4, 5) speaks of a love of jewellery, and this is amply borne out by archaeology. Men and women wore heavy gold necklets or torcs, armlets and brooches. We know also that some Celts painted their bodies, as recent investigations of Lindow Man demonstrate.

The Nature of the Evidence

The available data relating to Celtic society, religion and mythology falls into three main groups: archaeology; the remarks of contemporary Classical commentators on the pagan Celts; and the vernacular literature of dark-age and early medieval Wales and Ireland. All types of evidence are, to an extent, indirect; the pagan Celts did not write about themselves, so it falls to modern scholars to sift and interpret this evidence which is so far removed from today's world, both chronologically and culturally.

To a degree, the three categories of evidence have to be treated separately. The vernacular literature relates specifically to Wales and Ireland. The Classical writers comment mainly on Gaul. Most of the archaeological evidence for Celtic religion belongs to the period of Romano-Celtic influence on Celtic lands. It is therefore most useful for Britain (not Ireland) and Continental Europe. But distinct though these three groups of evidence may be, there are some religious themes which are shared; water ritual is attested in all three types of source; so is head-hunting; so is Otherworld feasting and the champion's joint of pork. The religious significance of cauldrons and the sanctity of 'three' are present in both the archaeology and the vernacular literature; and there are many other features common to more than one category of evidence.

Archaeology

Archaeological evidence has to be regarded as, in some sense, indirect, since it depends both upon accidents of survival and upon interpretation by modern people, far removed from the culture which the evidence reflects. This data will necessarily

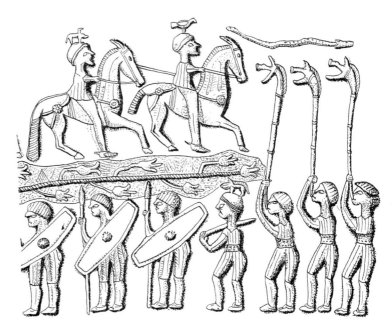

Scene on one of the plates of the Gundestrup Cauldron (see pages 108–10). The plate shows Celtic soldiers, wearing breeches and animal-crested helmets, carrying spears, La Tène shields and carnyxes (boar-headed trumpets). Above the footsoldiers is a sacred tree, and in front of the horsemen is the typically Celtic image of the ram-horned snake.

present ambiguities, and misunderstandings will inevitably occur. Any attempt at explaining such thought processes as religion by archaeological means will be particularly speculative, a construction rather than a reconstruction.

Archaeology embraces material remains of the Celtic religious past, such as built sanctuaries and other sacred places; burials; traces of ritual activity, like deliberate breakage, abnormal deposits of material and sacrifice of humans or animals; epigraphy (inscriptions relating to gods or beliefs); iconography – images of divine beings or symbols; liturgical and priestly regalia; and miscellaneous religious objects, such as amulets, curse tablets and votive offerings.

The relevant archaeological material, to which reference is made in the *Dictionary*, dates from the time that Celts or proto-Celts may first be recognized in terms of their material culture (about the 8th c. BC) until the demise of Celtic paganism, which is roughly synchronous with the end of the Roman occupation in Celtic lands (around AD 400).

Before the Romano-Celtic period, the time when Roman and indigenous traditions blended to produce a new hybrid culture, the evidence for belief in the supernatural powers has largely to be inferred indirectly. It was not until the period of Roman influence that the wide range of divine images appeared, and the tradition of dedicatory inscriptions, alluding to the gods by name, was introduced. In the pre-Roman, 'free' Celtic phase, then, the archaeological evidence for cult activity and religious beliefs is elusive. Built shrines were relatively few; Celtic art depended more on abstract designs than on anthropomorphic forms *per se*. But there are two geographical pockets where a sculptural tradition existed before the Roman phase: these are Provence and Central Europe. Here, as at Roquepertuse and Holzerlingen, Celtic gods were represented in human form from as early as the 6th–5th c. BC. Bronze images of animals, particularly boars, were made all over Celtic Europe during this pre-Roman phase; and the Gundestrup Cauldron may date as early as the 2nd c. BC. The relatively few wooden images which survive from this time in waterlogged conditions indicate that a vast amount of perishable iconography must once have existed. Indeed, the Roman poet Lucan mentions such wooden images (*Pharsalia* III, 412–17).

It is during the Romano-Celtic period that the great range of representations of the gods was produced, stimulated by Classical traditions of anthropomorphic depiction of the divine powers. But this wealth of evidence must imply a complicated set of belief systems pre-dating Roman influence, since much of the iconography is alien to Mediterranean cult imagery and must owe its genesis to indigenous, though previously largely silent, religious traditions. Paradoxically, the Celtic world needed the stimulus of Roman ideas for its own beliefs and cults to be fully expressed in iconographical form. In the same way, epigraphy was only introduced to Celtic lands on any scale during the Roman period, but the huge array of native god-names mentioned in dedicatory inscriptions must have had their origins in a free Celtic religious system.

Evidence for ritual and for places of worship occurs in the pre-Roman phase: cult activity manifests itself by behaviour which has no practical function, such as the deposition of valuable metalwork in water or the deliberate smashing or bending of votive objects before deposition. There is some evidence for human sacrifice, exemplified by Lindow Man, and the abnormal deposition of human bodies during the Iron Age, at such sites as Danebury. Head-hunting is indicated by, for example, the sacred Provençal sites of Roquepertuse and Entremont, where the skulls of young men were placed in niches within Celtic sanctuaries. The great majority of sacred structures or temples belongs to the Romano-Celtic phase, when special architectural styles were adopted for shrines. In the pre-Roman period, most religious buildings resembled secular dwellings and are only distinguishable as sacred either because they are overlain by known temples of Roman date or because they are associated with unequivocally ritual practices. Frilford is an example of the former occurrence: here two Roman temples were built on top of two Iron Age structures. At Hayling Island, a late pre-Roman shrine was associated with elaborate ritual which included deposits of martial equipment and the sacrifice of specific animal species. Apart from shrines, evidence for religious places includes ritual pits, where idiosyncratic depositions took place, and sacred lakes, like Llyn Cerrig Bach, whose cult character is demonstrated by the large numbers of prestigious objects cast into the water in the late Iron Age.

The Classical Writers on Celtic Religion

Many Greek and Roman authors chronicled the customs and religion of the Celts. These comments possess the value of contemporaneity, but they pose their own problems. Firstly, the observations of these writers are their perceptions about an alien people, whose traditions and thought processes were by no means fully understood by their more 'civilized' neighbours. Secondly, it is clear that these Mediterranean authors exercised considerable selectivity in the choice of things they thought worth recording. The druids were sensationalized by Julius Caesar for politico-propaganda purposes. Odd and cruel rituals, such as human sacrifice, were singled out for particular attention. But there is little information on the gods themselves, and where it does occur, the Romans tended to equate and confuse Celtic divine beings with their own deities. Celtic religious thought processes were

Chased gold bowl dating from the 6th c. BC, decorated with repoussé dots and with symbols of deer, sun and moon, from Altstetten, Zürich, Switzerland.

Detail of the 2nd c. BC bronze shield, decorated with red enamel or glass inlay, from the River Witham, Lincolnshire.

Carved granite pillar, decorated with La Tène designs, dating from the 1st c. BC or 1st c. AD, from Turoe, County Galway, Ireland.

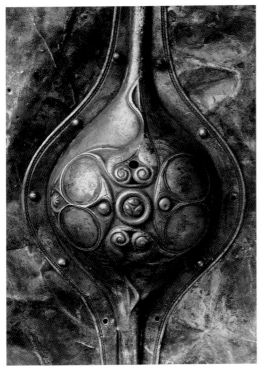

interpreted according to the parameters of the Classical world, and Celtic ritual activity was seen very much in terms of Roman concepts of the correct and contractual propitiation of the gods.

The Greek Stoic philosopher Posidonius lived and wrote during the 1st c. BC. His writings are lost, but he is the main source for many later Graeco-Roman observers on the Celts (Tierney 1959–60, 189–275). The authors whose works are of most use are Julius Caesar (writing in the mid 1st c. BC), especially *De Bello Gallico*, Book VI; Strabo (*c.* 40 BC–AD 25); Diodorus Siculus (writing between 60 and 30 BC); Dio Cassius (*c.* AD 155–230); and Lucan (1st c. AD). Between them, these writers present a considerable body of information on human sacrifice, beliefs in the afterlife and other aspects of Celtic religious activity, but no picture emerges of a pantheon or of a structure of belief. One of the interesting features of the evidence of the Mediterranean commentators is that sometimes there is a recognizable relationship between their observations and other sources. For instance, the emphasis on the divinatory powers of the druids is chronicled by both Graeco-Roman and vernacular literature. The religious cults associated with water and head-hunting which are recorded by Classical writers likewise manifest themselves in both the Irish and Welsh documents and in the archaeological record.

The Evidence of Irish and Welsh Literature

Ireland

The Irish oral tradition began first to be preserved in written form in the 6th c. AD. However, only a few fragments of manuscript survive from a time earlier than 1100. Most of the earliest extant manuscripts were compiled during the 12th c. by Christian monks. Although much of the material culture described in these sources probably refers to a period no earlier than the 7th c. AD, none the less, the basically pagan, pre-Christian character of the mythology presented in this literature cannot be disputed.

There are three groups or cycles of prose tales which contain persistent references to the world of the supernatural (Mac Cana 1983, 14–16, 54, 94, 104). One is the so-called 'Mythological Cycle', which includes the *Book of Invasions* (the *Leabhar Gabhála*) and the *History of Places* (the *Dinnshenchas*). The *Book of Invasions* was compiled in the 12th c., but its origins lie in the earlier compilations of monastic scholars who, in the late 6th–7th centuries AD, began to make a 'history' of the people of Ireland. The book describes the various mythological invasions of Ireland from before the Flood. The story was constructed in order to set the scene for the coming of the Gaels or Celts to Ireland. The book records the activities of the divine race, the Tuatha Dé Danann, who inhabited the island before being driven to create an Underworld kingdom by the Sons of Mil (the Milesians or Gaels). The *Dinnshenchas* also belongs to the 12th c.; it contains a collection of topographical lore and the names of places, which are often explained in mythological terms. The second relevant cycle of stories is known as the 'Fionn Cycle', the tales of which were given little recognition until the 12th c. The cycle tells the story of the hero Finn and his human and superhuman associates. The Fionn Cycle is closely associated with the natural world, but includes many references to the supernatural. Third is the 'Ulster Cycle', of which the most prominent group of tales is the *Táin Bó Cuailnge* (the *Cattle Raid of Cooley*). It is this group which contains the stories about the great conflict between Ulster and Connacht, King Conchobar and Queen Medb; the Ulster hero Cú Chulainn; Conchobar's druid Cathbadh; Conall Cernach; Ferghus; Deirdre; Naoise; and many other supernatural beings. Ancient Ireland was made up of five provinces, and in the pre-Christian period, there was great rivalry between the two most northerly ones, Ulster and Connacht (Lehmann 1989, 1–10). The struggles were chronicled in a cycle of tales which belongs to Ulster alone; there is no record associated with Connacht itself. Part of the earliest known form of the *Táin* is contained in a flawed and mutilated text in the oldest manuscript, called the *Book of the Dun Cow* or the *Leabhar na hUidre*, which was compiled in the monastery of Clonmacnoise in the 12th c. But the origins of the *Táin* are much earlier; the language of the earliest form of the story belongs to the 8th c., but some passages may be earlier still (Kinsella 1969).

There exists a great deal of controversy as to the value of the early Irish sources in a construction of pagan Celtic mythology. The tales were written down within a Christian milieu, the redactors or compilers being monks. The language used frequently suggests that the stories were produced no earlier than the 8th c. Some of the material is also strongly suggestive of medieval rather than prehistoric Ireland. None the less, there is irrefutable evidence that some of the manuscripts contain records of a society that is arguably pre-Christian. Archaism is particularly apparent in the Ulster Cycle, in that it describes an Ulster whose political status reflects a situation earlier than the 5th c. AD when it underwent a radical change. In the Ulster Cycle, the province is dominant, but in the 5th c., the greatness of Ulster was destroyed by the family of King Niall (who himself died in about AD 404) (Jackson 1964). There are other factors which are indicative of archaism. Although the stories were written down by Christian redactors, God is not worshipped. Instead, we are presented with a world whose perception of the supernatural was pre-Christian. So it is quite possible that the world described is that of the pagan Irish Iron Age. Certainly, the heroic society of the Ulster Cycle strongly reflects that chronicled for the Celts by their Classical commentators. In any case, it is clear that, whatever the date the cycles of tales were compiled, they contain large amounts of non-Christian material, which came down to the redactors from the oral traditions. Indeed, it is even occasionally possible to link the deities of the Mythological Cycle with Romano-Celtic gods: Nuadu–Nodens is one example; Lugh–Lug is another.

Notwithstanding the strong indications of early paganism reflected in the Insular tradition, its undoubted value for the study of the pre-Christian Celtic world has to be viewed in the light of constraining factors. In terms of religion, we have to ask the nature of the status enjoyed by these supernatural beings and how they relate to the pagan Celtic religion, of which we know from the genuinely contemporary material provided by archaeology and the Classical written sources. The Irish texts certainly contain the personalities of Celtic deities, but the forms of worship and the beliefs associated with them are not recorded. The divinities encountered in, for instance, the Mythological Cycle, are rarely directly identifiable with the gods we know from Gaul and Britain in the first few centuries AD. The problem here could be that of Christian 'laundering' of pagan oral tradition. The redactors may have been ignorant of or hostile to Irish paganism and may thus have deliberately redefined the world of the supernatural, to make it less potent. Thus, the superhuman heroes rather than proper gods who inhabit Ulster and Connacht may owe their existence, at least in part, to a deliberate dilution of paganism on the part of the Christian chroniclers. The other caveat on the general value of the Insular material is that it pertains specifically to Ireland: the sources are spatially far removed from much of the mainstream pagan Celtic world. Like the Welsh tradition, considered below, written Irish mythology relates only to what was, in the pagan period, the western periphery of a huge geographical area stretching as far east as Czechoslovakia and as far south as Italy.

Wales

Whilst there was undoubtedly a rich mythological tradition in early Wales, it is poorly documented and there is little in the written sources which is demonstrably very early. The mythology is present, but it has largely been reshaped within a different context, so that it is often barely recognizable. The material which is most relevant consists of the *Four Branches of the Mabinogi* and the *Tale of Culhwch and Olwen*, together with related poems such as the *Spoils of Annwn*. The *Four Branches* consist of four separate but related stories: the tales of Pwyll, Rhiannon and Pryderi, and Pwyll's sojourn in Annwn; Branwen and Bendigeidfran, children of Llŷr, and the battle between Britain and Ireland; Manawydan and the journey of himself, Pryderi and Rhiannon into England; and Math, Lord of Gwynedd, which includes the story of Gwydion, Arianrhod and Lleu Llaw Gyffes. The *Tale of Culhwch and Olwen* is a quest story, in which Culhwch has to perform a series of impossible tasks, set by Olwen's father, the giant Ysbaddaden, before he can marry his love.

The Bard, an oil painting by Thomas Jones, 1774, illustrating Thomas Gray's powerful romantic poem of the same title, written in 1758. As Edward I's conquering army approaches, the Welsh bard curses the marauding English before flinging himself from the mountain-top to the raging torrent below.

The *Four Branches of the Mabinogi* were probably first compiled in the 11th c. from material which may be a few centuries older. The *Mabinogi* is preserved in two Welsh collections: the *White Book of Rhydderch*, written in about 1300, and the *Red Book of Hergest*, which dates from the late 14th c. (Mac Cana 1983, 14–16; Jones & Jones 1976, ix–xli). The *Tale of Culhwch and Olwen* is earlier, perhaps 10th c. in its original form. But much of the subject-matter of both the *Mabinogi* and the *Tale of Culhwch and Olwen* may allude to traditions going back many centuries before their compilation. The tales chronicle the activities of euhemerized supernatural beings, whose divinity is not overt but is betrayed by their physical and moral stature. We are introduced here to magic animals, shape-shifting, heads with divine powers, cauldrons which can resurrect the dead and the pagan underworld, called Annwn. Some of the heroes and heroines of this Welsh tradition can be directly related to known Celtic divinities: thus Rhiannon may be Rigantona ('Great Queen') or Epona; Mabon is surely Maponus; Modron is the Great Mother-goddess.

It is undoubtedly true that, whilst there are strong links with Celtic religion, these Welsh tales have undergone more contamination than the early Insular material. It is possible to see that international story-motifs have been interleaved with the early tradition (Mac Cana 1983, 72). There is also a clear link between the Welsh evidence and the great Continental cycle of Arthurian Romance. Arthur himself appears as a superhuman hero, who braves the underworld and tries to acquire the magic cauldron of renewal. Within Welsh tradition, it is often possible to distinguish material which can definitely be associated with pagan traits observable in archaeology or other sources, but the inclusions which are clearly alien to the pagan Celtic tradition must be left out of account.

The Nature of Celtic Religion and Mythology

What is Mythology?

The term 'mythology' embraces a complex set of ideas and perceptions. A myth is a symbolic story, the method by which human imagination expresses something whose meaning is too profound for it to be conveyed in simple words (Roberts 1982, 5–9). So myths can be regarded almost as parables. Mythology is a sacred tradition which tells us who we are and why we are. Mythology embraces the whole range of stories, sacred beings and theologies which make up the religious backdrop of belief systems. Myths have many functions and concerns: of these the most important is to answer difficult and imponderable questions, where explanations cannot be rationalized in terms of human experience. Such questions may relate to the creation of the world, life, death, the afterlife, the seasons and the behaviour of natural phenomena, like the sun or thunder. These issues can thus be explained by means of the construction of a mythology; the personification of natural forces and their endowment with names often forms the foundation for polytheistic belief systems. In this way, the gods or supernatural entities themselves and the priests, who act as mediators between them and the commonality of humankind, are invested with considerable power. The other, related, function of mythology is to account for traditions existing within a given society and for habitual or extraordinary ritual practices, such as repeated festivals, or sacrifice.

Celtic Mythology and Celtic Religion

The belief systems of the pagan Celts are constructed by modern scholars using both written and archaeological sources. Celtic mythology and religion consist of anything pertaining to the Celtic perception of the supernatural. The different kinds of evidence paint a picture of a religious tradition which was especially rich, complex and diverse, bearing out Caesar's comment (VI, 16) that the Celts were a very religious people. This variety and complexity is due largely to the essential animism upon which Celtic religion was based. Everything in the natural world was numinous, containing its own spirit. Thus each tree, spring, stream, mountain and rock possessed its own divine force, and the gods were everywhere.

The nature-based character of Celtic religion pervades the whole spectrum of belief and worship. The pan-tribal divinities, such as the Sun-god and the Mother-goddesses, were venerated for their respective qualities as promoters of heat, light and fertility. Many deities were semi-zoomorphic, like Cernunnos and the horned gods, or demonstrate a close affinity with animals, like Epona or Nehalennia. At the lowest level, the topographical nature of some divine spirits is shown by the occurrence of a god whose name ties him to a particular sacred place: thus Nemausus is the name both of Nîmes and its spring-god; the city of Glanum was presided over by the water-deity Glanis. Of the more than 400 Celtic god-names known from inscriptions, 300 are recorded only once. Places of worship were often not built shrines but *loci consecrati*, or natural sacred places.

The prime concern of the druids, arguably the main Celtic priesthood, was to constrain and control what were perceived as the supernatural powers existing in the natural world, by means of propitiation and magic. This was perceived as necessary in order to provide a beneficial outcome to any circumstance, where the divine forces would act for rather than against humankind. All Celtic religious activity should be seen in this context. But the richness of Celtic religion is due partly also to its adaptability. The free Celtic traditions of open-air worship and aniconic perceptions of the gods – which allowed the Celtic king Brennus to scoff at anthropomorphic representations of Greek deities at Delphi (Diodorus Siculus XXII, 9, 4) – changed and developed in the Roman phase. Roman cults were accepted and absorbed into the Celtic religious system, but Celtic perceptions of the divine world remained fundamentally the same.

There is one final feature of pagan Celtic religion which should be mentioned, namely the transition into Christianity. The transference from polytheism to monotheism was made easy because the multiplicity of pagan deities could slip without difficulty into the characters of Christian saints. The goddess Brigit became Saint Brigid, with her cult virtually unchanged. Saint Ann was probably originally the Irish goddess Anu. The Virgin Mary took over many functions of the Celtic Mother-goddesses. In addition, pagan rituals were often adapted to Christian use: healing cults and holy wells exemplify this transformation. The pagan Celtic Otherworld corresponds very closely to the Christian Promised Land: pagan tales such as the *Voyage of Bran* have a parallel in the *Voyage of Saint Brendan*. Thus the religion of the pagan Celtic world not only survived, in adapted form, the Roman occupation, but was not even totally obliterated by Christianity.

Subject Index

Vichy
Vix
Walbrook
Wanborough
Welwyn
Willingham Fen

5.   Objects and symbols

axe
axe, double
barrel
boat
cart/chariot
cart/chariot-burial
cauldron
circle
coin
Coligny Calendar
cross
headdress
horns
Jupiter-Giant column
key
limb/organ, votive
mask
model tool/weapon
pillar
pit
rosette
S-symbol
sceptre
shrine
swastika
temple
torc
Viereckschanze
weapon
wheel
wine

6.   Natural phenomena

bog
bog-burial

conifer
earth
fire
grove
lake
mistletoe
moon
mountain
oak
pool
rain
river
sea
spring, healing
sun
thunder
tree
water
well

7.   Concepts and ideas

abstraction
afterlife
animism
Annwn
art
Avalon
Beltene
burial
couple, divine
curse
death
decapitation
divination
dualism
emphasis
feast
fertility
festival
geis
goblin
head
head, Janiform

head, triple
head-hunting
healing
hero
Himbas Forosnai
hunt(er)
Imbolc
infant-burial
interpretatio celtica
interpretatio romana
Lughnasad
magic
metamorphosis
monster
Nature (god of)
number
oracle
Otherworld
phallus
rebirth
ritual
ritual damage
sacral kingship
sacrifice, animal
sacrifice, human
Samhain
schematism
shape-changing
sídh
sovereignty (goddess of)
Tarbhfhess
territory (god of)
Tir na Nog
transmigration of souls
triplism
underworld
war
witchcraft

8.   Religious personages

bard
druid
fili
priest

A

Abandinus was a British deity, known only from a shrine dedicated to him at Godmanchester in Cambridgeshire. Godmanchester was a Roman town with a *mansio* or hostel for travellers. The settlement grew up at the river crossing of the Great Ouse by Ermine Street. To the west of the *mansio* was the shrine of Abandinus: three successive temples were built here. From the site came votive feathers or leaves and a plaque dedicated to the local god Abandinus. The text of the plaque reads 'to the god Abandinus, Vatiacus gave this from his own resources'. If the word 'Abandinus' has been read correctly, the first element is the Celtic rivername Abona or Afon. The temple is situated close to the River Ouse, and a well or cistern was present in one of the shrines, so it is possible that Abandinus was a water-god. The other possibility is that the name is related to 'Maband' or 'MABON' – the Divine Youth (*see also* MAPONUS).
□ H.J.M. Green 1986, 29–55.

Abnoba was a divine huntress, associated with the Roman goddess DIANA. She was a mistress of the forest, perhaps also possessing maternal or fertility connotations. Abnoba was worshipped in the region of the Black Forest during the Romano-Celtic period.
□ de Vries 1963, 98, 126.

Abstraction *see* SCHEMATISM

Aericura was a Celto-Germanic goddess, called variously Aericura and Herecura; a male counterpart, Aericurus, is also recorded at Corbridge in Northumberland. The name may be related to that of the Classical underworld goddess Hecate. Aericura was venerated in Baden Württemberg, in the vicinity of Stuttgart: a stone at Cannstatt is dedicated to her, and it depicts a MOTHER-GODDESS seated on a throne, with a basket of fruit in her lap; and there are other similar (though unnamed) images from Cannstatt and Rübgarten. Sometimes Aericura is depicted as one of a divine partnership in the area of South Germany and the Balkans. The couple are named Aericura and DISPATER (the god has taken his name from that of the Classical

underworld deity), and they probably protected humans in the afterlife. At Salzbach near Ettlingen, the goddess sits with her basket of fruit, whilst her partner unrolls the scroll of life, signifying its one-way span and its inevitable end. At Varhély in Dacia, the god is accompanied by a three-headed dog, reflective of the Graeco-Roman symbolism of Cerberus, the fearsome triple-headed canine guardian of the Roman Otherworld; Aericura here holds a key, a symbol of the entry to the gates of heaven.

Whilst it may appear strange that a goddess of the underworld is represented with the imagery of a Mother-goddess, it should be remembered that the Mothers were closely associated with death and regeneration, as well as fertility and prosperity.
□ Green 1989, 41; Espérandieu *Germ.*, nos. 347, 560, 562, 569, 634; Hatt 1945.

Afterlife *see* OTHERWORLD; REBIRTH

Ailill is one of the many consecutive husbands taken by the queen-goddess MEDB of Connacht. Medb chooses Ailill because he, like her, is without fear; he is generous; and he is not jealous of her sexual activities. This is ironic because, when Medb discovers Ailill's own infidelity, she prompts Conall Cernach to kill him, on the Feast of Beltene.

Medb and Ailill rule Connacht from the royal court of Cruachain. It is clear that Medb is the dominant partner and that Ailill is, to an extent, a cipher for her. The rivalry between them provokes the great Cattle Raid of Cooley, which results in a war between Connacht and Ulster. A story attached to the *Táin* tells of how both Medb and Ailill boast to each other of their possessions. All is fairly equal except that Medb has nothing to compare with Ailill's huge white-horned bull. It is to capture the great brown Ulster Bull of Cuailnge that Medb provokes war with the Ulstermen (*see* BULL).

Ailill does possess a certain character of his own; a number of stories point to his role as an arbiter. Thus before the last battle of the *Táin*, Ailill meets King Conchobar of Ulster to discuss a truce. He also acts as an arbitrator at the Feast of Bricriu when there is a quarrel between heroes as to whom should receive the champion's portion of pork.
□ O'Fáolain 1954; Kinsella 1969; Lehmann 1989, 1–10; Bhreathnach 1982, 243–60; O'Rahilly 1946, 176.

Aix-les-Bains There is evidence of a healing cult at the important spa of Aix-les-Bains: here a local version of the Mother-goddesses – known as the Comedovae (*see* MATRES COM-EDOVAE) – were venerated, their name referring specifically to health. At the site of the springs there was a shrine to the spring-deity Borvo, at which small bronze figurines of Hercules were offered. The Graeco-Roman 'strong-man' was presumably invoked here as a potent fighter against disease.
☐ Dayet 1963, 167–78; de Vries 1963, 130; Thevenot 1968, 166.

Albiorix *see* MARS ALBIORIX

Alesia During the late Iron Age, Alesia in Burgundy was a large fortified settlement or *oppidum*. It was the last real bastion of resistance of the Gaulish chief Vercingetorix, who fought the final major battle against the Romans in 52 BC. After the conquest, Alesia became a Roman town: archaeological evidence suggests that it was a thriving centre for native and Romano-Celtic religious cults.

Many sculptures depict divine couples; the Gaulish Hammer-god and his consort were invoked, and sometimes the male partner in the divine marriage is represented as a warrior–protector of fertility and abundance. One set of the partners was Ucuetis and Bergusia, to whom a dedication was made in a shrine and who may have been craft-deities. Gods of the wine harvest were also venerated. The horse-goddess Epona was worshipped here, as were the Mother-goddesses: on one carving, a seated matron holds huge fruits in her lap; she was found in a cellar which may have been a domestic shrine. On another stone, three Mothers are each accompanied by a naked toddler. Other divinities were worshipped at Alesia: several images depict a bearded god flanked by two doves or ravens. The solar god was venerated here too: a statue shows the Romano-Celtic Jupiter with his emblems of globe and eagle; on each side of his throne is carved a Celtic sun-wheel. A large number of model bronze wheels was found associated with deposits of more than 200 miniature pots, set in groups of nine. These objects were offerings made at a late pre-Roman wooden sanctuary. The healers APOLLO MORITASGUS and DAMONA were also worshipped here. *See also* ALISANOS.
☐ Espérandieu nos. 2347, 7114, 2348, 7518, 2356, 2375; Deyts 1976, no. 3; Pobé & Roub-

Standing stone near Minions, Cornwall. A stone like this stood at Tara; it cried out at the touch of legitimate kings such as **Ailill**.

Bronze plaque from **Alesia**, depicting the horse-goddess Epona in a chariot.

ier 1961, no. 180; Le Gall 1963, 174; 1985, 68, fig. 39, 41–4, fig. 17; Green 1989, fig. 12.

Alisanos is an example of Celtic animism, the belief that every natural feature in the landscape possessed a divine spirit. Alisanos was a Gaulish god of the rock; but a deity called Alisonus was invoked in Burgundy, and here he could be the eponymous spirit of Alesia, the two names being philologically related.
□ Duval 1976, 60.

Allonnes On the outskirts of a Roman *vicus* (civil settlement) and situated close to the theatre and baths at Allonnes (Sarthe) was a Romano-Celtic temple, with a circular *cella* or inner sanctum surrounded by a square portico or ambulatory. The shrine was set within a rectangular galleried *temenos* or sacred enclosure. This sanctuary appears to have been dedicated to MARS MULLO, a Celtic healer-god who specialized in the cure of eye disease. The temple contained more than 300 offerings of Celtic coins and three dedications to Mullo, at least one of which dates from the reign of Augustus. In a later period of the shrine, stone sculptures of pilgrims were dedicated to the god, the images clearly reflective of eye diseases.
□ Thevenot 1968, 65–6; Horne & King 1980, 374–5.

Amhairghin *see* CONALL CERNACH; ÉRIU

Ancamna was a Gaulish goddess who is known only from epigraphic dedications. She appears to have been a specifically Treveran deity, associated with the cult of the healer-god MARS LENUS, whose divine partner she was (*see* COUPLE, DIVINE). The couple were worshipped at Trier. But at a spring-sanctuary at Möhn, north of Trier, there was a dedication to Ancamna, this time linked with another god, Mars SMERTRIUS. At this rural shrine, clay figurines depict a Mother-goddess, perhaps identifiable as Ancamna herself. So Ancamna is known to have possessed two different consorts: Lenus and Smertrius, both venerated in the territory of the Treveri.
□ Wightman 1970, 211–23; Green 1989, 61, 64; C.I.L. XIII, 4119.

Andraste 'While they were doing all this [massacring Roman women] in the grove of Andate [Andraste] and other sacred places,

they performed sacrifices, feasted and abandoned all restraint (Andraste was their name for victory and she enjoyed their especial reverence)' (Dio Cassius 62, 7, 1–3).

Mediterranean authors tell us that Boudica, queen of the Iceni who led a rebellion against the Romans in AD 60, worshipped Andraste, goddess of victory. Dio Cassius informs us that Boudica released a HARE before setting out on a campaign, while invoking Andraste. Possibly this goddess is analogous to Andarte, a deity worshipped by the Vocontii of Gaul. *See also* SACRIFICE, HUMAN.
□ Allason-Jones 1989, 151; de Vries 1963, 122; Duval 1976, 59.

animal (*see also* individual species in Subject Index, part 3) Both wild and domesticated animals were revered for their particular qualities and were regarded as sacred companions or associates to a number of Celtic divinities. In Celtic belief, there was no rigid boundary between gods perceived in human form and supernatural animals. Celtic religion was based on the natural world and thus on the belief of the presence of spirits in all aspects of nature. This can be seen in the tradition of METAMORPHOSIS which is so prominent in the vernacular mythology. In the iconography, this fluidity in imagery is exhibited in the endowment of anthropomorphic figures with horns, antlers or hooves.

Of the wild animals, stags and boars seem to have attained greatest prominence. Stags are swift and virile and were revered as such. Boars are belligerent, ferocious and indomitable and were thus a natural symbol of war and aggression. Both were important symbols of hunting cults and the forest. The bull, horse and dog were singled out for especial reverence among the domesticated animals, once again for the particular qualities associated with each. The bull is aggressive and potent; the horse a symbol of speed and prestige; the dog was linked above all with healing and the underworld, because of its curative spittle and its scavenging habits.

In the archaeology of the Celtic world, evidence for the sanctity of animals takes the form of animal deposits (including sacrificial material) and iconography. Before the Romano-Celtic period, the Celts adorned their metalwork and coins with depictions of beasts, and the Celts of the Camonica Valley in North Italy drew pictures of the animals they revered and hunted on the rocks of the sacred valley. In the Romano-Celtic period, images of animals appear either alone (usually as small bronze or clay figurines) or in company with various divinities. Some of these, like Epona and Nehalennia, are nearly always depicted with particular zoomorphic associates. Whole or parts of animals were buried as part of ritual activity throughout the Celtic world, both before and during the Romano-Celtic phase. At Danebury in Hampshire, animals were interred in pits in a complicated series of ritual acts; pre-Roman shrines like Gournay-sur-Aronde (Oise) and Hayling Island (Hants) were sites of similarly specific religious practices.

□ Green 1986, 167–70; Brunaux 1986; Downey, King & Soffe 1980, 289–304; Anati 1965; Cunliffe 1983, 155–71.

animism *see* RIVER; SPRING, HEALING; TERRITORY, GOD OF

Annwn The kingdom of Annwn is featured in the *First Branch of the Mabinogi*. It was an underworld realm whose king was Arawn. A common Celtic theme was the enlistment, by OTHERWORLD rulers, of mortals to aid them in their struggles: the story is that Pwyll, Prince of Dyfed, met Arawn while hunting, in a quarrel over a stag. To make things right between them, Pwyll agreed to help Arawn in his conflict with a rival underworld king, Hafgan. Thus, at Arawn's request, he changed places with the king, ruling Annwn for a year, while Arawn, as Pwyll, presided over Dyfed. During that year, Pwyll resisted the temptation to sleep with Arawn's beautiful wife. At the end of the year, as instructed by Arawn, Pwyll met Hafgan and killed him with a single blow; he then met Arawn at the arranged trysting-place, and each returned to his respective kingdom. Pwyll's loyalty over Arawn's wife strengthened the bond of friendship between the two rulers, and they maintained their relationship, frequently exchanging valuable gifts. Indeed, Arawn sent Pwyll the first pigs to be seen in Dyfed. Because of his sojourn in Annwn and his uniting of the kingdoms of Arawn and Hafgan, Pwyll became known as Head of Annwn.

Annwn appears in a number of early Welsh tales and poems. In one story, a daughter of the king of Annwn was compelled to wash at the 'Ford of the Barking' until she had a son by a Christian. She was released from the

A 1st c. BC coin of the Iceni, worshippers of **Andraste**, showing a boar at bay.

The antlered god Cernunnos and his **animal** attributes, on the Danish Gundestrup Cauldron.

Engraved silver bowl showing **animal** symbolism; from a Bronze Age chief's grave at Maikop, South Russia.

spell by being seduced by Urien Rheged, to whom she bore twins, Owein and Morfudd. Poem 30 of the *Book of Taliesin,* the *Spoils of Annwn,* tells of a disastrous expedition to the Otherworld by Arthur and his men, who stole a magic, diamond-studded cauldron belonging to the chief of Annwn. This vessel was made to boil by the breath of nine virgins, and refused to boil food for a coward! The acquisition of the cauldron cost Arthur dear: out of three shiploads of men only seven survived.

The Cẁn Annwn or 'hounds of Annwn' were death omens, ghost-dogs who came at night and foretold death. They were small, speckled and greyish-red, chained and led by a black, horned figure. They were sent from Annwn to seek out corpses and human souls.
□ Jones & Jones 1976.

Antenociticus Iconography and epigraphy very frequently provide separate evidence for the presence of certain divinities: thus inscriptions mentioning gods are usually unaccompanied by images of these deities; and images often appear alone, with no evidence as to which god is being invoked. But Antenociticus is an exception: at Benwell, a fort on Hadrian's Wall, was a shrine dedicated to this local god. Here was also found a stone head of a youthful male deity, broken off what may have been the cult statue. On the neck were traces of a groove which would have held a metal torc, a Celtic symbol of status and prestige. The stylization of the hair suggests the presence of horns or antlers. The name defies interpretation: at Benwell, the name may be spelt 'Antenociticus' or 'Anociticus'. The head was found in a small apsidal temple outside the south-east angle of the fort.
□ Green 1989, 99; Ross 1967a, 163, fig. 51; Toynbee 1962, 146, no. 41; 1964, 106, pl. XXVIIIa; R.I.B. 1327–9.

Anu is frequently confused with DANU or Dana, the divine ancestress of the Tuatha Dé Danann. It is very uncertain as to whether Anu and Danu were or were not separate entities. Both were Mother-goddesses, associated with the founding and prosperity of Ireland. Anu was closely identified with the land, and she was especially associated with Munster. Her fertility role is demonstrated by the name of a mountain in County Kerry, called Dá Chích Anann (the Breasts of Anu).

She may have been adopted in early Christian Ireland as Saint Ann.
□ Mac Cana 1983, 86, 132; Ross 1967a, 209; Sjoestedt 1949, 24f.

Apollo (*see also* under Celtic surnames) The Graeco-Roman Apollo was a god of prophecy (*see* ORACLE), music, poetry, healing and hunting. He was also a sun-god, Phoebus Apollo. The god was adopted into the Celtic pantheon, where the sun and healing appear to have been his main concerns. Apollo was the presiding divinity of a number of healing sanctuaries in Gaul, especially in Burgundy: these include Sainte-Sabine, Essarois and Alesia. Apollo's surnames include Belenus, Grannus, Moritasgus and Vindonnus. In many of his sanctuaries, he seems to have combined a healing with a solar function. The name 'Belenus' means 'brilliant', but the god was venerated as Apollo Belenus at the curative shrine of Sainte-Sabine. Apollo Vindonnus at Essarois was a deity who restored light and vision to people with eye disease. Sometimes Apollo was linked with a native consort (*see* COUPLE, DIVINE): he was worshipped with Damona at Alesia; but he was most frequently venerated with SIRONA, and the couple had a wealthy and important sanctuary at HOCHSCHEID near Trier.

Apollo Atepomarus In Celtic Gaul, Apollo was sometimes associated with horses; at some of his healing sanctuaries (as at Sainte-Sabine, Burgundy) small figurines of horses were dedicated to him. This horse association may have arisen because Apollo was a sun-god, and horses were closely linked to the Celtic solar cult (*see* HORSE; SUN-GOD). At Mauvières (Indre), Apollo was called by the Celtic surname of Atepomarus. The root 'epo' refers to the word for 'horse'; and the epithet is sometimes translated as 'Great Horseman' or 'possessing a great horse'.
□ C.I.L. XIII, 1318; Ross 1967a, 324; Green 1986, 172–3.

Apollo Belenus 'Belenus' means 'bright' or 'brilliant'. The term was an epithet or descriptive surname given to the Celtic Apollo in parts of Gaul, North Italy and Noricum (part of modern Austria). Apollo Belenus was a healer, but he was also a sun-deity, like the Classical Phoebus Apollo. So he may have represented the beneficent, curative aspect of the sun's heat.

The cult of Belenus possessed a particular status in that it is mentioned in a number of Classical literary sources. Ausonius was a poet from Bordeaux, writing in the later 4th c. AD. He alludes to sanctuaries to Belenus in Aquitania, and he speaks of a temple priest of the cult named Phoebicius – this adopted name referring to the 'light' aspect of the Celtic Apollo. Tertullian talks of the cult of Belenus in the Norican Alps (*Apologeticus* 24, 7); and Herodian mentions Belenus' worship at Aquileia in North Italy (*History of the Empire after Marcus*, 8, 3.6).

Detail of a silver jewellery design by Rhiannon Evans, called 'The Hounds of **Annwn**'.

The cult of Belenus is attested archaeologically, in terms of epigraphic dedications, sometimes found in temples. In North Italy, he is known, for instance, in Venice and at Rimini. In Gaul, his cult was popular in Provence: inscriptions come from the Marseilles area; Créasque (Bouches-du-Rhône); and Calissanne (B-du-R). One interesting find was that of a gem at Nîmes, dedicated in Greek letters to Belenus and bearing the image of an old man decorated with star-like symbols. Belenus was venerated at Clermont-Ferrand; and he had a temple at the sacred healing springs of Sainte-Sabine in Burgundy. Here Apollo Belenus was invoked by pilgrims needing cures for their sickness. People dedicated stone images of swaddled infants at the shrine, presumably in the hope that they would thus be cured. Also offered as votives here were clay figurines of horses, probably because Belenus was a solar god and horses had a close affinity with sun-deities in the Celtic world.

Stone head from a 2nd–3rd c. AD statue of **Antenociticus**, a British god with a shrine at Benwell, on Hadrian's Wall.

The cult of Belenus was both important and popular. Belenus himself probably pre-existed the Roman period: dedications to him alone (without Apollo's name) mean that he was not totally dependent on the link with the Classical god for his identity. It is possible also that his cult was associated with the Celtic solar-fire festival of BELTENE on 1 May, when bonfires were lit to welcome the summer and magically encourage the sun's nourishing warmth.

□ Zwicker 1934–6, 105; C.I.L. V, 2144–6; XI, 353; XII, 402, 5693; XIII, 1461, 2386; Gourvest 1954, 257–62; Thevenot 1951, 129–41; 1952, 247; Aebischer 1934, 34–5.

Apollo Cunomaglus A temple at Nettleton Shrub in Wiltshire was dedicated to Apollo Cunomaglus ('Hound Lord'). The shrine existed soon after AD 69, but it was only later

A 2nd c. BC gold coin from Germany, with a horseman, perhaps **Apollo Atepomarus**, a patron of horses and riders.

developed into a major cult centre; in the mid 3rd c. AD a large polygonal shrine, hall, hostel, shops and a priest's house were built, attesting to the wealth and popularity of the cult. Diana and Silvanus were venerated here, suggesting that perhaps Cunomaglus himself was a hunter-god. But it is possible that Nettleton may have been a healing sanctuary: Apollo's main Celtic role was as a healer; the site is close to water; and such finds as tweezers and pins may denote the presence of a curative cult.
□ Wedlake 1982.

Apollo Grannus was a healing spring-deity equated with the Celtic Apollo in Europe. He is mentioned by Dio Cassius (*Historiae* 77, 15, 5) who remarks that the emperor Caracalla could not find a cure at the temples of either Grannus, Aesculapius (the Graeco-Roman healer-god) or Serapis (an Egyptian deity).

The name Grannus probably derives from the ancient name for Grand in the Vosges: there was a cult centre here, and another at Aachen, or Aix-la-Chapelle, the ancient Aquae Granni ('the waters of Grannus'). Grannus was associated with therapeutic spring water over a wide area, from Brittany to north-east Gaul and as far as the Danube, where a 3rd c. AD temple at Brigetio in Hungary was dedicated to Apollo Grannus and Sirona. Grannus is even recorded at Rome itself. A curious find is a pot discovered at Vestmanlund in Sweden, which bears a dedication to Apollo Grannus by a Roman temple official called Ammilius Constans, in fulfilment of a vow. Presumably such an offering came to be in Sweden as a result of either trade or looting.

Like Belenus, Grannus possessed a solar aspect: he was called Phoebus on an inscription from Trier, where the god is depicted driving a sun-chariot. But attempts to link the name of Grannus philologically with an Irish word for the sun (*grían*) do not work.

The ritual associated with the healing cult of Grannus probably took a form essentially similar to the other great healing religions. Pilgrims would visit the sanctuary, purify themselves in the sacred water, and give their offerings and pray. They might then enter the *abaton* or dormitory for the 'healing sleep', where they hoped to encounter the god in a vision or dream and be cured. This rite of incubation is suggested by an inscription at the temple of Grand. *See also* MOGONS.
□ Szabó 1971, 66; Thevenot, 1968, 97ff; de Vries 1963, 82–3.

Apollo Moritasgus At Alesia in Burgundy, the Celtic healer Apollo was surnamed 'Moritasgus', the epithet referring to 'masses of sea water'. His divine consort was DAMONA. A dedication to the couple alludes to the presence of a shrine at the curative spring, which possessed a sacred pool where sick pilgrims could bathe. The sanctuary itself was impressive, with baths and a polygonal temple. In addition, there were porticoes which were perhaps for the curative sleep, in which the sick hoped for a divine vision and a cure. Numerous votive objects, models of pilgrims and of the afflicted parts of their bodies were dedicated to Moritasgus: limbs, internal organs, breasts, genitals and eyes were all represented. The presence of surgeons' tools argues for the activities of priests who were also physicians.
□ Le Gall 1963, 147–58.

Apollo Vindonnus The Celtic Apollo had a temple at ESSAROIS near Châtillon-sur-Seine in Burgundy. The sanctuary was based on a curative spring, presided over by Apollo Vindonnus, meaning 'clear light'. Part of the temple pediment survives, bearing an inscription to the god and the spirit of the springs and, above it, the head of a radiate sun-deity. Pilgrims brought many votive objects to the shrine of Vindonnus, some made of oak, some of stone. Some offerings take the form of images of hands holding fruit or a cake as a gift; others represent parts of the body requiring a cure by the god. Most of all, the devotees of Apollo Vindonnus appear to have suffered from eye afflictions, which are represented by bronze plaques depicting eyes. It is appropriate that such unfortunates should venerate and propitiate a god of light, who could restore to them the clear vision reflected by his character and his name.
□ Thevenot 1968, 110–12.

Apollo Virotutis was one of the identities of the Gaulish Apollo. The epithet has been interpreted as meaning 'Benefactor of Humanity'. Apollo Virotutis was worshipped, for example, at Fins d'Annecy (Haute-Savoie) and at Jublains (Maine-et-Loire).
□ de Vries 1963, 81; C.I.L. XIII, 2525, 3185.

Arausio was the eponymous spirit of the town of Arausio (Orange) in southern Gaul. The town is first mentioned by the Roman historian Livy; it belonged to the Celto-Ligurian tribe of the Cavares, but was made into a Roman *colonia* in 35 BC. Inscriptions attest to the presence of this presiding deity who gave the town its name.
☐ Clébert 1970, 253; Rivet 1988, 272–5.

Arawn appears in the *First Branch of the Mabinogi*; he is a lord of the underworld. PWYLL, prince of Narberth, encounters Arawn while on a hunting trip; he sends his hounds after a stag, but then sees emerging from the wood another group of strange dogs, who have caught and are killing a stag. These hounds are curious to look at, shining white with red ears. Pwyll drives them away and calls his own pack to the stricken deer. At this point, a horseman appears, angry at the insult Pwyll has done him: the strange dogs are his. He is Arawn, king of Annwn, the Otherworld, and he tells Pwyll that they will be enemies unless Pwyll does something for him. Arawn explains that the lord of Narberth must take on Arawn's form and rule Annwn for a year, whilst Arawn rules Narberth as Pwyll. At the end of the year, Pwyll must fight and kill Arawn's enemy Hafgan, the lord of another underworld kingdom, and then return to the present meeting-place at Glyn Cuch. Arawn warns Pwyll to strike Hafgan only once; if he wounds him twice, Hafgan will recover and be stronger than ever. Pwyll is successful; the two keep their tryst, and thereafter the two rulers are firm friends, regularly exchanging gifts. Arawn is the lord of a united Otherworld.
☐ Jones & Jones 1976.

Altar to **Apollo Cunomaglus**, 'Hound Lord', at the Nettleton Shrub Romano-Celtic temple, Wiltshire.

Arduinna The local boar-goddess of the Ardennes Forest was named Arduinna, the name being related to the topographical word for the region. A bronze statuette from the area shows the goddess riding on a BOAR, a dagger in her right hand. She is probably a huntress, akin to the Roman DIANA, representative of the spirit of the forest and protectress of all its inhabitants, hunters and hunted. Arduinna is an example of Celtic ambiguity: she is at the same time a guardian of human hunters and the wild boars which are their prey.

    The idea may be similar to the belief systems of certain North American Indians,

The Celtic boar-goddess **Arduinna**, with her boar and hunting-knife, from the Ardennes.

who believe that hunting is acceptable as long as it is done with respect for the animal and the beast consents to being killed. Thus the harmony of nature is maintained, and the animal may be reincarnated to dwell in the forest and be hunted once again.

□ Boucher 1976, no. 292; Green 1989, 27.

Arianrhod In the *Fourth Branch of the Mabinogi*, Arianrhod appears as the daughter of Dôn and the sister of Gwydion. The legend is that MATH, Lord of Gwynedd, has the curious quirk that he has to have his feet resting on the lap of a virgin. Arianrhod becomes a candidate for the post of footholder; as a test of her virginity, she has to step over Math's magic wand. But as she does so, she gives birth to two boys. One of the children is named Dylan, but Arianrhod places three taboos on the other boy at his birth, including one that he will not be given a name until such a time as she chooses to give him one. However, Arianrhod is tricked by Gwydion into naming the boy LLEU LLAW GYFFES. Similarly, Arianrhod's oath that her son will not bear arms until she decides to equip him is revoked by trickery. Because of his mother's third oath, that Lleu will never have a human wife, Math and Gwydion produce a magical wife made of flowers, named Blodeuwedd.

□ Jones & Jones 1976; Mac Cana 1983.

Arnemetia Aquae Arnemetiae ('the waters of Arnemetia') was the name of the settlement which grew up around the sacred spa at Buxton in Derbyshire, in the tribal area of the Corieltauvi. This is the only evidence we have for the goddess Arnemetia, whose name contains the Celtic word 'nemeton', meaning 'sacred GROVE'; so her name is interpreted as being 'she who dwells over against the sacred grove'. Arnemetia must have presided over the curative waters of the Buxton springs, just as the better-known British goddess Sulis ruled over Aquae Sulis at Bath (*see* SPRING, HEALING). The springs at Aquae Arnemetiae may have possessed special potency for the Celts: they are close together in the valley floor and contain two kinds of water.

□ Richmond & Crawford 1949, 23.

Arras (Culture) This term refers to a distinctive material culture which appears to have been introduced into East Yorkshire and Humberside from the Marne area of eastern Gaul during the early 4th c. BC. This culture manifested itself particularly in specific burial traditions, including that of cart or chariot-burial. Men and women of high rank were interred, sometimes accompanied by rich grave-goods and with intact or dismantled two-wheeled carts or chariots (*see* CART/CHARIOT-BURIAL).

□ Stead 1979; Dent 1985, 85–92; Hodson & Rowlett 1973, 184–5.

art *see* CAULDRON; COIN; CROSS; EMPHASIS; LIMB/ORGAN, VOTIVE; MASK; MODEL TOOL/WEAPON; ROSETTE; S-SYMBOL; SCHEMATISM; SHRINE; SMITH-GOD; SWASTIKA; TORC; TRIPLISM

Arthur is not *sensu stricto* a figure of mythology but rather a historical personage, in all probability a war leader of late Roman or early Dark Age Britain. The medieval Arthurian histories and romances of, for instance, Geoffrey of Monmouth and Chrétien de Troyes, are not useful in the present context. But there is no doubt that Arthur is associated with Celtic myth: he is a warrior of superhuman stature, hunting monsters and visiting the Otherworld. In these respects, he closely parallels such heroes of pagan mythology as Finn. In the *Tale of Culhwch and Olwen,* Arthur helps Culhwch to hunt down the enchanted boar Twrch Trwyth (*see* CULHWCH AND OLWEN). In an old Welsh poem, the *Spoils of* ANNWN, Arthur visits the Otherworld to try and obtain the magic cauldron of regeneration. The AVALON of the Arthurian legends is a Happy Otherworld of healing and renewal which is indistinguishable from that of pagan Celtic tradition.

□ Alcock 1971; Luttrell 1974; Cavendish 1978; Ashe 1990; Jones & Jones 1976, xxii–xxvi.

Artio was a denizen of the forest, one of a large group of Celtic deities whose identities were inextricably entwined with animals. Her close link with the BEAR is demonstrated by her name, which means 'bear'. On a bronze group from Muri near Berne, Artio sits with a vessel of fruit beside her, offering more fruit to a large bear which faces her and at whose back is a tree; an inscription on the base of the bronze dedicates the group 'to the goddess Artio'. The fruit indicates that Artio was a goddess of plenty or fertility. But she may also have been both a huntress and, paradoxically, also a protectress of bears. Apart from the Swiss find, Artio was invoked by inscriptions in a remote valley near Bollendorf near Trier.

☐ Boucher 1976, fig. 291; Green 1989, fig. 10; Wightman 1970, 217.

Arvernus *see* MERCURY ARVERNUS

Assche-Kalkoven From this site in Belgium comes a cache or hoard of pipe-clay figurines of HORSES, probably originally from a temple. The statuettes could be associated with a number of cults, including Celtic versions of Apollo and Mars, but the presence of lunar amulets represented round the necks of some of the figures suggests their association with a celestial cult, perhaps that of the Celtic Sky-god or an unknown lunar deity.

☐ de Laet 1942, 41–54; Green 1986, 172.

Atepomarus *see* APOLLO ATEPOMARUS

Aufaniae *see* MATRONAE AUFANIAE

Aulnay-aux-Planches The ritual site at Aulnay (Marne) was constructed in the 10th c. BC but bears considerable resemblance to later European sanctuaries, for example the 3rd c. BC enclosure at LIBENIČE (Czechoslovakia). The sanctuary at Aulnay-aux-Planches consisted of a large, rectilinear, ditched enclosure, about 300 ft × 50 ft. Inside were four burials: one was that of an infant who was perhaps sacrificed to bless the site when it was established. Also present was a PIT containing an ox skull, placed opposite the entrance to the enclosure, and it may be that the skull was set on a wooden post bedded into the pit.

☐ Piggott 1965, 232; 1968, fig. 20; Schwarz 1962, 54–5.

Avalon is the Happy Otherworld of Arthurian romance, a magic island in the west, a paradise of apple trees. It was in Avalon that Arthur's sword was forged and whither Arthur was taken to be healed from his fatal wound. Avalon's association with apples may relate to a version of the Otherworld known from pagan Irish mythology. The sea-god Manannán presided over the Otherworld, especially in the form of the island of Emhain Abhlach ('Emhain of the Apple Trees'). This island is sometimes identified with Arran, off the coast of Scotland.

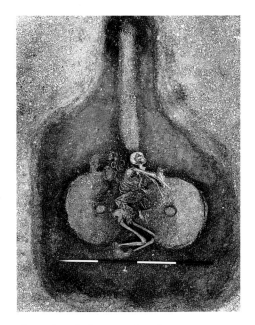

Chariot-burial of a young Iron Age princess, excavated at Wetwang Slack, East Yorkshire, in 1984, and belonging to the **Arras Culture**.

Statuette of **Artio**, with her bear, from Muri near Berne, Switzerland.

According to one tradition, Avalon was actually at Glastonbury: in 1191 monks at Glastonbury Abbey claimed to have discovered the bodies of Arthur and his queen in the cemetery of the abbey, accompanied by an inscribed lead cross identifying them and mentioning Avalon. This find is recorded by the contemporary Giraldus Cambrensis; Ralph of Coggeshall gives another contemporary account in which he alludes to the burial of Arthur in the Island of Avalon. It is quite possible that the whole Glastonbury association arises from a forgery by the abbey monks.

□ Alcock 1971, 74–80; Ashe 1968; Baswell & Sharpe 1988; Luttrell 1974, 218; Cavendish 1978.

Aveta was a goddess venerated at a shrine in the Altbachtal religious precinct at Trier, capital of the Treveri, on the Moselle. The sanctuary was visited by pilgrims who offered to the presiding goddess numerous small figurines of a Mother-goddess who is presumably representative of how Aveta was perceived by her devotees. These images vary in that some depict the goddess holding baskets of fruits, some lap-dogs and others swaddled infants, as if all these symbols were considered to be virtually interchangeable attributes of fertility and prosperity. The DOG may be present in reflection of Aveta's role as a healer or deity of renewal and rebirth. *See also* DEA NUTRIX.

□ Wightman 1970, 217, pl. 21d.

axe symbolism may be traced back in Europe at least to the Bronze Age. Urnfield graves contain bronze and clay miniature axes (*see* MODEL TOOL/WEAPON); and in the Mediterranean world, axe models were offered to the Greek sky-god Zeus at his temples at Dodona and Olympia, perhaps as early as the late 2nd millennium BC. In the very late Bronze Age and the beginning of the Iron Age, there is evidence for an association between axe symbols and the sun cult. Functional axes from North Italy may bear incised wheels or swastikas, and one pendant in the form of an axe is decorated with the motifs of a water bird and a disc, both solar symbols at this period. At Hallstatt itself, axe models were buried in graves: one has the image of a horseman on the top of the blade; another has a miniature horse perched on the blade edge. The link between horses and sun cults

is well established (*see* HORSE). At the Dürrnberg *oppidum* near Salzburg, a child was buried in the 4th c. BC with an axe and a wheel amulet.

The custom of manufacturing miniature tools and implements as votive offerings was extremely common in the Romano-Celtic world. These models take various forms, but most common of all are the axes. They were offered in temples and graves, and are found also on domestic sites. A group of Swiss axe models are engraved with the names of deities – Jupiter, Minerva and the Mother-goddesses. Many of the British axe models come from shrines: Hockwold (Norfolk), Brigstock (Northants) and Woodeaton (Oxon) are just samples of many such occurrences. At Woodeaton, three of the models may support the idea of a solar symbolism: one has an incised ligatured cross or broken-rimmed wheel on its blade; another is decorated with a swastika; the third has a concentric circle motif.

Miniature axes may reflect a number of symbolic perceptions: some certainly appear to possess a link with the sun cult; others may be good luck talismans. The symbol of an edged weapon or tool may have been efficacious in warding off evil and promoting the protection of the gods. The ubiquity of model axes is interesting: miniaturization may have occurred because of cost or convenience factors, but there may also have been a sense in which the making of a tiny replica of a functional object may itself have been an act of consecration, similar to the tradition of ritual damage. Certainly, painstaking care was sometimes taken to copy a full-size object in miniature: the Romano-British axe model from Tiddington (Warks) was such a faithful replica, with the blade and shaft (quite unnecessarily) cast separately, as if to copy the manufacture of a real axe of wood and iron.

□ Déchelette 1910, 409ff; Green 1991a; Sandars 1957, 275; Kromer 1959, 138, pls 137, 222; Pauli 1975, 18, figs. 3, 5; Forrer 1948; Stähelin 1931, 486; Green 1984a, 66–8, 99–101; 1975, 54–70; 1986, 220–2.

axe, double Like axes, double axes were made as votive offerings. Of course, the double axe is best documented as a symbol of Minoan Crete at the beginning of the 2nd millennium BC, but it was also of later importance in Europe.

Many of the oriental Baals, who were sky- and weather-gods, were associated with the double axe: Dolichenus of Mount Comma- gene in Syria and Zeus-Hadad of Nabataea are two examples. It is an enigmatic symbol: its link with storm-gods may endow it with the imagery of a thunderbolt; as a double-edged weapon, it could be perceived as a link between the upper and lower worlds; it could, instead, be simply a symbol of authority and prestige. Some scholars maintain that the resemblance of the double axe to a butterfly may be a deliberate evocation of rebirth symbolism (in recognition of the chrysalis 'death' of the creature before it renews itself in all its winged glory).

Early Iron Age bronze axe with horseman figure from Hallstatt, Austria.

In barbarian Europe, the double axe appears as a votive symbol as early as the later Bronze Age, occurring in the form of pendants at such sites as Fort Harrouard in France. The double axe was adopted into the Romano-Celtic panoply of images: a minia- ture example (*see* MODEL TOOL/WEAPON) comes from a temple precinct at Trier in Germany; and a pin with a double axe head has been found in Britain at Richborough, Kent. Most evocative of its possible celestial significance is the gold amulet at Balèsmes (Haute-Marne), which is in the form of a wheel with a crescent and a double axe motif soldered on. This talisman has been interpreted as being symbolic of sun, moon and storm energy.

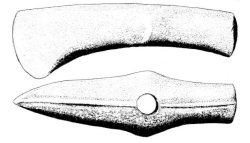

Stone Age **axe** from Jutland: these were sometimes used by Iron Age Celts as votive offerings.

□ Glück 1965; Speidel 1978; Sandars 1957, 275; Green 1984a, no. A102, 66–8; Cook 1925, 543–59.

Aylesford, Kent, is the site of a late Iron Age cremation cemetery. In one grave, which consisted of a circular pit cut into the chalk, was a stave-built wooden bucket, covered in sheet bronze, which had once contained the cremation burial. Similar bucket-burials are recorded from Swarling and Marlborough (Wilts). The Aylesford bucket is distinctive in that on opposite sides of the bronze rim are two free-standing Celtic bronze heads, identical to each other and decorated with helmets and lobed headdresses. These heads are good examples of the severed-head image, and have characteristics in common with earlier central European sculpture, for exam- ple the heads decorating the Pfalzfeld Pillar of the 5th or 4th c. BC.

□ Megaw 1970, no. 187; Megaw & Megaw 1989, 185–7.

Detail from the 1st c. BC bucket, found in a rich cremation grave at **Aylesford**, Kent.

B

Baco An inscription to this god reveals that he was invoked by Gauls living in the area of Châlon-sur-Saône. His name indicates that he was probably a boar-god, of whom many are recorded in the Celtic world (*see* ARDU-INNA; BOAR; MERCURY MOCCUS).
□ Duval 1976, 52.

Badbh is an Irish war-goddess, whose name denotes 'rage', 'fury' and 'violence'. She appears in the Ulster Cycle as a single or triple entity and, to an extent, interchangeable with other similar war-goddesses such as Nemhain. Like the MORRIGÁN, the Badbh often appears in the form of a RAVEN or CROW, 'Badbh Catha' (*see* METAMORPHOSIS). In Romano-Celtic Gaul (Haute-Savoie) a raven-goddess called Cathubodua must be the same divinity.

All the Irish war-goddesses had the power to confound armies, causing confusion by their appearance and their cries. They caused havoc especially among the forces of Connacht. Badbh herself is closely associated with the Ulster hero Cú Chulainn, whom she helps and encourages on a number of occasions. But three days after Cú Chulainn receives his death-blow, the Badbh flies over him in the guise of a crow, and the fact that he does not strike at her is proof that he is really dead.

Badbh is a crow of battle and of death. Her appearance can prophecy that someone is about to die. In the *Tale of Da Derga's Hostel*, she appears as an ugly, black, crow-like hag, harbinger of doom (*see* DA DERGA). The Badbh appears also as a 'washer at the ford' washing the arms of warriors about to die in battle.
□ Lehmann 1989, 1–10; Hennessy 1870–2, 32–55; Kinsella 1969; Mac Cana 1983, 86; Vallentin 1879–80, 19; Ross 1967a, 219, 244–5, 248; Stokes 1900, 156; O'Rahilly 1946, 126.

Ballachulish At the site of Ballachulish in Argyll was found one of the very few wooden images from the pagan Celtic period which have survived in Britain. It probably dates from the 1st c. BC and was found in peat in circumstances suggesting that it was originally within a wattled or wicker structure,

which could have been some kind of shrine. Wooden figures like this are preserved only in anaerobic, usually waterlogged conditions. The Ballachulish figure is a rare example of what appears to be a female wooden image: the statuette is oak, crudely carved, but it is naked, with the pudenda emphasized. The figure may serve to endorse the statement of the Roman poet Lucan (*Pharsalia* III, 412), who comments on wooden images of Gaulish divinities, roughly hewn on tree trunks.
□ Green 1986, fig. 5; Megaw & Simpson 1979, 477; Piggott & Daniel 1951, no. 33.

Balor was a king of the Fomorians, sea-robbers who pillaged Ireland and demanded crippling taxes of the Tuatha Dé Danann. He was called 'Balor of the Baleful Eye' because he had a single enormous eye whose glance meant instant death to an enemy. As Balor became old, the eyelid grew so heavy that it took four men to hoist it up with pulleys and ropes. Balor could not be killed with any weapon.

Balor lived on Tory Island: his one great dread was on account of an ancient prophecy – that he would eventually be destroyed by his own grandson. He had one daughter, Eithne, whom he had imprisoned in a cave on Tory with twelve serving women. But Kian, a member of the Tuatha Dé, was bitter against Balor because his family had been robbed by the Fomorians, and he sought revenge. So Kian disguised himself as a woman, entered Eithne's cave and seduced her. She bore triplets, and in his fear of the prophecy, Balor hurled them all into the sea. One, however, was saved and was taken in, reared by a blacksmith and given the name LUGH.

The feared prophecy came to pass: Lugh came to the aid of King Nuadu and the Tuatha Dé in their great war against the Fomorians. By magical means, Lugh managed to slay Balor by casting a sling shot at his eye, which drove it through the back of his head so that it massacred many of the Fomorian leader's followers.

Because of his great eye and of his being the ancestor of Lugh, Balor is often interpreted as a solar god, like his grandson Lugh himself. But in fact, Balor seems to have represented the negative forces of evil and the evil eye, whose power could only be neutralized by the positive light-force represented by Lugh.
□ Krappe 1927; O'Fáolain 1954; Carey 1984,

1–22; Ó'Cuív 1954, 64–6; O'Rahilly 1946, 308–16; Delaney 1989, 7–9.

Banbha The Irish *Book of Invasions* alludes to Banbha as one of the three eponymous goddesses of Ireland, the other two being ÉRIU and FÓDLA. She was an ancestor-goddess, in that she was the mother of Cesair, the leader of the first mythical invasion of Ireland, which occurred before the Flood. In a later invasion, that of the Sons of Mil (the Milesians, Gaels), Banbha is one of the three goddesses who each exact from the invaders the promise that the island will bear her name. Banbha is the wife of Mac Cuill, a member of the Tuatha Dé Danann (the divine invaders displaced by the Sons of Mil).
□ Mac Cana 1983, 54, 62; de Vries 1963, 135, 152; Ross 1967a, 204–5; Rolleston 1985, 132.

bard Classical writers such as Strabo (IV, 4, 4) allude to religious and learned classes among the Celts: the druids, the bards and the 'Vates'. Of these three, the bards were specifically concerned with singing and poetic eulogies. Diodorus Siculus (V, 31, 2) says that the bards were lyric poets. This threefold division is substantiated by the Irish literary tradition, which speaks of Druïdh, Filidh and Baird (bards). Once again, the Irish bards were praise-poets, but their role became increasingly subsumed by the filidh (*see* FILI). Singers and other musicians, including bards, played an important part in the ceremonies associated with Otherworld feasting. In the Fionn Cycle, the young hero Finn gains supernatural wisdom by eating a salmon caught by the bard Finnegas.
□ Mac Cana 1983, 12–13; O'Fáolain 1954; Ross 1986, 82–4.

Wooden image of a goddess, dating from the 1st c. BC, from the waterlogged site of **Ballachulish**, Argyll.

Relief of a god with hammer, dog, pot and a **barrel** by his left foot, from Monceau, Burgundy.

barrel Images of the Gaulish HAMMER-GOD in Burgundy and the lower Rhône Valley are distinctive in that the god is often accompanied by a wine barrel. In fact, the imagery of this cult is striking for the amount of wine symbolism – amphorae, pots, goblets, vine-grower's tools are all present. One interest of the barrel is that it has a close affinity with the Hammer-god's hammer: the two symbols may touch, and on some occasions, barrel and hammer may merge into one composite motif.

Barrels occur with two types of Hammer-god image: firstly, where the deity appears alone; secondly, where he is accompanied by a consort. The Burgundian iconography is the most evocative: here, hammer and barrel frequently appear together. At Monceau, the god is depicted with his dog, a wine goblet, hammer and barrel, which supports the base of the hammer shaft. On a stone at Cussy-le-Châtel, the Hammer-god is portrayed as a tipsy old man with a short-hafted, stocky hammer and his right foot resting on a barrel. At Toul near Metz, outside the region, a lost image portrayed a Hammer-god with his pot, dog, hammer and two wine barrels. Where the god is depicted with a consort, the barrel is frequently positioned between the two deities: this happens at Alesia; on a second stone from the same place, three wine barrels are present, two held by the god and a third adjacent to the leg of the goddess.

In the lower Rhône Valley, the most curious imagery is present, where hammer and barrel symbols merge into a single motif. A bronze statuette from Vienne (Isère) depicts a god wearing a wolfskin over his shoulders and accompanied by an object consisting of a long shaft, terminating in a barrel-like hammer-head with five smaller barrels radiating out on spokes from the main one.

It is a fair supposition that the barrel accompanies the Hammer-god as a symbol of wine and the florescence of the grape harvest in the great wine-growing lands of Burgundy and the lower Rhône. The relationship between the hammer and the barrel is enigmatic. But it is suggested that the hammer motif is associated with protection and regeneration (see HAMMER-GOD), and it may be that the wine in the barrel represents rebirth, in addition to its more obvious image of well-being. Red wine may be an allegory of blood and therefore perhaps resurrection. The ability of wine to lift one's mind away from reality may also have a connection here.

□ Green 1989, 42, 51–2, 70, 82–4; Espéran-dieu, 4568, 4708; Thevenot 1968, 133–42; Kent Hill 1953, 205–24; Boucher 1976, no. 301.

Bath The hot springs beside the River Avon at Bath in the west of England gush out of the ground at the rate of a quarter million gallons per day. The spot must have been sacred long before the Roman period; indeed, some Celtic coins have been found there. The goddess venerated at Bath was SULIS, equated in the Roman period with Minerva. She was a healing deity, but her Celtic name has philological links with the sun.

The Romans built a massive shrine to Sulis Minerva. Engineers converted the springs into an enormous ornamental POOL, enclosing it in a huge, imposing structure. Associated with the springs were a large Mediterranean-style temple and a vast bath suite. The temple itself may have been erected as early as the Neronian or early Flavian period (about AD 65–75). The central focus of the sanctuary was the springs and reservoir, into which numerous offerings were thrown, including many lead CURSE tablets or *defixiones* and more than 16,000 coins. The coins throw an interesting light on cult practice: there is evidence for deliberate selection of types, and many were ritually cut and 'killed' to consecrate them and render them unusable in the real world.

The great altar of the temple was carved with images of Roman gods, like Bacchus, Hercules and Jupiter. On the temple pediment was carved a male Medusa-head with flowing snake-hair and beard. The imagery here also evokes water and solar symbolism, appropriate for a shrine to a spring-deity with a solar name. The cult statue of Sulis herself is represented by a more than life-size gilded bronze head of the goddess as Minerva, hacked from the body sometime in antiquity.

The great temple at Bath displays a more regular Roman architectural style than is often found in Britain. It was wealthy and probably once possessed a theatre for the enactment of ceremonial. It was patronized by an international clientele: Romans, Romanized natives, Celts from the Gaulish provinces and Greek freedmen. The importance of the cult is shown too by the presence of religious officials: a *sacerdos* or priest had a tombstone here, and there was a school of *haruspices* (*haruspex* means 'gut-gazer') who examined the entrails of sacrifices and gave omens.

Numerous altars to Sulis or Sulis Minerva were set up at Bath. But many other Celtic deities are attested here too: Mars Loucetius and NEMETONA; Mercury and Rosmerta; the Suleviae; the triple Mothers; and Genii Cucullati. Sulis as a healer was offered a pair of votive model breasts made of ivory, perhaps worn by a woman during childbirth and lactation and then offered to the goddess in thanksgiving when her child was safely weaned.

Bath was a sanctuary of sufficient importance to be mentioned by Classical writers.
Ptolemy alludes to Bath in his *Geography* (II
3, 28), and in the 3rd c. AD Solinus speaks of
the place in his *Collectanea rerum memora-
bilium* (XXII, 10).
□ Green 1986, 154–5; Cunliffe & Davenport
1985; Cunliffe & Fulford 1982; Henig 1984,
43–7, 162; Toynbee 1962, no. 96.

bear There were dense forests in Gaul before
and during the Roman occupation: wild animals such as boar, deer and bear inhabited the
woodlands, and their presence gave rise to
cults associated with the beasts themselves
and with hunting.

One such cult concerned bears. A bear-
goddess ARTIO is known at Muri near Berne
in Switzerland. Her name means 'bear', and
she is depicted on a bronze group with a
basal dedication to her. The goddess is
depicted sitting on a chair, with fruit as
her main attribute, facing a large bear who
confronts her beneath a tree. Artio was
invoked also in a remote valley near Bollendorf in the land of the Treveri. Mercury was
surnamed 'Artaios' (*see* MERCURY ARTAIOS) at
Beaucroissant (Isère); and a Gaulish place-
name 'Artiomagus' reflects the high status of
bears. These bear-deities may have been
invoked by hunters to help them catch their
prey without harm to themselves. But there
is no doubt that Artio was also a protectress
of bears.

In Britain, the evidence for bear cults is
sparse, but in the north, small amulets attest
the veneration of these creatures. Several jet
talismans of bears come from North Britain
at, for instance, Malton, Bootle and York. A
sardonyx bear-cameo from South Shields may
also be an amulet, perhaps owned by a
hunter.
□ Boucher 1976, fig. 291; Green 1978, 63, 71,
74, pl. 91; 1986, 184–5; 1989, fig. 10; C.I.L.
XIII, 4113, 5160; Wightman 1970, 217: Thevenot 1968, 157.

Beire-le-Châtel was one of the many Romano-
Celtic healing spring sanctuaries of Burgundy. The hammer-god Sucellus was worshipped here, and so was an obscure goddess
named IANUARIA: the temple produced a
small stone statuette of a young female clad
in a heavy pleated coat and holding a set of
pan-pipes; the base is inscribed 'to the goddess Ianuaria'. Two carved heads may rep-

Pewter mask, perhaps belonging to a priest, from
a culvert of the baths at **Bath**.

Romano-Celtic jet **bear** amulet from Bootle,
Lancashire.

resent the Celtic Apollo; one has radiate hair and three horns, the other has two horns sprouting from his hair. Horn symbolism is important at this shrine: a number of stone figures of triple-horned bulls come from the sanctuary. The horn imagery is perhaps present as a symbol of fertility and well-being. Though bronze triple-horned bulls are common occurrences, especially in eastern Gaul (*see* BULL, TRIPLE-HORNED), stone examples are extremely rare. Stone images of doves from the shrine are indicative of peace, harmony and thus, perhaps, spiritual health.

□ Espérandieu, nos. 3620; 3622, 1 & 2; 3636, 1–3; Deyts 1976, nos. 9, 21–2, 44–6, 50–2; Green 1989, 180–1, fig. 81.

Beissirissa *see* JUPITER BEISSIRISSA

Belatucadrus The name 'Belatucadrus' means 'Fair Shining One'. Inscriptions to him appear in North Britain, his worship being confined to the Cumberland and Westmorland area of Hadrian's Wall. About twenty-eight dedications alluding to Belatucadrus have been found, referring either to the god's indigenous name alone or to Mars Belatucadrus, thus equating the native deity with the Roman war-god. At Carvoran, he is referred to as both 'deus Belatucadrus' and 'deus Mars Belatucadrus'; at Carlisle and Netherby he is Mars Belatucadrus; at Plumpton Wall the inscription is to 'the sacred god Belatucadrus', and at Burgh-by-Sands, where many dedications to him were made, he is invoked as 'most sacred'. Interestingly, only three of the dedications are demonstrably military, and furthermore, the diverse spellings of his name imply a low level of literacy among his devotees.

There is no iconography which is specifically linked with epigraphic dedications to the god, but in the same region, several nameless representations of horned, naked warrior-gods were set up, and it is more than likely that Belatucadrus can be identified with some of these depictions. The existence of indigenous war-gods like Belatucadrus clustering in the vicinity of Hadrian's Wall bears witness to the stimulus of native hostility to the presence of the Roman military in North Britain.

□ Ross 1967a, 181–2; Birley 1932; Fairless 1984, 224–42; R.I.B., 1776, 1784.

Belenus *see* APOLLO BELENUS

Beltene is the second of the four great Insular Celtic seasonal festivals; it was celebrated on 1 May. Beltene means 'bright FIRE' or 'goodly fire'. The festival was associated with the start of open pasturing, with the beginning of summer and the welcoming of the sun's heat to promote the growth of livestock and crops. Bonfires were kindled in sympathetic magic, to encourage the sun's warmth to penetrate the earth. According to the 9th c. glossator Cormac, two fires were lit by druids, and animals were driven between them in a magical fertility rite. Beltene was also known in Ireland as Cétshamain. It is possible that the festival was associated with the Celtic sun- and healer-deity Belenus: the names of both Belenus and Beltene contain the 'bel' element which refers to brilliant light. Beltene was a specifically Irish festival; the fact that it was linked with stock-rearing may mean that it was not an appropriate ritual activity for the whole of the Celtic world. *See also* CERNE ABBAS.

□ de Vries 1963, 334–5; Rhŷs 1901, 308–10; Ross 1986, 119–20; Green 1986, 15; 1991a; Binchy 1958, 113–38.

Bendigeidfran, or Brân the Blessed, appears as a huge, superhuman figure in the *Second Branch of the Mabinogi*, where he is described as being of such a size that no house could hold him. He is the son of Llŷr and brother of BRANWEN and Manawydan. When Branwen is humiliated by her husband Matholwch, king of Ireland, Bendigeidfran sets out with the army of the Britons to avenge her. He is so large that he wades in the Irish Sea alongside the ships of his men. There is bitter fighting, and the Britons only just prevail. But Bendigeidfran has been fatally wounded by a poisoned spear; he commands his seven surviving heroes to cut off his head, to bear it with them to the White Mount in London and bury it there, to guard the kingdom from invaders. On the way Bendigeidfran's followers spend seven years at Harlech and many more in the Happy Otherworld of Gwales. During the whole of this time, the head of Bendigeidfran remains alive, as a talisman, talking and encouraging his men. The story of Bendigeidfran demonstrates very clearly the magical and holy properties perceived in the human HEAD. *See also* CAULDRON; DECAPITATION.

□ Ross 1967a, 119, 252; Jones & Jones 1976; Mac Cana 1983, 78; Williams 1930.

Bergusia was the female element in a Celtic divine couple (*see* COUPLE, DIVINE), UCUETIS and Bergusia, who were venerated at Alesia in Burgundy and who may have been divinities of crafts. Their names are known from two epigraphic dedications, but there is also an image of a couple at Alesia which may represent them, and on which Ucuetis is depicted as a hammer-god. One of the dedications is inscribed on a large bronze vessel found in the crypt or cellar of a huge building. In this underground room were pieces of bronze and iron which could have belonged to metalsmiths. The building could have been a house belonging to a craft guild, and the underground room is suggested as having been the shrine of the presiding divine craft-patrons, Ucuetis and Bergusia.

□ Thevenot 1968, 125; Espérandieu, no. 7127.

Biliomagus 'Bile' is the Celtic word for a sacred tree. Biliomagus was a Gaulish place-name, meaning 'the plain' or 'clearing of the sacred tree'. The Irish queen-goddess Medb had her own sacred tree, called 'bile Meidbe'.

□ Ross 1967a, 34–5; Mac Cana 1983, 48.

bird (*see also* individual species in Subject Index, part 3) The veneration of birds by the Celts was associated both with the general characteristics of these creatures and with the particular qualities of individual species. The ability of birds to leave the earth and fly high in the heavens made them objects of worship in many religions of antiquity. This quality evokes ideas of freedom, and there is evidence that birds could represent the human soul liberated from the body at death.

Many species of bird were perceived as possessing prognosticatory powers: ravens and doves in particular, perhaps because of their distinctive 'voices'. Water birds reflected the link between air and water; carrion eaters represented death; and there are other examples of the veneration of specific types of bird. In the vernacular tradition, birds possessed supernatural powers, and divine entities frequently metamorphosed between human and bird form. The singing birds of the Welsh Rhiannon and Irish Clíodna possessed powers of enchantment and healing.

□ Green 1986, 186; 1989, 142–4; Ross 1967a, 234.

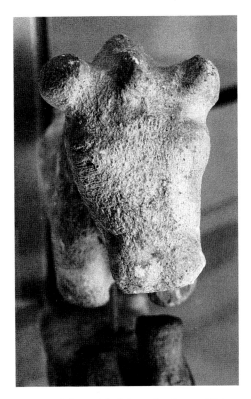

Stone triple-horned bull from the shrine of **Beire-le-Châtel**, Burgundy.

Bronze handle-mount in the form of a **bird**, from the early 3rd c. BC bronze Brå Cauldron, Denmark.

Blodeuwedd This mythical lady appears in 'Math', the *Fourth Branch of the Mabinogi*. She is created from the flowers of the oak, broom and meadowsweet, as a magical wife for LLEU LLAW GYFFES, son of Arianrhod. Blodeuwedd is conjured by the magician Gwydion and Math because of Arianrhod's oath that Lleu will never have a human wife.

Blodeuwedd is extremely beautiful, but she is faithless and has a lover, Gronw Pebyr. Together, they plot to kill Lleu; she manages to make her husband disclose how he can be killed, even though he is nearly immortal. The lovers are unsuccessful: Gronw is slain by Gwydion, and Blodeuwedd is turned into an owl.

□ Ross 1967a, 274; Mac Cana 1983.

Boann is the spirit of the River BOYNE: her story is found in the 12th c. *Dinnshenchas* or *History of Places*. Boann visits the forbidden well of Sídh Nechtan, which belongs to her husband NECHTAN, a water-god. Because Boann has disobeyed the taboo, the water turns into a torrential river, chases and engulfs her. Thus Boann becomes the River Boyne itself. Boann and the Daghda have a secret 'marriage' and produce OENGHUS, 'the young lad'. In order that their union should be concealed, the pair casts a spell upon the sun so that it remains motionless in the sky for nine months, until the baby is born: thus Oenghus is conceived and born on the same day. The name Boann has associations with 'cow'.

□ Mac Cana 1983, 32; Stokes 1894, 315; Rolleston 1985, 121; Gwynn 1913, 28ff; Bhreathnach 1982, 243–60.

boar Perhaps the most important zoomorphic symbol for the Celts. The boar represented war and hunting on the one hand and hospitality and feasting on the other. The creature is prominent in both the vernacular literature and the archaeological record.

Boars are natural war symbols. They are ferocious and indomitable, and it is significant that images of boars frequently emphasize the raised dorsal bristles of the attacking boar. Boars with prominent spinal crests are common on Celtic coins, where they may be war motifs. Boar-headed trumpets were used in warfare, and helmets were adorned with boar figurines as crests. One of the plates on the Gundestrup Cauldron shows both boar-crested helmets and carnyxes (trumpets).

Some of the Iron Age figurines of boars may well have come from helmets. The little Iron Age boar statuette from Hounslow may be such a fitment. Iron Age figurines of boars with ornate crests come from as far east as Báta in Hungary and Luncani, Romania. A hoard of bronze animal figures was deliberately buried at about the time of the Roman conquest of Gaul at Neuvy-en-Sullias (Loiret). They included three bronze boars, one of which, spinal crest erect, is nearly life-size. Definitely a war motif was the boar image attached to the later Iron Age shield from the River Witham (Lincs). Tacitus comments that the (Germanic or Celtic) tribe of the Aestii wore boar amulets as protection in battle (*Germania* 35).

Of the wild animals hunted by the Celts, boars and stags were the most common prey (*see* HUNT(ER)/HUNTER-GOD). On a Celtic coin at Maidstone in Kent, a boar and stag appear together, perhaps as hunting symbols. A 3rd c. BC bronze group at Balzars, Liechtenstein, represents warriors or hunters with a boar and stag. A Romano-Celtic bronze image of a dying boar at the Muntham Court temple (Sussex) may reflect a hunting cult. Various depictions of hunter-deities with boars include the bronze statuette of ARDUINNA in the Ardennes Forest, who rides a boar, her hunting-knife in her hand; at Reichshoffen near Strasbourg, a stone carving represents a god with a young pig under his arm. The late Iron Age depiction of the god at EUFFIGNEIX (Haute-Marne) shows the deity wearing a torc, with a boar striding along his torso: he may be a local hunter-god. The antlered nature-god Cernunnos is associated with boars on the Gundestrup Cauldron and on a relief at Nuits-Saint-Georges in Burgundy.

The association of boars with feasting, particularly the Otherworld FEAST, is very strong both in the evidence of archaeology and the literature. Strabo (IV, 4.3) says that the Celts particularly liked fresh and salted pork and that Gaulish pigs were large and fierce. Rich Iron Age graves in Britain and on the Continent attest to the funerary feast which involved pork. In the Irish mythological tradition, pork formed the basis of feasting both in this world and in the afterlife. Competition for the champion's portion of pork is amply attested. Diodorus Siculus (VI, 28) refers to this custom. An example of an Irish mythological banquet is the Feast of Bricriu, where squabbling over the best portion took place between heroes. Every 'bruidhen' or Otherworld hostel was ruled by a god who presided over the supernatural feast. Pigs were slaughtered and eaten each day, only to be reborn by magic and consumed afresh. The divine lord of the Otherworld banquet was often perceived as a man with a pig slung over his shoulder.

Enchanted or supernatural boars abound in the vernacular literature: in the Welsh tale of CULHWCH AND OLWEN, TWRCH TRWYTH is a huge enchanted boar, transformed from an evil king. The Irish hero DIARMAID has a foster-brother in boar form whom he hunts and by whom he meets his death. In the vernacular tradition, supernatural boars could be enormous and destructive, luring hunters to the Otherworld.

There is some archaeological evidence for boar sacrifice (*see* SACRIFICE, ANIMAL): at the shrine of Gournay-sur-Aronde (Oise), young pigs and lambs were butchered on site and consumed in ritual meals. Exactly the same choice of pig and sheep was made at the British Iron Age sanctuary of Hayling Island. At Sopron in Hungary, Iron Age ritual is attested by the burial of a complete boar, packed into a stone grave. A young boar was buried, perhaps as a foundation offering, at Chelmsford during the Romano-Celtic period; and at the Hockwold Romano-Celtic temple in Norfolk, the four column bases of the *cella* (inner sanctum) each had a pit containing pig and bird bones. The ritual shaft at Ashill (Norfolk) contained a sacred deposit of pots, antlers and boar tusks. *See also* BACO; MAC DA THÓ; MERCURY MOCCUS.
□ Boucher 1976, 161; Devauges 1974, 434; Green 1976, 204, 212; 1986, 179–81; 1989, 91, 133–41, figs 46, 57; Hatt n.d., pl. 23; Espérandieu, nos 2984, 7702; Allen 1976; Olmsted 1979, pl. 3E; Brunaux 1986; Downey et al. 1980, 289–304; Anon 1980, no. 76; Green 1990a; Jackson 1964; Mac Cana 1983, 51; Megaw 1970, no. 238; Foster 1977; Goodburn 1976, 342.

boat Celtic water ritual in western Europe was sometimes specifically associated with boats. Since the Middle Bronze Age, people in northern Europe had been conducting religious ceremonies involving boats and carved images of ships on granite rock slopes near the sea. At HJORTSPRING, in Denmark, in the 3rd c. BC, a boat was filled with war

Blodeuwedd, the magic Welsh woman made of flowers, an original design by Jen Delyth.

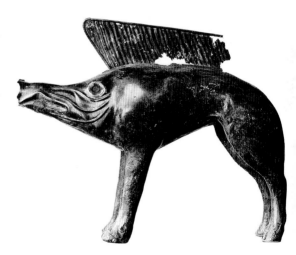

Late Iron Age bronze **boar,** nearly life-size, with emphasized dorsal bristles, indicating aggression, from Neuvy-en-Sullias, France.

booty, including more than 300 swords, spears and shields, and sacrificed animals. It was then dragged out into a bog and sunk as part of a ritual associated with war- and water-gods. A similar practice may be observed at Nydam in Schleswig-Holstein in the 4th c. AD.

Boat models were made as offerings to the gods all over north-west Europe: a hundred tiny, gold-leaf boats were deposited at Nors Thy in Jutland; and a similarly minute, gold miniature boat comes from the Iron Age *oppidum* at the Dürrnberg in Austria. A wooden, Iron Age boat model containing images of five warriors with shields was recovered from the Humber estuary at Roos Carr. At Broighter in County Derry, Northern Ireland, a hoard dating from the 1st c. BC consisted of gold jewellery, a bowl and a golden boat model, complete with mast and oars. This perhaps reflects boat ritual being practised on the western edge of the Celtic world. The Irish occurrence calls to mind the earlier deposit of the Kimmeridge shale bowl from Caergwrle in North Wales, a boat model decorated with inlaid tin and gold leaf to represent shields, oars, waves and boat ribs. The Caergwrle bowl dates from around 1000 BC.

Romano-Celtic religious iconography includes boat imagery. The Mother-goddesses at Nuits-Saint-Georges and Alesia in Burgundy are associated with boat symbolism; it has been suggested that it may reflect the journey of the soul to the Otherworld. Other Celtic goddesses, too, are linked with boats. NEHALENNIA, the marine deity who protected traders travelling across the North Sea from the Netherlands, often appears depicted with boats and rudders. Sequana, goddess of the Seine at its source near Dijon, appears on her cult image standing in a duck-prowed boat. *See also* MANANNÁN.
□ Cunliffe 1975, 89–92; Megaw 1970, no. 284; Mac Cana 1983, 93; Gelling & Davidson 1969; Green 1986, 145–8; 1989, 11.

bog Lakes and marshes were active foci of prehistoric European ritual, especially during the Celtic phase. It is not always easy to separate lakes from bogs since what is marshland in the present may originally have been a lake, when associated with Celtic ritual. Sometimes, though, it is possible to associate bogs with ritual activity. As was the case with lakes and rivers, bogs received offerings of

rich and prestigious material, especially metalwork. Bogs possess the particular property of being dangerous and treacherous, with the ambiguity of seeming innocuous, like firm ground. Their ability to suck in and engulf the unwary who strayed into them must have given rise to the perception of bogs as possessing lives of their own with a perhaps malign, supernatural power residing within them. These spirits had to be appeased and propitiated by means of gifts, both animate and inanimate.

The Iron Age bronze pony-cap and horns from Torrs in Kirkcudbright were from a bog. Many Irish cauldrons have been found, deliberately deposited in marshy ground. The great silver Gundestrup Cauldron was discovered dismantled in a peat bog in Jutland. Wagons and carts were deposited at Dejbjerg and Rappendam, also in Denmark. The Dejbjerg finds consisted of two Gaulish cult vehicles, dismantled and placed in a mound with a cremation-burial. There was a non-functional, throne-like structure in the centre of each; the finds suggest that the person interred was female. At Rappendam, quantities of wooden wheels were sunk in a peat bog; nearby was the body of a man, perhaps a human sacrifice, and parts of sacrificial animals (*see* BOG-BURIAL). The site may have been a shrine belonging to the local community. It is tempting to relate such finds to the remarks made by Tacitus (*Germania* 40) about the Teutonic goddess Nerthus, who rode through her cities on a wagon.
□ Glob 1969, 166–8; Green 1986, 144; Megaw 1970, 129, no. 203; Coles & Coles 1989.

bog-burial The most interesting feature about Iron Age ritual associated with BOGS is the evidence for human sacrifice. Most of the finds are from Denmark, where a number of human sacrificial victims were dedicated to the gods during the late 1st millennium BC. TOLLUND MAN was strangled with a sinew rope and deposited in the marsh at Tollund, wearing nothing but a leather cap and a girdle, in about 500 BC. Borre Fen Man was garotted in the same manner; Grauballe Man had his throat cut. One of the most horrifying sacrifices was that of a lady in Juthe Fen, Jutland: she was pinned down in the peat, perhaps while still alive, by wooden crooks which had been driven over each knee and elbow joint, and heavy branches clamped across her chest and stomach. She may have been a witch; certainly her killers wished to make very sure that she stayed in the bog and her spirit did not wander to plague the living.

These Danish bog-sacrifices show a striking similarity to a British example, found in 1984. This is Lindow Man, a young male who was hit on the head twice, garotted and his throat cut before being thrust face-down in a shallow pool within the bog at LINDOW MOSS in Cheshire. The man was about 25–30 years old when he died, probably during the 4th c. BC (though there is some controversy about the C14 dates). Lindow Man's despatch closely resembles that of Tollund Man: in each instance the garotte followed a distinctive knotting technique; both men partook of a kind of ritual meal before being killed; both were naked, apart from a cap and belt in the case of the Danish body and a fox-fur armlet for Lindow Man. The body of Lindow Man was painted.
□ Stead et al. 1986; Green 1986, 144–5; Glob 1969, 18–101; Coles & Coles 1989.

A 1st c. BC gold model **boat**, from Broighter, County Derry, Northern Ireland.

Borvo was a male healing spring-deity, who was worshipped in Gaul under the name of Borvo, Bormo, Bormanus or a similar derivative. The name is connected with 'bubbling water' and reflected the behaviour of springs, because of either their heat or gases. The god could be venerated simply under his native name, but he was also frequently invoked with the Romano-Celtic version of Apollo, who was associated in Gaul with thermal spring sanctuaries.

Borvo/Bormo/Bormanus was worshipped over a wide area, from Bourbonne-les-Bains (Haute-Marne) to Galicia in north-west Spain; he was invoked in the valleys of the Loire and Rhône, the Alps and Provence at, for instance, Aix-en-Provence. Borvo's name is reflected in that of many settlements where he was venerated: BOURBONNE-LES-BAINS and Bourbonne-Lancy are examples. At Entrains (Nièvre) in Burgundy, Borvo is known from epigraphic sources, and an image of the god shows him holding a goblet (perhaps filled with curative water) and with a purse and plate of fruit, reflective of his role as a god of prosperity and fertility. A sherd of terra sigillata found at the sacred spring site of Vichy (Allier) depicts a naked god seated on a rock; in his hand is a cup of liquid which bubbles over its brim.

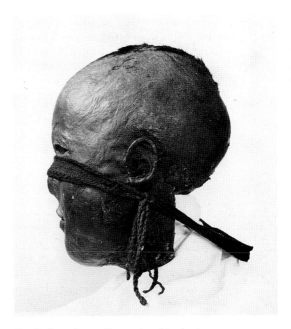

Head of a girl, ritually murdered in the 1st c. BC and committed as a **bog-burial** to the marsh at Windeby, Denmark.

Although Borvo is generally linked with Apollo, at Aix-les-Bains he may have been equated instead with Hercules. At this healing spring shrine, a marble torso was found in the swimming-pool of the bath: inscriptions give us the name of Borvo or Bormanus, but in one spring, not far from the baths, was discovered a series of eight small bronze figurines which had been thrown into the water by bathers in gratitude for their cure. These statuettes, which had been ritually damaged (to render them appropriate for the supernatural – see RITUAL DAMAGE), represented not an Apollo-like figure but Hercules brandishing his club. This Graeco-Roman hero may have been identified with the native spring-healer Borvo because it was believed that the 'strong man' of Classical mythology was powerful against disease.

Borvo was frequently associated with a divine consort: at Die (Drôme) in the south of France, Bormanus and Bormana were worshipped. At Bourbonne-les-Bains, there was a sanctuary to Borvo and Damona (she was also the partner of Apollo Moritasgus at Alesia): in the ruins of the shrine were two bronze snake's heads, reflective of the regenerative symbolism of the serpent. Finally, the female version of Borvo/Bormanus – Bormana – could be independent of her male consort: thus at Saint-Vulbas (Ain), Bormana was worshipped on her own, there being no mention of Bormanus.
□ C.I.L. XII, 2901; XIII, 5924; Espérandieu, 2262; Duval 1976, 77; Thevenot 1968, 99, 103–4; Dayet 1963, 167–78.

Bouray A bronze statuette of a god from Bouray (Seine-et-Oise) dates perhaps as early as the 2nd c. BC. The image is of a naked male deity wearing a torc (necklet) and seated cross-legged. The figure is notable in having an enormous head and diminutive legs which end in hooves, probably those of a stag. The over-emphasis of the head may reflect the Celtic belief in the religious importance of the human HEAD; the stag hooves and cross-legged attitude may identify the Bouray deity as CERNUNNOS, though there is no sign of antlers.
□ Green 1989, fig. 37; Pobé & Roubier 1961, no. 11; Joffroy 1979, no. 78.

Bourbonne-les-Bains (Haute-Marne) was an important Gaulish curative spring sanctuary. The name of the site derives from the local spring-god Bormo or BORVO, whose name means 'bubbling spring water'. The god and his consort Damona were worshipped here. Other deities associated with the therapeutic spring shrine included Maponus, the 'Divine Youth' and the Gaulish Hammer-god: on a depiction of him, he is accompanied not by his usual pot but with a billhook, perhaps a vine-grower's tool. The Sun-god was venerated too at Bourbonne-les-Bains; solar wheel-amulets were cast into the spring water as votive offerings, perhaps to the Sun-deity in his capacity as a healer.
□ Jubainville 1893, 152; Thevenot 1953, 293–304; Green 1989, 82; Duval 1976, 77, 117; C.I.L. XIII, 5924; Chabouillet 1880–1, 15ff.

Boyne, River Like many great rivers in the Celtic world, the River Boyne in Ireland had its own divine spirit: this was BOANN, who visited the forbidden sacred well of NECHTAN, her husband. In consequence of breaking this taboo, Boann was engulfed by the well-water, which flowed out and chased her: thus water and Boann combined to form the River Boyne. This story is told in the 12th c. Irish compilation known as the *Dinnshenchas*. According to one tradition, the hero Finn dies by drowning in the Boyne. *See also* SALMON.
□ Stokes 1894, 315; Rolleston 1985, 121.

Bran (Irish), son of Febhal, is an example of the archetypal mortal who is lured to the Otherworld by a goddess in the form of a beautiful woman. Bran is walking near his stronghold when he hears music of such sweetness that it enchants him and sends him to sleep. When he awakes, he finds an apple branch beside him, silver with white blossom. He returns to his fortress, and that night, the goddess appears and sings to him of the wonders of the Happy Otherworld: the land she speaks of is a series of islands far out in the western ocean; it is full of beauty, music, fine sport and agelessness. The goddess gives him the apple branch. The next day Bran sets off to find the goddess and the Otherworld of which she has sung, accompanied by his three foster-brothers and twenty-seven warriors. The magic symbolism of three and three times nine is probably significant.

The tale of Bran's journeying is told in the *Voyage of Bran* or *Immram Brain*, which probably dates from the later 7th or 8th c. AD. A lost manuscript compiled at the Monastery of Druim Snechta is the original source of the many extant texts of the *Immram*. On his sea voyage, Bran encounters Manannán mac Lir, the god of the sea, who is riding the ocean in a chariot. The journey continues until Bran and his followers arrive at the Land of Women, where he sees the beautiful goddess. They remain on this island for what they perceive as being one year, when some of Bran's crew become restless for home and beg their leader to leave. But the goddess warns them that, in human terms, many centuries have passed and that if they set foot on Irish soil, they will instantly age hundreds of years and crumble to dust. Notwithstanding, the crew persuade Bran to embark for home. When off the coast of Ireland, one of the sailors flings himself ashore, but the goddess' prophecy comes true and he turns to dust. Bran writes his story in ogham on wooden sticks and casts them ashore from his boat; he then continues his wanderings, and what befalls him eventually is not recorded.

□ Mac Cana 1983, 69, 89, 124; Berresford Ellis 1987, 45–6; Mac Cana 1976, 95–115; 1972, 102–42.

Bràn the Blessed *see* BENDIGEIDFRAN

Branwen gives her name to the *Second Branch of the Mabinogi*. She is the daughter of Llŷr and the sister of BENDIGEIDFRAN (Brân the Blessed) and of Manawydan. Their court is at Harlech in North Wales. Branwen is described as one of the three chief ladies (or matriarchs) in the land and the most beautiful woman in the world. MATHOLWCH, king of Ireland, travels to Harlech to seek the hand of Branwen in marriage. One of her brothers, Efnisien, is so angered by the betrothal that, as an insult, he mutilates Matholwch's horses in their stall. Branwen and Matholwch are married and return to Ireland. But in revenge for the insult done to the king, Branwen is humiliated and degraded: she is forced to act as cook and, moreover, her ears are boxed every day by the butcher. Care is taken that no knowledge of her fate travels to Wales, but Branwen rears a young starling, trains it, ties a letter to its leg and bids it fly to Bendigeidfran. It does so, and thus the Britons make war with the Irish.

We know little of Branwen herself: she and Matholwch have a son, Gwern. After Bendigeidfran is fatally wounded and his head cut off at his own command, Branwen

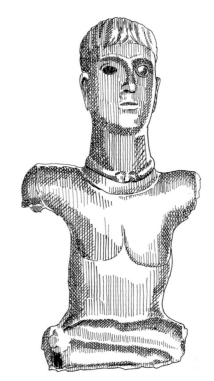

Bronze statuette of a god with a torc and hooves from **Bouray**, France.

Harlech Castle in North Wales, site of the court of **Branwen** and her family.

returns to Britain, lamenting that two islands have been destroyed because of her. She dies and is buried near where she landed, at Aber Alaw. There is little evidence for the divinity of Branwen, except inasmuch as she is described as one of three powerful women or matriarchs, a possible allusion to the Celtic triple Mother-goddesses. But her brother Bendigeidfran has a great deal of magic attached to him, and he is certainly of supernatural status.

☐ Jones & Jones 1976; Rolleston 1985, 366–72; Mac Cana 1983, 78, 80.

Bres King Bres ('the Beautiful') is mentioned in the *Book of Invasions* as one of the first kings of the Tuatha Dé Danann: he reigns as surrogate for Nuadu, since the latter has lost his arm in battle, thus no longer meeting the criterion of physical perfection demanded for Irish kingship. Bres is a curious, complex character, since his father was a king of the Fomorians, deadly enemies of the Tuatha Dé. The rule of Bres was oppressive, and Ireland fell under the influence of the Fomorians. Most important was the fact that Bres was mean and gave niggardly hospitality; this gave rise to barrenness in the land.

Nuadu's arm was replaced by Dian Cécht with one of silver, and with the support of Lugh, the Tuatha Dé joined battle with the Fomorians – the Second Battle of Magh Tuiredh. Bres was captured, and his life was spared in return for acting as adviser on the appropriate times of the year for ploughing, sowing and harvesting. This is interesting: the Tuatha Dé lacked farming skills, and this is why Bres, the half-Fomorian, was so valuable to them. The Fomorians understood agricultural matters, whilst the Tuatha Dé possessed craft skills.

☐ Macalister 1931; Mac Cana 1983, 54–61.

Bricriu appears in the Ulster Cycle as a trouble-maker, one of whose principal aims seems to have been to promote rivalry and dissension between heroes. He was nicknamed 'Nemhthenga' or 'Poison Tongue'. He is particularly associated with Cú Chulainn and appears in many tales about him. One important story is the 'Feast of Bricriu'. The mischief-maker invites the Ulstermen to a great feast, and when they show reluctance to attend (because of Bricriu's reputation), he threatens them with dire strife and trouble which he will brew up between them. Bricriu builds a special house in which to entertain King Conchobar and the Ulstermen. At the feast itself, Bricriu stirs up jealousy between three Ulster heroes, Conall Cernach, Loeghaire and Cú Chulainn, so that they turn upon each other. Bricriu does this by offering each of them the champion's portion of pork. Peace is eventually restored by Sencha, the peacemaker, and by Ailill of Connacht, who acts as arbitrator. Next, Bricriu promotes rivalry among the wives of the three heroes. The problem is settled when the three warriors are judged by ordeal in Connacht and primacy is awarded to Cú Chulainn.

☐ Mac Cana 1983, 97–100; Ross 1986, 40.

Bricta was the female companion of LUXOVIUS, the god of the spring at Luxeuil (Haute-Saône), there being epigraphic dedications to the couple from the site. Whilst it is known from the form of his name that Luxovius had associations with light and with the site of Luxeuil itself, little of Bricta's nature is evidenced. It has been suggested that she may be linked with the Irish goddess BRIGIT, who became St Brigit when Ireland became Christian.

☐ Wuilleumier 1984, no. 403; Green 1986, 153; 1989, 45–6.

Brigit The name of this Irish goddess was originally an epithet meaning 'exalted one'. Brigit is of especial interest because she appears to have undergone a smooth transition from pagan goddess to Christian saint.

Brigit was both one goddess and three: she is sometimes linked with two eponymous sisters. She was a divinity of healing, crafts and poetry; she was expert in DIVINATION and prophecy (*see* ORACLE), and she was invoked by women in childbirth. The goddess was the territorial deity of Leinster, though she was venerated all over Ireland; and she was the daughter of the Daghda. There was a strong fertility aspect to Brigit's cult: her festival was on 1 February, the feast of Imbolc, which was associated with the lactation of ewes and was one of the four great Celtic seasonal festivals. It is possible that the Irish goddess was linked with the great northern British deity Brigantia.

As a saint, Brigit took over many of the attributes of the pagan goddess. Her birth and upbringing were steeped in magic: she was born in a druid's household and fed on the milk of magical, Otherworld cows. As a

saint of Kildare, her FERTILITY symbolism is intense, even though she herself was a virgin: she supplied limitless food without her larder ever dwindling; she could provide a lake of milk from her cows, which were milked three times a day; and as presider over ale brewing at Easter, one measure of her malt made enough ale for her seventeen churches. But most significant is that the feast day of St Brigit took place on 1 February, the pagan Imbolc, which was the festival of Brigit the goddess.
☐ Rolleston 1985, 103; O'Riain 1978, 138–55; Vendryes 1924, 241–4; Bray 1987, 209–15; Mac Cana 1983, 32–4, 93.

Brixianus *see* JUPITER BRIXIANUS

bull The strength, ferocity and virility of the untamed bull was revered and admired by all the Celtic peoples. From the beginning of the free Celtic period in Europe, there is evidence for the veneration of bulls. In addition, the domesticated ox had its own symbolism of agricultural wealth and its power as a draught animal. Bull figurines occur as early as the 7th c. BC: a small bronze bull statuette comes from a grave at Hallstatt in Austria; its huge horns serve to emphasize its aggressive nature. A similar figurine comes from a 6th c. BC context at the cave of Býčiskála in Czechoslovakia. In the later Iron Age, the repeated application of bull-head escutcheons to metal buckets and the bull-heads decorating firedogs may reflect the feasting symbolism associated with the bull.

There is evidence for the sacrifice of bulls and oxen (*see* SACRIFICE, ANIMAL) during the Iron Age. At GOURNAY-SUR-ARONDE (Oise), a temple was built associated with the pre-Roman *oppidum*. Here there is abundant evidence for the burial of elderly cattle, perhaps as offerings to the chthonic gods. Here, whilst some animals were slaughtered and butchered, horses and cattle were allowed to die naturally and offered whole to the gods. Bull sacrifice is amply attested on the Iron Age silver cauldron at Gundestrup in Jutland: the abundant iconography of the cauldron includes an image of a slain bull on the base plate and another scene where three bulls are being attacked by three sword-bearing warriors: the huge size of these creatures in relation to their killers may reflect their supernatural status. Bull sacrifice among the Celts is recorded by Pliny (*Natural*

The Well of St **Brigit**, Fouchart, Ireland. People still hang rags by the spring in honour of the saint.

Bronze **bull** figurine, 6th c. BC, from a cave at Býčiskála, Bohemia.

History XVI, 95) who gives an account of a festival on which the druids climbed a sacred oak, cut down some mistletoe, caught it in a white cloak and sacrificed two white bulls, on the sixth day of the moon (horned or crescent-shaped at this time). Mistletoe was concerned with fertility and was regarded as an antidote to barrenness; the bulls may also be involved with fecundity.

There is a great deal of bull symbolism in Romano-Celtic Europe. The Bull-with-three-Cranes, TARVOSTRIGARANUS, was venerated at Paris and Trier, where the bull may be associated with seasonal imagery and the Tree of Life. Triple-horned bull images emphasize the efficacy of the horn in terms of the symbolism of fertility and aggression; and many gods of human form adopted bull horns (*see* BULL, TRIPLE-HORNED; HORNS). In Classical and Oriental religions, the bull was associated with the sky-gods; the link is also demonstrated in the Celtic world by such images as the Willingham Fen (Cambs) sceptre, where a triple-horned bull's head accompanies the image of the sky-god. Bulls were also frequently associated with the antlered god Cernunnos, occurring in company with this deity at Nuits-Saint-Georges in Burgundy, Reims and Saintes. Bulls were also connected with Gaulish healing shrines; their images appear, for instance, at Sequana's sanctuary of *Fontes Sequanae*; at Forêt d'Halatte; and at Beire-le-Châtel.

Ireland had a predominantly pastoral economy in antiquity, and cattle figure prominently in the written mythological tradition. Bulls were important images here, having close associations with the supernatural. In one tradition, the high king of Ireland was chosen by means of the TARBHFHESS or bull-sleep: a bull was killed, and a chosen individual ate his fill of its flesh and drank the broth. He then slept, and a truth spell was chanted over him; he would then dream of the person who should be elected king.

The greatest bull story in Irish mythology concerns the Donn Cuailnge or the Brown Bull of Cooley. This is a great Brown Bull of Ulster, an animal capable of human reason. The great Ulster tale of the *Táin Bó Cuailnge* or the *Cattle Raid of Cooley* is based on this bull. In a foretale to the *Táin*, Medb and Ailill, the queen and king of Connacht, are each boasting of their possessions. They are equal in every respect save that Medb has nothing to compare with Ailill's famous

white-horned bull. Medb searches all Ireland to find an equal but to no avail. Then she hears of the Brown Bull of Ulster. The bull's owner, Daire mac Fiachniu, at first agrees to part with him on loan in return for substantial treasure, but he changes his mind on overhearing the drunken brags of Medb's men that they would have seized the creature anyway, with or without Daire's permission. The Brown Bull is sent off into hiding within Ulster.

Both the Brown Bull of Ulster and the White-Horned Bull of Connacht are famed for their huge size and phenomenal strength: the Brown is said to be so large that fifty boys can play on his back. The hero Ferghus commented that the two bulls had been sent to Ireland by jealous gods on purpose to cause strife and destruction among men. He said that they were enchanted bulls, having been metamorphosed from swineherds and then ravens. They had always caused war and ruin.

Queen Medb decides to invade Ulster and take possession of the Brown Bull by force. There then follows a long and bloody war between Connacht and Ulster. The night before the great rout of Ireland by the Ulstermen, the Brown Bull of Ulster is sent into Connacht for safety. Once there, he bellows with excitement at the sight and smell of a new land; the White-Horned Bull of Ailill hears him – no one but he has ever before dared to make such a noise in his territory. Medb's people name Bricriu as judge between the two animals: they fight all day and all night, all over Ireland. The Brown Bull eventually kills Ailill's bull and carries the carcass impaled on his horns. But as he turns back to Ulster in triumph, he rushes head-on at a mountain and perishes (an alternative ending is that his heart bursts with his exhaustion). The fight is a symbol of the great struggle between Ulster and Connacht, and the death of the two creatures brings peace between the two lands.

□ O'Fáolain 1954; Olmsted 1982, 165–72; Kinsella 1969; Maugard 1959, 427–33; Green 1986, 176–9; 1989, 149–51; Espérandieu 1319, 3134, 4929; Ross 1986, 91; Planson & Pommeret 1986; Mohen et al. (eds) 1987, no. 26; Megaw 1970, 35.

bull, triple-horned Images of bulls in Romano-Celtic Europe are frequently depicted with the addition of a third horn. Nearly forty examples of triple-horned bulls are recorded, mainly from Gaul, with a few British images. They appear mainly as bronze figurines, though both stone and clay three-horned bulls occur. Their distribution indicates that they were indigenous to the Gaulish provinces, being found most frequently among the Lingones, Sequani and the eastern tribes generally. The unequivocally sacred character of triple-horned bulls is indicated by their appearance in shrines and by occasional votive dedications associated with them. Stone bulls were offered at the shrine of BEIRE-LE-CHÂTEL in Burgundy. A bronze three-horned bull at Auxy (Seine-et-Loire) was dedicated to the Emperor. Some of the British bull images have interesting associations: a clay figurine of a triple-horned bull was found in a child's grave at Colchester; a bronze example comes from a late temple at Maiden Castle, Dorset. The head of a bronze bull is part of the complex iconography of the WILLINGHAM FEN (Cambs) sceptre.

The triple-horned bull, then, occurs in association with a number of other images. At Beire-le-Châtel, one deity was Ianuaria; the occurrence here of depictions of an Apollo-like god and of doves suggests that this was a healing and possibly oracular sanctuary. The Maiden Castle bull is curious in having the busts of three female divinities on its back, an image which may possibly relate to TARVOSTRIGARANUS, the Bull with three Cranes. At Willingham Fen, the bull is the associate of the Celtic Sky-god, with his eagle and wheel.

TRIPLISM was a powerful religious symbol in the Celtic world. The number three had an efficacy which cannot be explained simply by its multiplicity. HORNS were also potent symbols of aggression and virility; thus the addition of a third horn to the image of a BULL must have considerably increased the potency of its symbolism. Boucher suggests that the artistic origin of the triple-horned bull image may derive from a Pompeii–Herculaneum type, where bull figurines have birds perched between their horns. It is easy to see how, in a Celtic milieu, the bird could become a third horn. The addition of a horn to a conventional bull image possesses a symbolism over and above the emphasis on the horns and the introduction of a triplistic element. The unnatural extra horn serves to remove the image from nature and give it a supernatural, supranormal status.

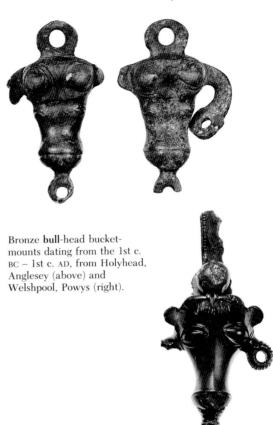

Bronze **bull**-head bucket-mounts dating from the 1st c. BC – 1st c. AD, from Holyhead, Anglesey (above) and Welshpool, Powys (right).

Bronze **triple-horned bull** from Glanum, Provence.

The bull itself was revered as a creature of great power, fertility and invincibility. But it was also a creature of good fortune. The Beire-le-Châtel bulls were associated with a beneficent, healing cult; the little bronze three-horned bull from GLANUM in Provence prances with joy; and the Willingham bull is associated with light and the sun. Finally, the occurrence of triple-horned bull figurines in such graves as that of a child at Colchester may have represented good luck in the after-life.

□ Green 1986, 190–2; 1989, 180–2; 1984a, no. C6, pl. LXXXI; Colombet & Lebel 1953, 112; Boucher 1976, 170ff; Thevenot 1968, 154–6; Charrière 1966, 155ff; Lebel & Boucher 1975, 108; Deyts 1976, nos 21, 22, 44–6.

burial *see* BOG-BURIAL; CART/CHARIOT-BURIAL; CAULDRON; DEATH; DECAPITATION; DOG; INFANT-BURIAL; OTHERWORLD; REINHEIM; SÍDH; TRANSMIGRATION OF SOULS; VIX; WELWYN

Býčiskála was an important Czechoslovakian cult centre, situated in a cave and associated with local iron working. In the 6th c. BC, religious activities, apparently connected with human and animal sacrifice, took place. Areas of the cave were used for funeral pyres; wagons, vessels, grain and beasts were offered, perhaps to the infernal powers. Forty people, mostly women, were interred here, many with their heads, hands or feet missing; nearby were the ritually quartered bodies of two horses. Inside a cauldron was a human skull; another had been made into a drinking cup. A votive offering found here consisted of a small bronze bull figurine.

□ Megaw 1970, no. 35.

  C

Camonica Valley In an isolated valley in the forests of the Italian Alps is a series of sacred rock carvings which date from the later Neolithic to the end of the Iron Age. The practice of carving on the Camunian rocks was already dying out before the Romans occupied the region in the 1st c. BC. The art is in such a remote area that its primary purpose must have been religious: it can only have been seen by deliberate visitors to the valley. Camonica Valley is a natural corridor in difficult, mountainous terrain, a pass used by wild herds in migration or in harsh weather. The area was prime hunting country and a rich source of food. The Camunian people were great hunters and they portrayed themselves and their prey on the rock faces.

The Iron Age Camunians were Celts. During the preceding Bronze Age phases, the dominant images on the rocks included oxen, weapons and the sun. In the Celtic period, the stag and the sun predominated. The hunters are depicted, sometimes aggressively masculine, ithyphallic, with huge muscles and large weapons. The close affinity between hunter and victim is demonstrated in scenes where an image is semi-human, semi-animal: on a 7th c. BC carving at Naquane, an ithyphallic hunter is accompanied by a creature with enormous antlers who is half man, half STAG. Even more significant is the creature depicted on a 4th c. BC carving at PASPARDO, a large standing man dressed in a long garment, a torc around each arm and antlers on his head. He is accompanied by a ram-horned snake and a small ithyphallic devotee. This figure may be the earliest known representation of the antlered Celtic god CERNUNNOS.

Besides the sun and hunting cults, the Celtic Camunians also portrayed their funerary ritual on the rocks: death scenes are drawn, with four-wheeled wagons bearing urns (perhaps containing the ashes of the deceased) and accompanied by processions of worshippers or mourners. Indeed, a whole way of life and death, traditions, customs and religious perceptions are described at Camonica, in a series of ritual acts which spanned a period of perhaps 3000 years.

□ Anati 1965; Green 1989, figs. 35, 54, 71.

Camulus *see* MARS CAMULUS

cart/chariot The practice of CART- or CHARIOT-BURIAL which took place in Hallstatt and La Tène Europe may have links with Celtic and proto-Celtic religion involving vehicles. In the pre-Celtic Bronze Age Urnfield tradition in Europe, model carts bearing sheet-bronze vessels may reflect a ritual designed magically to induce rain or drive it away. The Trundholm 'sun car', buried in a Danish field in about 1300–1200 BC, consisted of a six-wheeled cart bearing a gilt bronze sun disc and borne by a horse. The model cult wagon from STRETTWEG in Austria dates from the 7 c.

BC. On the vehicle stands the image of a goddess holding a vessel aloft, accompanied by scenes of a ritual hunt, with stags, horsemen and footsoldiers.

Chariots were prestige vehicles for the Celtic military aristocracy. They were fast and manœuvrable in warfare, showing off the skill of chariot driver, horse and soldier. By Caesar's time, chariots had fallen into disuse for fighting, though he encountered them in Britain. But as religious transport they remained important. Tacitus (*Germania* 40) describes the Teutonic earth-goddess NERTHUS who travelled on a wagon in cult processions. A goddess portrayed on the Gundestrup Cauldron is flanked by two stylized wheels, which may represent a chariot. Queen Medb of Connacht drove round her camp before the battles with Ulster. A Romano-Celtic image of two Mother-goddesses at Essey in Burgundy depicts the deities seated in a chariot. Finally, the Graeco-Roman chariot of the sun-god Apollo was occasionally adopted for the transport of the Celtic Sky-god: at Besigheim, Stuttgart, the normal mounted horseman-giant group on a Jupiter-column is replaced by the Sky-god driving a chariot, with the chthonic monster on the ground. Here, the vehicle represents the solar element in the cult, in place of the sun-horse. □ Reinach 1917, 157; Green 1984a, 177; 1991a, Espérandieu, 2325; Megaw 1970, no. 38; Glob 1974; Coles & Harding 1979, 367–8; Gimbutas 1965, 341–2.

A 7th c. BC rock-art scene at Naquane, **Camonica Valley**, depicting a four-wheeled cart pulled by two horses.

A 2nd c. BC coin from Germany, showing a charioteer driving a two-wheeled **cart** or **chariot**, pulled by two horses.

cart/chariot-burial During the Hallstatt and La Tène Iron Age, the élite in Celtic society were traditionally interred in rich graves, some of which are characterized by the presence of a wagon or light cart. During the Hallstatt period (the earliest Iron Age of non-Mediterranean Europe) members of the highest rank in society were buried in wooden mortuary chambers beneath earthen barrows, accompanied by four-wheeled wagons, sometimes partly dismantled. In some burials, three sets of horse harness or trappings have been found, representing the chieftain's own charger as well as the wagon team itself. Very occasionally, the HORSE team itself was buried with the dead. Hallstatt men and women were both interred with vehicles. The 6th c. BC Höhmichele Barrow (Germany) contained two wooden chambers, one with a female wagon-burial, the other a male interment with a wagon and horse trappings: he was

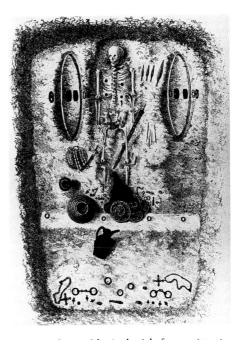

Drawing of a **cart/chariot-burial** of a warrior, at La Gorge Meillet, Marne, 4th–3rd c. BC.

laid on a bull hide, with a woman beside him. With him were his quiver, two bows and fifty iron-headed arrows. The wealth of this grave is indicated by the resplendent grave furniture – vessels, jewellery and rich textiles, including Chinese silk. This is just one example of a rich Hallstatt cart-burial. Another is the late Hallstatt princess' grave at VIX in Burgundy, where a lady of high rank was interred on a dismantled wooden cart and accompanied by an enormous Greek *krater* or wine-mixing vessel, imported from Corinth or Tarentum. Further east, at BÝČISKÁLA in Czechoslovakia, a Hallstatt funerary wagon was found, sheathed in bronze and decorated with swastikas. When new, the metal would have gleamed like gold and would have been an awe-inspiring focus of the funeral ceremonies.

In about 500 BC the centre of Celtic power shifted north and west to areas like the Marne in eastern France. The tradition of vehicle-burial continued, but now, high-status interments were accompanied by light, two-wheeled carts or chariots, again sometimes dismantled and occasionally with the horse team itself. On the Continent, such burials are demonstrably those of warriors: in Britain, the evidence is less clear. Two-wheeled vehicle-burials began in Europe in the 5th c. BC, early in the La Tène period. An example of a Marne chariot-burial is 'La Gorge Meillet', which consisted of two contemporary inhumations: the upper body was that of a man with a sword; the lower one was a youth, lying on a two-wheeled vehicle and dressed in a tunic. He had rich grave goods – jewellery, a toilet set, a long sword, four spears, food and wine.

In Britain, a group of Continental Celts appear to have established themselves in the north-east early in the 4th c. BC and then spread elsewhere within England. They brought with them a distinctive material culture (the so-called 'Arras Culture') which manifested itself in specific burial traditions, including cart-burial. Vehicles were interred with their owners, sometimes complete, sometimes dismantled, but rarely with weapons. Both men and women were thus buried. The 'Lady's Barrow' contained an extended skeleton, a joint of pork, a dismantled chariot, a whip and a mirror: the inference is that this was a female's grave. The 'King's Barrow' also contained an extended skeleton, but with the vehicle were the bodies of the horse team,

who had been sacrificed at the death of their master. Recent discoveries at Wetwang Slack (E. Yorks) include two chariots, each at the centre of a square barrow, accompanying a male and a female burial. Both vehicles were dismantled before interment, and both burials exhibit a formalized and organized ritual: the iron tyres and chassis were deposited first, then the dead person with the side of pork, and finally the wheels and the rest of the vehicle. In the woman's tomb most of the grave goods were made of bronze: she was buried, crouched, with her meat, a mirror, a swan's-neck dress-pin and what appears to be a work box. By contrast, the man's grave was accompanied almost exclusively by objects of iron: he was a warrior, and he took with him to the afterlife his sword, seven spears and a shield of early La Tène type. The Wetwang Slack graves may well be dynastic burials of, perhaps, the ruling chieftain and chieftainess.

The practice of vehicle-burial was widespread in the Iron Age. In the 1st c. BC two dismantled Gaulish cult vehicles were buried in a bog deposit, accompanying a female cremation at Dejbjerg in Denmark. Far away, in North Italy, the Iron Age Celts of CAMONICA VALLEY depicted scenes including funerary wagons bearing urns and funeral processions accompanying them.

□ Burgess 1980, 277; Champion et al. 1984, 270–3; Green 1986, 3, 123–6; Olmsted 1979, 130–2; Glob 1969, 167; Megaw 1970, no. 7; Megaw & Megaw 1989, 46–7; Stead 1979; Dent 1985, 85–92; Collis 1984, 118, 138; Hodson & Rowlett 1973, 184–5; Cunliffe 1974, 287–99; Anati 1965.

Cathbadh In the Ulster Cycle of prose tales, Cathbadh is a DRUID during the reign of King Conchobar of Ulster. Cathbadh's primary role seems to have been concerned with prophecy (*see* ORACLE) and DIVINATION, and he appears time and again to foretell good or evil to the Ulstermen. Cathbadh was a powerful figure, who on occasions took precedence over the king himself.

In the *Cattle Raid of Cooley* or *Táin Bó Cuailnge*, Cathbadh is an instructor of young heroes in the arts of divination, telling them of good and bad omens and which days were auspicious or inauspicious for certain activities. During one of these instruction sessions, Cathbadh prophecies that that particular day was lucky for anyone taking up arms, that his life would be short but glorious. The young hero Cú Chulainn hears this prophecy and immediately demands arms of the king, even though he is still a young boy.

On another occasion, Cathbadh warns the Ulstermen against the bitter and destructive satire of the poet Aithirne. An important prophecy of the druid concerned the birth of Deirdre. She was born to Fedlimid, King Conchobar's storyteller; Cathbadh was present at her birth and accurately foretold that she would be extremely beautiful but that she would cause ruin and slaughter among the Ulstermen.

□ Dunn 1914, 60; Ross 1967a, 54–5; Kinsella 1969; O'Fáolain 1954; O'Hógáin 1990; Mac Cana 1983, 94.

The La Gorge Meillet warrior, interred with his vehicle in a **cart/chariot-burial**, Marne, France.

Caturix *see* MARS CATURIX

cauldron As early as the later Bronze Age of pre-Celtic Europe, sheet-bronze vessels were used in ritual associated with feasting and the dead. The cauldrons of the later Bronze Age (from the end of the 2nd millennium BC) were primarily ceremonial cooking vessels, perhaps used for heating drink as well as for boiling meat. They were undoubtedly used at large feasts: some have a capacity of 13–16 gallons. They appear in Continental European contexts, and many come from Ireland. In later Bronze Age Europe and during the Iron Age, cauldrons seem to have been associated with both funerary and water ritual. Urnfield sheet-bronze vessels, sometimes mounted on wheeled wagons, carried the cremated remains of the dead. During the Iron Age, cauldrons were deliberately buried in watery contexts: in Denmark, the Gundestrup and Brå Cauldrons come from bogs. A huge bronze cauldron filled with more than 2,000 pieces of bronze jewellery comes from Duchcov in Czechoslovakia, an Iron Age spring sanctuary. In Britain, there are several lake deposits containing cauldrons: that at Llyn Fawr in Mid-Glamorgan dates from about 600 BC, though the cauldrons themselves are older; the Llyn Cerrig deposit on Anglesey contains material dating from the 2nd c. BC to the 1st c. AD. The Scottish cauldron-lake finds at Carlingwark Loch and Blackburn Mill date from the very late Iron Age. Some of the Iron Age cauldrons are very large: the silver cult vessel from Gundestrup has a capacity of 28.5 gallons; the bronze cauldron at Brå could hold 132.

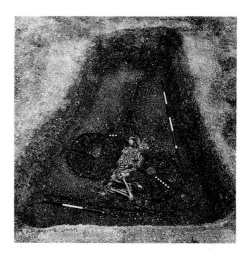

Cart/chariot-burial of a warrior at Garton Slack, East Yorkshire.

Late Iron Age **cauldron**, found filled with ironwork, with another vessel inverted over it and buried as a votive deposit in the bog at Blackburn Mill, Scotland.

There is evidence for cauldrons and for the pork boiled in them on many archaeological sites: Danebury in Hampshire is an example. Furthermore, the feasting associated with these vessels is amply attested in the vernacular mythological tradition, both in Ireland and in Wales. Here, cauldrons were particularly concerned with Otherworld feasting and with rebirth or resurrection. Each Otherworld 'bruidhen' (Irish Otherworld hostel) possessed its own inexhaustible cauldron of plenty and regeneration. The Irish god most closely associated with the cauldron of abundance is the Daghda, but the healing cauldron of rebirth is a regular attribute of the tribal god, epitomized by the Daghda himself. He has a club of destruction and a cauldron of restoration. Some scholars suggest a similarity between the Daghda with his club and cauldron and the Romano-Celtic god Sucellus, who bears a hammer and pot – perhaps interpretable as implements of death and resurrection. The Daghda's vessel is so enormous that in it the Fomorians (enemies of the Tuatha Dé) could make a porridge containing goats, sheep, pigs and eighty measures each of milk, meal and fat.

The cauldron of REBIRTH is recorded in the Welsh literature, though the vessels alluded to are frequently of Irish origin. In 'Branwen', the *Second Branch of the Mabinogi*, the Irish, under King Matholwch, possess a magic cauldron into which they cast their dead warriors and cook them on a fire every night, so that they might rise the next day as fighting men, as good as new. These soldiers are whole and healthy, except that they have lost the power of speech. This cauldron has to be destroyed before Bendigeidfran's Britons can overcome the Irish. The cauldron itself was originally in the possession of Bendigeidfran who had given it to Matholwch as a gift before hostilities broke out between Wales and Ireland. But Bendigeidfran obtained this cauldron from Ireland: he recounts how it emerged from the Lake of the Cauldron, borne on the back of a huge man, accompanied by an even larger woman.

A magic Irish cauldron appears in the Welsh *Tale of Culhwch and Olwen*; one of the tasks set for Culhwch by Olwen's father Ysbaddaden is to obtain the magic cauldron of Ireland, which belongs to Diwrnach, overseer to the king of Ireland. This cauldron, full of all the treasures of Ireland, is obtained for Culhwch by Arthur.

Cauldrons are of particular interest since the archaeological and literary evidence have so many features in common. The feasting, regeneration and water symbolism which is so prominent in the vernacular mythology is present, or at least implied, by the archaeological material. A final piece of evidence perhaps illustrates the closeness of the two groups of data. One of the repoussé plates on the Gundestrup Cauldron depicts a scene where a god accompanied by soldiers holds a man over a vat of liquid, perhaps in the act of resurrecting a dead warrior.

□ Olmsted 1979; Ross 1967a, 179, 223; Sterckx 1985, 295–306; Ross 1986, 17; Cunliffe 1983; Manning 1972, 224–50; Mac Cana 1983, 65, 78; Jones & Jones 1976, 29–31, 37, 130; Gerloff 1986, 84–115; Green 1986, 141–7; Megaw 1970, no. 134; Lynch 1970, 249–77.

Cerne Abbas (Giant) Above the village of Cerne Abbas in a lonely remote valley in the Dorset hills is carved a giant, 180 ft high, cut through the turf to the chalk beneath. The figure belongs to the small group of hill figures in southern England which may be of Celtic origin (*see also* UFFINGTON). The image is of a naked, ithyphallic man, brandishing a knotted club in his right hand, his left arm extended as if there were once something hanging from it. The sideways position of the feet and the knee joints suggests movement.

In the 13th c. the giant was known locally as Helith. It is possible that the founding of Cerne Abbey in AD 987 took place as a countermeasure against the paganism represented by the giant. It is known that periodic scourings have kept the figure in good condition, but it is uncertain how far back these scourings go. Late documents assert that the cleaning of the Cerne Abbas Giant was performed at intervals of a certain number of years and that the day was a holiday in the village and in the surrounding countryside. Certainly, in the enclosure 70 ft above the giant's head a maypole was erected, and on 1 May (the Celtic festival of Beltene) villagers went up the hill and danced round the pole, in a fertility ritual which was presumably stimulated by the presence of the overtly virile image. This ceremony is recorded in the early 1900s, but the origins of the tradition are unknown.

It is very probable that the Cerne Abbas Giant was carved during the Romano-British

period. If this is correct, then it could belong
to the late 2nd c. AD. The figure with the club
closely resembles Hercules, and his left arm
may once have supported the lion skin which
is the second specific emblem of the Graeco-
Roman demigod. It was towards the end of
the 2nd c. that the Roman Emperor Commodus declared himself to be an incarnation
of Hercules, calling himself Hercules Romanus. Many small bronzes of Hercules from
East Anglia may date from this time.

But even if the carving of the Cerne Abbas
figure was stimulated by the imagery of
Hercules, it is quite likely that what was in
fact represented was a Celtic fertility god.
The maypole and its ritual post-dates the
carving, but it may reflect a fertility cult which
had been going on for centuries, perhaps for
two millennia. The 1 May connection is
interesting: it is on that day that Beltene, one
of the four major seasonal festivals, was
celebrated with fertility rites, the lighting of
bonfires to welcome the summer and the heat
of the sun. The Cerne Abbas figure may well
have been at the centre of such fertility ritual.
□ Petrie 1926; Piggott 1938, 323–31; Grinsell
1958, 227–8, pl. XII.

Huge chalk figure of a giant carved on the
hillside above **Cerne Abbas** in Dorset. He could
be a Celtic Hercules, probably of the 2nd c. AD.

Cernunnos The name 'Cernunnos' means
'horned' or 'peaked one'. On a monument
dedicated by Parisian sailors in the reign of
Tiberius, the name is inscribed above the
head and shoulders of a balding, bearded
elderly god wearing antlers, from each of
which hang a TORC or neck ring. In addition
to the antlers, the god has the ears of a
stag. Although the association of name and
antlered image occurs only on this one monument, 'Cernunnos' has served to identify
numerous other images of an antlered deity
which occur before and during the Romano-
Celtic period in the Celtic world.

Cernunnos is remarkable in that, unlike
most Celtic divinities, he appears in the
pre-Roman, free Celtic period. The earliest
recorded manifestation is on a 4th c. BC rock-
carving at Paspardo in Camonica Valley in
North Italy, where an antlered god bears a
torc on each arm and is accompanied by a
ram-horned snake and a small ithyphallic
being. On the Gundestrup Cauldron, which
could date as early as the 2nd–1st c. BC,
Cernunnos appears cross-legged, with two
twisted torcs and antlers; he is accompanied
by a stag, a ram-horned snake and other
creatures. So already, in the pre-Roman per-

Altar depicting the antlered god **Cernunnos**,
flanked by Apollo and Mercury, from Reims,
France.

iod, there are associations between certain symbols: stags, multiple torcs, ram-horned snakes and fertility, all of which are reflected by imagery which appears in the Romano-Celtic world.

It is the images of Cernunnos which occur in Gaul that present the most striking symbolism. Here, the god is lord of animals (just as he is on the Gundestrup Cauldron), fertility, abundance and regeneration. In terms of monument distribution, Cernunnos was most popular in north-central Gaul, but he was venerated also in the Charente region of western France, at Saintes, and in Britain.

In Romano-Gaulish imagery, Cernunnos is repeatedly associated with ram-horned snakes (see SNAKE, RAM-HORNED) and there are other recurrent motifs. On a relief at Sommerécourt (Haute-Marne), the god is depicted feeding a ram-horned snake from a bowl of gruel on his lap; there are holes on the god's head for the insertion of metal or real antlers. This imagery is repeated at Étang-sur-Arroux in Burgundy on a bronze statuette, but here, an interesting feature is the presence of two subsidiary heads attached to the main head of the god. This links Cernunnos with the distinctive groups of triple-headed or three-faced images so popular among the Remi and elsewhere (see TRIPLISM; HEAD, TRIPLE). Cernunnos is associated with this triplistic symbolism elsewhere in Burgundy: at Nuits-Saint-Georges he is triple-faced; and at Beaune nearby, whilst Cernunnos is himself not triple-faced, his companion depicted on a carved stone is thus shown. On both these monuments, the dominant symbolism is that of fertility. The separate and removable antlers noted above may reflect seasonal ritual, where the antlers were inserted or removed in imitation of spring growth and autumn shedding of antlers on a stag.

Other Gaulish images reinforce his association both with animals and with the symbolism of abundance: on a relief at Reims, Cernunnos appears as a cross-legged, seated deity, flanked by Mercury and Apollo. He has a large bag or sack on his lap from whose open mouth pour coins or grain, consumed by a stag and bull at his feet; a rat crouching on the pediment above Cernunnos' head may symbolize an underworld association for the god. At Saintes, Cernunnos appears twice on one monument: on the main surface, he is accompanied by a female consort; on the

reverse of the stone the god sits cross-legged, in company with bull images. This link with a female partner is interesting, especially because we know of a female equivalent of Cernunnos: at Clermont-Ferrand (Puy-de-Dôme) and Besançon (Doubs) bronze figurines represent antlered goddesses. A final Gaulish depiction of especial note comes from Vendoeuvres (Indre), where Cernunnos appears as a young boy flanked by two older youths who balance on snakes and each grasp one of the central god's antlers. The striking thing about this carving is that the snakes, though not ram-horned, have human faces, in reverse balance to the zoomorphic imagery of Cernunnos himself.

Two British representations of the antlered deity deserve mention. First, from Cirencester, there is a small stone relief of the god whose legs are actually replaced by two large ram-horned snakes which rear up their heads, tongues protruding, next to two open purses of money on either side of the god. The second object is a recent discovery of a Celtic silver coin, dating from around AD 20, from Petersfield in Hampshire, which displays on its obverse the head of an antlered being between whose horns is a solar wheel.

Cernunnos is one of the most striking examples of a semi-zoomorphic Celtic god, perhaps one of those beings who regularly underwent transmogrification or shape-shifting from human to animal form (see METAMORPHOSIS), mentioned so frequently in the vernacular literature. His close affinity with his forest companion, the STAG, is demonstrated by his adoption of antlers, and sometimes cervine ears or hooves. His other intimate associate is the snake, frequently ram-horned, which wraps itself around his body, eats from his hand and, at Cirencester, actually merges with the image of the god himself. The SNAKE was a symbol of renewal or regeneration; the stag a woodland animal, fast and aggressive in its sexuality. In many of his images, Cernunnos displays a role as god of abundance and fertility, with cornucopiae, fruit, bowls of grain or money, and at Camonica, his small companion is ithyphallic. Cernunnos' link with ordinary people may be shown by his cross-legged pose: Mediterranean writers remark that the Gauls commonly sat on the floor (Diodorus V, 28, 4; Athenaeus VI, 36). Finally, Cernunnos is above all lord of animals. In addition to his stag and snake, he is sometimes depicted in company with many different species of beast, wild and domesticated, all enhancing his symbolism as a god of wild and tamed nature, fecundity and a Noah-like beneficence. His intimate rapport with the animal world is displayed above all by his image, whereby he is both man/god and beast.

□ Espérandieu, nos. 3132, 3133, 2083, 3653, 1539; C.I.L. XIII, 3026; Anati 1965; Thevenot 1968, 144–53; Bober 1951, 13–51; Olmsted 1979, pl. 2A; Green 1989, 86–96; Wightman 1985, 179; Autun 1985; Devauges 1974, 434; Planson & Pommeret 1986, fig. 44; Musée Archéologique de Saintes 1984, no. 30; Boon 1982, 276–82.

Early 1st c. AD relief of **Cernunnos**, with his antlers ringed by torcs and an inscription to the god, on the *Nautes Parisiacae* monument, Paris.

Chamalières A Celtic healing shrine at the Source des Roches de Chamalières (Puy-de-Dôme), south of Clermont-Ferrand, was built at the place where two natural springs possessing genuine mineral, therapeutic properties welled out of the ground. The name of the Chamalières god is unknown; no cult image has been discovered, though a lead *defixio* mentioning the god MAPONUS has recently been found. But wooden images dating from the immediate pre-Roman period show pilgrims, sometimes with the head or eyes emphasized, reflecting appeals to the deity for a cure for blindness, failing sight or eye disease. A deposit of more than 2,000 wooden votives was found, lying more than a metre deep in the area of the two springs. Coins suggest that the shrine was in use only for about 100 years or so after Caesar's conquest of Gaul (i.e. 1st c. BC – 1st c. AD). There were apparently no built structures at the sanctuary, merely a sacred pool and an enclosing wall in a marshy valley. The wooden offerings may, as at *Fontes Sequanae*, have been set up around the spring and pool. *See also* SPRING, HEALING; VICHY.

□ Bémont 1984, nos. 269, 270; Vatin 1969; Green 1986, 151–2; Deyts 1983.

circle Of the many motifs and symbols which decorate metalwork and other material in Europe during the later Bronze Age and earlier Iron Age, the circle, particularly the concentric circle, is perhaps the most ubiquitous. Care needs to be taken in interpreting such motifs as religious symbols, but there is some evidence that before and during the Celtic period in Europe, circles were associated with specific cults. Circles were important symbols associated with the sun

Late Bronze Age swords from Germany: one has a **circle** decorated grip.

Late Bronze Age dress-fastener with concentric **circle** decoration from Clones, County Monaghan, Ireland.

cult: on Celtic coins, images of horses (themselves solar emblems) occur in association with wheels and circles which seem to be interchangeable solar motifs (see WHEEL/WHEEL-GOD). Circles and sun wheels occur together on many Romano-Celtic tombstones from Alsace. Different kinds of celestial symbols, including suns and circles, appear as decoration on pipe-clay figurines of Celtic goddesses; and there is a similar array of symbols on some bronze statuettes of the hammer-god Sucellus.

It is likely that in certain circumstances, circles and concentric circles could represent the sun, or a 'short-hand' version of a spoked wheel. But the circle also stands on its own, as a ring of eternity, and may have possessed its own significance over and above its solar associations.

□ Powell 1966, 155; Allen 1980; Linckenheld 1927; Green 1984a, 162–3; 1990a; 1991a.

Cissonius see MERCURY CISSONIUS

Clíodna This mythological woman was an Irish queen-goddess who belonged to Carraig Clíodna in County Cork. Clíodna was a goddess of the Irish Otherworld, a happy place full of beauty, feasting and hunting and without pain, death or ageing. Clíodna took the form of a most beautiful woman: she possessed three magical birds decked in bright plumage, which ate from the apples of the Otherworld tree. These birds had the reputation of uttering such sweet music that the sick would be lulled to sleep and be healed.

□ Mac Cana 1983.

Cocidius The local northern British god Cocidius was equated variously with MARS and SILVANUS. In North and West Cumbria, he was invoked as Mars; in the more easterly region of Hadrian's Wall he was linked instead with the Roman woodland god and with hunting. The name 'Cocidius' is obscure, but it is possible that it may refer to 'red', perhaps reflective of bloodshed (appropriate both to warfare and the hunt).

The association of Cocidius in the east of the Wall area with forests and hunting is demonstrated by both epigraphy and certain imagery: at Ebchester, South Tyne, he was called Cocidius VERNOSTONUS (alder tree); an altar at Risingham shows the god hunting deer against a forest background; a red jasper

intaglio from Wall is decorated with a hunter with his hare, hound and tree, who may be Cocidius. Other imagery of woodland scenes on altars may refer to the cult of Cocidius in his 'peaceful' hunting role. Hunting would have been both a sport and an economic necessity, and Cocidius, like so many HUNTER-deities, may have been both a slayer and guardian of the occupants of the forest.

Further west, in Cumbria, Cocidius was more martial: equated sometimes with Mars, he may be one of the gods who are so frequently represented in this region as crudely incised horned war-gods who are unnamed. Dedications have been found at the fort of Birdoswald, but more significant is the evidence of the cult of Cocidius from Bewcastle: here, two repoussé silver plaques, epigraphically dedicated to Cocidius, show a crudely depicted native warrior-god with spear and shield. So at Bewcastle we are actually able to identify the name of Cocidius with the image of a WAR-GOD. The combination of evidence from both Birdoswald and Bewcastle make it quite likely that the *fanum Cocidi* mentioned in the *Ravenna Cosmography* was situated somewhere in the valley of the River Irthing.

□ Ross 1967a, 372–5; Richmond 1943, 127–224; Tomlin 1985; Green 1986, 113, 183; Fairless 1984, 224–42; R.I.B., 1102, 1872.

cockerel Julius Caesar remarks (*de Bello Gallico* V, 12) of the Celtic Britons: 'They think it wrong to eat hares, chickens or geese, keeping these creatures only for pleasure and amusement.' This may imply the presence of a sacred taboo on the flesh of all three creatures.

The Roman MERCURY is often depicted accompanied by a cockerel; the reason may be that Mercury was the herald of the gods, just as the cockerel heralds the new day. In a Celtic context, Mercury retained this imagery. At Gloucester, the god is accompanied by his native consort Rosmerta; a large cockerel struts by his side. The group of Celtic triple heads at Reims is distinctive in bearing the emblems of a ram's head and a cockerel on the top surface of the stones. Both these creatures belonged to Mercury's cult, and their presence may imply an equation between the Remic triple-faced images and the cult of the Gaulish Mercury. Other specifically Celtic deities are occasionally depicted with cockerels: a British goddess at

Corstopitum has next to her an altar with a cockerel perched on it, perhaps the representation of a sacrifice to her. At Nîmes, a figure of the Gaulish Hammer-god is accompanied by a cockerel, perhaps symbolic of the welcome daylight and of spring.

☐ Green 1989, 58, fig. 22; Hatt 1984, 287–99; Espérandieu, 437; Ross 1967a, pl. 72a.

coin Pre-Roman Celtic coins frequently bear iconography which is religious in content, even though it may possess no cult significance in the context of its presence on coins. It is probable that the predilection for horse images on the reverse of coins reflects the religious importance and prestige accorded to horses within Celtic society, even though the prototype for this coin image comes from the motif of Apollo's chariot on coins struck by Philip II of Macedon. Some Celtic coins bear very specific motifs: Breton issues show horses ridden by huge birds of prey; scholars have linked this obscure iconography with early Irish mythology, where the war-goddess Badbh takes the form of a crow and harries armies. An issue of the Aulerci Eburovices depicts a human HEAD with a boar on its neck, an image which is similar to the stone cult statue of a boar-god at Euffigneix (Haute-Marne). Coins of the Osismi show a human head surrounded by other smaller heads joined to the main head by means of chains. This has been related to the image of the Celtic god Ogmios to whom Lucian refers in a poem. Many animals which are common in Celtic religious iconography and mythological tradition occur on coins: apart from horses, these include boars, cranes, stags, bulls and ram-headed snakes. Images of female charioteers presumably represent divinities, bringing to mind such deities as the Irish Medb in her chariot surveying her armies. *See also* SULIS.

☐ Allen 1980; van Arsdell 1989; Green 1990a.

Coligny Calendar At the end of the 19th c. was found the oldest piece of evidence for the written Celtic language which survives. The Coligny Calendar comes from Coligny near Bourg-en-Bresse (Ain). It consists of a huge bronze plate, now fragmentary, measuring 5ft × 3ft 6in, engraved with a calendar of sixty-two lunar and two intercalary months. It probably dates from the 1st c. BC – 1st c. AD. Whilst the lettering and the numbers themselves are of Roman form, the language is Gaulish.

Silver repoussé plaques of war-gods, dedicated to **Cocidius**, from Bewcastle, Cumbria.

Gold **coin** of the Parisi, 1st c. BC, showing a schematized human head, from France.

The **Coligny Calendar**, a bronze tablet written in Gaulish in the 1st c. BC and perhaps belonging to the druids, from Bourg-en-Bresse, France.

The inference is that the calendar was drawn up by the druids, in order to calculate the right and wrong times for certain activities. Each month is divided into a lucky and an unlucky half, demarcated by the abbreviations MAT (good) and ANM (not good); the reckoning is by nights rather than days. It is probable that the druids used this calendar in judging the most auspicious times for important religious and secular activities – such as making war, planting and harvesting or major sacrifice. We know from early Irish literature (especially the Ulster Cycle) that the druids had the power to promote or delay certain actions taken by kings or queens. An example of this is the occasion when Medb of Connacht wishes to join battle with the Ulstermen and is prevented from doing so by her druids, for a fortnight.

☐ Piggott 1968, 53, fig. 5, 123; Cunliffe 1979, 106–10; Mac Cana 1983, 90, 91.

Colijnsplaat On 4 April 1970, fishermen working off Colijnsplaat, on the estuary of the East Scheldt River in the Netherlands, recovered three fragments of two altars from 85 ft below the surface of the water. Since then, more than 120 altars and sculptures have been salvaged from the sea. In Roman times, there would appear to have been a temple at a site called in antiquity Ganuenta on the bank of the river, which was submerged by the waters of the North Sea at the end of the Roman period when the shore-line receded. Epigraphic information from the stones indicates that the sanctuary was at its most popular in about AD 200.

The goddess whose shrine flourished at Colijnsplaat during the 3rd c. was called NEHALENNIA; she was a goddess of seafarers, who gave protection to traders journeying across the North Sea and blessed their business transactions. Another major temple to Nehalennia was set up at DOMBURG on the Island of Walcheren. However, the goddess seems only to have been venerated in this region, by the tribe of the Morini. That Nehalennia was considered a powerful divinity is indicated both by the number of dedications to her and by the fact that suppliants visited her sanctuaries from all over the Celtic world.

☐ Green 1986, 87; 1989, 10–16; van Aartsen 1971.

Comedovae see MATRES COMEDOVAE

Conall Cernach is one of the three great warrior-heroes of Ulster, in the mythological tradition of the Ulster Cycle. He is the son of Amhairghin, the poet, and Fionnchaomh, daughter of Cathbadh, the druid. His name denotes his warrior status: Conall is suggested as meaning 'strong, like a wolf'; Cernach is usually interpreted as 'victorious'. His supernatural character is demonstrated by many stories associated with him. He is sometimes regarded as an ancestor-deity, one of three ancestors of north-east and central Ireland; and he seems to have held a position as guardian of Ireland's borders.

Conall Cernach is closely associated with the hero Cú Chulainn: he is one of the three great warriors of Ulster, the other two being Cú Chulainn himself and Ferghus. Both Conall Cernach and Ferghus are Cú Chulainn's foster-fathers and tutors; and both are dispatched by King Conchobar with a false pardon to the fugitives Naoise and Deirdre.

Two different traditions associate Conall Cernach with the court of Queen Medb of Connacht, the great opponent of the Ulstermen. One describes how the hero defects from Conchobar's court, along with Ferghus and Cormac, after Conchobar's treachery towards Naoise. The second tells of Conall Cernach's exhaustion (after the great war between Ulster and Connacht was over and Cú Chulainn and Conchobar were dead) and his sojourn at Medb's court at Cruachain for a year. Whilst in Connacht, Conall Cernach is persuaded by Medb to kill her unfaithful husband Ailill, but she also betrays Conall by informing on him to the Connachtmen. This sets the scene for his own death.

Many of the stories of Conall Cernach emphasize his supernatural status. There are great feats of bravery and strength, such as the slaying of the fierce Ceat mac Mághach and the combat with the four-headed monster Cimme. In one tale, Conall Cernach attacks a fort whose treasure is guarded by a great snake. The creature does not oppose Conall but, instead, dives into his waist-belt. After the fort is destroyed, Conall releases the snake, neither having done harm to the other. At the Feast of Bricriu, Conall Cernach boasts that he always sleeps with the head of a Connachtman beneath his knee, and in the *Tale of Mac Da Thó's Pig*, he is described as wearing the head of Connacht's foremost warrior at his belt.

The story which most clearly demonstrates Conall Cernach's superhuman status concerns his decapitated head. This is described as enormous, capable of holding four calves, four men or two people in a litter. The head has magic powers, in that it was prophesied that the Ulstermen would gain strength by drinking milk from it.

☐ Ross 1967a, 121–3, 150–3; Dillon 1933; Mac Cana 1983, 97–8; O'Fáolain 1954; Lehmann 1989, 1–10; Bhreathnach 1982, 243–60; Kinsella 1969.

Conchobar mac Nessa is the king of Ulster, the focus of the society of superhuman heroes and warriors depicted in the Ulster Cycle. Conchobar had his royal seat at Emhain Macha, and it was from there that he conducted the great campaign against Medb and Ailill of Connacht. Conchobar is closely linked with the hero CÚ CHULAINN: he is his foster-father, and in some stories there is a close blood tie between them. Conchobar is variously represented as Cú Chulainn's father, uncle and grandfather.

The character of Conchobar is complex and not entirely honourable. He demonstrates both cruelty and treachery in the affair of DEIRDRE, when he falsely pardons NAOISE and his brothers, luring them back from Scotland to Emhain Macha and engineering their deaths. His behaviour is so reprehensible that the great Ulsterman FERGHUS defects to Connacht, together with Conchobar's own son Cormac.

Conchobar is surrounded by the imagery of warfare: he possesses a strong band of warrior-heroes, called the Red Branch Knights, of whom Cú Chulainn becomes the chief. Conchobar also trains a corps of boy fighters. During the war with Medb of Connacht, Conchobar comes face to face with his arch-enemy Ferghus, who strikes Conchobar's shield three times, causing the shield to shriek, as it always does when its royal bearer is in danger. Conchobar's son Cormac persuades Ferghus to spare his father.

Several features of Conchobar's character mark him out as a complex figure with many facets, some of which are indicative of his supernatural status. He, like his druid, Cathbadh, is a prophet: he foretells that Cú Chulainn's son Conla will mean trouble for his kingdom, and for the honour of Ulster Cú Chulainn kills him. Conchobar is also recorded as being the first consort of Medb,

Altar to Nehalennia, goddess of sea travel, from her shrine at **Colijnsplaat** on the Dutch North Sea coast.

The Mountains of Mourne, County Down, part of the Ulster kingdom of **Conchobar**.

before she reigns as queen of Connacht at Tara. Conchobar finally meets his death by means of a brain-ball, made out of the head of a Leinster king, Meas Geaghra: brain-balls were made by mixing brains with lime and letting them harden. This weapon was hurled at Conchobar by Ceat mac Mághach. Thus, the symbol of the severed head, such an important sacred object to the Celts, is associated with the death of the mythical king of Ulster.
□ O'Fáolain 1954; Lehmann 1989, 1–10; Hull 1956, 243–5; O'Máille 1928, 129–46; Meyer 1907, 112ff; Stokes 1887, 47–64.

Condatis The British god Condatis was some-times equated with the Celtic MARS. He was the god of the watersmeet or confluence ('condate') in the Tyne-Tees region of North Britain, one of the many examples of divine personifications of water; and this spirit may have been especially revered because of the power perceived in the meeting of two rivers (*see* RIVER). Four dedications to the god are recorded in County Durham from, for example, Piercebridge and Chester-le-Street; and Condatis appears also at Bowes. Although the equation with Mars in the frontier zone of Britain would appear to associate Condatis with war, his Celtic name implies a water symbolism, perhaps even evocative of healing.
□ R.I.B. 1024, 1045, 731; Ross 1967a, 182, 376; Fairless 1984, 224–42.

conifer As evergreens, conifers were a nat-ural symbol of life and fertility. Exempt from the seasonal 'death' and 'rebirth' of deciduous trees, they were sometimes adopted as special symbols of eternity. The stone Mother-god-dess at Caerwent holds what is probably a stylized conifer in front of her, enhancing her own imagery of everlasting life and flores-cence. An altar at Glanum in Provence bears no dedication but is carved with a conifer. We know that further west, in the French Pyrenees, altars were dedicated simply to trees, and it may be that in southern Gaul, conifers possessed a cult significance of their own. In some of the small Pyrenean mountain shrines to the Celtic Jupiter, such as Le-Mont-Saçon, altars carved with the solar signs of wheel and swastika were also sometimes decorated with conifer symbols. *See also* TREE.
□ Green 1989, figs. 14, 67; Brewer 1986,

14, pl. 6; Fouet & Soutou 1963, 275–95; Espérandieu, nos. 859–65.

Cormac *see* BELTENE; CONALL CERNACH; CON-CHOBAR; DIVINATION; FERGHUS; GRAÍNNE; MACHA

Corotiacus *see* MARS COROTIACUS

couple, divine A feature of the Romano-Celtic pantheon was the pairing of male and female divinities. Gods of Graeco-Roman origin, when imported to Gaul, the Rhineland and Britain, frequently acquired female partners, even though consorts for the deities are unknown to Classical mythology. The usual pattern is for the intrusive Roman god to marry an indigenous goddess with a Celtic name; the reverse is never true. The names of divine couples may take one of three forms: the god may have an entirely Roman name; he may have a Roman first name and a Celtic descriptive surname; or he may bear a native Celtic name. Thus we have MERCURY and ROSMERTA, APOLLO GRANNUS and SIRONA, SUCELLUS and NANTOSUELTA. Some deities, like those just mentioned, occur commonly and were clearly popular in many parts of the Celtic world. But others are very localized and may appear only once or twice, like UCUETIS and BERGUSIA who seem only to have been venerated at Alesia.

This concept of the divine marriage, which is demonstrated archaeologically, may have its parallel in Irish mythology, where there existed the tradition of the territorial goddess marrying a mortal consort, to bless the land and ensure its fertility (*see* TERRITORY, GOD OF). In Gaul and Britain we may be witness-ing the marriage of a protecting deity of the tribe with the Mother-goddess. What is apparent from a study of the iconography is that though many divine couples enjoy a very close relationship, they nevertheless exhibit a certain independence one from the other.

Taking all types of divine couple occurring in the iconography and epigraphy of mainland Europe, the dominant imagery of the goddess is that of fertility – both of humans and animals – abundance and earthly florescence. Rosmerta's name, indeed, means 'the Great Provider'. These goddesses may possess varied symbols to demonstrate this essential preoccupation with well-being and plenty: *cornucopiae*, wine vessels, buckets, honey-combs, fruit, animals and many others. The

male appears in many guises, but his major function appears to be that of a protector: he may be in the form of a warrior, a hammer-god or a healer; he guarded the wine harvest, and sometimes his imagery reflects interest in successful business transactions. What is also important is the fact of the divine marriage itself: there is acknowledgment that the partnership promoted fertility and fulfilment in all senses. Perhaps there was the perception that Roman conqueror and Celtic conquered were joined in harmony, protector-god to Mother–goddess, or simply man to woman. But the result of the marriage was, in any case, success, whether in promoting plenty, healing, a good wine harvest or flourishing herds. Above all, the Burgundian tribe of the Aedui worshipped divine entities whom they chose to perceive as a pair of partners, with the potency that the mutual support of male and female could generate. But all over the Celtic world, different couples were worshipped, in public or private shrines and houses, and often the couples were peasant deities, who understood the hopes, fears and problems of everyday life. *See also* INCIONA, VISUCIUS.
☐ Lambrechts 1942, 117–20; Green 1989, 45–73.

Altar decorated with a **conifer** symbol, from Glanum, Provence.

Coventina The personification of the holy spring at Brocolitia or Carrawburgh on Hadrian's Wall was called Coventina. The spring which fed a small POOL or WELL was enclosed by a high sanctuary wall, and the pool forms a replacement for the *cella* or inner sanctum in a normal Romano-Celtic shrine. The pool was initially constructed as a functional cistern early in the 2nd c. AD, but then it quickly acquired religious significance. Devotees visited Coventina's water sanctuary and cast coins, jewellery and figurines into the pool as offerings to the goddess. The number of pins found is suggested by some scholars as being indicative of offerings given by women for a safe childbirth. The figured bronzes dedicated to Coventina included a statuette of a horse and another of a dog. Coventina may have been a healer, but the water over which she presided contained no genuine medicinal properties (*see* SPRING, HEALING).

Coventina's name is known from the many dedications to her, some of which were, at some time in antiquity, cast into her well, perhaps reflecting either attack or simply disuse. Whilst she is first and foremost a

Stone carving of a **divine couple**, with pot, hammer, *cornucopia* and *patera*, from Pagny-la-Ville, Burgundy.

The water-goddess **Coventina**, who had a sacred spring and well at Carrawburgh on Hadrian's Wall.

British goddess, she was known in Gaul, at Narbonne, and in north-west Spain. Where we are provided with information from her dedicatory inscriptions, worshippers in Britain came from the Celtic and German provinces. The high status and importance with which Coventina was regarded is indicated by some of her titles, 'Augusta' and 'Sancta'.

Images of Coventina tell us how she was perceived by her dedicants: most prominent is her water imagery; on one relief, the goddess is depicted like a Classical water nymph, semi-naked and reclining on lapping waves, brandishing a water-lily leaf in one hand and resting one elbow on an overturned pitcher. On another sculpture, Coventina is represented as a triple nymph, pouring water from a beaker. While her imagery owes its form to Graeco-Roman iconography, the style of the goddess' representations is Celtic, with little attention being paid to realism in anatomical proportions, rudimentary facial features and hair depicted as schematized strokes.

A sinister deposit from Coventina's pool is a human skull. Skulls were frequently placed in pits and wells, perhaps so that the deceased would find easy passage to the afterlife or be renewed in the Otherworld (see HEAD).
□ Green 1986, 80, 149, 154–5, 165–6; 1989, 40–1, 155–6; Allason-Jones & McKay 1985.

crane Long-legged wading or marsh birds, cranes or egrets, figure in both the iconography and the written mythological tradition. Images of cranes appear on Celtic coins, for example on an issue of the Lemovices, where they are associated with horses. Most important in Romano-Celtic imagery are two reliefs figuring egrets or small cranes, from Paris and Trier respectively. Both stones date from the 1st c. AD, and they show striking similarities with one another. On each monument three cranes are associated with a bull, a willow tree and a woodcutter who chops at the tree. The interpretation of these scenes is difficult: on the Paris stone, the bull has three cranes on his back, and there is an accompanying dedication to TARVOSTRIGA-RANUS (the Bull with three Cranes). The imagery on both reliefs has specific links, in that egrets eat parasites from the hide of cattle, thus having a symbiotic relationship with their host. Egrets and cranes have an affinity with willow trees, and both willows and cranes like water. The imagery of the

woodcutter and the tree is sometimes explained as the Tree of Life being cut down in a seasonal allegory of winter; the birds may thus be perceived, perhaps, as the soul of the tree released at its death.

Cranes appear elsewhere in Romano-Celtic iconography: an altar carved with a wading bird was found in a ritual pit at Biddenham, Bedfordshire; at Risingham, Northumberland, a stone depicts Mars and Victory accompanied respectively by the Celtic symbols of a goose and a crane. Interestingly, this war association is repeated in Irish vernacular tradition: in the *Book of Leinster*, the Tuatha Dé Danann god Midhir possesses three hostile cranes who guard his sídh, Brí Léith, from visitors, but also have the reputation of robbing warriors of their courage and will to fight; they are thus birds of ill omen. Giraldus Cambrensis alludes to the taboo against eating crane flesh in early Ireland (*Expugnatio Hibernica* I, 33), and this may have been because these creatures brought bad luck.

Elsewhere in the Insular mythological tradition, cranes are particularly associated with the shape-changing or METAMORPHOSIS of females, usually ill-natured women. The derivation of this may be the comparison between the shriek of a crane and the screech of a scold. In one account of Manannán, the Irish sea-god has a crane-bag full of treasures, the remains of a crane which had once been a woman, transformed because of her jealousy. But crane-women were not always malevolent: the Irish war-hero Finn is associated with cranes: as a small child he is saved from falling to his death over a cliff by his grandmother who is transformed into a crane. Finn is also associated with cranes of death, four enchanted sons of an old woman, the 'Hag of the Temple'.
□ Allen 1980, 141ff; Espérandieu, nos 3134, 4929; Duval 1961, 197–9; Wightman 1985, 178; Phillips 1977, no. 215; Green 1976, 206; Ross 1967a, 279–92; 1986, 130.

Creidhne see GOIBHNIU

cross The motif of the four-armed cross is, at its most simple, basic level, a sign which evokes images of space and the radiation of light. The arms of a cross stretch out in four different directions; it commands space, and the radiating lines of the symbol may reflect the sun. Two kinds of cross were used as religious motifs in the Celtic world – the vertical/horizontal, equal-armed cross and the diagonal or St Andrew's cross. The simple, right-angled cross, in fact, resembles a schematized, rimless wheel, and may have been depicted on occasions to represent this sun-sign (*see* WHEEL/WHEEL-GOD). Hallstatt Iron Age sheet-bronze vessels were decorated with repoussé crosses and solar wheels in association.

In the later Iron Age, and particularly in the Romano-Celtic phases, the St Andrew's cross was adopted as a religious symbol, probably as a celestial motif, to represent the sun or the stars. Romano-Celtic swastika-brooches may be decorated with diagonal crosses (the SWASTIKA was itself a solar motif). Bronze figurines of the Gaulish Hammer-god were sometimes ornamented with celestial signs, including diagonal crosses. An image of the Celtic Sky-god at Scarpone (Moselle) bears a St Andrew's cross on his chest. A number of bronze model axes, like those from the Woodeaton temple, bear 'X' symbols on their blades.
□ Green 1984a, 163–5; 1991a; Reinach 1894, 171; Kirk 1949, 32ff.

crow Many Celtic divinities were associated with carrion birds, usually ravens, though iconographically it is sometimes difficult to distinguish between crows and ravens. The Irish war-goddess Macha was called 'Crow', and another female war-deity, Badbh, has a name which also denotes 'crow'. Many of the Irish war-goddesses, such as the Morrigán, were crow- or raven-deities who could change between the forms of woman and bird. The Morrigán is described in the literature as 'battle crow' or 'battle raven', and this is also true of Badbh Catha – Battle Crow. Both crows and ravens were birds of death, because of their colour and their scavenging habits, and the Irish crow-raven goddesses prophecied disaster, death and defeat for armies to whom they appeared. On certain Celtic coins, there are images of crows or ravens perched on horseback, as though in reflection of the Irish tradition. In terms of iconography, many divinities were associated with carrion-birds, and small images appear in such British contexts as the religious caches at Willingham Fen, Cambs, and Felmingham Hall, Norfolk. *See also* RAVEN.
□ Ross 1967a, 95, 244; Duval 1987; Green 1986, 108; 1976, 205, 210; Gilbert 1978, 159–87.

Silver jewellery design, by Rhiannon Evans, based on the **crane**, showing two birds with intertwined beaks.

Two model bronze axes from the Romano-Celtic shrine of Woodeaton, Oxfordshire, decorated with the symbol of the diagonal **cross**.

Two **crow** or raven figurines from the hoard of religious bronzes at Felmingham Hall, Norfolk.

Cruachain in County Roscommon was the royal court of Queen MEDB of Connacht. She reigned from there with her consort Ailill, having been established at Cruachain by her father, the high king Eochaidh Feidhleach. Cruachain was also the site of a cave which was thought to be an entrance to the Otherworld. Spirits, many of them malevolent, emerged from the cave at the Festival of Samhain on 1 November, when the boundaries between the worlds of the living and the dead were temporarily dissolved.
□ Ó'Máille 1928, 129–46; O'Rahilly 1946, 176; Ross 1967a, 122.

Cú Chulainn (The Hound of Culann) is the epitome of the superhuman war-hero of the mythological tradition. Cú (hound) is a common title for a great war-hero. Typically, he is destined to have a short, brilliant life covered with glory. He is unsurpassed in battle, young, valorous, of superhuman strength and beautiful. He is closely associated with the gods, and he himself is of supernatural origin. The oldest literature pertaining to Cú Chulainn is the part of the Ulster Cycle known as the *Táin Bó Cuailnge* (the *Cattle Raid of Cooley*). His introduction into the narrative probably dates from the 7th c. AD. His identity may derive from a warrior cult, and he, like Medb, was euhemerized into a 'historical' figure.

Cú Chulainn's birth and youth are steeped in the supernatural. His mother was Deichtine, but his father was variously the divine Lugh, Deichtine's brother CONCHOBAR (birth due to incest was sometimes a mark of divinity) or the mortal Sualtaimh. He had many superhuman foster-fathers, including FERGHUS and CONALL CERNACH. At the time of Cú Chulainn's birth, two foals are born; they become his chariot horses, the Grey of Macha and the Black of Saingliu. This close birth affinity with animals is closely paralleled in the story of Pryderi in the *Mabinogi*.

Until he is seven years old, Cú Chulainn's name is Setanta. He arrives at the court of King Conchobar of Ulster, at Emhain Macha, having fought off 150 of Conchobar's boy-warrior troop on the way. He kills the fierce hound of Culann the Smith and pledges to act as a guard for the smith in the dog's place. This may be how he acquired his name, Cú Chulainn. When still very small, he demands arms from Conchobar, having heard a prophecy of the druid, Cathbadh, that anyone taking up arms on a particular day should have great glory. Cú Chulainn breaks fifteen sets of weapons before he accepts arms which have been specially strengthened. As soon as he is armed, he goes out and slays the three fierce sons of Nechtan, enemies of the Ulstermen.

Cú Chulainn's war prowess is prodigious: he is larger than life, and the *Táin* is full of his incredible feats of battle. He is trained by a female warrior/prophetess SCÁTHACH. He is one of the heroes who quarrel over the champion's joint of pork at the Feast of Bricriu. Cú Chulainn kills the monster CÚ ROI and his own son Conla. The latter tragic deed is done because he is bound to his king, and Conchobar foretells that Conla is a threat to him.

Cú Chulainn has a scythed chariot in which he goes to war, a charioteer, Laegh, who himself has supernatural power, and he has magical weapons: these include his Gae Bulga, a barbed spear given to him by Scáthach, from whose wound no one can recover; and a visor, a gift from the sea-god Manannán.

In the great conflict between Conchobar of Ulster and MEDB of Connacht, there is personal enmity between Cú Chulainn and Medb, who constantly seeks to trick and bribe him. For much of the *Táin*, Cú Chulainn fights the Connacht forces single-handed, since he is the only Ulster hero unaffected by MACHA's curse of weakness. In the *Táin*, there are constant references to Cú Chulainn's supernormal warrior skills: he kills large numbers of men sent against him in single combat and then despatches 100 fighters sent against him at once.

One characteristic of Cú Chulainn in battle is his habit of going berserk or into 'warp spasm'. On these occasions, he becomes a monster: his body revolves within its skin; his hair stands out from his head; one eye sinks into his head, the other bulges out onto his cheek; his muscles swell to enormous size, and a hero-light rises from his head. On one occasion, he gives a great howl and all the local spirits howl with him, driving the Connachtmen mad with fear. One aspect of the berserk fit is that when it is on him, Cú Chulainn cannot distinguish between friend and foe. To bring him to his senses in one episode, the Ulsterwomen appear naked before him, so shaming him that he can be seized by the warriors of Ulster: he is then thrust into three vats of cold water – the first of which bursts, the second bubbles, and the third grows warm.

Cú Chulainn's close link with the supernatural is a constant theme in descriptions of his life. His weapons are magical; his charioteer is able to cast spells of invisibility over his chariot; his tutor Scáthach foretells his destiny; a special light radiates from his head, which dims when he dies; he uses magical symbols to halt the advance of the Connachtmen; and he has magical power over animals. The severed head of his father Sualtaimh is able to rebuke the Ulstermen for not coming to Cú Chulainn's support. Cú Chulainn himself is linked with sacred numbers: he has tri-coloured hair; seven pupils in each eye; seven fingers and toes on each extremity (*see* NUMBER). He has three faults: those of being too young, too brave and too handsome. Cú Chulainn's future wife, Emere, imposes superhuman tasks on him before she will consent to marry him. There is a close parallel between this story and Culhwch's labours in the *Tale of Culhwch and Olwen*. Cú Chulainn has various encounters with the divine world: his Otherworld father Lugh appears to heal and comfort him after combat; he encounters the MORRIGÁN as a beautiful woman and, when he spurns her, narrowly defeats her when she attacks him in the forms of an eel, a wolf and a heifer.

Cú Chulainn has associations with the Otherworld during his lifetime. In one story, he is approached by the Otherworld king, Labhraidh, who invites him there, offering him the love of a beautiful Otherworld woman, Fand, in return for Cú Chulainn's killing of Labhraidh's rivals, other rulers of the Underworld. In one tradition, Cú Chulainn travels (like the Trojan Aeneas of Virgil) to the Otherworld. He describes fortresses with palisades decorated with impaled heads, monsters, snakes and other horrors.

The death of Cú Chulainn is devised by Medb: she uses the Children of Cailatin, whom she has trained in sorcery, to lure the hero to his death, and she pits against him the entire force of Ireland. He dies fighting alone at Magh Muirtheimne. Many portents surround Cú Chulainn's end: there is a 'geis' or bond on him not to eat dog flesh (perhaps because he is the 'hound' of Culann); he breaks this taboo, and this weakens him.

The death of **Cú Chulainn**, the raven-goddess of death on his shoulder. Bronze sculpture by Oliver Shepherd, 1916, in the main Post Office, Dublin.

When the Grey of Macha is saddled up for him to go to battle, the horse cries tears of blood; and when Cú Chulainn mounts his chariot, his weapons all fall at his feet. Finally, he encounters the 'Washer at the Ford', who washes his armour, thus presaging his imminent death. The hero is killed with a spear forged by Vulcan. His death is signalled by the presence of the BADBH, the 'Battle Crow', alighting on his shoulder.

□ O'Fáolain 1954; Lehmann 1989, 1–10; Stokes 1876–8, 175–85; 1908, 109–52; Olmsted 1982, 165–72; O'Rahilly 1946, 61; Jackson 1961–7, 83–99; 1964; Sjoestedt 1936, 1–77; Baudiš 1914, 200–9; 1921–3, 98–108; Best 1911, 72; Meyer 1907, 112ff; Kinsella 1969; de Vries 1963, 72–87; Mac Cana 1983, 29, 36, 101–3; Ross 1967a, 235.

Cuda Cirencester in Gloucestershire, the tribal capital of the Dobunni, was an important centre for the cult of the Mother-goddesses, in both their singular and their triadic form. Here they were frequently associated with the hooded triplets, the Genii Cucullati (*see* GENIUS CUCULLATUS). One sculpture depicting a MOTHER-GODDESS and three Cucullati bears a dedication inscribed on the base to 'Cuda', a name which refers directly to prosperity and well-being. Cuda is depicted seated, with an object in her lap, perhaps a loaf or an egg; with her are three standing hooded figures, of whom the one nearest the goddess seems to be offering something to her or receiving a gift from her.

□ Green 1976, 172, pl. XVIIe; 1986, 85–6.

Culhwch and Olwen The Welsh mythological story known as the *Tale of Culhwch and Olwen* was probably first written down in the 11th c. AD. Culhwch is a cousin of the British hero Arthur. His mother Goleuddyd, when pregnant with Culhwch, finds herself near the home of a swineherd; she develops a violent aversion to the pigs, gives birth there and then flees. The swineherd rescues the baby, names him 'Culhwch' ('pig run') and brings him to the royal court of his father, Cilydd.

When Culhwch's mother is dying, she fears that her husband the king will marry again and dispossess her son. So she exacts a promise that Cilydd will not take another wife until a briar with two heads appears growing on her grave. To prevent this happening, she instructs a monk, her personal confessor, to check on her grave and ensure any suspect plant is cut down. After seven years, the monk grows lax and forgets to tend the grave, and King Cilydd remarries.

Culhwch's new stepmother has a daughter by her previous husband. On learning of Culhwch's existence, she demands that he marry this daughter. Culhwch refuses, saying that he is too young to marry. So the new queen puts a curse on Culhwch, saying that the only person he will ever marry is Olwen, daughter of Ysbaddaden, king of Giants. Culhwch, on hearing Olwen's name, immediately falls in love with her. Culhwch's father sends him off to visit Arthur: the description now given of Culhwch's appearance paints a picture of a young god or hero. He is dressed as a champion, in a purple cloak with boots made of sheets of red gold. His face shines; he has a battle-axe, a hatchet capable of drawing blood from the air, a gold sword, an ivory hunting-horn and two greyhounds. When Culhwch arrives at the court of Arthur, the doorkeeper forbids him access to his lord, because he is unannounced. Culhwch then begins to show his superhuman powers: he threatens to shout three times and that his cries will cause pregnant women to abort and other women to be barren. Culhwch gains entry to Arthur's court and persuades him to help him find Olwen.

Culhwch, Arthur and certain of Arthur's knights search for Olwen for a year without success. She is finally located, and Culhwch tells her of his love. Olwen herself appears as a queen or goddess, wearing a heavy gold torc. She explains that her father, the giant Ysbaddaden, will never give his consent to their marriage because once Olwen weds, he will die. Culhwch desires Olwen to run away with him, but she persuades him to approach her father instead. The giant tries hard to put Culhwch off, including several attempts to kill him and his companions with poisoned javelins. Eventually Ysbaddaden states a list of virtually impossible tasks Culhwch must perform in order to win Olwen. These Herculean 'labours' include burning down a hill; obtaining the magic birds of Rhiannon; getting the magic CAULDRON filled with the treasures of Ireland; and retrieving a pair of scissors or a razor and comb from between the ears of TWRCH TRWYTH. This last is a huge, supernatural beast who has been transformed from a king because of his wickedness. Before Culhwch and Arthur can begin to track down

Twrch Trwyth, they must find and enlist the help of MABON, the divine hunter, who is imprisoned in a castle at Gloucester. Culhwch and Arthur are aided in this task by supernatural animals: these include the Blackbird of Kilgowry, the Eagle of Gwernabwy; the Stag of Rhedenure and the Salmon of Llyn Llyw. Culhwch, Mabon and Arthur chase Twrch Trwyth through South Wales, Cornwall and part of Ireland. They finally overcome him and obtain the razor and comb from between his ears. Arthur himself fulfils the final 'labour', that of obtaining the blood of the Hag of Hell. Culhwch and Olwen finally marry.

The tale has a number of supernatural elements. In some senses, Culhwch himself is a pig; he is named as such, and his subsequent association with a transformed boar is perhaps significant. The shape-shifting between human and animal form is a product of myth, as is the ability of animals to aid and communicate with humans. All the main characters are larger than life – Culhwch, Olwen, Arthur, Ysbadadden and Twrch Trwyth. Mabon is definitely divine. Culhwch himself appears like a god or hero, shining from head to toe and able to threaten the fertility of women.

□ Delaney 1989, 185–95; Jones & Jones 1976; Mac Cana 1983, 16; Hamp 1986, 257–8; Gruffydd 1912, 452–61.

Cunomaglus *see* APOLLO CUNOMAGLUS

Cú Roi mac Dairi, the 'hound of Roi' is a mythical character in the Ulster Cycle. He is a sorcerer and a shape-shifter, sometimes appearing in normal form, at other times in the guise of a monstrous peasant. He is portrayed as a great traveller, but wherever he went, he invoked a spell so that his Kerry stronghold revolved at great speed, and its gateway could never be found after dusk. Cú Roi had an enormous cauldron into which could be fitted thirty oxen.

Cú Roi is especially associated with Cú Chulainn: he acts as judge between three heroes of Ulster after the disruptive Feast of BRICRIU, and accords primacy to Cú Chulainn. But in another encounter, Cú Roi humiliates the young hero, causing him to hide away for a year. Cú Roi is eventually killed by Cú Chulainn, the archetypal slaying of a monster by a youthful hero. Cú Roi can only be killed by his own sword, and according to one

The Mother-goddess **Cuda**, accompanied by three Genii Cucullati, from Cirencester. There is a worn dedication to her on the base.

Bronze boar from the late Iron Age Lexden tumulus, near Colchester. The main theme of the tale of **Culhwch and Olwen** is the pursuit of an enchanted boar.

version of the story, Cú Chulainn uses Cú Roi's weapon to kill a certain salmon in whom resides the soul of Cú Roi. *See also* SALMON.
☐ Mac Cana 1983, 98–101; Baudiš 1914, 200–9.

curse The gods could be invoked for dark purposes. Curses could be employed to damn people and to ask the powers of the supernatural for punishment to be inflicted on those who had injured the suppliant. Curses or *defixiones* were made of lead and inscribed in cursive writing, sometimes back-to-front. Such objects were not particularly of Celtic origin, but they were employed, for example, in the province of Roman Britain, and the curses frequently called upon Celtic as well as Roman divinities.

Many so-called curses may also be regarded as forms of *nuncupatio*, a Latin term meaning a declaration on the part of a devotee to a god, promising to do something for that deity if the suppliant receives the divine aid he requests. Still, these lead tablets are distinctive in that they usually require punishment and revenge for a wrong done to the perpetrator of the inscription. Most of the injuries involved theft: at the temple of Uley (Glos) one Cenacus (probably a Celt) complains to Mercury about two men who had stolen a draught animal. Cenacus begs Mercury that neither will enjoy good health unless they repay the animal and offer devotion to the god. On a *defixio* from Ratcliffe-on-Soar (Notts), Jupiter is requested to work on parts of a thief's body, forcing him to repay money stolen. The devotee promises to pay Jupiter a tithe of the sum recovered. The curse which was also a *nuncupatio* or declaration needed to present the most precise information possible: the name of the god and, if possible, the identity of the wrongdoer. If the latter were uncertain, then the catch-all formula 'whether man or woman, slave or free' was employed.

Recently, major groups of *defixiones* related to the worship of specific gods have been recovered. Perhaps most important is the large collection of curse tablets found in the reservoir at the great temple of Sulis at Bath. These all mention Sulis by name, thus invoking the great Celtic goddess of healing as a deity also of revenge, particularly against theft. The tablets were thrown into the sacred spring, thus being removed from the real world and committed to the goddess. Secrecy

was also maintained by the rolling up of the lead sheets.

Certain *defixiones* were specifically curses; they do not necessarily mention a god or goddess, and they actually use the word 'curse'. Two tablets from London are good examples: one reads 'Titus ... solemnly cursed, likewise Publius'. The other is very vengeful: 'I curse Tretia Maria and her life and memory and liver and lungs mixed up together, and her words, thoughts and memory, thus may she be unable to speak what things are concealed.'

Lead is a heavy, earthly metal; it is likely to have been specially selected for the sinister purposes of punishing and cursing, whilst less punitive dedications to the gods were inscribed on bronze, silver or even gold. The difficult script, too, and its occasional inversion, adds to the dark, spell-like magic of the invocation. Such tablets were perhaps powerful ways of exacting retribution and maybe the very knowledge that he/she had been so denounced would sometimes be enough to hasten the malefactor to repent.
☐ Henig 1984; Green 1986, 24–5, 37, 155; 1976, 165, 225.

  D

Da Derga The Irish OTHERWORLD could sometimes be represented as houses or hostels in the countryside. These places were known as 'bruidhne'; and one was the Hostel of Da Derga, literally the House of the God Derga. The story of the destruction of Da Derga's hostel concerns King Conaire, whose doom awaits him at the house. On his journey, the king meets harbingers of death in the form of three red-garbed horsemen on red horses, who come from the Otherworld. Even this warning does not deflect the king, who continues towards his destiny and enters the hostel, where he is foredoomed to die. Derga is, in fact, the god of the dead, the same being as DONN, and only the dead or those destined to die can enter his house. 'Derga' can also mean 'red', perhaps evocative of blood and death, and this is probably the significance of the red horsemen. Associated with Da Derga's hostel was the Irish goddess of destruction, the Badbh, who appears as black and ugly, a triple image who are naked, bleeding and have ropes around their necks

to signify death and maybe even human
sacrifice.

☐ Mac Cana 1983, 127; Ross 1967a, 170, 222;
Knott 1936; Stokes 1900; 1901.

Daghda The Daghda was an Irish tribal
father-god, the chief of the Tuatha Dé Danann. His title means 'the good god'. The
Daghda was associated with magic and with
abundance. He had two special attributes, a
huge club of which one end killed the living
and the other revived the dead, and an
inexhaustible CAULDRON: both were of supernatural size. The Daghda is a paradoxical
character: endowed with great wisdom, he
is portrayed as gross and uncouth; he wears
a ridiculously short tunic, and in an encounter
with the Fomorians, displays a capacity for
outrageous overeating. In his fertility role,
the Daghda mates with BOANN, the spirit of
the River Boyne, exemplifying the union of
tribal god and Mother-goddess. He also mates
with the destructive war-goddess, the MORRI-
GÁN, which ensures security for his people.
The goddess BRIGIT was his daughter. *See
also* SÍDH.

☐ Mac Cana 1983, 64–6.

Damona The name of this goddess means
'Great' or 'Divine Cow'. She was venerated
in Burgundy and inscriptions show her to
have been linked both with Apollo Moritasgus
and a related deity, Borvo, both associated
with curative spring sanctuaries. Damona and
Apollo were worshipped at Alesia, where a
spring shrine was dedicated to the couple,
who presided over a small pool in which sick
pilgrims bathed in the hope of a cure. All
that remains of Damona's image is a carved
stone head crowned with corn-ears and a
hand with a serpent curled round it. The
name of the goddess and the presence of corn
symbolism indicates a fertility role; the snake,
occurring in a context very similar to that
associated with Sirona, may reflect Damona's
function as a healer, the skin-sloughing habit
of the snake being perceived as an allegory
of rebirth. The polyandrous character of
Damona is indicated by her connection with
other native gods linked with Apollo, namely
Borvo or Bormo, another water-god, at
Bourbonne-les-Bains and Bourbonne-Lancy.
Here an inscription associates Damona specifically with the healing sleep or incubation
undergone by pilgrims at curative shrines, in
the belief that in this sleep they would dream,

Lead **curse** tablet invoking Sulis, from the Roman
reservoir, Bath.

Alise-Ste-Reine, ancient Alesia, the centre of the
cult of **Damona**, a goddess of fertility and
healing.

see visions, be visited by the god and be cured. At Arnay-le-Duc (Côte-d'Or) Damona was associated with the indigenous god Abilus: in the votive pit which contained the inscription was a variety of objects including sculpture, a piece of which depicts the head of a snake and a human arm entwined in a serpent's coils, a similar imagery to that of Damona's statue at Alesia. At Bourbonne-les-Bains, and in the Charente region, Damona was also invoked alone, showing that on occasions, she could be independent of her male companion.

□ Le Gall 1963, 157–9; C.I.L. XIII, 5924; Duval 1976, 77, 177; Thevenot 1968, 104–7.

Danebury is a major Iron Age hillfort in Hampshire. The first defended settlement was established in the mid 6th c. BC. Here, substantial evidence of ritual activity has been found, much of which appears to have been associated with important events which took place at the site. A major work, such as the building of the rampart, appears to have been accompanied by a complicated series of religious acts, sacrifices and foundation burials. An example of this is the interment of three men at the bottom of a quarry hollow when the rampart was constructed. These may be seen as appeasement offerings to the gods of the territory on which the hillfort was built.

Much of the ritual activity at Danebury was concerned with the digging, use and abandonment of grain-storage pits. The gods of the underworld were perhaps perceived as being disturbed by the intrusion of pits into their territory, and thus they had to be propitiated. Indeed, the storing of grain underground implies a certain trust of the chthonic powers, and these seem to have co-operated, in that pit storage was remarkably successful in keeping corn uncontaminated and ungerminated. The ritual involved with storage pits included filling these pits with particular types of material: groups of pots, iron implements, layers of charred grain and animals. Each instance, taken in isolation, can be explained away in secular terms, but taken cumulatively, this repeated activity must be significant in religious terms. The crucial time for the propitiation of the gods may have been at the end of the storage period, when the PIT was emptied. Now the gods needed acknowledgment and thank-offerings. About one-third of the total number of pits at Danebury contained some evidence that ritual had taken place.

Some of the animal deposits in the grain pits are interesting: the ritual burials include dogs, horses and ravens, which were all important in Celtic mythology. Skulls and limbs were buried as well as whole animals. One early pit contained the bodies of two dogs accompanied by a deliberately selected collection of bones representing at least seven species, though consisting of just twenty bones in all. The remains were of cattle, sheep, pigs, red and roe deer, voles and either frogs or toads. Once the bones and bodies were in position, chalk blocks were laid over them and a massive timber post erected centrally over the hole. In all the animal deposits, the type of beast and the part of the body to be interred were significant. Horse skulls or mandibles were a particular choice (*see* SACRIFICE, ANIMAL).

The disposal of human bodies at Danebury presents the most fascinating evidence for ritual behaviour. In central-southern England formal burial accounts for no more than six per cent of the given population in the early Iron Age. So when interments were made at Danebury or elsewhere in the region, they may have been in some manner abnormal. It has been suggested that the people buried were socially outside the norm, sacrificial victims (*see* SACRIFICE, HUMAN) or in some way unclean, the result of murder, suicide or some other violent death. The bodies at Danebury consist either of complete skeletons, skulls or other parts of the body. Some whole skeletons were weighted down with stones, perhaps to prevent their spirits rising. The presence of dismembered bodies suggests that they may have been ritually exposed to allow the spirits time to depart. One specially dug pit contained three human legs, a lower jaw and part of a trunk. The skulls are almost exclusively those of adult men. Perhaps they had belonged to warriors who had died in battle, their heads offered to the gods as war trophies. We know that this was a widespread tradition among the Celts (*see* HEAD-HUNTING).

□ Cunliffe 1983, 155–71, figs 85–92; Green 1986, 30–1.

Danu or Dana is the mother of the Irish divine race, the Tuatha Dé Danann, who bear her name 'the people of the goddess Danu'. As a mother-goddess, Danu is often

confused with ANU, and it is unclear as to whether Danu and Anu were separate divinities or not. As Anu is specifically connected with the fertility of Ireland and Danu was the mother of the Tuatha Dé, it is highly likely that the two were always in fact one goddess with two slightly different names, or that they merged very early in the oral tradition.
□ Mac Cana 1983, 132; Sjoestedt 1949, 24f; Ross 1967a, 209.

Dea Nutrix is the Latin for 'nursing goddess'; the term is used to describe a particular manifestation of the Celtic MOTHER-GODDESS in western Europe. The image type of this goddess may have been derived from representations of the Italian nursing divinities or from the concept of the deified empress, who was sometimes perceived as a fertility goddess. Images of a seated female figure appear as pipe-clay statuettes, which were manufactured in central Gaulish, Breton and Rhineland factories during the 1st and 2nd c. AD. The goddess sits, often in a high-backed wicker chair, suckling one or two children. Images of this deity appear in domestic contexts, graves and shrines. At Dhronecken near Trier, a shrine was dedicated to this nursing goddess, containing numerous figurines both of the deity herself and of children whom she protected. The Dea Nutrix occurs at a number of other sanctuaries, including the temple of St Ouen de Thouberville (Eure), a shrine at Trier, where the goddess was named AVETA, and at Alesia. Grave finds of the figurines, including examples at Ballerstein in Alsace and Hassocks in Sussex, may have been placed in tombs to comfort the dead and bring promise of renewal and rebirth in the afterlife.
□ Jenkins 1957b, 38–46; 1956; 1978, 149–62; Green 1986, 89; 1989, 30; Rouvier-Jeanlin 1972; de Vesly 1909; Wightman 1970, 217; Le Gall 1963, 161; Linckenheld 1929, 67.

death There is abundant evidence from the Classical and vernacular literature and from archaeology that the Celts believed death was not the end of everything. TRANS-MIGRATION OF SOULS and REBIRTH are constant themes. Iron Age tombs may contain rich grave goods, attesting to the need for earthly equipment in an afterlife, perceived as essentially similar to the human world. Elaborate ritual associated with some Celtic

The 5th c. BC pit-burial of a young man, from the Iron Age hillfort at **Danebury**, Hampshire.

Clay **Dea Nutrix** figurine, together with the two-piece mould used in its manufacture, from Toulon-sur-Allier, France.

burials displays the importance attached to death. In the Marne region and East Yorkshire, for instance, high-ranking individuals were buried with two-wheeled carts or chariots (see CART/CHARIOT BURIAL). In the very late Iron Age of south-east Britain, Celtic aristocrats were buried with all the provisions needful for Otherworld feasting (see FEAST). But before the 1st c. BC in central-southern England, only about six per cent of the population were accorded formal burial. It has been suggested that these interments were perhaps the result of abnormal death.

Various deities were associated with death and the underworld. The Romano-Celtic DIS-PATER is an example; the Irish DONN is another. The Welsh OTHERWORLD was Annwn, presided over by Arawn. In Ireland, there were many Otherworld places, islands in the sea or SÍDHE under the earth. See also DA DERGA.

□ Green 1986, 121–30; Cunliffe 1983, 155–71; Wait 1985; Mac Cana 1983, 128–31; Whimster 1981.

decapitation The Celts practised HEAD-HUNT-ING; they frequently decapitated their war victims and offered their trophies up to the gods in temples or kept them as precious possessions preserved in their homes. Diodorus Siculus, Livy and Strabo all record these practices (Livy XXIII, 24; X, 26; Diodorus V, 29, 4; XIV, 115; Strabo IV, 4, 5). Pre-Roman shrines attest the Celtic custom of decapitating their vanquished enemies, though it is unclear whether this always took place before or after death. Such sanctuaries as ROQUEPERTUSE and ENTREMONT in Provence have pillars with niches containing the heads of young adult men, some of whom certainly received serious battle wounds.

There is evidence for decapitation in Roman Britain: seven of the burials in the Lankhills cemetery at Winchester contained beheaded bodies, all of later 4th c. AD date. Most of these were elderly women, who had been interred with the head placed by the legs. All of these bodies were associated with elaborate or abnormal graves of other people who may have met a violent end. One grave containing a decapitated body also had two dogs. The beheading process was prescribed by a very specific ritual: it was always performed from the front, with care taken as to where the vertebrae were severed; it was always done with a knife.

Ritual decapitation occurred at other late Romano-British sites, perhaps reflective of an increased anxiety that the dead might not reach the Otherworld unless helped by certain ritual practices. At Odell (Bucks) a woman's decapitated head was placed behind the wicker lining of a well. Curbridge (Oxon) produced three beheaded burials from a later cemetery, all with the heads between the legs. Similar ritual is documented at Kenchester (Hereford & Worcester) and Stanton Harcourt (Oxon). At Orton Longueville (Cambs) a cemetery of the 2nd c. AD produced the body of an elderly woman, beheaded and with her head positioned at the foot of her grave. A late group of burials at Alcester consisted of ten infant interments and the body of a decapitated young girl, her head placed between her legs; and at the shrine of Springhead in Kent, infants were themselves beheaded.

A group of 3rd and 4th c. burials in Dorset may betoken of the presence of WITCHCRAFT: the ritual here involved the beheading of middle-aged or elderly women, the heads then placed by the knees after the lower jaw had been removed; the bodies were accompanied by spindle-whorls. At Kimmeridge, the ritual was especially complicated: a late 3rd c. burial in a cist was that of an old woman, head by her feet, with her lower mandible removed and a spindle-whorl placed by her body. On top of the cist a second body had the jaw from the cist-burial placed with her, together with a second spindle-whorl.

In all these instances of female decapitation, the common denominator may be a specific characteristic common to all the women: perhaps this was witchcraft, leading to a need to ensure that the body of the dead woman went speedily on her way to the underworld and did not linger in spirit form to make mischief on earth. In Dorset, the removal of the lower jaw may have been to prevent the woman talking after death and casting spells. Alternatively, the ladies may have been simply village scolds rather than witches. But the decapitation rite as a whole is probably best interpreted as a form of religious ritual designed to ease entry to the Otherworld.

Decapitation features frequently in the vernacular mythology: here are a few examples. In the *Second Branch of the Mabinogi*, the head of BENDIGEIDFRAN is cut off and brings good fortune to his companions. In the Irish story of Finn, Lomna, Finn's fool, is decapitated and the head, impaled on a stake, is still able to speak. The HEAD of the Ulster hero Conall Cernach is enormous and has magical properties; it is prophesied that the men of Ulster, smitten by the weakness curse of Macha, will regain their vigour if they drink milk from Conall's head.

☐ Green 1986, 29–31, 130–1; Benoit 1955; Macdonald 1979, 415–24; Simco 1984, 56–9; Goodburn 1976, 336; 1978, 438, 444; Wilson 1975, 252; Green 1976, 228, 48–9, 202; Ross 1967a, 118–22.

Deirdre The story of Deirdre and NAOISE appears in a text of the 9th c. AD. It was subsequently introduced into the Ulster Cycle as a foretale of the *Táin Bó Cuailnge*, in order to explain the defection of Ferghus from Ulster to Connacht.

Deirdre is the daughter of FEDLIMID, the chief storyteller to CONCHOBAR, king of Ulster. Before her birth, the druid Cathbadh prophesies that Deirdre will be very beautiful but that she will bring death and ruin to the Ulstermen. The warriors of Ulster wish her to be killed at birth, but Conchobar decides to foster her in secret and then marry her himself when she is of age. One day, the young Deirdre sees her foster-father skinning a calf in the snow, its blood being drunk by a raven. She remarks to her companion, the poetess Leabharcham, that the man she loves will have the same combination of colouring: black hair, white skin and red cheeks. Leabharcham informs Deirdre that one Naoise, the son of Uisnech, has all these attributes. Deirdre breaks out of her purdah, meets Naoise and, by challenging his honour, persuades him to go away with her. Naoise, his two brothers and Deirdre flee first to Ireland and then to Scotland. Conchobar treacherously sends a pardon, which Deirdre distrusts; the three brothers are lured back to the royal court of Emhain Macha in Ulster and are killed by Eoghan, son of Duracht. Deirdre herself is kept by Conchobar for a year. At the end of that period, the king asks her whom she hates most of all the Ulstermen; she replies that she most loathes Eoghan, for it was he who slew her beloved Naoise. Conchobar forthwith announces that she shall go and live with Eoghan. But as Deirdre is travelling in Conchobar's chariot, between the king and Eoghan, she hurls

Death by beheading was a common fate for prisoners of war. The head of this young man was dedicated to the gods at Roquepertuse in Provence in the 3rd c. BC.

Stone figure of a warrior-god holding a severed head, from Entremont, Provence, illustrative of **decapitation**.

herself from the chariot, dashing her head to pieces against a boulder.

The tale of Deirdre and Naoise has several points of interest. Firstly, Cathbadh's prophecy is fulfilled, for it is Conchobar's treachery which leads to the desertion of his son and the great hero Ferghus to the court of Medb of Connacht. Deirdre herself is noteworthy in the strength of her personality and in her ability to foresee Conchobar's duplicity. She stands out among the women of Irish mythology in that she questions the powerful honour code by which Irish heroes live. She herself also displays honour by killing herself rather than being dishonoured by her lover's killer. It is impossible to ascertain whether or not Deirdre is herself of divine origin, but the story conforms to the familiar archetype of young girl, elderly suitor and youthful lover. It also belongs to a common theme whereby a divine or superhuman heroine unites with one of a trio of brothers.
□ O'Fáolain 1954; Cormier 1976–8, 303–15; O'Leary 1987, 27–44; Mac Cana 1983, 94–7.

Diana is the Roman goddess of the hunt and of the MOON. The latter association, with its imagery of waxing and waning, gave Diana a role as a protectress of women, especially in childbirth. The moon and women were held to have a close affinity because of the female monthly cycle.

Where Diana is represented and invoked in Gaul and Britain, she generally appears in Classical guise. But there is some evidence for her association or conflation with indigenous cults. At the shrine of Nettleton Shrub (Wilts) the Celtic hunter, Apollo Cunomaglus, was accompanied by Diana; and at the late Romano-Celtic temple at Maiden Castle (Dorset), an image of Diana occurs with a statuette of a Celtic triple-horned bull.

In certain instances, Celtic female deities of the hunt were conflated with the Roman Diana. ABNOBA of the Black Forest, and ARDUINNA of the Ardennes are examples of this natural equation. The fertility aspect of the moon-goddess is exhibited in images of Celtic Mother-goddesses wearing lunar amulets: this occurs on a small clay figurine of a Mother-goddess at Cologne, who holds a small dog on her lap; and in the shrine at Gripswald, an image of the three Mothers depicts them each wearing a crescent-shaped amulet. At Mainz, the Gaulish Hammer-god is accompanied by a consort with a bow and quiver, a Celtic version of Diana. In Ireland, the goddess Flidais may be the Insular equivalent of the Roman Huntress.
□ Ristow 1975, no. 42; Espérandieu, no. 6616; Ross 1967a, 215–16.

Dian Cécht In the Irish *Book of Invasions*, Dian Cécht appears as the god of the craft of healing: indeed, he is at one and the same time a healer and a kind of smith. Nuadu, king of the Tuatha Dé Danann, lost his arm at the First Battle of Magh Tuiredh. Because he was no longer physically perfect, Nuadu had to relinquish the kingship. But Dian Cécht and his son made him a silver arm and hand, and thus Nuadu could rule once more.

The second great act of Dian Cécht occurred after the Second Battle of Magh Tuiredh, when the Tuatha Dé inflicted a final defeat on the Fomorians. Dian Cécht and his three children sang incantations over a certain well; all the fatally wounded of the Tuatha Dé were immersed in the water and restored to full health.

Dian Cécht belongs to a group of Irish gods who had a definite and specific divine function, as one of the craft-gods. His curative powers appear to have derived from a combination of magic and the knowledge and use of healing herbs.
□ Carey 1984, 1–22; O'Rahilly 1946, 308–16; Krappe 1932, 90–5; Mac Cana 1983, 58, 61.

Diarmaid ua Duibhne appears in the Fionn Cycle. He is a lieutenant of the ageing hero Finn, leader of the war-band, the Fianna. Diarmaid is loved by the beautiful GRÁINNE, who is betrothed to Finn. At first, he refuses her because of his bond of loyalty to his leader, but Gráinne binds him with a 'geis' to take her away from the court of Tara. The fugitives are pursued by Finn all over Ireland, but they are aided by Diarmaid's foster-father, Oenghus, the god of love. The couple reach the Forest of Duvnos which contains a magic tree of immortality, guarded by a giant, Sharvan the Surly. Finn sends two warriors after Diarmaid, but he overcomes them. The young hero then slays Sharvan and collects berries from the magic tree for Gráinne and himself. Finn discovers the forest, but Oenghus again helps Diarmaid by taking his shape and luring his companions to 'kill' him instead. Eventually, after seven years of unsuccessful pursuit, the hero is pardoned by Finn, and he and Gráinne live together

happily for some time, producing five children. But Finn still thirsts for revenge. A
boar hunt is organized, in which Diarmaid is
invited to take part. However, the boar is the
magic boar of Boann Ghulban in County
Sligo; this creature had once been Diarmaid's
foster-brother, and it was prophesied that
Diarmaid would meet his death through him.
Finn knows the prophecy and deliberately
exposes Diarmaid to danger. In one version
of the story, the boar kills Diarmaid; in
another, the boar is killed, but the hero is
fatally wounded by one of its poisonous
spines, through Finn's trickery.

The elopement of Diarmaid and Gráinne
is first mentioned in the 10th c. *Book of
Leinster.* The stories of the Fionn Cycle
were developed during the 12th c.; and the
tradition concerning Diarmaid's death dates
from between the 12th and 15th c.

Diarmaid's story belongs to a well-known
group of Irish mythological tales involving a
tragic plot whereby there is conflict between
an elderly person of high rank and a young
hero over a young and beautiful girl. Diarmaid himself may be divine in origin: he is
closely linked with the god Oenghus, and he
is sometimes known as Diarmaid Donn (Dark)
or Diarmaid, son of Donn. Thus, he is associated with Donn, the god of the dead. He
is irresistibly attractive and is described as
'Master and Charmer of Women'. His destiny
and death are prophesied, and his foster-
brother is a supernatural boar. In his own
behaviour, Diarmaid displays supernatural
characteristics: he is a great warrior, able
to kill the giant Sharvan who is virtually
immortal. Diarmaid eats the berries of the
tree of immortality, and he can thus perhaps
only be killed by means of magic.
□ O'Fáolain 1954; Meyer 1897a, 458–62;
Lloyd, Bergin & Schoepperle 1912, 41–57;
Campbell 1870–2, 193–202; Mac Cana 1983,
109–12.

Dispater was the Roman god of the dead.
There is evidence that his identity was
adopted by the Celts, because it conformed
to divine perceptions of their own. Caesar
(*de Bello Gallico* VI, 18) mentions that the
Gauls considered themselves to be descended
from Dispater and that, moreover, they
reckoned time by nights rather than days.
One of the 9th c. Berne commentaries on
Lucan's 1st c. AD *Pharsalia* equates the thunder-god Taranis with Dispater.

Altar to the hunter-goddess **Diana**, with her
hound, bow and quiver, London, 2nd c. AD.

Ben Bulben or Boann Ghulban, County Sligo,
home of the enchanted boar, killer of **Diarmaid**.

In South Germany and the Balkans there are dedications to Dispater and a native consort, AERICURA. Their imagery shows a goddess with the emblems of a Mother-goddess, but the god holds a scroll, perhaps the 'Book of Life' with its symbolism of the passage from youth to old age and death. On a stele from Varhély in Romania, Dispater is accompanied by a triple-headed dog, perhaps a native variant of Cerberus, the canine guardian of Virgil's Hades.

The fact that Dispater was apparently an ancestor-deity as well as god of death links him closely with the Irish DONN, who also combines these two functions.
□ de Vries 1963, 88–92; Duval 1976, 103; Green 1986, 66; 1989, 69; C.I.L. XIII, 6322; Espérandieu, no. 347; Zwicker 1934–6, 50.

divination is a method of foretelling the future, the will of the gods and the presence of good or bad omens, by means of observation of human and animal behaviour and that of natural phenomena. Thus, augury (the study of birds in flight) may be considered as a form of divination. The DRUIDS gained an adverse reputation from Classical writers because of their perpetration of human sacrifice (see SACRIFICE, HUMAN). The purpose of such practices was not so much the appeasement or propitiation of the gods but rather for divination. Thus, ritual murder of various kinds was carried out. Diodorus Siculus (V, 31, 2–5) and Strabo (VII, 2, 3) allude to the custom of Celtic and Teutonic priests of stabbing human victims and examining their movements in the throes of death. Tacitus remarks on the sacred grove of the druids on the island of Anglesey, where altars were drenched with human blood and festooned with entrails; he says it was by observation of these that the druids consulted their gods (*Annals*, XIV, 30). Other human sacrifice included death by impaling, being shot with arrows, burning or drowning. All of these may have had a divinatory purpose. Caesar (VI, 16) implies that it was the belief of the druids that the power of the supernatural could only be neutralized and controlled if human life was sometimes sacrificed.

The druids of Irish literary tradition had a divinatory or prognosticatory role: the Ulster druid, CATHBADH, foretold the fate of Ulster if Deirdre were born and reared. He also knew the lucky days for taking up arms, and this caused Cú Chulainn to demand that the king should equip him on a particular day. Medb of Connacht's druid forebade her to give battle for a fortnight because the omens were unfavourable. The 9th c. AD glossator Cormac comments on the practice of chewing the flesh of pigs, dogs or cats in divination, which was known as 'Himbas Forosnai'. Also involved with divination in Ireland were the filidh, members of the learned class of Irish society who took over many of the functions of the druids after Christianity was adopted in the land (see FILI). Their particular goddess was Brigit, who was an expert in learning, poetry and divination. *See also* ORACLE.
□ Mac Cana 1983, 96; Ross 1967a, 301; 1986, 114; Green 1986, 27–9; Beard & North 1990, 49–72.

dog In both Classical and Celtic mythology and religion, dogs possessed composite symbolism in which the animals could represent hunting, healing and death. The significance of the hunt speaks for itself, but healing symbolism derives from the belief that the saliva of the animal contains curative properties. The death role may come from observation of the dog's carrion habits. Certainly Virgil (*Aeneid* VI) paints a grim picture of Hades, with its fierce three-headed canine guardian. In early Welsh mythology, as expressed in the *Mabinogi*, the Underworld god ARAWN had a pack of white red-eared dogs. The 'Cŵn Annwn' or Hounds of ANNWN (the Welsh Underworld) are elsewhere described as omens of death.

In the archaeology of Celtic religion, dogs feature in two distinct ways: in the iconography they appear as companions of many different divinities; and dogs were buried with a specific set of rituals, attesting, perhaps, their chthonic symbolism.

Dogs appear in the imagery of Celtic Europe as associates of both male and female deities. They occur with hunter-gods, as at Le Touget (Gers), where a stone statue portrays a Gaulish hunter with a hare in his arms and a hound by his side; and at London, where the god has a bow and quiver. As hunting companions, dogs have the dual role of aggressive fighter and guardian of their masters; and it is as protectors that the creatures frequently appear in the iconography. The Dutch goddess of the North Sea, NEHALENNIA, is almost invariably depicted in company with a large, benign-looking hound who sits beside her, obviously present as a domestic protector, just as the goddess herself guards her devotees in their journeys across the North Sea. The Gaulish Hammer-god frequently appears with a small dog at his feet. He was a god of prosperity and well-being, and the dog may be again present in the capacity of a benevolent, domestic guardian. But at Varhély in Dacia, the god appears with a three-headed dog, perhaps, like Cerberus, reflective of underworld symbolism.

Many of the Celtic Mother-goddesses, whether triple or single images, are accompanied by dogs. The *Deae Matres* at Cirencester (Glos) and Ancaster (Lincs) appear with small dogs. In the Rhineland, especially at Trier, stone and clay images of single Mothers depict the goddesses with lap-dogs: the shrine of AVETA at Trier produced many small clay statuettes of a goddess holding a small dog. Sirona at Hochscheid is similarly portrayed; it may be that the dog is here in its capacity as a healer. The great curative shrine at LYDNEY (Glos) was dedicated to the British god NODENS. Dedications to him were found, but no anthropomorphic image. Instead, nine images of dogs were offered at the temple. Here the creature is almost certainly present as a healer. At Nettleton Shrub (Wilts) a shrine was dedicated to a god who may have been both hunter and healer: he is Apollo Cunomaglus ('Hound Lord'); the temple was probably a healing sanctuary, and it is known that Apollo did combine the two roles. The divine hunt was perceived as associated with renewal and rebirth, so it is appropriate that the two concepts should be linked and that the dog represents both aspects to a hunter-healer cult. It is as a healer that the animal appears on an image of a god at the curative shrine of Mavilly: here the deity sits with a dog and raven, while a pilgrim with his hands over his eyes may reflect his suffering from eye disease. At the therapeutic sanctuary of Sequana at *Fontes Sequanae* near Dijon, images of pilgrims holding dogs in their arms were offered to the goddess; and at the healing shrine of Apollo Belenus at Sainte-Sabine in Burgundy, a stone image of a baby in a cot shows the child with a dog curled up on his legs, as if it were there to cure some affliction of the infant's limbs.

Some iconography suggests that the dog may have possessed a combined healing and underworld role. The Greek god Asklepios was both a healer and a chthonic deity, and

Bronze figure of a Celtic god, decorated with circles, possibly **Dispater**, from Cologne.

Bronze **dog**, probably a deer-hound, from the Romano-Celtic shrine at Lydney, Gloucestershire.

he had sacred dogs which symbolized both these roles. An image of a goddess at Xertigny is accompanied by a dog and a snake: this latter creature had a chthonic role, but in addition, it was a symbol of regeneration. The Celtic horse-goddess Epona is sometimes shown with a dog; at Altrier she appears with both dog and raven, as if here the chthonic element may be paramount.

Apart from the iconography of Celtic gods and goddesses, archaeology has produced considerable evidence for the association of dogs with ritual, which was perhaps associated with the Otherworld (see SACRIFICE, ANIMAL). Pits and wells may contain dog-burials: at Muntham Court in Sussex a 200-ft-deep pit associated with a 1st c. AD circular temple was found to contain multiple dog skeletons. A well at Caerwent had five dog skulls; and a bronze figurine of a dog was thrown into Coventina's Well at Carrawburgh in North Britain. At the Iron Age hillfort of Danebury, a pit associated with the earliest phase of the settlement contained two dogs accompanied by the carefully selected bones of about seven other species of animal. The small Roman site at Staines near London had a well containing sixteen dogs and a complete Samian bowl. At the Iron Age and Roman site of Ivy Chimneys (Essex) a ditch contained the bodies of a horse and a sheep or goat, accompanied by a row of dog teeth 'set as though in a necklace'. Seven puppies, one with an adult bitch, were each buried in an urn in the Upchurch Marshes in Kent; and at the Elephant and Castle in London, the bodies of two dogs were placed in a wooden box with 2nd c. pottery and buried in a shallow pit. The practice of peculiar or abnormal dog-burial continued throughout the Roman period in Britain: in the late Roman cemetery at Lankhills, Winchester, a decapitated human body was accompanied by two dogs, one complete, the other dismembered and with the ends of the bent-over backbone tied together.

All the foregoing evidence of ritual associated with the bodies of dogs points to a complex series of religious activities which must have been concerned with the appeasement of the powers of the underworld. See also MAC DA THÓ.

□ Dehn 1941, 104ff; Wightman 1970, 217ff; Wheeler & Wheeler 1932; Thill 1978, nos 45, 46; Espérandieu, no. 4219; MacDonald 1979, 415–24; Cunliffe 1983, 46, 155ff; Allason-

Jones & McKay 1985; Ross 1968, 255–85; Thevenot 1968, 68; Green 1986, 175–6; 1989, 10–16, 53–4, 69, figs 30, 31; Linckenheld 1929, 40–92; Hondius-Crone 1955; van Aartsen 1971; Turner 1982, 15.

dolphin These sea creatures are traditionally associated with Classical mythology, where they symbolize the journey of the human soul across the sea to the Isles of the Blessed. Dolphins occur with a number of Celtic divinities: they are present as part of the imagery of the Netherlands North Sea goddess Nehalennia, who was a marine deity, protectress of sea travellers and traders. Here, the creatures may simply be marine symbols, although they may also represent rebirth after death. Another water-goddess, the British Coventina, was invoked on an altar bearing a dedication to her and decorated with two dolphins. One of the depictions of the three Mothers at Cirencester in Gloucestershire portrays the lower part of their robes twisted into the form of dolphins, a deliberate symbolism which may once more refer to the chthonic role of the Mothers. A dolphin appears on the WILLINGHAM FEN mace, which bears composite sky and underworld imagery, including a solar wheel, an eagle, a triple-horned bull's head and a chthonic monster being driven into the ground under the foot of the Sky-god. A dolphin is depicted ridden by a godling on one of the plates of the Gundestrup Cauldron. □ Stebbins 1929; Toynbee 1962, no. 73, pl. 84; Hondius-Crone 1955, no. 3; Green 1986, fig. 29; Ross 1967a, pl. 86b.

Domburg On 5 January 1647, the sand-dunes around Domburg on the Island of Walcheren, off the Dutch North Sea coast at the mouth of the Rhine, were partly destroyed by storms. Thus were revealed a group of some thirty altars from a temple to the local goddess of the Morini, NEHALENNIA, dating from the 2nd–3rd c. AD. Many of these stones were destroyed in a fire in 1848, but a few survive, and drawings remain as testimony to some of those which perished. That the site of Domburg was on a trade route is suggested by finds of imported pottery and coins.

Nehalennia was a marine goddess: she was venerated at two shrines, Domburg and COLIJNSPLAAT, by sailors, traders and other professional people who prayed to her before undergoing the hazards of journeys across the North Sea, and who, on their return, gave thanks to the goddess for their safety and for successful business transactions. The two shrines were visited by people whose homes were all over western Europe: one altar from Domburg was offered to Nehalennia by a trader in pottery between Gaul and Britain.

The imagery of Nehalennia at both Domburg and Colijnsplaat show her as a sea-goddess, associated with boats and rudders, but also as a goddess of plenty, with baskets of fruit and *cornucopiae*. Her most distinctive symbol is a large, benevolent hound who sits protectively by her side. Both Nehalennia's shrines were engulfed by the North Sea some time shortly after the end of the Roman period.
□ Hondius-Crone 1955; Jenkins 1956, 192–200; Green 1989, 10–16.

Donn is the Irish god of the dead. His name means 'the Dark One'. Originally, Donn was the chief of the Sons of Mil, a mythological race who invaded Ireland, ousting the divine Tuatha Dé Danann. But Donn made the mistake of slighting Ériu, one of the three eponymous goddesses of Ireland, and he was drowned off the south-west coast of Ireland. A place near this spot, on a small rocky island named 'Tech nDuinn' ('the House of Donn'), became Donn's dwelling-place as god of the dead. The house was the assembly place for the dead before they began the journey to the OTHERWORLD. The fact that Donn is both an ancestor-deity and god of death means that he has a close affinity with DISPATER, who was the Roman lord of the dead. Caesar (*de Bello Gallico* VI, 18) remarks that the Gauls revered Dispater from whom they believed they were descended. Donn is probably also the same entity as the Irish DA DERGA, who appears as a death-god in the story of Da Derga's Hostel.
□ Mac Cana 1983, 36–8, 62; Berresford Ellis 1987, 89.

dove This bird was the attribute of Venus, the Roman goddess of love, and was a symbol of peace, harmony and affection between individuals. In a Celtic context, doves seem above all to have been associated with curative cults, particularly those of the Celtic Apollo. This may have been, at least in part, because doves have distinctive 'voices' and were linked to Apollo in his capacity as an oracular divinity as well as a healer (*see*

Boy riding a **dolphin**, on one of the silver plates of the Gundestrup Cauldron.

Terracotta pigeon or **dove**, symbol of love and peace and attribute of the Romano-Celtic Venus, from London.

ORACLE). At a number of Gaulish therapeutic sanctuaries, especially in Burgundy, representations of doves carved in groups of two, four or six were offered to the presiding deity: they occur thus, for instance, at Beire-le-Châtel and at Alesia. At the healing shrine of Apollo Vindonnus at Essarois, images of pilgrims carry doves as presents to the god; and depictions of children hold birds as offerings to Lenus Mars, the curative god at Trier who was a particular benefactor to the young. These birds may have seemed especially appropriate as thank-offerings at healing spring sanctuaries since they were perceived to reflect harmony, peace of mind and thus good health in spirit and in body, the very antithesis of harm.

□ Espérandieu, no. 3636; Green 1989, 142–4; Deyts 1976, nos 50–2; Thevenot 1968, 149–64; Wightman 1970, 213.

druid The evidence for the druids as a powerful group of religious leaders is mainly contained within the comments of Classical writers on the Gaulish Celts. The most famous material is chronicled in writings of Strabo (IV, 4, 4), Diodorus Siculus (V, 31, 2–5) and Caesar (*de Bello Gallico* VI, 13–14), but all these writers derive their material from a lost shared source, Posidonius. Caesar is our most useful source. He divides the high-ranking Gauls into knights and druids. He says that the druids controlled religion and all sacrifices, giving rulings on all religious questions. Caesar further remarks that druidism belonged originally to Britain, whence it came to Gaul. On a fixed date each year, the druids assembled in a sacred place in the territory of the Carnutes, considered to be the centre of Gaul. Caesar speaks of the rigorous training of the druids, mainly learning the oral traditions by heart, which could go on as long as twenty years. He alludes to the druids' interest in the study of the natural world as well as religion. They taught that the souls of the dead underwent transmigration, apparently in order to prevent warriors from being afraid of death and thus make them more valorous in battle (see TRANSMIGRATION OF SOULS). Caesar comments that the druids acted as judges or arbitrators in all disputes.

It is clear from the Classical sources that the druids' main concern was the control of supernatural forces. They did this mainly by means of DIVINATION, which included the perpetration of human sacrifice. Victims were stabbed and their death throes and the flow of their blood examined, and many other forms of ritual killing took place (see SACRIFICE, HUMAN). Tacitus (*Annals* XIV, 30) alludes to the consultation of the innards of victims for divinatory purposes in the druidic grove on Anglesey. An interesting remark by Caesar (VI, 16) is relevant here: he says that the gods could be neutralized or controlled only if one human life were exchanged for another. Thus, if illness or other crises threatened the Gauls, the druids would organize human sacrifice. Pliny (*Natural History* XVI, 95) speaks of a fertility ritual involving MISTLETOE, thought to be a cure for barrenness. He describes how, on the sixth day of the moon, the druids climbed a sacred oak tree and cut down a growth of mistletoe with a golden (surely gilded) sickle which was then caught in a white cloak; two white bulls were then sacrificed.

Classical writers allude to the history of druidism after the arrival of the Romans in Celtic lands. Augustus tolerated it; Tiberius opposed it, and Claudius tried to eradicate it. Though there are late references to druids (for example in the works of the 4th c. Bordeaux poet Ausonius, who speaks of druidic succession from father to son), it is clear that once the main free Celtic heirarchy of chiefs and knights had broken down, the druids would have lost much of their influence.

The druids make frequent appearances in the Irish mythological tradition. Here, the same three classes of druids, bards and seers (filidh) which occur in the Classical literature appear again. The druids largely disappeared from Ireland under Christian influence, many of their functions being taken over by the filidh (see FILI). But early Irish mythology contains many druids. In the *Book of Invasions*, an early leader, Partholón, comes to Ireland with three druids; the goddess Brigit was born in a druid's household; Finn was reared by a druidess. The Daghda was credited with being a god of druidism, which may refer to magic or prophecy.

The Irish druids were powerful royal advisers and prophets. CATHBADH, the druid attached to the household of King Conchobar of Ulster, sometimes wielded greater influence than the king himself. He was a clairvoyant, prophesying, for instance, that the unborn Deirdre would be Ulster's ruin. The druids of Queen Medb ordered her not to engage battle with the Ulstermen until they were able to foretell a propitious day. Druids were also involved in the choice of the rightful king of Ireland: they supervised the TARBHFHESS or 'bull-sleep', in which the correct king-elect would be foretold.

Finally, the druids of Ireland were involved in magic, sometimes used for evil. In the Fionn Cycle, the Black Druid turns Finn's future wife, Sava, into a fawn. Eva, the stepmother of Lir's children, uses a druidic wand to turn them into swans.

The real significance of the druids for Celtic religion cannot be estimated with any degree of accuracy. They probably possessed powerful religious and political influence during the free Celtic period. Certainly, the notion of a powerful religious leadership in later European prehistory is entirely comprehensible. Whilst there is no direct evidence to support this, it is not impossible that the druids were pan-Celtic before the Roman period, surviving in Ireland until the coming of Christianity. *See also* ORACLE.

□ O'Fáolain 1954; Bray 1987, 209–15; Watson 1981, 165–80; Cormier 1976–8, 303–15; Green 1986, 26–8; Piggott 1968; Le Roux & Guyonvarc'h 1978; Drinkwater 1983, 38–9; Harding 1974, 96–112; Nash 1976, 124; Jackson 1964; Cunliffe 1979, 106–10.

Drunemeton The word means 'sacred oak grove' or 'oak sanctuary' (*see* GROVE; OAK). The Greek geographer Strabo (XII, 5, 1) tells us that Drunemeton was the meeting-place of the Council of the Galatians, a group of Celts who settled in Asia Minor during the early 3rd c. BC. Clearly, this sacred meeting-place is precisely comparable to the holy site that Caesar mentions (VI, 13) in the land of the Carnutes, regarded as the centre of Gaul, where druids met at a fixed time each year to discuss intertribal matters of religious and political importance.

dualism is a term used to describe the interdependent relationship between opposing concepts of life and death, good and evil, positive and negative forces, day and night, light and dark. Many Celtic and Romano-Celtic cults demonstrate this ambiguity and a close interaction between apparently opposite aspects of the supernatural. A good example of this is the imagery of the mounted Sky-god of the Jupiter-columns (*see* JUPITER-GIANT COLUMN). Here the forces of good, life and light represented by the horseman

Drawing of a **druid**, taken from Henry Rowlands' *Antiqua Restaurata*, 1723.

A sacred grove, perhaps **Drunemeton**, taken from a 17th c. book on the German gods by Elias Schedius, printed in Amsterdam.

interact closely with the negative, dark forces, depicted in the form of a chthonic giant with snake limbs. The Sky-god's horse often appears to trample the monster into the earth, but the relationship is ambivalent, and the giant sometimes supports the horse. In a sense, what is displayed is a kind of seasonal imagery, where death is necessary for life, winter for spring, dark for light. Similar dualism may be observed in other cults, such as that of the Mother-goddesses, who are concerned with life, growth and fertility, but who may also preside over death and the afterlife.
□ Green 1989, *passim.*

Duchcov The 'Giant's Springs' at Duchcov in Czechoslovakia was a natural spring which in the 3rd or 2nd c. BC was the site of specific ritual activity, presumably associated with a divinity of the spring waters. Here people dedicated a huge bronze cauldron containing more than 2,000 bronze objects, mostly bracelets and brooches. This evidence for cult activity is interesting not simply because of the richness of the deposit but because, in general, aquatic ritual deposition is associated with martial equipment, arguably representative of an essentially masculine activity. Here at Duchcov, by contrast, jewellery was the main type of votive offering. Whilst men did wear ornaments in the Iron Age, it could be argued that Duchcov may have been the site of a cult where women were the major participants. The other feature of interest about Duchcov lies in the presence of the CAULDRON: the association of a large bronze vessel with aquatic ritual is one of a number of instances where this takes place (*see* LLYN FAWR; LLYN CERRIG BACH).
□ Megaw 1970, 20, no. 134; Piggott 1968, 83ff; Fitzpatrick 1984, 178–90.

duck The tradition of using duck images as religious symbols goes back in barbarian Europe to the Middle Bronze Age, around 1300 BC, when the image was adopted to decorate sheet metalwork. In this Urnfield art, ducks are often shown flanking a solar wheel or forming the prow and stern of a boat which carries the sun-disc. This solar-duck symbolism carried over into the Celtic La Tène period where it is found, for example, on bronze torcs in the Marne region. The duck may here reflect the link between sky and water, because of the bird's ability both to fly and to swim. It is known that solar cults had a close affinity with water (*see* SUN/SUN-GOD).

At the Iron Age hillfort of Milber Down (Devon), three bronze figurines – of a raven, a duck and a stag – are recorded, the duck having a water-line clearly demarcated along its body. The bird has a cake or pellet in its beak, which may signify fertility or sacrifice. Elsewhere in Britain, bronze ducks come from Ashby-de-la-Launde (Lincs) and Rotherly Down (Wilts), where a curious statuette depicts a duck with a human head on its back. The most important duck image from Celtic Europe is the bronze statuette of SEQUANA, spirit of the Seine, at her shrine of *Fontes Sequanae* near Dijon. The goddess stands in a boat in the form of a duck, a ritual pellet or cake in its beak. It is assumed that Sequana appears thus in order to intensify the imagery of water, the boat and duck combining to form an augmented symbol of the potency of the river at its source.
□ Sprockhoff 1955, 257–81; Green 1989, 41, fig. 16; 1991a; Fox et al. 1948–52, 27ff; Deyts 1985.

 E

eagle The most important symbolism of eagles concerns their association with the Roman sky-god Jupiter. With their great size and wingspan, their majestic mien and their ability to fly at a great height, these birds were appropriate creatures as emblems for the celestial king of gods. The Celtic Sun-god, whose identity was to an extent merged with that of the Roman sky-god, adopted the eagle as one of his attributes. Thus, Romano-Celtic images of the Sun-god frequently appear in western Europe with the Celtic solar wheel and the Roman eagle. Many instances of this association are documented: examples can be cited at Alesia in Burgundy; Alzey in Germany and Willingham Fen in Cambridgeshire. Bronze bucket-mounts at Thealby (Lincs) and the River Ribble (Lancs) exhibit curious imagery in the form of eagles emerging from bulls' heads. Bulls were also companions of the sky-god, and it is possible that we are witnessing either intensification of celestial symbolism or a shape-shifting between bull and eagle.

The eagle appears in early Welsh mythology, in 'Math', the *Fourth Branch of the*

Mabinogi, where it does possess a shape-changing role. In this tale, LLEU LLAW GYFFES, son of Arianrhod, marries Blodeuwedd, a non-human woman conjured from flowers by Math, lord of Gwynedd, and Gwydion the magician. Lleu is struck a mortal spear-blow by Gronw, Blodeuwedd's lover, and immediately he changes into an eagle, flying off into a sacred oak tree. Lleu may himself have a celestial or solar aspect to his cult. His name means 'Bright One of the Skilful Hand'; and his association with the eagle and the oak (Jupiter's sacred tree) links him closely with sky symbolism.
□ Green 1984a, 189; Mac Cana 1983, 74–5; Ross 1967a, 277–8; Jones & Jones 1976.

Bronze **duck** figurine with a sacred cake in its beak, from the Iron Age hillfort of Milber Down, Devon.

Earth *see* MOTHER-GODDESS; TERRITORY, GOD OF

Emhain Macha, situated at Navan Fort near Armagh, was the seat of the royal court of Ulster, the stronghold of King Conchobar mac Nessa. The name means 'the twins of Macha' and relates to the legend of the Irish goddess MACHA, who died in a horse race after giving birth to twins. It was from Emhain Macha that the great war was conducted between the people of Ulster and Connacht (the *Táin Bó Cuailnge*). One of the stories of the Ulster hero Cú Chulainn's early life was his arrival at Emhain Macha, having routed the 150 youths reared there under the tutelage of Conchobar.

Various tales exist, explaining the fall of Emhain Macha: one dates its destruction to AD 281, but it is generally thought that the fort was finally conquered under Niall of the Nine Hostages, the first historically recorded king of Ireland, who reigned in the 5th c. AD.

In excavations at Emhain Macha, the main period of occupation was found to be about 700 BC. There was a large round house on the hill, which was replaced again and again. It stood beside a larger enclosure. In around 100 BC this perhaps royal residence was replaced by some kind of sanctuary, when an enormous structure was built with five circles of oak posts. In the middle was a massive PILLAR of oak which could be seen for miles.
□ Ross 1986, 109; Lehmann 1989, 1–10; Kinsella 1969; O'Rahilly 1946, 230–3; Mac Cana 1983, 101.

Bronze statuette of an **eagle**, from the Woodeaton Romano-Celtic temple, Oxfordshire.

Aerial view of Navan Fort, County Armagh, built about 300 BC. This was the ancient stronghold of **Emhain Macha**, royal seat of the kings of Ulster.

emphasis relates to the treatment of religious imagery. Very frequently, Celtic artists deliberately over-emphasized certain attributes or parts of the body of a cult image, in order to endow the depiction with particular potency. In animals, horns or antlers are often large in proportion to the rest of the body: this happens on rock carvings in Camonica Valley, where stag antlers may be extravagantly large; or on the Strettweg cult wagon, where the antlers are as big as the stags themselves. On boar images, the dorsal bristles are exaggerated, in order to demonstrate ferocity: this occurs, for instance, at Neuvy-en-Sullias (Loiret) and at Hounslow in southern England. On anthropomorphic images, it is the head which is over-emphasized. On the bronze statuette at Bouray in northern Gaul, the head takes up more than half the whole figurine. Eyes, hands or genitals may also be stressed: at *Fontes Sequanae*, the images of pilgrims frequently have exaggerated eyes, to let the healing goddess know it was the part of the body which required a cure.

Sometimes the inanimate attributes of a deity were emphasized or exaggerated: Epona's platter of fruit on a monument at Trier is huge; so is the *cornucopia* of the Hammer-god's consort at Pagny-la-Ville (Burgundy). This kind of exaggeration is very common on Celtic images. The same phenomenon occurs in the vernacular tradition of Ireland and Wales: the Daghda has an enormous club and cauldron. The reason for this kind of over-emphasis is to make the image more efficacious, to give particular power to the most important attribute or part of the body and to acknowledge that power to the god concerned. In a sense, the emphasis of an emblem or of part of a divine image has the same effect as doubling or tripling that image (*see* TRIPLISM). It stresses the importance of the deity both to the god himself and to the worshipper.

☐ Green 1986, 211–16; 1989, 207–14; Anati 1965; Mohen, Duval & Eluère 1987, no. 27; Megaw 1970, no. 238; Pobé & Roubier 1961, pl. 11; Deyts 1983; 1985; Espérandieu, no. 2066; Schindler 1977, 37, fig. 101.

Entremont was the capital of the Celto-Ligurian tribe of the Saluvii: the *oppidum* is about 3 km north of Aix-en-Provence. The Celtic town was sacked and the tribe conquered by Rome in 124 BC. Here there was a native shrine which displays evidence of ritual associated, above all, with HEAD-HUNT-ING. The sanctuary was situated on the high-

est point of the hill, and consisted of a stone structure whose porticoes were decorated with carvings of severed heads and adorned with real skulls nailed into niches; one of the latter had a javelin head embedded in the bone, supporting the view that the skulls were those of battle victims which were offered to the gods of the shrine. Many sculptures depict head imagery, and it may be that if genuine human heads were unavailable, the gods were offered carved replicas instead. One stone, the so-called 'head PIL-LAR', consists of a tall block with twelve severed heads incised on it: these are depicted with no mouths and with closed eyes, perhaps suggestive of death; the bottommost head is upside-down, maybe leading the others to the Underworld. The stone probably dates from the 3rd–2nd c. BC. Another portico carving comprises a relief of a horseman with a human head dangling from the neck of his mount; this is very evocative of the comments of such Classical writers as Livy (X, 26; XXIII, 24), Diodorus Siculus (V, 29, 4) and Strabo (IV, 4, 5) who all allude to Celtic head-hunting.

Noteworthy also at Entremont are the stone images of warriors who sit cross-legged wearing cuirasses and helmets and often hold severed human heads in their hands. These may be war-gods with the heads of their victims, or alternatively they may be the gods of the dead. Images like these are found elsewhere in Provence, at GLANUM and ROQUEPERTUSE. The evidence for offerings and head imagery is repeated at Roquepertuse. *See also* NAGES.

☐ Benoit 1955; 1981, 54, 87, fig. 49; Green 1986, figs. 10, 11.

Epona The name 'Epona' derives from the Celtic word for 'HORSE'. Epona was a Celtic horse-goddess whose iconography was inextricably linked with equine symbolism. Epona was a popular deity to whom many epigraphic dedications and images were set up throughout the Celtic world during the Roman period. She was especially venerated in Gaul and the Rhineland: the Burgundian tribes of the Aedui and Lingones, and the Mediomatrici and Treveri of eastern Gaul were particularly devoted to her. But she appears further afield: Epona was worshipped in Britain, Yugoslavia, North Africa and even in Rome. Here, uniquely for a Gaulish divinity, she had a festival on 18 December, demonstrating her official acceptance in the capital of the Empire. In addition, there are Classical literary allusions to Epona's cult (for example: Minucius Felix, *Octavianus* XXVIII, 7; Apuleius, *Metamorphoses* III, 27).

Epona attracted worshippers during the 1st–4th c. AD from a wide spectrum of Romano-Celtic society; an important contingent came from the military installations of the Rhine and Danube. But other prominent groups of devotees venerated Epona in Burgundian houses and small shrines: indeed, in Burgundy is the only specific evidence for the existence of a shrine to Epona; found in the ruins of a temple at Entrains (Nièvre) were two inscriptions, one of which dedicates the sanctuary to the goddess.

The special interest of Epona's cult lies in her images, for she is never represented without her equine companion(s). Epona's iconography falls into two main groups: most important are the depictions of the goddess riding side-saddle on a mare; specific to the tribal areas of Burgundy is the presence of a foal either asleep beneath its mother, suckling the mare or being fed from a *patera* offered to it by the goddess. The other main image type was particularly favoured along the German frontier: here Epona is depicted between two or more horses. At Beihingen in Germany the goddess sits between two groups of three and four horses which walk towards her as if in homage. Of the same type is one of the few British representations of Epona, a small bronze from Wiltshire in which Epona is seated between two ponies (one of either sex); she has a yoke and a *patera* filled with corn from which she feeds the ponies.

Much of Epona's imagery displays the symbolism of FERTILITY and the earth's abundance. Many of her representations depict the goddess with baskets of fruit or corn (for example at Kastel in the Rhineland and Dalheim in Luxembourg). The Burgundian imagery of mare and foal is especially evocative: the foal gains nourishment from Epona's *patera* (for instance at Autun) or suckles its mother (as at Santenay). The fact that Epona's mount is a mare is important: the lands of the Aedui and Lingones of Burgundy were famed for horse breeding, and Epona presided over this aspect of fertility. In addition, there seems to have been a definite association between Epona and the Mother-goddesses: she was linked with them

Rock carving of the 7th c. BC from Camonica Valley, depicting a figure, half-man, half-stag, with **emphasis** placed on the antlers.

Stone head of a deity from the *oppidum* of **Entremont**, France.

on a dedication dating from the 3rd c. AD at Thil Châtel in Burgundy; and at Hagondange (Moselle) Epona is portrayed in triple form, as if in imitation of the three Mothers.

Epona was associated both with water/healing and with death: she was venerated at such Gaulish spring shrines as Sainte-Fontaine-de-Freyming (Moselle) and at Allerey (Côte-d'Or), where she was depicted in the guise of a water nymph. The goddess is frequently represented with a DOG, which could reflect either healing or death: at Altrier in Luxembourg, she is accompanied by a dog and a raven, the latter a specifically chthonic symbol. At Agassac in south-western Gaul, Epona appears as a Nereid on horseback, on a marble tombstone, and at the great cemetery of La Horgne au Sablon near Metz, Epona's image occurs several times: on one stone Epona on her mare is depicted with the image of a man behind her; this has been interpreted as a human soul being led by the goddess to the Otherworld. This symbolism of the afterlife may also be represented on images where Epona carries a large KEY; this occurs, for instance, at Gannat (Allier) and Grand (Vosges). The motif could represent the key to the stable, but at a deeper level, it could reflect the ability of the goddess to unlock the gates of heaven and the happy Otherworld. On other images, as at Mussig-Vicenz near Strasbourg, Epona holds a *mappa* or napkin which, we are told by Suetonius (*Nero* 22), was used to start off horse races. Again, at a more profound level of meaning, the *mappa* may reflect Epona's presiding over the beginning of man's journey through life.

The symbolism of Epona is complex and multifaceted. Mediterranean commentators speak of her purely as a goddess of horse and stable. Horses were of fundamental importance to the Celts, in terms of economics, transport, war, power, prestige and religion. The Gaulish cavalry in the Roman army formed a large group of worshippers; Epona may have been perceived as a protectress of horsemen and their mounts. After all, the intelligence and speed of horses were crucial to the safety of the cavalryman; and it should be remembered, too, that pre-Roman Celtic society was based on a hierarchy of chiefs and knights, on whom the society and prestige of the tribe depended. Horses were important in Celtic religion, being linked with the high deities of sun and warfare. But Epona's cult possessed a greater profundity than her equine symbolism alone would suggest. The femininity of her imagery and that of her horse are significant, as is her overt fertility symbolism. But her key, her *mappa* and her association with the dead suggest that here was a goddess who guarded her devotees throughout this life and into the next world. She was a patroness of horses, cavalrymen and the craft of horse breeding at one level; at another, she reflected the deep mysteries of life, death and rebirth. *See also* RHIANNON; ROSETTE.

□ Johns 1971–2, 37–41; C.I.L. III, 5192, XIII, 5622; Duval 1976, 50; Linduff 1979, 817–37; Oaks 1986, 77–84; Green 1989, 16–24; Magnen & Thevenot 1953, nos. 2–3, 117; Thevenot 1968, 187–91; Hatt 1945, no. 23; Espérandieu, nos. 1618, 1855, 4219, 4350–5, 7290, 7513, 8235; Espérandieu *Germ.*, no. 404.

Ériu is an earth MOTHER-GODDESS who is identified with the land of Ireland. When the divine race of the Tuatha Dé Danann are defeated by the Sons of Mil (the Gaels), the invaders encounter the three eponymous goddesses of Ireland – BANBHA, FÓDLA and Ériu. Each of them extracts a promise from the Milesians that the island will bear her name. The fili (poet, seer) Amhairghin assures Ériu that hers will be the main name for Ireland (Éire); in return, Ériu prophesies that the land will belong to the Sons of Mil for all time.

There is some evidence that Ériu was a solar divinity: the sun was perceived as a golden cup filled with red wine which Ériu, as goddess of the land, hands to successive mortal kings of Ireland, to signify their marriage and the fertility of the country (*see* SACRAL KINGSHIP). In addition, Ériu was the wife of the Tuatha god Mac Grené, his name reflecting his solar role.

□ Rolleston 1985, 132; Pokorny 1925, 197–202; Mac Cana 1955–6, 76–114.

Essarois The Burgundian shrine at Essarois (Côte-d'Or) was the sanctuary of the Celtic healing god APOLLO VINDONNUS; Vindonnus' name means 'clear' or 'white'. The stone pediment of the temple building shows the image of the god as a radiate-headed solar god, associated with a dedicatory inscription to Vindonnus and the springs. This divinity was associated with healing springs, and pilgrims came to his shrine to be cured particularly of eye diseases (*see* SPRING, HEAL-ING). Bronze eye models displaying their afflictions were offered to Vindonnus in the hope that sick eyes would be replaced by healthy ones. In addition, wooden votive limbs and internal organs were dedicated with similar hopes in mind (*see* LIMB/ORGAN, VOTIVE). Images of hands holding gifts to the god were also found. The association of sun, light, water and the healing of eyes recurs at other shrines; Luxeuil is one example. Here at Essarois, it is probably no accident that appeal for eye cures was made to a divinity whose name and image symbolized clarity of light and vision and the idea of pure, translucent water.

☐ Thevenot 1968, 110–12, fig. on p. 111; Espérandieu 3417–33; Green 1989, 163.

The horse-goddess **Epona**, carrying fruit or bread, from Dalheim, Luxembourg.

Esus The Roman poet Lucan described in a poem, the *Pharsalia*, dating from the 1st c. AD, the last great battle in the civil war between Pompey and Caesar. In it, he alludes to the journey of Caesar's troops through southern Gaul and their encounter with three Gaulish gods: Taranis, Teutates and Esus (*Pharsalia* I, 444–6). Lucan describes this triad as cruel, savage and demanding of human sacrifice: 'horrid Esus with his wild altars'. In later commentaries on Lucan's poem, probably dating from the 9th c. from Berne, Esus is mentioned as being propitiated by human sacrifice (*see* SACRIFICE, HUMAN): men were stabbed, hung in trees and allowed to bleed to death. The two commentators equate Esus with Mars and Mercury respectively, but this may not pose as great a problem as first appears, since the word 'Esus' is not so much a name as a title, meaning 'Lord' or 'Good Master'.

Whilst the implication of Lucan's description is that Esus was an important and powerful Gaulish divinity, this is belied by the archaeological evidence in which Esus may be traced to only two monuments. The more significant stone forms part of the pillar dedicated to Jupiter by Parisian sailors in the reign of Tiberius. The block from Paris was found with five others in 1711 on the site of Nôtre-Dame. The Esus stone itself is inscribed with his name, and beneath this is a depiction of a muscular god chopping at a branch of a willow tree. On a juxtaposed scene is another willow, a bull and three cranes or egrets, with the inscription 'TARVO-STRIGARANUS'. Essentially similar iconogra-

The god **Esus**, whose name is inscribed above his image, from the *Nautes Parisiacae* monument in Paris, early 1st c. AD.

phy recurs on a 1st c. AD stone at Trier, where an unnamed woodcutter attacks a willow in which repose three egrets and the head of a bull.

The symbolism of the two monuments, whilst not identical, is sufficiently similar and idiosyncratic for it to be possible to identify the presence of Esus on both. In addition to the image of the woodman, the willow, marsh birds and bull appear on the Paris and Trier images. The iconography is obscure, but there is a natural association between bulls, birds and willows: egrets feed on parasites in cattle hide; they, like the willow, are inhabitants of marsh or water margin, and egrets nest in willows. The woodcutting scene is problematical in terms of interpretation. It has been suggested that Esus prunes the tree for sacrificial purposes. It may be that there is cyclical imagery in the destruction and rebirth of the Tree of Life in winter and spring: the birds may represent the soul in flight, perhaps the soul of the tree itself; the bull could himself be a sacrificial beast. Seasonal imagery may also be present in the symbiotic relationship enjoyed between bull and birds, which are of mutual benefit to one another. Finally, it should be recalled that trees are associated with Esus not simply in the iconography but also in the Berne commentaries which describe the fate of Esus' human sacrificial victims.
□ Mac Cana 1983, 29, 33; Zwicker 1934–6, 50; Duval 1976, 26–7; 1961, 197–9; Ross 1967a, 279; Espérandieu, nos. 3134, 4929; C.I.L. XIII, 3656.

Étain The Irish story of Étain is fragmentary: it concerns the love of MIDHIR, a god of the Tuatha Dé Danann, for a beautiful girl. Midhir's attentions to Étain stimulate the jealousy of Midhir's wife Fuamnach, who casts a spell on the girl, turning her into a butterfly. Even thus transformed, Étain possesses magical powers: she can hum Midhir to sleep and warn him of the approach of an enemy. Fuamnach causes a magical wind to blow Étain away; she is harboured for some time by OENGHUS, god of love, but she is buffeted abroad once more and finally falls into a cup of wine belonging to the wife of Edar, an Ulster hero. The woman drinks the wine, and Étain is reborn as a new child, more than 1,000 years after her initial birth. Midhir has continued searching for Étain throughout this period; he finds her again,

married to Eochaidh, king of Ireland. By trickery, Midhir wins Étain and flees with her to his sídh (Otherworld palace), having turned both her and himself into swans.

Étain is closely associated with the supernatural: she is linked to two gods, Midhir and Oenghus. She is reborn with the same identity as her original self. Most important of all, it is clear that in her marriage to Eochiadh, she is fulfilling the role of goddess of sovereignty, legitimizing his rule by her union with the king (see SACRAL KINGSHIP).
□ Nutt 1906, 325–39; Müller 1876–8, 342–60; Bergin & Best 1938, 137–96; Mac Cana 1983, 90–2.

Euffigneix A late pre-Roman image of a native deity comes from Euffigneix (Haute-Marne) in eastern Gaul, perhaps dating from the 2nd or 1st c. BC. The image consists of a stone block or pillar roughly formed into a human torso, surmounted by a large head with stylized Celtic features. Round the neck is a massive torc; each side of the trunk is decorated with a large human eye in low relief. Most interesting of all is the carved figure of a BOAR, dorsal bristles erect, which stalks along the body of the god, facing towards his head. The name of the god represented here is unknown, but he may be a hunter-deity associated with boars and the forest. The depiction may even reflect METAMORPHOSIS, the shape-changing between human and animal form in which Celtic divinities indulged, as we know from the vernacular sources. The same god may be represented on certain Celtic coins minted by the tribe of the Aulerci Eburovices of the Evreux region, which show images of a human head with a boar along its neck. The eye motifs on the Euffigneix stone give it a special potency, perhaps exhibiting the all-seeing power of the god and, in addition, the ability to ward off the evil eye. It is possible that the form of the image itself may reflect wood-carving techniques translated into stone.
□ Allen 1980, fig. 25; Espérandieu, no. 7702; Green 1989, 105–6, fig. 46; Pobé & Roubier 1961, no. 6; Megaw & Megaw 1989, 160.

Fagus Trees held extreme sanctity for the Celts; certain species of TREE were person-

ified in specific areas of Gaul and given a
spiritual identity as local divinities. People
living in the French Pyrenees dedicated altars
to 'the god Fagus', the name meaning 'beech
tree'; and at Croix d'Oraison an incised bust
of a man, executed in simple Celtic style, may
represent an anthropomorphized version of
Fagus.
☐ Green 1989, 153; C.I.L. XIII, 223, 224;
Thevenot 1968, 220.

Fates were Roman divine personifications
who were invoked as goddesses concerned
with the destiny of humankind, normally
occurring in triplicate (*see* TRIPLISM). It may
have been this triple form which encouraged
a fusion between the Fates and Celtic belief
systems. Thus, there is sometimes a link
between the three Fates or *Parcae* and the
triadic MOTHER-GODDESSES. In Burgundy and
among the Treveri, the imagery of the
Mothers sometimes attests the merger of
their cult with that of the Fates. Thus at Trier
and Metz, the Mother-goddesses possess,
not their normal fertility emblems but instead
a spindle, distaff and scroll, signifying their
role as measurers of men's lives. This symbolism recurs on certain Burgundian reliefs of
the three Mothers, where the goddesses
might hold a balance or the scroll of life.
In Britain, at Carlisle, there is epigraphic
association between the three Mothers and
the Fates, where the Celtic goddesses are
actually named as *Parcae*.
☐ Espérandieu, nos 4937, 7233; Deyts 1976,
no. 170; Thevenot 1968, 173–6; R.I.B., 951,
953.

feast Both the archaeology of the European
Iron Age and the vernacular tradition feature
the concept of the OTHERWORLD feast, demonstrating the very strong Celtic belief in an
afterlife. The rich, late pre-Roman graves of
south-east Britain exhibit a preoccupation
with this post-death banquet. These graves –
exemplified by those at WELWYN – may contain amphorae, once full of wine, and drinking
vessels. They also contain fire-dogs, used
perhaps for spit-roasting or for containing
fires. At Winchester, a 1st c. AD grave was
furnished with a meal consisting of poultry
and a young pig. Pork was buried with some
of the high-status individuals interred with
two-wheeled vehicles in East Yorkshire. This
kind of evidence for provision of food and
drink in the afterlife is reflected by graves all

A 2nd or 1st c. BC stone
carving of the Boar-god at
Euffigneix. The figure
wears a torc, and a boar
strides along his torso.

Bronze flagon, relic of a
funerary **feast**, from the
Iron Age chariot-burial at
La Gorge Meillet, Marne,
France.

Iron Age bronze jug, once
holding wine for a ritual
feast, from Waldalgesheim,
Germany.

over the Celtic world. Marne burials attest this custom; goose bones found in Czechoslovakian graves may reflect the consumption of these creatures in a ritual banquet.

Irish mythology is full of references to Otherworld feasting, where pork was eaten and quantities of liquor consumed. Each 'bruidhen', or Otherworld hostel, was presided over by a god who provided the supernatural feast. Every bruidhen had its own inexhaustible CAULDRON; animals, especially pigs, were killed and resurrected to be eaten again. It was at one of these hostels that the smith-god GOIBHNIU had his feast – his 'Fledh Ghoibhnenn'. Those who ate and drank at his table neither aged nor died (a feature of the Celtic Otherworld). *See also* MAC DA THÓ.
□ Mac Cana 1983, 34–5, 127; Megaw 1970, 17; Hodson & Rowlett 1973, 186; Green 1986, 129–30; Stead 1985b, 36–43; Dyer 1990, 157–9, pl. 58.

Fedelma was a prophetess and poet at the court of Queen Medb of Connacht, when the latter was plotting the invasion of Ulster to capture the Brown Bull of Cooley. Fedelma told Medb of the brave young Ulster hero Cú Chulainn, who would wreak grievous harm on Ireland and that Medb's host of warriors would be covered in blood.
□ O'Fáolain 1954; Kinsella 1969.

Fedlimid In the Ulster Cycle tale of DEIRDRE, King Conchobar and the Ulstermen are drinking at the house of Fedlimid the storyteller, when the unborn Deirdre cries out in the womb of Fedlimid's wife. When the druid Cathbadh foretells the doom surrounding the child, Conchobar saves her from being put to death and fosters her.

There is another Irish historico-mythical character of this name, one Fedlimid mac Crimthainn, a 9th c. king of Munster.
□ Mac Cana 1983, 121; O'Hógáin 1990.

Fellbach Schmiden was a religious site near Stuttgart in Germany, one of a well-known group of ritual structures known as VIERECK-SCHANZEN. The 'sanctuary' consisted of a shaft or well within a square enclosure. The shaft is especially interesting since it contained oak carvings, including those of a stag and two rams or goats, the latter once held by a missing human figure whose hands survive curled round the animals' torsos. Dendrochronological tests on samples of the oak suggest that the tree was felled in the late 2nd c. BC. The imagery of anthropomorphic figures holding up effigies of animals recurs on the Gundestrup Cauldron, but here the creatures are represented much smaller than the supporting human figure. It is possible that the effigies were not votive offerings but rather were part of the structure of a shrine.
□ Webster 1986a, 95; Planck 1982; 1985; Megaw & Megaw 1989, 162–3.

Ferghus mac Róich is a mythical, heroic figure who appears in the Ulster Cycle of prose tales. The first part of his name is cognate with the Latin 'vir' ('man') and he appears to have been a fertility figure. Ferghus was the first mate of the notoriously promiscuous MEDB of Connacht. He was also the husband of Flidais, a goddess of deer and cattle: it was said that she was the only woman, apart from Medb, who could satisfy Ferghus' rampant sexual appetite and that, in her absence, he required seven ordinary women to take her place.

Ferghus was king of Ulster before King CONCHOBAR; he was the lover of Nessa, Conchobar's mother, who would grant him her favours only if her son was made king for a year. This took place, and Conchobar proved so popular that the people chose him for their permanent king. Ferghus preferred hunting and feasting to kingship and gave in gracefully. Ferghus is described as of superhuman status: he had the strength of 700 men; he was as tall as a giant; he could, at one meal, consume seven pigs, seven deer, seven cows and drink seven vats of liquor. He possessed a magic sword which could stretch as long as a rainbow.

Ferghus figures most prominently in the *Táin Bó Cuailnge* and its foretales. He defects to Connacht and the court of Queen Medb, having been disgusted by the treacherous behaviour of King Conchobar of Ulster in the affair of Naoise and Deirdre. Ferghus is one of Conchobar's ambassadors, despatched to Scotland with a false pardon for Naoise and his brothers. He is the pledge of safe conduct for their return to Emhain Macha, but before they arrive, Ferghus is lured away by the promise of a feast. Thus, the hero is caught between two bonds of honour or 'geissi': his oath never to refuse a feast and his pledge to guard Naoise from harm. There is some suggestion that the Deirdre and Naoise story was introduced into the Ulster Cycle at a later date than the *Táin* in order to explain the defection of Ferghus from Ulster to Connacht.

After his defection to Connacht, Ferghus acts as adviser to Queen Medb, as scout and as go-between from Connacht to the Ulstermen. He is, to an extent, a prophet and an interpreter of the supernatural: it is he who explains that the two great bulls, the Brown of Ulster and the White-Horned Bull of Connacht (over whom the *Táin* is fought) are in fact enchanted creatures, metamorphosed men, sent to Ireland to wreak havoc by jealous gods.

Though no longer at the court of Ulster, Ferghus retains some links with the kingdom of the North. He is one of the foster-fathers of the Ulster hero Cú Chulainn, and he warns Medb of his foster-son's prowess. Medb sends Ferghus to parley with Cú Chulainn and various terms are agreed, though these are later broken by Medb. Ferghus' affection for Cú Chulainn is demonstrated by his fulfilment of his promise never to confront his foster-son in battle. When the situation arises, he retreats, and most of the Connachtmen go with him. He also allows Cormac, Conchobar's exiled son, to persuade him to deflect the sword blow directed at the king. The magic sword, instead, lops off the tops of three hills. Ferghus finally meets his end at the hands of Ailill, Medb's husband, when bathing in a pool with the Connacht queen.

Some traditions credit Ferghus with the authorship of the *Táin Bó Cuailnge*.

□ Kinsella 1969; O'Fáolain 1954; O'Leary 1987, 27–44; Lehmann 1989, 1–10; de Vries 1963, 139; Rolleston 1985, 234, 245; Berresford Ellis 1987, 119–20; Ross 1967a, 215.

fertility of crops, livestock and humans was, quite naturally, a major concern of the Celtic peoples, and this is clearly reflected in cults and ritual. Most of the goddesses chronicled in the Irish vernacular tradition combine attributes of fertility and sexuality with that of war. In the iconography, goddesses like EPONA and NEHALENNIA were associated with well-being and florescence, but the *Matres* or MOTHER-GODDESSES above all were concerned with all aspects of fertility. Divine couples were invoked as purveyors of abundance in all its forms (*see* COUPLE, DIVINE). Many of the male deities, too, were primarily gods of fertility: SUCELLUS, the GENII CUCULLATI and CERNUNNOS were all venerated in their capac-

Iron firedogs and frame, equipment for a burial **feast**, from a late 1st c. BC cremation-grave at Welwyn, Hertfordshire.

A 2nd c. BC wooden image of a stag from the ritual *Viereckschanze* at **Fellbach-Schmiden**, near Stuttgart, Germany.

ity of providers and promoters of procreation. Certain images of war-gods in North Britain were depicted as ithyphallic (*see* PHALLUS) and with HORNS, thus associating virility and aggression. Horns themselves appear to have been potent symbols of fertility. *See also* BULL; IMBOLC; MISTLETOE; MOON; RAM; SIRONA; SNAKE; SNAKE, RAM-HEADED; STAG.

festival *see* BELTENE; COLIGNY CALENDAR; FIRE; IMBOLC; LUGHNASAD; SAMHAIN.

fili The filidh (singular fili) were members of the learned class in Ireland: they had both secular and religious functions, and were largely responsible for the Irish mythological traditions which survive from the early centuries of the 1st millennium AD. The repertoire of the filidh included stories which were specifically concerned with the supernatural world. Filidh correspond to *vates* who are alluded to in Classical literary comments on Celtic society. They were experts in storytelling and in composing learned poetry, but they were also seers and practised DIVINATION. Filidh also had the reputation of possessing supernatural power to blemish or cause death by means of satire.

In Ireland, the novice fili had to undergo a learning period in a special school for between seven and twelve years. Whilst there, he would be taught to compose in various rigid poetic metres; he mastered and committed to memory genealogies and heroic tales; he learned prophecy and the skills of praising rulers.

The filidh took over many of the powers and functions of the DRUIDS, who faded out of importance after the coming of Christianity to Ireland. As learned poets, they also usurped the role of the BARDS, who were relegated to a minor role within society. They were remarkably long-lived as a class: filidh continued to possess the functions of seers, poets, teachers, royal advisers and witnesses of contracts until the 17th c. in Ireland. Brigit was the favoured deity of the filidh; her expertise was in learning, poetry, divination and prophecy. *See also* ORACLE.
□ Mac Cana 1983, 12–19; Watson 1981, 165–80; O'Rahilly 1946, 323; Ross 1986, 97–8.

Finn mac Cumhaill is the hero of the Irish Fionn Cycle. He is the leader of the élite war-band, the Fianna, who are selected for their strength and valour, bound by strict rules and pledged to fight for the high king of Ireland against foreign invaders. In peacetime the Fianna devote themselves to hunting and other outdoor pursuits.

Finn is the greatest leader of the Fianna. Born after the death of his father, Cumhaill, he is reared by a druidess and a wise woman, and he develops a great affinity with the natural world. When Finn grows into a young man, he ousts his father's killer, Goll, from the Fianna leadership and acquires a bag of craneskin containing a spear, helmet, shield and pigskin belt. This is the heritage of his father and of the leadership of the Fianna. Finn goes to Finnegas, the bard, in order to learn poetry, and it is from Finnegas that he acquires wisdom and the gift of prophecy: the bard catches the SALMON of Knowledge and gives it to Finn to cook. The young hero burns his thumb on the hot fish, puts it in his mouth and thus gains supernatural knowledge. On his arrival at the royal court of Tara, Finn is granted leadership of the Fianna by the high king, as a reward for saving Tara. The stronghold has been burned down each year on the Feast of SAMHAIN by a goblin named Aillen, who first enchants the court and then sets fire to the palace. Finn keeps awake during Aillen's visit by laying against his cheek an enchanted spear made by Len, swordmaker to the gods, and he is able to kill the goblin.

Under Finn, the Fianna prosper and become even more élitist, with severe initiation tests and ordeals. Both Finn and the Fianna perform supernatural deeds: one Keelta (the runner) overcomes an enchanted boar single-handed and kills a five-headed giant who has been ravaging crops. Finn himself hunts supernatural boars whose aim is to lure him and his men to the Otherworld. The hero also encounters a supernatural horse who entices him to the underworld. The association between Finn and cranes is interesting: apart from the episode of the craneskin bag, Finn as a young child is saved from death by his grandmother in CRANE form.

There are a number of pointers to the divine or superhuman character of Finn. He marries Sava, a woman who has been transformed into a fawn, and he is able to cancel the enchantment. By her, he has a son, OISIN. Finn has various encounters with supernatural beings, including the triple Morrigán as three old hags. He has the gift of clairvoyance, and he has supernatural fighting prowess. In one story, Finn successfully challenges the Tuatha Dé Danann god, Nuadu, for lordship of the sídh of Almu.

Sadly, the great character of Finn is marred by his jealousy of DIARMAID, his rival in love over GRÁINNE. He falls into dishonour by arranging Diarmaid's death. Finn's wife has prophesied that Finn will die only if he drinks from a horn; according to one tradition, the ageing Finn, abandoned by his Fianna, tests his strength by attempting to leap the Boyne. But he has broken his 'geis' by drinking from a horn; he falls into the river and dies.
□ O'Fáolain 1954; Bhreathnach 1982, 243–60; Meyer 1897a, 462–5; 1893, 241–7; Campbell 1870–2, 193–202; O'Rahilly 1946, 271, 279; Ross 1967a, 228, 284, 318, 328; Mac Cana 1983, 104–13.

Fir Bholg In the early Irish *Book of Invasions*, successive populations of Ireland are described. The fourth group of people to invade were the Fir Bholg. It is suggested that these pre-Goidelic groups took their name from a god 'Builg'. The next invaders were the divine race of the Tuatha Dé Danann, who challenged the power of the Fir Bholg and defeated them at the First Battle of Magh Tuiredh, County Sligo. The vanquished Fir Bholg fled to the Aran Islands, and there erected the massive stone-built fort of Dun Aonghusa on Inishmore. Tradition also has it that the Fir Bholg were permitted by the victorious Tuatha Dé to retain the province of Connacht.
□ Macalister 1931; Even 1956, 81–110; O'Rahilly 1946, 43–8, 141, 380; Mac Cana 1983, 59.

fire In antiquity, a religious link was frequently made between fire and the sun. Fire was perceived as the terrestrial element which corresponded to the sun in the heavens. Fire was a supernatural force, able to warm and to illuminate the darkness, but its destructive properties were also acknowledged. Fire was perceived as a purifying, cleansing element, a gift to mankind from the sun.

The veneration of fire is something particularly associated with the cold areas of Europe, with their long, dark winters and overcast skies. Many pagan European fire festivals are recorded, some of which have continued until the present day. Bonfires were lit at the great Celtic festivals of Beltene on 1 May and

Clay *Dea Nutrix*, a Romano-Celtic goddess of fertility, suckling twin babies.

The stone fort of Dun Aonghusa on Inishmore, Aran Islands, said to have been built by the **Fir Bholg**.

Samhain on 1 November, in acknowledgment of the critical points in the solar year, to welcome and encourage the sun as a fertile and warming force. There were Midsummer bonfire rituals, which copied the solstitial activity of the sun in the sky. These pagan fire festivals were replaced by such Christian festivals as that of the celebration of St John the Baptist's birth. He was born at Midsummer, and the tradition of bonfires may have developed because there existed a tradition that the saint's bones were burnt by the Roman emperor Julian the Apostate in the mid-4th c. AD. Thus the 'bone-fire' was a fitting festival for the saint.

Ritual bonfires served several purposes: they acknowledged the power of the sun by replicating its heat and light on earth, but the rich ash from the fires was spread on the fields to help fertilize the seed and promote its germination.

Linked to the bonfires were the Celtic and Germanic customs of wheel-rolling. The Christian St Vincent, living in the 4th c. AD, observed a pagan Celtic festival which took place in Aquitaine. The ritual consisted of rolling downhill to a river a flaming wheel, which was then reassembled in the shrine of the Sky-god. An almost identical practice is chronicled in descriptions of St John's festival, where a great wooden wheel covered in straw was rolled down the mountainside to a river. The idea was that if the wheel reached the water unimpeded, a good harvest and a propitious year would be ensured.

A less pleasant fire ritual pertaining to the Celts is recorded by such Classical authors as Strabo (IV, 4) and Caesar (VI, 16). These writers describe a ritual in which huge man-shaped wicker images were filled with human and animal sacrificial victims and set alight. A 9th c. AD scholiast or glossator on Lucan's *Pharsalia* links this rite with the Celtic thunder-god Taranis. So the power of lightning may have been reflected. Interestingly, 'straw-men' are recorded as being burned in post-pagan European spring festivals: these images, which were burned at Easter time, were known as 'Judas men'.
□ Zwicker 1934–6, 50; Hole 1940, 63–72; Hatt 1951, 82–7; Frazer 1922, 614–15.

Flag Fen Sometime in the Middle Bronze Age (circa 1200 BC), an artificial island was constructed in the Fen wetlands of eastern England, on which a settlement was estab-

lished. Shortly afterwards, a timber alignment of large oak posts was erected, which marched from the dry land at Fengate across to the island and beyond it. The alignment may have been almost 1,000 yards long and originally consisted of some 2,000 posts.

What is particularly interesting about Flag Fen is its evidence for intense ritual activity, which began about 1200 BC and went on into the Celtic Iron Age, perhaps ending in the 2nd c. BC. Deposited adjacent to or alongside the timber alignment, mainly to the south, were found more than 300 items of metalwork, including many prestige/high-status and martial objects such as swords, daggers and spears. Many of these objects had been ritually broken and cast into the water (*see* RITUAL DAMAGE). Some of the items were of tin, and there is evidence that these were made on the site, perhaps especially for deposition.

In addition to the metalwork, pottery and shale objects were also thrown into the water: near the timber alignment, too, were a human skeleton and other human bones, and there was also a number of dog-burials. The inference is that people over a considerable period of time were making offerings to their gods by casting in their precious possessions, especially their weapons. These acts have been likened to the casting of Excalibur into the mere, perhaps associated with ceremonies in which the deities of the watery Otherworld were appeased, in times of disaster or rejoicing.

The alignment has been interpreted as a boundary rather than any kind of trackway, and it is significant that the ritual activity was centred on this liminal structure. Francis Pryor has suggested that it may represent a pre-Roman version of 'beating the bounds'.
□ Pryor 1990, 386–90.

Flidais *see* DIANA; FERGHUS; STAG

Fódla In early Irish mythology, there was a close association between certain goddesses and the land. One of these deities was Fódla, one of the three eponymous goddesses of Ireland. At the time of the Coming of the Gaels (or the sons of Mil), who displaced the Tuatha Dé Danann, the three goddesses – BANBHA, Fódla and ÉRIU – each exacted a promise from the Milesians that the island would bear her name.
□ Mac Cana 1983, 62, 86.

Fomorians These beings appear in the 12th
c. Irish *Book of Invasions*, which contains an
account of the mythical invasions of Ireland.
The second invasion, led by Partholón, fought
against a race of demonic beings, the Fomorians or Fomhoire, whose name means 'under-
demons': this was the first battle of Ireland.
When the TUATHA DÉ DANANN inhabited the
land, the Fomorians pillaged their territory
and imposed crippling taxes; anyone default-
ing was punished by having his nose cut from
his face. The king of the Fomorians was
BALOR, the glance from whose single eye
could strike an enemy dead.

The king of the Tuatha Dé was Nuadu, but
since physical perfection was a requirement
for leadership, he was deposed after losing
his arm. His successor was BRES, who was
in fact a Fomorian, and his rule became
increasingly oppressive. Now Nuadu was fitted with an artificial silver arm and was
reinstated by the Tuatha Dé. He was urged
by the young warrior LUGH of the Long Arm
to throw off the Fomorian yoke once and for
all. Lugh appeared in Ireland and, as his first
act, joined battle with a band of Fomorian
tax gatherers. In this conflict, the Fomorians
were routed, and many were killed.

A major confrontation between the Fomorians and the Tuatha Dé was inevitable: all
the magicians and craftsmen of the land
contributed their special skills against the
enemy. In the Second Battle of Magh Tuiredh, both sides suffered grievous losses, but
the slain people of Danu (the Tuatha Dé)
were restored to life by being cast into a
magic well, while the Fomorians stayed dead.
Balor himself was killed by a slingstone cast
by Lugh: with satisfying irony, his evil eye
was thus driven through the back of his
head and its destructive gaze turned on the
Fomorians themselves! The Fomorians were
decisively defeated and driven out of Ireland
for all time.

The struggle between the Tuatha Dé Danann and the Fomorians may reflect the archetypal dualistic conflict between light and
the chthonic powers. Curiously, it was the
Fomorians under Bres who provided the skills
of agriculture. Though called 'demons', the
Fomorians probably had divine status and
were, in a sense, necessary to the Tuatha Dé,
just as darkness and light, death and life,
winter and summer are mutually dependent.
□ Mac Cana 1983, 54–8; Krappe 1927;
O'Fáolain 1954.

The 'straw-man', burnt in **fire** festivals to the
Sun-god. This is a modern re-enactment of the
ceremony, in the film *The Wicker Man*.

The wetland site of **Flag Fen**, where votive
offerings of weapons were made in the later
Bronze Age and early Iron Age.

Fontaines Salées, Les (Yonne) is an example of a sacred thermal spring which was venerated before the Roman period in Gaul. The site possessed medicinal springs (*see* SPRING, HEALING) which were apparently visited from the early Iron Age, evidenced archaeologically by an oval structure. In the 1st c. AD, a double-walled enclosure was built, replacing the earlier structure and encircling a paved pool.

☐ Brogan 1973, 192–219; Piggott 1968, 71.

Fontes Sequanae The veneration of water-spirits is demonstrated throughout Celtic Gaul and Britain, especially rivers at their source. SEQUANA was the personification of the SEINE, and she presided over a healing sanctuary, *Fontes Sequanae*, (the 'springs of Sequana') at the source of the river, where water bubbled up as springs, in a valley to the north-west of Dijon in Burgundy. The shrine seems first to have been established in the late Iron Age. During the Roman period, the existing sanctuary was monumentalized by the building of an extensive religious complex centred on the springs and POOL.

The shrine's main interest lies in the evidence which it presents of the pilgrims who visited Sequana's temple in the hope of a cure from their afflictions (*see* SPRING, HEALING). The springs themselves have no mineral curative properties, only offering a source of fresh, clean water. In 1963, a rich deposit of 200 wooden (mainly OAK, which seems especially to have been chosen) votives were found in waterlogged ground during the excavation of the Roman structures, which they appear to pre-date. As early as the 1st c. BC, pilgrims were making the journey to the healing springs, offering models of themselves as simple rural peasants, dressed in heavy-weather hooded cloaks, reflecting perhaps their outdoor lives as farmers, mule drivers or hunters, or simply the fact that they were travellers. They offered to Sequana wooden models of their afflicted limbs or internal organs in the hope that they would be healed (*see* LIMB/ORGAN, VOTIVE). Eye troubles seem to have been rife, judging from the representations of eyes and blindness, and chest diseases – asthma or pneumonia – are suggested by curious models of thoracic cavities. Empirical medicine was practised here: doctors as well as priests were present. The ritual seems to have been centred on recipro-

city, whereby the votive leg or liver offered to Sequana was replaced, after prayer, with a whole organ, by the grace of the goddess.

During the Roman period, when the shrine was upgraded, the wooden offerings and images were replaced by stone sculptures. But the pilgrims represented were the same: they still wore heavy cloaks, and they still depicted themselves carrying symbolic gifts to the goddess – fruit, a purse of money or a favourite pet dog or bird. When the suppliants entered the sanctuary, they purified themselves at one of the springs, dedicated an image bought at the shrine-shop, immersed themselves in the sacred pool near the main temple, and thence proceeded to a long colonnaded building for the healing sleep, where they hoped for a dream, vision or revelation, the moment when the goddess inspired and healed them.

☐ Deyts 1983; 1985; Green 1986, 150–1; 1989, 152–61.

Forêt d'Halatte was the site of a Romano-Celtic temple near Senlis (Oise), which was associated with a healing cult. Here, images of pilgrims, parts of human bodies and representations of animals were fashioned in simple but powerful Celtic style, in both wood and stone. Heads predominate among the offerings, and on some figures, the torso is completely devoid of features apart from the delineation of the breasts. One image of a human hand holds a dove as an offering to the presiding divinity; and depictions of beasts – horses, pigs and bulls – were also dedicated in the shrine. The importance of the sanctuary at Forêt d'Halatte lies in the incredible degree of SCHEMATISM with which the figures have been carved, bearing witness to a vigorous religious art in which only the essential elements of a body were depicted.

☐ Green 1989, 220–2, figs 89, 94–6; Espérandieu, nos 3876–88; Ross 1967a, 63, pls 14a, b.

Fortuna was the Roman personification of Luck, Chance, Fortune, who was represented as a goddess, with a *cornucopia* (to signify the good things of life), a rudder and globe or wheel. All the last three symbols could change direction in an instant and alter good luck to bad and vice versa.

Fortuna is interesting within a Celtic context, since iconographical evidence indicates that her identity or some of her attributes were adopted as part of Celtic religious imagery. Thus, Rosmerta and Mercury at Gloucester are accompanied by Fortuna; and on a stone at Glanum in Provence, Rosmerta, herself a goddess of prosperity, has actually adopted Fortuna's distinctive attributes of a rudder on a globe. The Celtic Mother-goddesses, too, were touched by Fortuna's function: at Nuits-Saint-Georges in Burgundy, an image shows the goddesses associated with a globe and rudder; and at Gripswald in Germany the Mothers are again linked with these attributes of Fortuna. Both the Hammer-god and Nehalennia are also sometimes depicted as if they have borrowed some of Fortuna's imagery.

Fortuna is often represented with the symbol of a wheel in place of her spinning globe. Like a roulette wheel, it rotated and stopped at random, governing which direction the fortunes of men would take. But Fortuna's wheel may have given her links with the Celtic Sun-god whose solar symbol was the WHEEL. Thus, where Fortuna appears with her wheel at such places as Wiesbaden in Germany and Agey in Gaul, she may have been perceived as a goddess associated with the cult of the sun, perhaps the consort of the Sun-god.

□ Green 1986, fig. 48; 1989, 11, 50, 192, fig. 23; Salviat 1979, 49; Deyts 1976, no. 170; Espérandieu, nos 6616, 7526; Webster 1986a, fig. 17; Green 1984a, cat. no. B1; Hondius-Crone 1995.

Schematized stone figures, representing pilgrims or gods, from the Celtic sanctuary of **Forêt d'Halatte** near Senlis, France.

G

Gaels The dominant people in historical Ireland were the Gaels, speakers of the Goidelic Celtic language. They were traditionally the descendants of the mythical Sons of Mil, who came from Spain to Ireland and pushed out the previous ruling caste, the divine Tuatha Dé Danann, forcing them to make a new kingdom underground. The story of the Coming of the Gaels is recorded in the *Book of Invasions*.

□ Mac Cana 1983, 61–3.

Gebrinius *see* MERCURY GEBRINIUS

geissi are magically binding bonds of honour, taboos or prohibitions, which affected Irish kings and heroes. Cú Chulainn, for instance, was subject to a number of such bonds.

Relief of Mercury, Rosmerta and **Fortuna** (to Rosmerta's right) from Gloucester. The goddess holds a *cornucopia* and a rudder on a globe.

Infringement of these taboos meant inescapable catastrophe for their violator. When Finn goes against his geis and drinks from a horn, he dies. Insular sacral kings were surrounded by geissi, which went with high office (*see* SACRAL KINGSHIP). The original significance of these prohibitions is unknown, but some relate to the sanctity of kingship, in much the same way as priests, in some cultures, may be forbidden to do or see certain things.

☐ Lehmann 1989, 1–10, O'Leary 1987, 27–44; Mac Cana 1983, 117.

Genius Cucullatus This is a name given to certain distinctive cult images in Celtic Europe during the Roman period. A *cucullus* is a hood fastened to a cloak or coat. In a Romano-Celtic shrine at Wabelsdorf in the Austrian province of Carinthia, two large altars were erected with epigraphic dedications which read 'genio cucullato' ('to the hooded Genius'). The term Genius Cucullatus has been adopted to describe figural representations of particular deities who are typified and indeed identified by being dressed in hooded outdoor garments.

On the Continent, Genii Cucullati appear as single images, often in the form of giants or dwarves, but in Britain, the deities are idiosyncratic in being frequently depicted as triple dwarfs. Continental representations display very overt fertility symbolism; the figures often carry eggs, for instance on a wooden image at Geneva, or moneybags, as at the shrine of the maternal Xulsigiae at Trier. On occasions, the cucullus itself could be removed to expose a phallus; and Cucullati may appear as lamp fittings, the lamp holder being formed by the god's penis. Some Continental Cucullati appear with scrolls; and this is repeated on an image at Reculver in Kent. The parchment may reflect imagery borrowed from that of the Classical god Telesphorus, who represented wisdom and the craft of writing.

British Genii Cucullati are distinctive in their triplistic imagery (*see* TRIPLISM). They occur in two main distributional clusters: in the region of Hadrian's Wall and among the Dobunni of the Cotswolds. At Housesteads in Northumberland, a triple image from a small shrine, of perhaps 3rd c. AD date, in the *vicus* (the civil settlement) attached to the Roman fort, displays the trio swathed in heavy hooded capes reaching to their feet.

The interest in this particular group is that the face of the central divinity is clearly masculine, whilst his companions have softer, rounded facial contours, suggestive rather than female physiognomy. An alternative is that the faces instead reflect differing ages, an older deity flanked by two youths. This imagery may thus reflect either the presence of both male and female aspects of a given divine concept or the span of life, from youth to maturity. This latter pattern occurs among the Germanic Mother-goddesses.

The Cucullati occurring among the tribe of the Dobunni are interesting in that they, like many Continental examples, reflect clear fertility symbolism. Triads from a temple at Wycomb (Glos) carry eggs, as does an image at Cirencester. There was a cult centre at this tribal capital, where many images of Cucullati have been found, frequently represented in the company of a Mother-goddess, stressing their association with abundance and fecundity. On one relief, one of the three hooded gods turns to a seated Mother-goddess as if offering her a gift: the goddess' name is CUDA. On another Cirencester stone, three Cucullati accompany a Mother, two of whom carry swords, perhaps to protect her from the blights of barrenness, disease or famine. Outside the Dobunnic region, Genii Cucullati are associated with healing spring sanctuaries at Springhead in Kent and at Bath, where they accompany the prosperity-deities, Mercury and Rosmerta.

The cult of the Genii Cucullati appears to have embraced profound and sophisticated belief systems. Fertility, evidenced by phallic symbolism and association with the Mothers, is prominent. Some scholars have even seen breast imagery in the hooded shape of the figures. The association with eggs and with springs may represent healing, renewal and rebirth. A striking feature of the iconography of the Cucullati is the homogeneity of dress; the hood is always present, and this may reflect the normal outdoor clothing of a rural, peasant community. Pilgrims visiting the shrine of Sequana near Dijon are depicted in stone or wood wearing this heavy-weather cloak, and the imagery of the Cucullati may have been deliberately chosen to reflect an affinity between the gods and their devotees. In addition, the hooded shape may itself express phallic symbolism, or a hidden, shrouded image redolent of mystery, death or mourning. The triadism of many British

Cucullati serves to enhance their symbolic potency; the magic of 'three' was displayed, and it is perhaps significant that triplism was associated with many Celtic divinities – the Mother-goddesses are a prime example – whose main role included a fertility function.
☐ Egger 1932, 311–23; Heichelheim 1935, 187–94; Stähelin 1931, fig. 145; Wightman 1970, 213; Loeschke 1919, 157–60; Green 1976, 228; 1978, 66; 1986, 90–1, figs. 39, 40, 71; 1989, 185–7, fig. 83; Toynbee 1962, pl. 83; Cunliffe & Fulford 1982, no. 103, pl. 27; Deyts 1983; 1985.

Representation of the tripled **Genius Cucullatus** from Housesteads on Hadrian's Wall.

Glanis was the eponymous spirit of the sacred springs at the town of GLANUM in Provence. The settlement was occupied by the Greeks as well as the Romans and Celts; Glanis may well have been worshipped in some form as early as the 3rd c. BC. There are cisterns at the site of the springs, where pilgrims may have bathed. Near one of them an altar to Glanis and the Glanicae was set up. The Glanicae were a triad of local Mother-goddesses associated with the healing springs.
☐ Salviat 1979.

Glanum Sited in a valley which cuts through the mountain chain of the Alpilles in Provence, Glanum was a Celtic, Greek and Roman town. Here, there was a sacred spring which was a native, pre-Roman holy place. The basin or reservoir of the spring, in which pilgrims may once have immersed themselves to be cured (*see* SPRING, HEALING), may still be seen beneath an arch which once supported a covering for the pool. The reservoir was fed by a subterranean gallery leading from the spring itself.

The names of some of the divinities worshipped at this shrine and elsewhere in Glanum are known. The local spirit GLANIS and three Mothers, called the Glanicae, had altars set up to them. Other Celtic deities invoked in the town included Epona, the divine couple Mercury and Rosmerta and the Gaulish HAMMER-GOD, to whom a figurine and numerous small stone altars with hammer symbols were dedicated. On one such stone, the hammer is associated with representations of a human arm and leg, presumably models of diseased limbs which required a cure from the spring-god Glanis.

Dating from the pre-Roman period, when Glanum belonged to the tribe of the Saluvii, are enigmatic statues of warrior-gods, seated

The sacred spring dedicated to Glanis at **Glanum**, Provence.

in the cross-legged position. Remarkably similar images come from the nearby sanctuaries at ENTREMONT and Roquepertuse. These figures wear cuirasses and torcs, and sometimes they carry severed heads in their hands. The heads have closed eyes, and it is generally considered that the representations are of victorious war-gods with the heads of their vanquished and dead enemies.

One other Celtic divine image was important at Glanum: this is the triple-horned bull, a concept which was more at home in north-east Gaul than Provence (see BULL, TRIPLE-HORNED). None the less, it appears here as a beautiful little bronze figurine, wearing a decorated girth belt and closely resembling the small, agile, black Camargue bulls which still inhabit the region.
□ Salviat 1979; Rolland 1944, 167–223; Green 1989, 80, figs. 23, 32, 68a, b.

goat In both Classical and Celtic religious imagery, goats appear to have represented fertility. This is the creature's role when he accompanies Mercury, and here he is interchangeable with the ram, also a fertility emblem. Mercury appears in a Celtic context with his goat, as at Glanum in Provence, where he is accompanied by his native consort Rosmerta.

Goat-horned Celtic divinities are recorded in Britain and Gaul. At Colchester, an urn decorated with a human face has an applied phallus and goat horns. The fertility association is present also in Germany where, at Bonn, an altar dedicated to the triple *Matronae* has on the reverse a carving of a snake-entwined tree and a triple-bodied goat. The antlered god Cernunnos has goat legs on a relief at Beaune; and at Yzeures-sur-Creuse (Indre-et-Loire) is an image of a god seated on a goat, accompanied by a ram-horned snake. All these images demonstrate the essential association between the symbolism of the goat and other motifs which explicitly reflect fertility and abundance. The goat is a sexually active animal, and the horns reflect both virility and aggression. An interesting recent discovery from south-western Scotland is a little bronze image of a goat with enormously exaggerated horns.
□ Green et al. 1985, 43–50; 1976, 217; 1989, fig. 23; Ross 1967a, fig. 78; Louibie 1965, 279–84; Espérandieu, nos 2083, 7772.

goblin see FINN

Gofannon was a Welsh smith-god, son of Dôn, and the equivalent of the Irish GOIBHNIU. Smiths were particularly important in Celtic society, ranking equally with druids in the hierarchy. This was partly because such craftsmen were able to produce bright, strong metal from rough ore, by means of fire, water and skill. Up to the present day, certainly in Wales, blacksmiths were and are thought to possess the magic art of healing everyday ills such as warts. Gofannon features in the *Tale of Culhwch and Olwen*: his help is sought to delineate the furrows and clean the ploughshare.
□ Mac Cana 1983, 34–5; de Vries 1963, 98; Rhŷs 1901, 645.

Goibhniu, Luchta, Creidhne There was a triad of Irish craft-gods who belonged to the Tuatha Dé Danann: these were Goibhniu the smith, the most important of the three, Luchta the wright and Creidhne the metalworker. The three gods are called upon to forge weapons for Lugh and the Tuatha in the Second Battle of Magh Tuiredh, fought against the Fomorians. Each god makes a different part of the weapons: Goibhniu the head or blade, Luchta the shaft and Creidhne the rivets. Goibhniu's weapons are guaranteed always to fly true and always to inflict a fatal wound.

Goibhniu had another role, that of host of the Otherworld FEAST: at this meal, the god provides a special ale, and those who drink it become immortal. *See also* GOFANNON.
□ Mac Cana 1983, 34–5; Hull 1930, 73–89; O'Rahilly 1946, 308–16.

Goldberg Like the GOLORING, the Goldberg was a sacred enclosure in Germany, belonging to the Hallstatt period, 7th–6th c. BC. Here, there was a large settlement of rectangular wooden structures, houses and barns. In one corner, a sub-rectangular enclosure bounded by a wooden palisade contained two massive buildings, which may perhaps be interpreted as temples within a sacred *temenos* or precinct.
□ Piggott 1965, 90, fig. 46; 1968, 70.

Goloring A rare piece of evidence for the presence of a sacred enclosure, perhaps dating as early as the 6th c. BC, exists at a site known as the Goloring near Koblenz in Germany. The sanctuary consists of a large enclosure 625 ft in diameter, open to the sky, containing a central post which, from the depth of its hole, may have stood 40 ft high. The post may have symbolized a sacred tree or PILLAR, and the Goloring earthwork was probably erected for religious gatherings and ceremonies centred on this pillar. *See also* GOLDBERG.

□ Piggott 1968, 71; 1965, 232.

goose On a lintel of the pre-Roman Celtic shrine of Roquepertuse in Provence stood a huge stone goose, a symbol of watchful alertness and aggression, guarding the sanctuary from intruders. To the Celts the goose symbolized war and protection: thus, geese were buried with warriors in Iron Age Central and East European graves. Celtic war-deities were accompanied by geese in the iconography: a bronze figurine of a warrior-goddess at Dinéault in Brittany depicts her wearing a helmet with a goose crest. The Celtic Mars was associated with geese: he appears thus at Risingham in North Britain; and a goose was the companion of MARS THINCSUS (a Germanic deity) at Housesteads. The bird accompanies the peaceful healer-god Mars Lenus at Caerwent, presumably being present here as a guardian against disease. That the goose was sacred to the Britons is implied by Caesar's statement (*de Bello Gallico* V, 12) that there was a taboo on eating the creatures.

□ Hodson & Rowlett 1973, 189; Green 1989, 143; 1986, 187; Ross 1967a, 270–3, pls. 19a, 58a; Megaw 1970, 17.

Gournay-sur-Aronde (Oise) was a pre-Roman Celtic sanctuary built in an *oppidum* of the Bellovaci. Recent investigations have thrown considerable light on the ritual activity that took place on such sites. Firstly, hundreds of weapons were deliberately broken to 'kill' them before they were offered to the god (*see* RITUAL DAMAGE). The second feature of interest concerns the evidence for animal sacrifice (*see* SACRIFICE, ANIMAL). Two main groups of animal debris are present: one consists of the complete skeletons of horses and elderly cattle, with no sign of butchery; the other of young butchered animals, lambs and young pigs. The cattle were buried in pits (*see* PIT), and it has been suggested that these were sacrifices to the gods of the underworld. The horses were apparently buried with honour, as befitted the prestige value of these creatures, when they died of

A druidical **goat** sacrifice, from a drawing by William Stukeley of 1759.

Late Bronze Age vessel in the shape of a **goose**, from Hungary.

natural causes. But pigs and lambs were deliberately chosen as beasts to be sacrificed and the best portions consumed in ritual feasts. This bias towards these two species may be paralleled, for example, at Ribemont and Mirebeau in Gaul, and at the British shrine of HAYLING ISLAND. The entrance to the sanctuary at Gournay was guarded by flanking bull or ox heads, perhaps originally nailed to gateposts.
□ Brunaux 1986.

Gráinne appears in the Fionn Cycle of early Irish mythological tales; the story of the elopement of Gráinne and DIARMAID is mentioned as one of the chief tales in the *Book of Leinster*.

Gráinne is the daughter of Cormac; she is betrothed to Finn, the ageing leader of the war band known as the Fianna. At the wedding feast, she sees and falls in love with Diarmaid, one of the young Fianna. She approaches him, but he rejects her because she is promised to Finn. Gráinne shows her supernatural power over Diarmaid, in that she binds him with a magic oath or 'geis' to take her away from Tara. Diarmaid's companions urge him that this bond is stronger than his honour code with regard to Finn and must be kept. Diarmaid and Gráinne flee all over Ireland, pursued by Finn. The lovers are aided by OENGHUS, god of love, who spirits Gráinne away when she is in greatest danger, and gives the pair many pieces of advice, including a warning never to sleep two nights in one place. The couple arrive in the Forest of Duvnos, an enchanted wood guarded by a giant, Sharvan the Surly. There is a particular tree in the forest, a tree of immortality whose berries Sharvan is particularly anxious to guard. Gráinne desires some of the berries and presses Diarmaid to defy Sharvan and obtain some of the fruit for her. Diarmaid kills Sharvan, and both he and Gráinne eat some of the berries. Finn discovers the forest and the couple's hiding-place; Oenghus intervenes once again and spirits Gráinne away to safety a second time. Eventually, Finn pardons Diarmaid after Oenghus intercedes on their behalf; the pair settle in Kerry and produce five children.

The story of Gráinne and Diarmaid is one of a number of instances in Irish mythology of the eternal triangle of young man, young girl and ageing suitor. The situation is very similar to the tale of Naoise, Deirdre and Conchobar. There are many supernatural elements in the story: Gráinne herself is powerful and superhuman, though not herself divine. The intervention of the god Oenghus is important; and the presence of a tree of immortality, whose fruit is eaten by the lovers, raises the couple above human status.
□ O'Fáolain 1954; Meyer 1897a, 458–62; Lloyd, Bergin & Schoepperle 1912, 41–57; Mac Cana 1983, 109–12.

Grannus see APOLLO GRANNUS

Griselicae see MATRES GRISELICAE

grove Whilst the Celts sometimes worshipped in built temples, their cult foci were frequently natural features in the landscape, like trees, forests or groves. The term 'nemeton' refers to a sacred place and, in particular, a sacred grove. Certain Celtic place-names reflect the veneration of such places: examples include Aquae Arnemetiae (the 'spa of the grove goddess') at Buxton; Vernemeton (the 'especially sacred grove') and DRUNEME-TON in Asia Minor, the Galatian oak sanctuary alluded to by Strabo (XII, 5, 1), and there are many others. The Irish term for 'nemeton' or grove is 'fidnemed'. Tacitus speaks of the sacred groves on the island of Anglesey, where the druids performed acts of human sacrifice (*Annals* XIV, 30). Dio Cassius refers to a wood or grove sacred to the British goddess Andraste (LXII, 2). Lucan makes reference to groves near Marseille, where again human sacrifices were carried out (*Pharsalia* III, 399–452).

In addition to the evidence for sacred groves themselves, goddesses with 'grove-names' were venerated. Thus we know of ARNEMETIA of Buxton and NEMETONA, who was worshipped, for example, at Altripp near Speyer and at Bath. The Celto-German tribe of the Nemetes (in whose territory Nemetona was venerated) suggests that the tribe adopted this sacred name. At Grenoble, a group of female divinities was known as the Nemetiales (goddesses of the grove). *See also* OAK; SACRIFICE, HUMAN; TREE.
□ Green 1986, 21–2; 1989, 203; de Vries 1963, 144; Ross 1967a, 36–7.

Gundestrup From the Raevemose peat bog at Gundestrup in Jutland came the famous silver cult vessel known as the Gundestrup Cauldron. The vessel is some 14 in. high, with a diameter of about 25.5 in., and holds 28.5 gallons. It is made of 96 per cent pure silver and was originally gilded. The cauldron is composed of a base plate, five inner and seven outer plates, bearing mythological scenes, and it had been dismantled into its component silver sheets before being deliberately buried in the marsh.

There is some controversy concerning the origins and date of the Gundestrup Cauldron: it was probably manufactured between the 2nd and 1st c. BC. In terms of the artistic style of its decoration, the vessel could have been made in Romania or Thrace. The silversmiths (and it is possible to detect several hands at work) had access to a wide range of symbols, some of which have no parallel in the Celtic iconography of western Europe, but certain of the motifs and images are very definitely Celtic. Examples of these are the depictions of Celtic weaponry: the carnyx or boar-headed war-trumpet, shields, animal-crested helmets and others. In addition, certain cult images are represented which belong to the mainstream of Celtic iconography and are too idiosyncratic to be otherwise interpreted.

The plates on the Gundestrup Cauldron appear to depict a mythological narrative which is impossible meaningfully to explain. Gods, people and animals are portrayed, some of the latter of exotic species such as leopards. A convention was that divine beings were depicted larger than humans. Many of the images are familiar Celtic cult figures, which relate very closely to later Romano-Celtic religious iconography. The ram-horned snake appears twice; on one plate the creature is grasped by the stag-horned god Cernunnos, who sits in his normal cross-legged position, with his two torcs – one round his neck and one in his hand – and accompanied by his stag and other animals. On another plate, the solar Wheel-god appears to be present: here, the bust of a bearded god is offered a chariot or cart wheel by a small acolyte wearing a bull-horned helmet. One scene depicts a procession of Celtic footsoldiers and cavalry, with a sacred tree: the ram-horned snake is present, and there is a curious scene in which a tall god holds a small human being over a vat or bucket. This could represent a human sacrifice: the Gaulish god TEUTATES allegedly accepted drowned human victims. But the scene may instead reflect the resurrection of a dead soldier by immersion

Two Irish dolmens, at Kilcooley, County Donegal, and Proleek, County Lowth, c. 2000 BC. According to old tradition, these burial chambers were the homes of such deities as **Gráinne**.

A druidical **grove** sanctuary on Anglesey, from William Stukeley's *Itinerarium Curiosum*, 1775.

in a CAULDRON of immortality, such as is recorded in the vernacular literature of Ireland and Wales.

There is further important iconography on the cauldron: various goddesses are depicted, and on one plate, a female deity is flanked by wheels, as if she is travelling in a cart. It is tempting to speculate that she may be a similar figure to the Irish queen-goddess MEDB, who drives round her armies in a chariot, or the Germanic Nerthus who was mentioned by Tacitus (*Germania* 40). On an inner plate is a scene of three divine bulls about to be sacrificed by three sword-bearing warriors: the animals are huge in relation to their killers, which marks their holy status, and it is interesting that the Celtic tradition of triplism is present. A similar sacrifice is also depicted on the base-plate, where an enormous BULL sinks dying to the ground.

Apart from its rich and indisputably religious iconography, the deposition of the cauldron in the Danish marsh was itself a ritual act. Recurrent instances of cauldrons being deliberately placed in watery contexts during the later Bronze Age and Early Iron Age are widely evidenced in barbarian Europe. But the presence of this cult cauldron, with its Celtic iconography, in a Jutland bog is a problem. It is possible that craftsmen from south-east Europe were commissioned to make the vessel specifically for a Celtic clientele, to be used in religious ceremonies, perhaps by a priesthood. The vessel may have been looted from Gaul by Teutonic raiders, who later buried the dismantled cauldron either for safety or as a sacrifice to their gods. □ Olmsted 1979; Bergquist & Taylor 1987, 10–24; Green 1986, fig. 9; 1989, fig. 1.

Gwydion The *Fourth Branch of the Mabinogi* tells the story of MATH, lord of Gwynedd. He has two nephews, Gwydion and Gilfaethwy. Gwydion is a magician and takes prominence in the story: it is he who by magic contrives war between Math and Pryderi, lord of Dyfed, so that while Math is away, Gilfaethwy can sleep with Goewin, Math's virgin footholder. When Math learns of this treachery, he strikes his nephews with his magic wand, turning them into a stag and hind for one year, a boar and sow for a second and for a third, a male and female wolf.

When after the three years Gwydion is restored to human form, he still possesses his powers as a magician. One of his acts was to help Math fashion a wife out of flowers, Blodeuwedd, for LLEU LLAW GYFFES, whose mother Arianrhod swore at his birth that he would never have a human wife. □ Mac Cana 1983, 72–6; Jones & Jones 1976.

Hammer-god The Gaulish Hammer-god was an important and popular Celtic divinity: his images appear on more than 200 stone monuments and bronze figurines. His iconography is complex, showing him to be a god with a wide and varied sphere of influence. One or two representations of the Hammer-god are accompanied by a dedication to SUCELLUS 'the Good Striker'. The best documented of these is the stele at Sarrebourg which is dedicated to the divine couple Sucellus and Nantosuelta.

Representations of the Hammer-god fall into two main types: the first is the group in which he appears with a consort; in the second, he is depicted alone. The monuments group into four main distributional clusters: north-east Gaul, among the tribes of the Leuci and Mediomatrici: Burgundy, in the lands of the Aedui and Lingones; the region of Lyon; and the mouth of the Rhône, around the city of Glanum. Apart from representations of the god himself, stone votive hammers are found on Burgundian sites, especially at spring sanctuaries; and numerous little altars decorated with hammer symbols come from such southern Gaulish sites as Nîmes and Glanum.

Most images of the god display a remarkable homogeneity: they depict a bearded, mature male, wearing a short, belted tunic and a heavy Gallic cloak or *sagum*. In Gallia Narbonensis, the god appears differently, naked except for a wolfskin over his shoulders and a leaf crown. This is because in this region the Hammer-god was identified with the Roman nature-deity SILVANUS. Most portrayals of the god, wherever located, show him with two main inanimate attributes, a hammer with a long shaft and often a mallet-like head, and a small pot or goblet. In many cases the Hammer-god appears with a small dog, which sits close to his feet and gazes up at him.

In Burgundy and the lower Rhône Valley, a significant feature of the Hammer-god's iconography is his association with WINE and the grape harvest: thus, he frequently appears with a wine BARREL, goblet, amphora or vine-growers' tools. On Burgundian images of the god with his consort, this wine imagery is especially important, occurring, for instance, on more than one depiction at Alesia. At Vienne on the lower Rhône, a bronze statuette depicts the god with a curious combination of hammer and barrel symbol, an implement which consists of a barrel-like hammer-head set on a long staff, with five smaller barrels radiating out from the main one, on short stalks or spokes.

On many occasions, the Hammer-god appears at the sites of healing springs. This happens at Nîmes and Glanum in Provence, and on many Burgundian sites, as at Cussy-le-Châtel and the source of the Arroux. The Hammer-god had a solar association as well: at such places as Lyon and Prémeaux (Burgundy), bronze figurines of the deity appear decorated with celestial symbols; and the Vienne god's hammer-barrel has radiating spokes, like a sun or wheel. This solar association is supported by a find from a British temple, that at Farley Heath in Surrey. Here, a sheet-bronze sceptre-binding, decorated in repoussé, depicts schematized figures of gods and animals, including an image of the Hammer-god and a head of the Sun-god associated with a wheel sign.

The Hammer-god frequently appears with a divine consort (*see* COUPLE, DIVINE): at Sarrebourg, the image of god and goddess is named Sucellus and Nantosuelta. But many representations of an essentially similar couple are unnamed, and may or may not have been known by these titles. The divine partners appear in the Rhineland and among the Mediomatrici. But it is in Burgundy, among the Aedui, that the couple were at their most popular, and they were associated particularly with wine growing, the well-being which may come from drinking, and the prosperity of the land and its people. The partners appear once in Britain, on a small stone relief from East Stoke in Nottinghamshire.

The significance of the Hammer-god was profound and complicated. Overtly, his concerns were those of earthly prosperity and plenty. His association with wild nature is seen in Provence, but it is with the cultivated vine that he has greatest affinity in the wine-growing lands of Burgundy. The hammer

The great decorated silver **Gundestrup** Cauldron, from Jutland. Of 2nd – 1st c. BC date, it could have been looted from Gaul by Teutonic tribesmen.

Bronze figurine of the Gaulish **Hammer-god** from Orpierre, Hautes Alpes, France.

itself is clearly the god's most important symbol. It is a noisy, striking implement whose presence may have a number of meanings. It can symbolize authority, like a SCEPTRE, perhaps accounting for the long shaft; it may be a weapon, but if so, it is to protect people and to combat disease and infertility. The hammer may strike the earth and renew it after winter; or it may hammer in fence posts and thus be a symbol of boundaries and property. The god's other main emblem, the pot or goblet, may reflect plenty and the ever-replenishing vessel of regeneration which figures so prominently in the vernacular sources. It is probable, in any case, that the god looked after his followers both in life and after the grave. His wine imagery may symbolize not only the earthly drink but the red of blood and perhaps of resurrection. The Hammer-god's simple clothes denote him as a peasant's deity, and his was a homely, essentially domestic cult followed by ordinary artisans or rural people whose anxieties were to do with life, health, prosperity and care after death.
□ Espérandieu, no. 4566; C.I.L. XIII, 4542; Green 1989, 46–54, 75–86.

hare There are two brief Classical literary allusions to hares associated with Celtic religion and ritual in Britain. Julius Caesar (*de Bello Gallico* V, 12) comments on the sanctity of certain animals to the Britons – the cockerel, the goose and the hare; he remarks that these creatures were never eaten. Dio Cassius (LXII, 2) mentions that Boudica, queen of the Iceni, released a hare whilst invoking Andraste, goddess of battle and victory, before setting out on her campaign to defeat the Roman army under its general, Suetonius Paulinus, in AD 60.

There is some archaeological evidence that hares were treated in an abnormal fashion which may reflect ritual activity (*see* SACRIFICE, ANIMAL). Certain pre-Roman Iron Age or Romano-British ritual pits were filled with idiosyncratic deposits or layers of material, and some of these contain remains of hares: thus, hare bones occurred in a pit at Ewell (Surrey) and in the curious well at Jordan Hill, Weymouth, which is filled with layers of tiles, each pair containing a bird skeleton and a coin. At Ipswich, two pits each contained a deliberate deposit of matted hare fur.

Small figurines of hares are recorded in Romano-British contexts: a jet statuette comes from the fill of a grave at Colchester; a minute bronze figurine of a hare on a square base or pedestal comes from the vicinity of a 3rd c. AD temple at Thistleton (Leics). A ritual shaft at Winterbourne Kingston (Dorset) contained a sheet-bronze plaque with the outline of a hare crudely punched on the surface.

Hares are sometimes associated with the imagery of hunter-gods in Romano-Celtic contexts: thus at Chedworth (Glos) a god is accompanied by a hound and his quarry, in the form of a stag and hare. Similar symbolism occurs on Gaulish sculptures, such as is present on a stone at Touget (Gers) where a hunter-god carries a hare in his arms.

Apart from the clear association of hares with hunting, there are other characteristics of the creature which may have stimulated religious symbolism and ritual. Hares are swift animals; they display peculiar and aggressive behaviour in the spring, with their 'mad March hare' antics. They may also have reflected chthonic symbolism, in that they forage for food only at night.
□ Ross 1968, 264, 266; Hassall & Tomlin 1980, 410; Green 1989, 100–1, fig. 42; 1991b; Farrar 1953, 74–5; Toynbee 1962, 78; Pobé & Roubier 1961, 190.

Harlow The presence of a Romano-Celtic temple at Harlow in Essex has long been known. What is becoming apparent from recent excavations is that the site was sacred from the Bronze Age, when burials were made on the hilltop. Sacral activity during the Iron Age was intensified immediately before the Roman occupation, when deposits of gold and bronze Celtic coins, in mint condition for offerings, were made. The first-phase Romano-Celtic temple was built in the Flavian period, its wall overlying a late Iron Age penannular ditch which was probably itself a Celtic shrine, and the Roman structure was erected directly over the gold-coin deposition. The beasts sacrificed and eaten as part of the ritual at the shrine show the same distinctive pattern of behaviour at both Iron Age and Roman sacred sites, namely their killing and consumption either at six to nine months old or at eighteen months plus.

The divinity invoked at Harlow may have been a warrior: a worn sculpture depicts a war-god, and a large, stone, helmeted head may represent either Mars or Minerva, herself a war-goddess. In addition, some of the finds endorse this suggestion: four miniature

swords of 1st c. AD type have been found, one in its bronze scabbard (*see* MODEL TOOL/WEAPON). Other votive objects include a tiny pewter cup or chalice and a bronze leaf or feather, one of a well-known group of religious finds, which would have been nailed on the door of the shrine or placed on an altar as an offering. The most curious find from Harlow is what appears to be a tiny votive ivory breast set on a circular bronze plate: if this interpretation is correct, then it may imply the presence of a healing cult at Harlow.
□ France & Gobel 1985; Wheeler 1928, 300–27.

Romano-Celtic Hunter-god, with his hound and a **hare** in his arms, from Touget, Gers, France.

Hayling Island The shrine at Hayling Island (Hampshire) presents a striking example of continuity between the late Iron Age and the Roman period in Britain. A timber circular shrine surrounded by a courtyard was built during the 1st c. AD. All the ritual activity associated with this sanctuary was concentrated on the courtyard which contained offerings of martial equipment and horse gear, some ritually broken to 'kill' them and make them appropriate as offerings (*see* RITUAL DAMAGE). There was substantial evidence of animal sacrifice (*see* SACRIFICE, ANIMAL), but interestingly, there are no cattle bones. This may mean that cattle were deliberately avoided as 'taboo' animals at this particular sanctuary (*see* GOURNAY-SUR-ARONDE).

About fifteen years after the Roman conquest, a massive stone-built circular structure was erected on the site of the pre-Roman building which was cleared away and the ground levelled to receive the new temple. The round *cella* had a small porch, and the building was decorated inside and out with wall plaster. The *cella* was linked by a pathway to the main *temenos* entrance which had a complex set of rooms. The carrying of weapons by natives was now forbidden by the Romans, and this is reflected by the offerings, which now consisted of pottery, coins, jewellery and animals.

The Hayling shrine is especially interesting in that it may link with known historical events. The pre-Roman temple could have been built by Commius, leader of the Gaulish Atrebates, who was originally pro-Roman and an envoy to Britain prior to Caesar's visit in 55 BC. Commius changed sides in 52 BC and fled to Britain, to the Insular branch of

Reconstruction drawing of the Romano-Celtic temple at **Harlow**, Essex. The shrine was erected in the later 1st c. AD and replaced an earlier Iron Age shrine.

the Atrebates, in whose lands Hayling was situated. He may well have established this major cult centre. The Roman shrine was an important sanctuary and could have been part of the building programme of the romanized King Cogidubnus of Chichester, who was also probably responsible for building the palace at Fishbourne.

☐ Downey, King & Soffe 1980, 289–304.

head That the human head was perceived as a potent symbol for the Celts is attested by both literature and archaeology. Classical authors speak of HEAD-HUNTING, and heads were offered in Provençal shrines. In the Irish and Welsh vernacular sources, the heads of heroes possess magical, talismanic properties even after death. In the *Second Branch of the Mabinogi*, the head of BENDIGEIDFRAN (Brân the Blessed) is cut off by his companions at his own request but continues to speak to them and brings them good fortune on their travels. The huge head of the hero CONALL CERNACH has the magic power to bring strength to the Ulstermen if they use it as a drinking vessel. Irish warriors collected brain-balls (the brains of their enemies hardened with lime) as treasured trophies.

The emphasis on the human head is well attested in Celtic imagery. La Tène metal-work consistently uses the head as a decorative or symbolic motif: one can see this on the Waldalgesheim wine flagon, the Weiskirchen brooch, and the buckets from Aylesford (Kent) and Marlborough (Wilts) to name only a few of many examples. In the pre-Roman sculpture of Central Europe and Provence, the human head is a prominent symbol: the 5th–4th c. BC Pfalzfeld Pillar, decorated with four stylized heads; the Heidelberg head; and the carved heads at the southern Gaulish sanctuaries of Roquepertuse and Entremont may be cited.

In Romano-Celtic contexts, gods are frequently represented with over-large heads, or by heads alone. The bronze hooved god at Bouray (Seine-et-Oise) has a head grossly out of proportion with his diminutive body. Many North British deities were depicted simply as rough stone heads, sometimes horned, as at Carvoran in Northumberland. The stone head at Caerwent (Gwent) is interesting in that it was found on a platform in a chamber which was evidently a shrine.

All the evidence suggests that the human head was special to the Celts, perceived to be a potent symbol of the divine persona. By representing deities solely by means of heads, the Celts were acknowledging that the head was the most powerful part of an image. *See also* COIN; CONCHOBAR; HEAD, JANIFORM; HEAD, TRIPLE; HEADDRESS; WELL.

☐ Jones & Jones 1976; Powell 1966, 198; Megaw 1970, nos. 75, 171; Duval 1977, 137; Boon 1976, 163–75; Green 1986, 216–20; 1989, 211–14; Ross 1959, 10–43; 1961, 59ff.

head, janiform The power of two, of twins or of being able to look in opposite directions at once may have given rise to the depiction of janiform human heads. Some of these are demonstrably of an early date within the Celtic period: the 5th–4th c. BC stone image at HOLZERLINGEN in Germany is surmounted by a horned and janiform HEAD. The shrine at Roquepertuse was decorated with two conjoined heads linked by the huge beak of a bird of prey, which may date from the 4th c. BC or earlier. Celtic coins in Gaul and Britain have janiform heads: a British issue of Cunobelinus is decorated with a double head.

Many so-called Celtic stone heads are undatable, since they have no definite archaeological context, though the treatment of the features may make it probable that they belong to the Celtic period. Such is the case with the Irish janiform heads from Boa Island, Fermanagh and Kilnaboy, County Clare. The janiform head at Great Bedwyn (Wilts) is probably authentic. Undoubtedly of Roman date is the stone double-head at Corbridge, found on the site of the Roman military supply depot. One curious object is the head from Lothbury, London, which consists of two faces, one carved on either side of the crown of an antler. *See also* ROQUEPERTUSE.

☐ Megaw 1970, nos 14, 236; Benoit 1955; Ross 1967a, 78–83; Richmond 1956, 11–15; Laing 1969, 154–5; Powell 1958, pl. 75a; Cunliffe & Fulford 1982, no. 138.

head, triple A particular aspect of TRIPLISM was the practice of producing images of gods with three heads or three faces on one head. It is known that the HEAD was a potent symbol for the Celts, and thus it is logical for the head sometimes to have been represented with its power multiplied to the power of three.

The triple head may appear in iconography in several ways: sometimes the image consists of the triplicated head alone. Another group comprises an entire human body surmounted by three conjoined heads or faces.

The most important heads in the first group, where they are represented as severed heads, are those occurring in the territory of the Remi in north-east Gaul. In the area of Reims occur about eight examples of a homogeneous type, where a quadrangular block is carved with three faces, the central one full-face, the two flanking ones in profile. The faces have shared features and are bearded. Often the faces are decorated with a leaf crown, and the top surface of the stones frequently carries relief images of a ram's head and a cockerel. The presence of these emblems may link the Remic triple-faced images with the cult of the Celtic Mercury. This idea is supported by the presence on a monument at Paris of a depiction of Mercury, who is himself triple-faced. The so-called 'planetary' pots of the Sambre and Meuse valleys of north-east Gaul are sometimes decorated with triple heads. These vessels are distinguished by being ornamented with a number of heads of deities, one of which may be triple-faced. A number of triple heads occur in British contexts: examples are recorded at Wroxeter (Salop) and Braden-stoke (Wilts). On the very edge of the Celtic world, a triple head in granite comes from Sutherland in northern Scotland, and another has been found at Corleck in County Cavan, Ireland.

The second group of triple-faced images consists of whole bodies with three heads or faces. These occur especially in the Burgundy region, where there was sometimes an association between this image and Cernunnos, the antlered god. CERNUNNOS is himself triple-headed on a bronze statuette from Étang-sur-Arroux. Here, the god sits cross-legged, with two torcs and two ram-headed snakes feeding from a basket of fruit on the god's lap. He has one main head but also two small subsidiary faces near his ears. This symbolism recurs on a stone at Nuits-Saint-Georges, where the antlered deity is three-faced; at Beaune a triple-headed deity accompanies Cernunnos and a third divinity. Sometimes the triple-headed god is associated with other symbolism: at Dennevy (Saône-et-Loire) a three-faced deity shares a monument with a Mother-goddess and a third image bearing a *cornucopia*. The Paris three-faced Mercury has already been mentioned.

Stone phallic **head** of Romano-Celtic date from Eype, Dorset.

Stone **janiform head** from Leichlingen, Germany, 4th c. BC.

Stone **triple head**, found at the Romano-British town of Wroxeter, Shropshire.

Three-headed images had particular power. Such heads could look in three directions and possessed the normal potency of the human head, but tripled. It appears that images of certain gods were sometimes endowed with three heads in order to give these representations especial force. In the case of the Remic triple heads, these seem to reflect a specific choice of this tribal area. Indeed, pre-Roman Celtic coins of the Remi depict a triple-headed being, as if this image had long been regarded as reflective of their own tribal divinity.
□ Green 1986, 208–9, fig. 94; 1976, pl. XXd; 1989, 171–9, figs 76, 77; Ross 1967b, 53–6; Harding 1974, 102; Thevenot 1968, 144–9; Devauges 1974, 434; Lambrechts 1942, 33–4; Espérandieu, nos 2083, 2131, 3137.

headdress Evidence for priests and their ceremonial regalia is scanty, but in Britain, some items of liturgical garb demonstrate that the Romano-Celtic clergy, on occasions, might effect special dress in order to officiate at sacrificial or processional cult activities.

Temples and hoards (probably also originally from shrines) attest the wearing of crowns or other headdresses on ritual occasions. These take the form of either rigid bronze diadems or chain headdresses, perhaps worn over a leather helmet. The Hockwold temple (Norfolk) and the ritual hoard at Cavenham (Suffolk) have each produced several crowns: at Hockwold, six crowns are recorded, each with an adjustable headband. The finest of these consists of a diadem decorated with applied silver plaques and with four roundels on the headband depicting busts of divinities; the headdress is topped with a spike. Of the three crowns found at Cavenham, two were rigid diadems, high in the front with the band narrowing at the back. The third headdress comprises five bronze discs with serrated edges joined by a set of eight metal chains formed of S-shaped links, which would have fitted over a leather cap. Part of a similar chain-crown has recently been found at the Harlow temple (Essex) where the links are mainly of bronze, but some are of brass. Another example is known from the religious hoard at Stony Stratford, found with silver feather-plaques dedicated to a number of deities.

The most spectacular discovery of headdresses has been made recently at the WAN-BOROUGH temple (Surrey). These are of the chain-and-disc variety, but two are unique in that they are topped by a cast bronze wheel. This occurrence may mean that the Wanborough temple was a centre for the Celtic solar cult and that the headdresses were worn by priests of the sun.
□ British Museum 1964; Green 1976, 212–13; Layard 1925, 258ff; Surrey Archaeological Society 1988.

head-hunting is one of the few Celtic rituals for which evidence is provided by archaeology, Classical literary sources and the vernacular literature. It therefore forms an important link between the three categories of information.

Many Mediterranean observers of the Celts allude to head-hunting, mostly within the context of battle. Several authors speak of warring Gauls collecting the heads of their enemies slain in battle; they fastened them onto the saddles of their horses or impaled them on spear points. The Senonian Gauls are recorded as doing this in 295 BC when they defeated a Roman legion at Clusium. The reverence for the human HEAD as the source of power and the human spirit is demonstrated by allusions to what the Celts did with these trophies once collected. The North Italian tribe of the Boii killed the Roman general Postumius in 216 BC, cut off his head, cleaned it out, gilded it and used it as a cult vessel. Heads of important victims were embalmed in cedar oil and cherished above all other possessions. The heads of despatched enemies were also offered up to the gods in temples (Livy X, 26; XXIII, 24; Diodorus Siculus V, 29, 4; XIV, 115; Strabo IV, 4, 5).

Archaeological evidence supports the comments of the Graeco-Roman authors: in such Celto-Ligurian pre-Roman shrines of southern Gaul as ROQUEPERTUSE, NAGES and ENTRE-MONT, niches in the temple porticos held skulls of adult men, some of whom were certainly war victims: at Entremont, one skull had a javelin embedded in it. Iconography from these sanctuaries exhibits similar ideas: the head-pillar at Entremont displays a number of severed heads; the same site produced images of multiple severed heads piled one on top of the other; and there is a sculpture depicting a horseman with a human head suspended from his harness. In many of these Provençal shrines are images of warrior-gods, holding severed heads in their hands. These may represent the deities to whom the Gauls offered these war trophies.

Elsewhere in the free Celtic world, heads were offered to the gods: at the Iron Age *oppida* (fortified towns) of Bredon Hill (Worcs) and Stanwick (Yorks), the position of some human skulls suggests their original attachment to poles at the gates of the forts. This is reflected, too, in northern Spain, at the Celtiberian *oppidum* of Puig Castelar. In Britain, there is substantive evidence that the human head was on occasions consecrated to the supernatural powers: at the hillfort of DANEBURY (Hants) adult male skulls were buried in disused grain storage pits, perhaps to appease the spirits of the underworld, into whose territory the pits had penetrated. A simple rectangular shrine at Cosgrove (Northants) was found to have a human head buried in one wall. Iron Age coins sometimes portray severed heads: a coin of Cunobelinus at the Harlow shrine depicts a warrior brandishing a human head.

A 2nd c. AD bronze **headdress**, perhaps worn by a priest, from Hockwold, Norfolk.

There is more evidence than has been cited for the abnormal disposal of human skulls and for DECAPITATION. What is not clear, however, from either the archaeological or historical sources, is whether or not human sacrifice was involved (*see* SACRIFICE, HUMAN). The heads of battle victims could have been taken off after death, or decapitation may have been the method of killing.

Head collection is widely attested in the mythological traditions of Ireland and Wales. A few examples will suffice. In the *Táin Bó Cuailnge*, the Ulster hero Cú Chulainn smites off twelve heads in the plain of Murthemne and arranges them on stones. In the *Tale of Mac Da Thó's Pig*, another Ulster champion, Conall Cernach, boasts that he sleeps every night with the head of a slain Connachtman under his knee. Brain-balls (which consisted of a hardened mixture of brains and lime) were hoarded as trophies and were sometimes used as weapons. Occasionally, the head of a hero or superhuman being was revered as being endowed with magical properties: in the *Mabinogi*, Bendigeidfran is mortally wounded, and he orders his followers to cut off his head, promising that it will bring them luck, which it does. Similarly, Conall Cernach's huge head, when filled with milk, provides strength for the Ulstermen in their weakness. In the *Dinnshenchas*, there are stories of heads in wells which magically affect the water.

The skull portico at the pre-Roman Celtic sanctuary of Roquepertuse in Provence. The heads belonged to young warriors who fell victim to the practice of **head-hunting** in the 4th–3rd c. BC.

☐ Jones & Jones 1976; Jackson 1964; Cunliffe 1983, 155–71; Ross 1967a, 61–127; Filip 1960, 157; Lambrechts 1954; Benoit 1955; 1981; Miles 1970, 9; Green 1986, 29–32; Ross & Feacham 1984, 338–52; Wheeler 1928, 306.

healing *see* SPRING, HEALING; APOLLO; MARS LENUS; SEQUANA; SULIS

Heidelberg Pre-Roman Celtic sculpture is comparatively rare, but a group exists in Central Europe, dating from the 5th–4th c. BC. A fragmentary stone human head comes from Heidelberg, Baden, in Germany. The head is decorated with a lotus bud carved on the forehead and a leaf crown consisting of two balloon-like lobes or swelling leaves which meet above the centre of the head. Both leaf crown and lotus bud recur on other Central European stone sculpture (*see* PFALZFELD). It is suggested that the Heidelberg head may once have surmounted a pillar, forming a cult statue. The leaf-shaped headdress and lotus suggest that the carving represents a deity.
☐ Megaw & Megaw 1989, 74.

Hercules Most images of the Graeco-Roman divine hero which occur in the Celtic world depict him in his normal Roman guise, as a well-muscled, bearded man, wielding his club and sometimes the worse for wine. There are, nevertheless, some indications of a Celtic version of Hercules' cult. In this context, the strength of the god and his consequent potency in whatever capacity was his important quality.

The Greek writer Lucian, who travelled in Gallia Narbonensis during the 2nd c. AD, came across a picture of an elderly, bald man with a club, drawing behind him a band of joyous men attached to him by chains linking their ears to his tongue. Lucian's Gaulish informant told him that the Celts called the god OGMIOS; he was the god of eloquence, and the Celts identified him with Hercules because the latter was so strong.

The great strength of the Celtic Hercules manifested itself in other spheres of religious perception: at the healing springs of Aix-les-Bains, dedicated to the Celtic god, Borvo, pilgrims cast votive offerings into the water in the form of bronze statuettes of a Hercules-like figure. Here, the Mediterranean 'strongman' seems to have been adopted by the Celts as a powerful combattant against illness.

On the Tiberian pillar dedicated by Parisian sailors at Paris, a god with the Gaulish name, SMERTRIUS, closely resembles Hercules, with his beard and club. 'Smertrius' means 'Provider of Abundance', and at the Treveran shrine of Möhn, it is a title conferred on the Celtic Mars.

On inscriptions, Hercules' name is linked to a number of Celtic surnames or epithets. Most popular was Hercules Magusanus in north-eastern Gaul, where eleven invocations are documented. He was called Ilunnus in Gallia Narbonensis, a topographical name; at Silchester in Britain, he was Hercules Saegon, a name related to SEGOMO, which means 'victorious'. Finally, if the CERNE ABBAS Giant is of Celto-Roman origin, as seems likely, then we have in Dorset a huge image of a native, club-bearing Hercules.
☐ Dayet 1963, 167–78; C.I.L. XII, 4316; XIII, 3026; Espérandieu, nos 3132, 3133; Duval 1976, 79–82; de Vries 1963, 69–79; Thevenot 1968, 117–24; Ross 1967a, 381; R.I.B., 67.

hero *see* BENDIGEIDFRAN; CONALL CERNACH; CÚ CHULAINN; CULHWCH AND OLWEN; DIARMAID; FERGHUS; FINN; HERCULES; PWYLL

Himbas Forosnai *see* DIVINATION

Hjortspring In the 3rd c. BC a BOAT containing a hoard of more than 300 swords, spears and shields was deliberately sunk as a ritual act in a peat bog at Hjortspring on the Danish island of Als. The boat had been filled to the gunwales not only with war booty but with the carcasses of sacrificed animals, before being dragged out into the bog. Aquatic ceremonies associated both with boats and with weapon deposits are well documented in later European prehistory. Arms were considered items of power, prestige and security, fitting offerings to the supernatural forces. The deity at Hjortspring may have been a god of war or of water, but the offerings were probably deposited in the watery context because it was inaccessible and therefore the gifts would be inviolate and separated from the world of humankind.
☐ Harding 1978, 15; Fitzpatrick 1984, 178–90.

Hochscheid The Romano-Celtic healer APOLLO and his native consort SIRONA were the presiding deities at the curative spring sanctuary (*see* SPRING, HEALING) at Hochscheid in the Moselle Basin between Trier and Mainz. In the 2nd c. AD, a shrine was constructed around a spring, the waters of which fed a small cistern. Many votive offerings of figurines, coins and other items were made to the divinities, and two superb cult statues have been discovered. Apollo was represented in Classical guise as a young, naked god with his lyre and griffon; Sirona is robed and wears a diadem: a snake is entwined round one forearm, and in her other hand she holds a bowl of eggs. Both her attributes proclaim her as a goddess of fertility and renewal as well as healing. Several small clay figurines of Sirona depict her as a seated Mother-goddess, holding a small DOG in her lap or in her arms; the animal presumably appears here in its capacity as a healing image. The sanctuary was a wealthy one for so remote a region, and it could have been endowed by a rich villa-owner.

□ Dehn 1941, 104ff; Green 1989, 43–4, fig. 17; Wightman 1970, 220–1, pl. 22; Jenkins 1957a, 60–76.

Holzerlingen Of Hallstatt or early La Tène date (6th–5th c. BC) is a stone pillar statue from Holzerlingen, consisting of a tall, sandstone block, crudely shaped into a human torso, with a belt at the waist and an arm folded across the body. The statue is janiform or double-sided, with a dual head surmounting the stone. The facial features are highly stylized, with a gash-like mouth, wedge-shaped nose and heavy brows. The janus-head (*see* HEAD, JANIFORM) was surmounted by HORNS. The figure presumably represents a god, but his identity is unknown. The method of sculpture suggests imitation of wood-carving techniques. The Holzerlingen figure provides one of the earliest pieces of evidence for horned gods, who were so prevalent in the later Iron Age and Romano-Celtic period, especially in northern Britain. Janiform heads, too, can be paralleled elsewhere, for example at Roquepertuse in southern Gaul. A janiform god was able to look both ways, and this would have enhanced the efficacy of the image.

□ Megaw 1970, no. 14; Megaw & Megaw 1989, 74.

Holzhausen in Bavaria is one of a group of late Iron Age ritual sites which occur in Continental Europe, especially in South Germany. They are called VIERECKSCHANZEN, and

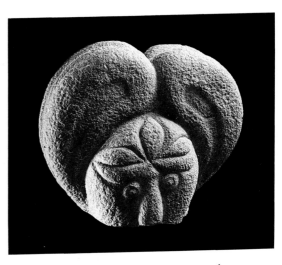

Stone head of a god, wearing a leaf crown and with a lotus symbol on his forehead, 5th c. BC, from **Heidelberg**.

Statue of **Hercules** slaying the Nemean Lion, from Cologne, Germany.

they consist of ditched rectilinear enclosures containing deep shafts which were the centre of religious activity. At Holzhausen, a single enclosure contained three shafts of which one, 26 ft deep, had at its base remains of a wooden pole surrounded by traces of human blood and tissue. This may be sinister evidence of human body disposal, probably human sacrifice (*see* SACRIFICE, HUMAN). One interesting point about the apparent occurrence at Holzhausen is that it shows evidence of an almost identical cult activity to that occurring 1,000 years earlier at Swanwick in Hampshire, where a deep shaft, dating from 1000 BC, also contained traces of a wooden stake with human organic remains adhering to it. The inference is that in both instances, ritual behaviour took place which involved a human sacrifice to appease the gods of the underworld. *See also* PIT.

□ Piggott 1963, 286–7; 1968, 80–2; Collis 1975, 101; Cunliffe 1979, 92ff; Megaw & Simpson 1979, 272; Green 1986, 20, 133.

horns were frequently added to representations of Celtic deities in human form. There appears to have been no rigid division, in Celtic perceptions of divinity, between the human and animal form. Thus, gods could be depicted with hooves, antlers or the horns of a bull, goat or ram.

An early horned sculpture is the janiform pillar-stone from Holzerlingen in Germany, which perhaps dates from the 6th–5th c. BC. Horned male heads occur as motifs in La Tène metalwork. A horned head is portrayed on the late Iron Age bronze bucket-mount at Boughton Aluph in Kent. The Gundestrup Cauldron shows a figure wearing a bull-horned helmet; and a genuine horned helmet comes from the Thames at Waterloo Bridge. Horned helmets are carved on the 1st c. AD triumphal arch at Orange. Iron Age coins depict horned beings: horns sprout from the hair of a horseman whose image is portrayed on certain Hungarian coins; horned figures appear on coins of Cunobelinus at Colchester; and an Iron Age coin at Marseille depicts an ithyphallic figure bearing horns.

In the Romano-Celtic world, horned images are widely distributed. A Gaulish god at Blain near Nantes bears enormous horns; and at the Burgundian shrine of Beire-le-Châtel two horned gods are depicted. But it is in Britain, especially among the northern confederacy of the Brigantes, that horned images predominate. Frequently, as at Maryport in Cumbria, horned gods are shown as warriors with spears and shields, naked and ithyphallic. The horns appear to symbolize a combination of aggression and virility, like the concept of a bull or ram. Sometimes, non-warrior gods have horns. The shrine dedicated to Mercury at Uley (Glos) yielded several conventional figures of the god, but there is a bronze one which is horned. A god at High Rochester may be a hunter-god, Cocidius. At Icklingham in Suffolk and Richborough, Kent, female horned deities are portrayed. Sometimes, as at Carvoran, the horned god is depicted simply as a human head.

Certain images of gods seem to have been endowed with horns on particular occasions in order to increase whatever symbolic power the god already possessed. Thus Mercury, Mars, hunter-gods and other divinities could be depicted with the Celtic symbol of horns. The tradition of horned and zoomorphic imagery was very strong in the Celtic world. Cernunnos was an antlered god; the triple-horned bull (*see* BULL, TRIPLE-HORNED) possessed an additional horn, to augment the symbolism and to add the magic efficacy of three; the ram-horned snake (*see* SNAKE, RAM-HORNED), too, is an example of horn endowment. The image of the horn contained great potency, in terms of war, aggression, virility and FERTILITY.

□ Megaw 1970, nos 14, 110; Megaw & Megaw 1989, 74; Espérandieu, no. 3015; Green 1986, 190–9; Allen 1980, nos 477–80; Laing 1969, 156; Wright & Phillips 1975, no. 197; Bailey 1915, 135–72; Ross 1961, 59ff; 1967a, 127–68; Ellison 1977; Deyts 1976, nos 21–2.

horse During the 8th c. BC, the Dorian invasions of Greece led to the introduction into Central Europe of the use of the horse for riding as well as traction. Horses became a symbol of an aristocratic warrior élite; riding was prestigious, and from the Hallstatt Iron Age, the horse was important in warfare. In the Celtic world, both the HORSEMAN and the charioteer were people of high status within society. In addition to the association with battle, the horse was revered because of other aspects of its secular status: qualities such as beauty, speed, sexual vigour and fertility were acknowledged with reverence; and the horse was valued, too, for its economic

importance. Thus, it is no surprise that horses
were of great significance within Celtic belief
systems. There is substantial evidence for
ritual associated with horses; equine imagery
abounds, and many different Celtic deities
adopted the horse as their emblem.

Horse sacrifices and ritual practices concerned with the disposal of dead horses
appear in the archaeological record throughout Celtic Europe (*see* SACRIFICE, ANIMAL).
At Býčiskála in Czechoslovakia, a 6th c. BC
cave produced abundant evidence of funerary
ritual which included the interment of forty
people (mainly women) who were buried
minus their heads, hands and feet. Nearby
were the quartered carcasses of two horses.
At the pre-Roman La Tène shrine at Gournay-sur-Aronde (Oise) complete horses were
interred, perhaps reflecting honourable burial within a sanctuary of revered animals.
Some of the British Iron Age 'Arras' chariot-
or cart-burials (*see* CART/CHARIOT-BURIAL)
consisted not only of the dead person and
his/her vehicle but also the horse team itself,
killed and interred in a kind of Celtic suttee.
This occurred, for instance, in the King's
Barrow in East Yorkshire; similar horse ritual
has been recorded at Mildenhall (Suffolk)
and Fordington near Dorchester (Dorset).
Hillforts have produced evidence of horse
ritual: at Danebury, from about 400 BC,
disused corn storage pits had horse mandibles
placed in them; at South Cadbury Castle,
horse and cattle skulls were carefully buried
in pits associated with an Iron Age shrine.

Ritual associated with the bodies of horses
persisted into the Romano-Celtic period:
beneath the threshold of a basilical building
associated with a Romano-Celtic shrine at
Bourton Grounds (Bucks) were horses, buried
perhaps as foundation deposits. A pit at
Newstead in southern Scotland dating from
the 2nd c. AD contained the skulls of humans,
oxen and horses; and a ritual shaft at Bekes-
bourne in Kent contained several complete
pots with, beneath them, a flat stone on which
a circle of horse teeth had been arranged.
Whilst all this evidence of ritual activity tells
us little or nothing about associated belief
systems, it does demonstrate reverence for
the horse, and where sacrifice was involved,
this represents a considerable economic loss
to the community, arguing for there being a
pressing reason for this action.

Images of horses, sometimes of a specifically sacred nature, appear during the Iron

The 1st c. BC display helmet with **horns** from the
Thames at Waterloo Bridge, London.

Lead plaque depicting a British god with **horns**,
from the Chesters Roman fort, Northumberland.

Celtic gold coin from Germany, depicting a **horse**
with female rider.

Age. Occasionally, it is possible to make an association between the horse and particular kinds of cult. Coins consistently depict horses in a close relationship to solar symbols, anticipating the unequivocal link between Romano-Celtic SUN/sky-gods and horses. Some of the Provençal pre-Roman sanctuaries were decorated with horse images: at ROQUEPERTUSE there was a frieze of four stylized horse heads in profile; a stone at Nages is carved with alternating horses and human heads; and at Mouriès many horse images, including a horned depiction, are incised on stones. At these shrines, the horse was probably associated with warrior cults. At the very end of the Iron Age, a cache of bronze animal statues was buried at Neuvy-en-Sullias (Loiret), near to a shrine. The images included a fine horse dedicated to a Celtic god, RUDIOBUS. In Britain, the best claimant to pre-Roman horse depiction is the UFFINGTON white horse.

In the Romano-Celtic period, the horse was associated with a number of deities. Celtic versions of Roman gods were linked with horses in a manner alien to their Classical iconography. Thus, the Celtic Jupiter appears as a sky- and sun-god, often on horseback, on the JUPITER-GIANT COLUMNS. That the horse is definitely a solar animal here is shown by the fact that the sun symbol of the wheel occasionally replaces the horse on the giant's back. The solar association is repeated on the quarry face at Bad Dürkheim in Germany, which was scratched with images of men, horses, wheels and swastikas. Some of the clay horses found in a hoard at ASSCHE-KALKOVEN (Belgium) bear lunar amulets round their necks, again indicative of celestial symbolism. Horses were associated with water and with healing spring shrines. Horse figurines were offered at curative sanctuaries dedicated to the Celtic Apollo, for instance at Sainte-Sabine. This god, worshipped as Belenus, had a solar connection, and the horse may well be present here as a solar animal. Romano-Celtic warrior-gods, equated with Mars, are depicted on horseback, especially in eastern Britain, a direct reflection of the status of the horse in Celtic warfare.

The Romano-Celtic horse deity *par excellence* was EPONA, who was a goddess of horse breeding and fertility and a patroness of cavalry officers. The association of horses with female deities can be traced back to the Iron Age, where coins depict horsewomen

and female charioteers who are almost certainly divinities. The Irish tradition, too, links goddesses and horses: the war/mother-goddess MACHA had equine associations. The fact that horses were linked with so many different Celtic cults suggests that they enjoyed an independent reverence and were acknowledged in their own right as symbolic of their own particular qualities. *See also* PRYDERI; RHIANNON; SWASTIKA.

□ Green 1976, 111; 1986, 49, 59, 170–8; 1989, figs 62, 63; 1990a; Megaw 1970, 13, no. 35; Linduff 1979, 817–37; Magnen & Thevenot 1953; Cunliffe 1974, 287–99; Thevenot 1951, 129–41; Cunliffe 1983, 155–71; Alcock 1972, 136–53; Benoit 1955; de Laet 1942, 41–54; Ross & Feacham 1976, 230–7; Ross 1968, 255–85; Brunaux 1986.

horseman The prestige and veneration accorded to the HORSE by the Celts manifested itself in images of a divine horseman, generally perceived as a warrior. Mounted war-gods are not part of the general repertoire of Roman religious imagery, but certain divinities of Roman origin, in particular Mars and Jupiter, were endowed, in Celtic lands, with the imagery of a horseman.

Pre-Roman Celtic horsemen (and horsewomen) were venerated: on Celtic coins, they appear on the reverse of many tribal issues. Southern Gaulish sanctuaries were furnished with stone images of mounted warriors: at Mouriès, horsemen were incised on stones; the shrine at Entremont, with its abundant imagery of severed heads, has produced a relief of a horseman carrying a severed head. A curious pre-Roman depiction comes from St-Michel-de-Valbonne (Var), where a stone menhir bears a representation of a horseman with a huge head riding over five severed heads (*see* RUDIANUS). These warriors are probably to be interpreted as warrior-gods, their vanquished enemies represented by the heads.

Mounted war-gods were worshipped particularly in eastern Britain, among the tribes of the Catuvellauni and the Corieltauvi. As early as the later 1st c. BC a shrine at Kelvedon (Essex) was associated with a pot stamped with horsemen. In the Romano-Celtic phase, there seems to have been an important horseman cult: a temple complex at Brigstock (Northants) was dedicated to a divine horseman, many small bronze figurines of whom have been found. A similar statuette comes

from Westwood Bridge, Peterborough. A find
from Martlesham (Suffolk) specifically associates the mounted war-god with a Celtic
Mars cult: a bronze figure depicts a god on
horseback riding down a prostrate enemy;
the accompanying inscription dedicates the
image to 'MARS COROTIACUS'. On a stone at
Stragglethorpe (Lincs) a horseman with a
spear rides down a serpent. The town of
Margidunum (Notts) has produced a stylized
stone relief of a horseman with spear and
shield, riding a diminutive beast. The imagery
of a mounted warrior riding down a human
enemy is strongly reminiscent of that occurring on early Imperial cavalry tombstones
of the Rhineland. Celtic divine warriors on
horseback were worshipped among the
Dobunni of Gloucestershire. At Kingscote, a
mounted god is accompanied on a relief by
a seated goddess; and at Bisley another
horseman brandishes a large shield and an
axe. Brooches in the form of horsemen occur
at several temple sites, including the shrine
at Lamyatt Beacon in Somerset.

The Celtic SKY-GOD appears in eastern Gaul
and the Rhineland as a celestial warrior: on
the summit of JUPITER-GIANT COLUMNS, a
stone group comprises the Sky-god on a
galloping horse, his thunderbolt in one hand
and often a solar wheel held like a shield in
the other. His horse rides down a monster,
representative of the dark forces, who is semi-
human, semi-serpentine. Here, the Sky-god
is a horseman because the horse was a solar
symbol for the Celts.

Other deities sometimes appear on horseback. The Celtic Apollo, a healer and solar
deity, was also depicted as a horseman: clay
figurines of horses and horsemen were offered
at Apollo Belenus' sanctuary at Sainte-Sabine
in Burgundy. APOLLO ATEPOMARUS, whose
surname reflects the concept of a horseman,
was invoked at Mauvières (Indre). Finally,
EPONA should be recalled here, the Celtic
horse-goddess who rides side-saddle on a
mare and who was worshipped all over the
Celtic world.
□ Ross 1967a, 168–203, fig. 138; Espérandieu,
nos 38, 105; Thevenot 1951, 129–41; 1968,
56–7; Benoit 1955; 1981, fig. 49; Allen 1980,
133–48; Green 1976, 181, 218; 1986, 108, figs
58–9, 61–5, 90; 1989, 123–9; Ambrose &
Henig 1980, 135–8; Greenfield 1963, 228ff;
Bauchhenss & Nölke 1981; Rodwell 1973,
265–7, pl. XXIXa; Leech 1986; C.I.L. XIII,
1318.

Stone decorated with four incised **horse** heads,
6th c. BC, from Roquepertuse, Provence.

French Celtic coin of the Aulerci Cenomani,
depicting a **horseman** or charioteer riding down
an enemy.

Figurine of a **horseman** from Peterborough,
Cambridgeshire.

hunt(er)/Hunter-god There was a special relationship between the Celts and the animals they hunted: reverence and a sense of protection as well as destruction. The wild beasts of the forest – stags, boars and bears in particular – all had deities associated with them, and all appear in imagery which reflects the hunt. Dogs, as companions to hunters, also figure in this iconography.

Hunter-deities may be distinguished by their weapons or their role inferred by their relationship with certain zoomorphic creatures. The goddess accompanying the Hammer-god at Mainz has a bow and quiver; at Risingham in the vicinity of Hadrian's Wall, a stag hunter, COCIDIUS, also has a bow and quiver; the same weapons are displayed on the carving of the Hunter-god found in a late Roman well beneath Southwark Cathedral.

Of all the hunted beasts, the STAG seems to have been most prominent. Many rock-art scenes at Celtic CAMONICA VALLEY in North Italy depict stag hunts. The concept of the stag hunt may likewise be portrayed on the 7th c. BC bronze cult wagon at STRETTWEG, Austria, where images of a goddess and soldiers are accompanied by two stags. The London god is shown with a stag and a hunting dog, as is the Risingham deity. At the LE DONON (Vosges) sanctuary, a local Hunter-god wearing a wolfskin and boots decorated with animal heads has the weapons of hunting – knife, spear and chopper. He rests his hand on the antler of his stag quarry.

Other beasts are depicted as hunted animals. The BOAR must frequently have been hunted for food and for sport: pork was the favourite meat of the Celts. But boar hunts are rarely portrayed, though a bronze of a slain boar comes from a shrine at Muntham Court in Sussex, and many boar images display the creature with erect dorsal spines, as if at bay. A representation at Reichshoffen near Strasbourg shows a god wearing a Gaulish *sagum* (coat), with a young pig tucked under his arm. The goddess ARDUINNA rides a boar on a bronze statuette, with a hunting knife in one hand. The hunter of a hare is depicted at Touget (Gers): he is accompanied by his hound and holds a hare in his arms.

Dogs often accompany Hunter-gods (*see* DOG): this occurs, for instance, on images at Touget, Risingham and London. Nodens SILVANUS at Lydney, who was offered representations of dogs at his sanctuary on the Severn, may have had a hunting role. Apollo Cunomaglus (Hound Lord) at Nettleton Shrub (Wilts) may have been a hunter. Both Silvanus and Apollo had hunting roles in the Classical world.

What is striking about the Celtic Hunter-gods is their close relationship with their quarry: thus the divinities at Le Donon, Touget and Reichshoffen appear to protect the beasts which are their prey. North British Hunter-gods frequently bear horns, exemplifying the close affinity between god and animal. This apparent ambivalence between hunter and hunted may be explained in terms of perceptions of the Divine Hunt, which had connotations not only of death but also of rebirth. The act of killing led to immortality. In vernacular sources, this concept of the Divine Hunt was reflected in stories of enchanted beasts – boars or stags – luring hunters to the Otherworld. It is clear that the Celts revered the beasts they hunted, and Hunter-gods protected them, as well as their hunting devotees. The success of the hunt depended on harmony and the correct relationship between hunters and hunted. The Classical writer Arrian (*de Venatione* 34) remarks that the Celts never went hunting without being accompanied by the gods. *See also* DIANA; VOSEGUS.

□ Webster 1986a, 46; Mac Cana 1983, 50; Espérandieu, nos 5752, 7800; Green 1986, fig. 73; 1989, 79–80, 100–2; Boucher 1976, fig. 292; Pobé & Roubier 1961, no. 190, Hatt n.d., 42, pl. 33; Hatt 1964, pls 150, 151; Phillips 1977, no. 234, pl. 63; Merrifield 1983, 188, fig. 86; Anati 1965; Megaw 1970, no. 38; Wheeler & Wheeler 1932; Wedlake 1982.

Ialonus The name 'Ialonus' refers to the personification of a concept associated with the land. The name has been interpreted as that of a deity of the cultivated field or clearing. It is also suggested that he could be the god of the glade, since 'ialo' means 'glade'. In Britain, Ialonus was invoked at Lancaster, where he is called 'Ialonus Contrebis'. Contrebis ('he who dwells among us') was venerated also at Overborough (Lancs). A female version, 'Ialona', was worshipped at Nîmes in Provence.

□ Duval 1976, 60, 105; Ross 1967a, 376; Bémont 1981, 65–88; R.I.B., 600, 610.

Ianuaria was a Gaulish goddess venerated at the Burgundian sanctuary of BEIRE-LE-CHÂTEL, a spring shrine at which images of the Celtic Apollo, triple-horned bulls and doves were also dedicated. A small stone statuette from the temple depicts a young girl with curly hair, clad in a heavy pleated coat and holding a set of pan-pipes. On the base of the statue is inscribed 'Deae Ianuariae'. Nothing else is known about this goddess. The shrine was a curative sanctuary, and it is known that Ianuaria's companion, Apollo, was a healer in a Celtic as well as in a Classical context. But Apollo was also a divine patron of music, and the Celtic goddess Ianuaria, with her pipes, would fit in well as a deity associated with music, which was perhaps perceived as a means of inducing the healing sleep (*see* SPRING, HEALING).
□ Espérandieu, no. 3620; Deyts 1976, no. 9.

Bronze group of **Hunter-gods** with their quarry, a stag and a boar, 3rd c. BC, from Balzars, Liechtenstein.

Icovellauna was an eastern Gaulish deity who was venerated at Metz and Trier, where a number of epigraphic dedications to her have been recorded. There are no images of the goddess, but her name and the context of the dedications tell us something of her character and function. 'Ico' can mean 'water', and this interpretation accords well with Icovellauna's presence at Metz, where she presided over the sacred healing spring (*see* SPRING, HEALING) of Sablon, at which an octagonal shrine was built during the Romano-Celtic period.
□ C.I.L. XIII, 4924; Wightman 1970, 217; Toussaint 1948, 207–8.

Imbolc was one of the four main Celtic festivals of Insular tradition. The festival was celebrated on 1 February and is thought to have been connected with the lactation of ewes. The feast was linked with the Irish goddess BRIGIT, a Mother-goddess and protectress of women in childbirth. All the festivals seem to have been related to fertility and seasonal ritual.
□ Vendryes 1924, 241–4; Bray 1987, 209–15.

Round tower in the churchyard of St Brigit's Cathedral, County Kildare. Brigit was associated with the pagan spring festival of **Imbolc**.

Inciona is the female partner of a divine couple (*see* COUPLE, DIVINE), Veraudinus and Inciona, who were apparently worshipped in only one place, at Widdenberg in Luxembourg. These deities are just one of many examples of names which occur only once in the archaeological record. We know nothing of their function, but we may assume that they represented the spirit of a particular locality.

□ Thill 1978, no. 11; Green 1989, 45.

infant-burial Of the large number of babies who must have died in pre-Roman and Romano-Celtic Britain, a few attest to the presence of a specific ritual associated with their burial and perhaps also with their deaths. Some infant-burials may have been the result of human sacrifice (*see* SACRIFICE, HUMAN); others perhaps died naturally, but their bodies were subsequently subjected to ritual activity.

There is some evidence for the bodies of infants being interred as foundation offerings in shrines: just outside the entrance to a late Iron Age circular sanctuary at Maiden Castle (Dorset) a baby was buried, perhaps to bless the building and to propitiate the gods on whose territory it was erected. Four infants, one of whom was decapitated, were buried as foundation deposits at the temple of Springhead in Kent. Other curious occurrences include the late Romano-British burial at Alcester (Warks) of ten babies with a young girl who had been beheaded and her head placed between her legs. At a Cambridge shrine, dead infants were interred with shoes which were much too large for them, as if it was envisaged that they would grow in the Otherworld.

□ Lewis 1966; Green 1986, 131–2; 1976, 228; Anon. 1978, 57–60; Penn 1960, 113ff.

interpretatio celtica This is a term used by modern scholars to describe the fusion or hybridization of Celtic and Roman religious cultures, whereby Roman gods were, to an extent, perceived by Celts in terms of their own belief systems. This is exhibited, for example, by Romano-Celtic inscriptions which record the veneration of a god with a Roman name but also a Celtic epithet or title. Such deities as Apollo Grannus, Mars Teutates, or Jupiter Taranis are instances of this marriage of Roman and indigenous names.

interpretatio romana is a term used by Tacitus (*Germania* 43, 3) to describe the process whereby the Romans interpreted the gods of the Celts as if they were in fact Roman divinities. Caesar (*de Bello Gallico* VI, 17) speaks of the gods he learned about in Gaul as if they were the divinities familiar to the

Roman pantheon – Jupiter, Mercury, Mars, Minerva and Apollo. In the iconography and epigraphy of the Romano-Celtic world, there is evidence of *interpretatio romana*. The Celtic goddess Sulis of Bath is named Sulis Minerva, her cult statue depicting her as a Roman goddess, and the great Treveran healing god Lenus is also called Mars, though healing is not a function traditionally associated with Mars. There are numerous other examples of such equation and hybridization.

□ Green 1976, 2; 1986, 36–8; Henig 1984, 22, 36.

Iovantucarus was the name by which the great Treveran healer-god, Lenus, was invoked at his important sanctuary at Trier (*see* MARS LENUS). The name Iovantucarus reflects the deity's function as protector of youth; and the temple was visited by pilgrims who brought with them images of children, often depicted holding pet birds as offerings to Lenus. At Tholey, also in Treveran territory, Iovantucarus was equated with Mercury.

□ Green 1986, 158; Wightman 1970, 211–17.

Iunones The triple Mothers of the Celtic world derive ultimately from the Roman concept of the Iuno, the essential spirit of the female, which represented the feminine principle, just as the Genius was the essence of a male being. The concept of the Iuno itself derives from the goddess Iuno or Juno, wife of Jupiter and an earth-deity who protected women especially during pregnancy, childbirth and lactation. The Roman Iuno Lucina was a nursing goddess, concerned especially with birth and breast-feeding, very like some of the Celtic MOTHER-GODDESSES. The Iunones were a triple version of the Iuno (*see* TRIPLISM), adopted as an epithet for the three Mothers in the land of the Treveri. *See also* SULEVIAE.

□ Wightman 1970; Green 1986, 80.

Jupiter The Roman SKY-GOD was adopted by the Celts, not only as a SUN-GOD but also as a high MOUNTAIN deity; as such, he was given a number of local territorial epithets or surnames in the Celtic world, of which the most important follow. *See also* JUPITER-GIANT COLUMN; SWASTIKA; WHEEL-GOD.

Jupiter Beissirissa Jupiter was given this name in southern Gaul at Cadéac (Hautes-Pyrénées) among the tribe of the Bigerriones, where a dedication to Jupiter Best and Greatest Beissirissa is recorded.
□ C.I.L. XIII, 370; Toutain 1920, 143ff.

Jupiter Brixianus Brixianus is a local, descriptive epithet relating to the name of Brescia, a town in Cisalpine Gaul (modern North Italy). The local god was equated with Jupiter.
□ Pascal 1964, 76–83.

Jupiter Ladicus The Roman sky-god was identified with a Celtiberian MOUNTAIN-god in north-west Spain, and was invoked as Jupiter Ladicus, the spirit of Mount Ladicus.
□ C.I.L. II, 2525; Toutain 1920, 143ff.

Jupiter Parthinus Also known as Partinus, on the borders of north-east Dalmatia (Yugoslavia) and Upper Moesia (Bulgaria), Jupiter was worshipped as Parthinus, perhaps associated with the local tribe or clan known as the Partheni.
□ C.I.L. III, 8353, 14613; Wilkes 1969, 165; Čremošnik 1959, 207ff; Green 1984a, 259–60.

Jupiter Poeninus was worshipped in the Alps around the Great St Bernard Pass, where there was a sanctuary as early as the Iron Age, and where votive plaques were offered to Jupiter Poeninus in the Romano-Celtic period.
□ de Vries 1963, 39.

Jupiter Taranis *see* TARANIS

Jupiter Uxellinus was a high MOUNTAIN god, worshipped in Austria. The name may indicate supremacy.
□ C.I.L. III, 5145; Alföldy 1974, 135; Green 1986, 68.

Jupiter-Giant column A composite type of stone monument, set up to honour the Celtic SKY-GOD in the western provinces of the Roman Empire, was the so-called Jupiter-column or Jupiter-Giant column. About 150 monuments are known, mainly from eastern Gaul and the Rhineland. The columns were erected especially in the lands of the Lingones, Mediomatrici and Treveri, along the Moselle and on both banks of the Rhine.

Infant-burial played a part in many rituals. This image from a shrine in Burgundy may represent a dead baby in its burial wrappings.

Gilt bronze head of Sulis Minerva, from Bath. Sulis' cult is a supreme example of **interpretatio romana**, the conflation of Roman and Celtic divinities.

The **Iunones** were a triple version of the Iuno, the spirit of the female principle. The goddesses were often triplicated, as on this relief of a water-goddess at Carrawburgh, Northumberland.

The Jupiter-columns consist of four- and eight-sided stone plinths, carved with images of deities which are generally related to the sun, moon and planets, and inscribed with dedications to JUPITER or Juno. Above the octagonal stone is a tall PILLAR, often decorated so as to suggest the bark and foliage of a TREE: the column at Hausen-an-der-Zaber specifically copies an OAK tree, being adorned with oak leaves and acorns. The column is surmounted by a figured Corinthian capital; on top of this, at the summit of the monument, is a sculptured group comprising a celestial HORSEMAN, sometimes holding a solar WHEEL like a protective shield, and a thunderbolt (*see* THUNDER), often of metal to catch the light. The sky-warrior's mount tramples down a gigantic anthropomorphic monster whose legs are in the form of serpents (*see* SNAKE). There is some Mediterranean influence in this imagery, which may derive ultimately from the Greek gigantomachy, but in a Classical context, the Sky-god is not a horseman, and there is no doubt that the symbolism is Celtic. This is borne out by the entirely Celtic distribution of the monuments.

The idea of erecting an image of the Celtic Sky-god on a tall pillar may have been partly in order to raise him as high into the sky as possible. There is additional tree symbolism: oaks were sacred to both Jupiter and the native Sky-god. The pillar may also have been perceived as a bridge between the upper and lower worlds. There are possible literary allusions to the Jupiter-columns: Maximus of Tyre, writing in the 2nd c. AD (*Logoi* VIII, 8) remarks that the Celtic image of Zeus was a high oak tree. Valerius Flaccus (*Argonautica* VI, 89) comments that the tribe of the Coralli (probably a Celtic tribe) worshipped effigies of Jupiter associated with wheels and pillars.

It is the iconography of the horseman group which is of greatest interest. The Sky-god is galloping, his cloak streaming behind him. He may carry his solar wheel as a shield to protect him, as at Luxeuil (Haute-Saône), Meaux (Seine-et-Marne), Obernberg (Bayern) and Quémigny-sur-Seine (Côte-d'Or). He is in opposition to the monster beneath the hooves of his mount, who writhes in distress and whose stricken face and straining muscles show the intolerable burden he carries. What we appear to be witnessing is the everlasting struggle between sky and underworld, life and death, good and evil, light and darkness. The giant with his snake

limbs represents the negative, chthonic world, subjugated by the positive powers of the Sky-god. But there is a dualistic, interdependent relationship between god and giant (*see* DUALISM): sometimes the monster seems to support the Sky-god's horse; and it is important to point out that rarely do either god or giant carry a weapon.

Very few remains of Jupiter-columns are documented from Britian, which is well outside the main distribution area. But there is possible evidence at Cirencester: from here comes a rectangular stone base with an inscription which refers to the restoration 'under the old religion' of a statue and column to Jupiter, by a Governor of Britannia Prima, Julius Septimius, a citizen of Reims. The date of the dedication has to be after AD 296, when the Emperor Diocletian divided Britain into four provinces. The reference to the 'old religion' may even tie the stone to Julian's Apostasy in the 360s.

Variations on the mainstream Jupiter-Giant columns exist: some monuments consist of a pillar surmounted by a seated image of the Sky-god, with no giant present. In other imagery, only the giant and the solar symbol of the wheel are depicted, to illustrate the balanced forces of light and darkness. Whatever the individual differences, the message of the Jupiter-columns is a paean of triumph to the Sky-god. The monuments are large: the column at Merten near Metz was more than 45 ft high when complete. The pillars must have been costly to erect, and it may be assumed that they reflected corporate worship. But in addition to their presence in towns, they were set up on private estates and in such remote sanctuaries as LE DONON in the Vosges.

□ Green 1984a, 173–8; 1986, 61–6; 1989, 123–9; Bauchhenss 1976; Bauchhenss & Nölke 1981; Phillips 1976, 35–41; Espérandieu, nos 3207, 4425, 7098; Kellner 1971, pl. 85; Espérandieu 1917, 72–86.

key The symbol of a key appears on images of a number of Celtic goddesses, and it may perhaps be interpreted as reflective of the ability of these deities to open the gates of heaven, or to lead their suppliants through the barrier between death and the afterlife.

The Germanic and Balkan goddess AERICURA, herself perhaps an underworld divinity akin to Hecate, may carry a key. At Winchester (Hants) a wooden image of a goddess wearing a cloak and torc bears a *mappa* (napkin) and a large key. The *mappa* was regularly used by the Romans to signal the start of horse races; Webster has suggested that, in a symbolic context, the *mappa* may reflect the beginning of life. If this is so then the key may symbolize the end of earthly existence and the journey through the entrance to the underworld. A sculpture at Naix (Meuse) shows a Mother-goddess with two younger attendants, one of whom has a vessel and key. The pot may be concerned with renewal (*see* CAULDRON), and the key may again refer to the gates of heaven. On some monuments, the horse-goddess EPONA is depicted holding a key, as at Grand (Vosges) and Gannat (Allier). Here, the symbol may reflect at one level the key to the stable door, and more profoundly, it may signify the unlocking of the doors to the Otherworld.
□ Green 1989, 69; Cunliffe & Fulford 1982, no. 115, pl. 31; Webster 1986a, 70–2; Thevenot 1968, 168ff; Espérandieu, nos 4678, 4894; 1618.

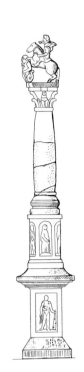

(Above left) Reconstruction of the **Jupiter-Giant column** at Bad Cannstatt, Stuttgart, Germany. (Above right) The **Jupiter-Giant column** at Hausen, near Stuttgart.

 L

Ladicus *see* JUPITER LADICUS

lake WATER held great sanctity for the Celts: rivers, lakes, bogs, springs and wells were all venerated during later prehistory and the Romano-Celtic period. Lakes particularly had the quality of inaccessibility for the offerings cast into them. The act of committing objects to lakes and bogs was in itself a holy thing, a way of reaching the supernatural powers.

The religious practice of lake deposition is alluded to by the Greek geographer Strabo (IV, 1, 3) who mentions a sacred lake in the tribal territory of the Volcae Tectosages near Tolosa (Toulouse). He describes a great treasure of silver and gold, consisting largely of ingots, which was deposited in the lake in great masses and which none dared to tamper with. No Celt was willing to profane this holy place. Sadly, the treasure was plundered by the Roman general Caepio in 106 BC. Strabo remarks that a number of similar sacred lakes existed at the time he was writing. Gregory

The horse-goddess Epona, with the **key** both to the stable and to the gate of the Otherworld, from Gannat, Allier, France.

of Tours (*In Gloria Confessorum*) alludes to an annual pagan three-day festival at Lake Gévaudan in the Cevennes, where peasants cast food, clothing and sacrificed animals into the lake.

Archaeological evidence for the deposition of objects in sacred lakes is substantial. At LA TÈNE in Switzerland, a wooden platform was built, from which deposits were made during the later Iron Age into a small bay at the eastern end of Lake Neuchâtel. The god of the lake received several hundred brooches, spears, shields and swords. The central date for deposition is 100 BC. A similar occurrence took place at Lake Biel, also in Switzerland. British lakes, too, were holy places around which ritual activity took place. At LLYN FAWR in mid-Glamorgan was found a hoard of metalwork which was deposited around 600 BC, at the very beginning of the British Iron Age. The material included exotic Hallstatt objects, harness and vehicle fittings, socketed axes and sickles and two bronze cauldrons. LLYN CERRIG BACH on Anglesey was the centre of religious activity later in the Iron Age. Here, the items cast into the lake range in date between the 2nd c. BC and the 1st c. AD. The metalwork includes prestige goods such a chariot fittings, weapons, ironworkers' tools and slave gang-chains, some of the objects being ritually broken before being cast into the water (*see* RITUAL DAMAGE). The wealth of the deposit and, for instance, the number of chariots represented suggest more than localized sanctity for this lake. It is even possible that Llyn Cerrig was associated with the druidic sanctuary on Anglesey alluded to by Tacitus. Both Llyn Fawr and Llyn Cerrig contained cauldrons; and there is other evidence associating metal vessels with lake deposition. Two southern Scottish lochs, Blackburn Mill and Carlingwark, had ritual CAULDRON deposits, made in the late Iron Age. *See also* POOL.
□ Vouga 1923; Fox 1946; Lynch 1970, 249–77; Savory 1976, 49; Sauter 1976; Green 1986, 141–3.

La Tène is the name given to the material culture of the Celts at the time of their maximum development and expansion, from the earlier 5th c. BC until the time of the Roman occupation. The term 'La Tène' is taken from the type site in Switzerland, a holy spot on the shores of a sacred LAKE which has produced literally hundreds of weapons and other metalwork, of a type sufficiently distinctive to enable archaeologists to relate their style and decoration to objects found in association with material culture which existed throughout most of the Celtic world. This culture is represented not only by metal objects but also by pottery and settlement types as well.

But La Tène on the shores of Lake Neuchâtel was primarily an important religious site. Here, a huge deposit of metalwork was found in offshore peat in a small bay at the east end of the lake. Wooden platforms or bridges had been built out into the water, and offerings of metalwork and other items had been cast into the lake in a series of ritual acts. Some of these bridges have been dated by dendrochronology to the 2nd c. BC. The god of the WATER received some 400 brooches, 270 spears, 27 wooden shields and 170 swords, in addition to other votive gifts – chariots, dogs, cattle, pigs, horses and human beings.
□ Megaw & Megaw 1989, 133; Sauter 1976; Vouga 1923; Ross 1986, 13–19, fig. 6.

Latis was a British goddess, local to Cumbria and probably a deity of watery places, pools and bogs (*see* POOL). Anne Ross sees a link between the name of Latis and a Celtic word for beer. The goddess was invoked at Birdoswald and Fallsteads.
□ Ross 1967a, 215; R.I.B., 1987, 2043.

Latobius The Celtic people of Noricum (modern Austria) worshipped a sky- and mountain-god who was equated with the high Roman deities, Jupiter and Mars. On the highest peak of Mount Koralpe between the Lavant and Mur valleys, 2,000 metres above sea-level, a votive inscription was set up to the sky-god Latobius who was here venerated as Mars.
□ Green 1984a, 259; Alföldy 1974, 9; Leber 1965, 25f; 1967, 517–20.

Le Donon The high mountain-top sanctuary in the Vosges at Le Donon flourished during the 2nd and 3rd c. AD. The shrine was deliberately situated where three tribal territories met, those of the Triboci, Leuci and Mediomatrici. The shrine seems to have been dedicated to the Celtic Mercury: many crudely carved images of a naked male deity with a purse or bag attest the worship of the Romano-Celtic god of prosperity. Some of these images are ithyphallic, in reflection of the god's additional role, promoter of human fecundity. One figure shows Mercury with a cloak, purse and a drawn sword, an attribute alien to the Roman god, but indicative of a local divinity, guardian-protector of abundance and well-being.

A woodland, nature and hunter-god was venerated at the Le Donon sanctuary. He may be the local god of the Vosges, VOSEGUS: two images display a male deity carrying the fruits of the forest – a pine-cone, acorns and nuts – in an open bag under his arm. He wears a wolfskin and his boots are decorated with the heads of small animals. This god is both a hunter and protector of the forest and its creatures: he has a long hunting-knife at his side, a large curved chopper for smiting beasts, and a lance. But he rests his hand in benediction on the antler of a stag which stands fearlessly at his side. The god's role as a forest-deity is enhanced by the presence of foliage.

Other divinities were worshipped at Le Donon: among them was the Celtic Sky-god, represented by at least four JUPITER-GIANT COLUMNS, with their summit groups of the mounted Sky-deity riding down his semi-serpentiform opponent. The lord of the sky was an appropriate power to be venerated at this elevated sanctuary, so close to his celestial element.
□ Hatt 1964, pls 150–1, 162–4; Espérandieu, no. 7800; Hatt n.d., 65–7, pl. 64; Green 1989, fig. 43; Duval 1976, 52.

Leno This obscure Gaulish god is not to be confused with the great Treveran healer-deity, Mars Lenus. Leno was the eponymous spirit of Lérins in Provence. We know nothing about him except for the presence of epigraphic dedications mentioning his name.
□ Clébert 1970, 253.

Lenus *see* MARS LENUS

Libeniče The Czechoslovakian ritual site at Libeniče in Bohemia dates from the 3rd c. BC. It consists of an elongated sub-rectangular enclosure surrounded by a ditch and measures 300 × 75 ft. Some kind of shrine was present at the south-east end, half sunk into the ground but unroofed. This contained a stone block and two post holes set close together; near these holes were the burnt remains of two timbers and two bronze torcs or neck-rings. The inference is that the tim-

The **lake** of Biel or Bienne, Switzerland, where, during the Iron Age, votive offerings were made to the water-spirits.

A 2nd c. BC wooden yoke from Lake Neuchâtel, **La Tène**, Switzerland.

Bronze bucket from Waldalgesheim, Germany, displaying typical **La Tène** art on the handle-mounts.

Relief of a Hunter-god, with his stag, from the mountain sanctuary of **Le Donon** in the Vosges, France.

bers were roughly carved into human form and adorned with the torcs, presumably representations of deities. Sacrifices within the enclosure are suggested by the presence of deposits of human and animal bones, and in the sanctuary was also found the body of a woman, perhaps a priestess who was buried in her shrine. The floor of the ritual structure within the enclosure had pits dug into it over a period of around twenty-four years, perhaps for repeated religious ceremonies such as libation. The holy site at Libeniče has parallels with such other Continental sanctuaries as AULNAY-AUX-PLANCHES (Marne) and MSĚ-CKÉ ŽEHROVIČE (Czech), which dates from the 6th c. BC.

□ Rybová & Soudský 1962; Piggott 1965, 234, fig. 132; 1968, 73–4, fig. 21, pls 16–17.

limb/organ, votive At the great healing cult establishments of Gaul and Britain, there developed a tradition whereby sick pilgrims visiting these spring sanctuaries offered models of the afflicted parts of their bodies to the presiding divinity. The idea was that of reciprocity: the diseased model of a limb, eye or internal organ would, it was hoped, be replaced by a whole and healthy one. It must be emphasized that this practice was by no means confined to the Celtic world: it occurred at the great Classical therapeutic shrines, such as those of Asklepios at Epidauros and of Hera at Paestum in southern Italy. In Catholic Mediterranean countries to this day, pilgrims offer replicas of the afflicted parts of their bodies to God or the Virgin Mary in the hope and expectation of a cure.

The practice of offering votive models of this kind is attested at a number of the Celtic healing shrines: in Britain, a pair of ivory model breasts was offered to SULIS at Bath, perhaps by a young mother; model limbs were offered at the shrines of Muntham Court (Sussex), Lydney (Glos) and Springhead (Kent). At LYDNEY, the model arm showed signs of disease. In Gaul, anatomical models are attested at many of the great curative sanctuaries. At Glanum in Provence, an altar was carved with arms and legs; ESSAROIS and Chamalières are both examples of shrines where wooden and stone models were offered to the presiding god. The most prolific material comes from FONTES SEQUANAE, a sanctuary dedicated to Sequana, goddess of the River Seine at its source. Here,

models of eyes, breasts, heads, limbs and internal organs were fashioned in oak, bought at the temple shop and cast into the spring pool as gifts to Sequana. Some of the models showed evidence of particular ailments: eye disease and respiratory problems were two major scourges of the pilgrims who prayed to the goddess.

□ Deyts 1983; 1985; Green 1986, 150–66.

Lindow Moss In August 1984, a mechanical digger turned up part of a human body in a peat bog at Lindow Moss in Cheshire. The body was that of a young man who had been placed, crouched and face-down, in a shallow POOL within the marsh. The man was not a peasant: his finger-nails were manicured and his moustache carefully clipped with a razor. He was probably deposited in the bog sometime during the 4th c. BC. His body had been painted in different colours.

Lindow Man is our best piece of evidence for the practice of human sacrifice in Celtic Britain (*see* SACRIFICE, HUMAN): the young man had been pole-axed, garotted and his throat cut, before being kneed in the back and thrust into the pool. He wore nothing but an armlet made of fox fur when he met his death.

Just prior to being sacrificed, Lindow Man had consumed a kind of wholemeal bread consisting of many different kinds of grains, perhaps a ritual meal. The most striking feature of the stomach contents was the presence of MISTLETOE pollen, which has led to speculation that the man may have been the victim of a druidic sacrifice. Bog bodies occur most frequently in Denmark, but the water-logged conditions at Lindow Moss preserved this body in astonishing condition and have thrown important light on the practice of sacrifice in Iron Age Britain.

Certain Irish mythological stories allude to a ritual threefold killing of the sacral king – by wounding, drowning and burning. It is tempting to link this with the triple injuries to Lindow Man; he was hit on the head, strangled and his throat cut. *See also* BOG; BOG-BURIAL; TOLLUND MAN.

□ Stead et al. 1986; Stead & Turner 1985, 25–9; Green 1986, 128, 144; Mac Cana 1983, 27.

Linsdorf Like the 'Tarasque' of NOVES, the Linsdorf monster from Alsace consists of a giant stone figure of a beast, perhaps a lion

or wolf, with its huge clawed forepaws each resting on a severed human head. The MONSTER has gaping jaws showing enormous pointed teeth, large round eyes and its pelt is represented as jagged points. The sculpture may date as early as the 3rd or 2nd c. BC, but some doubt has been expressed as to its authenticity. If it is Celtic, then its theme owes something to Roman funerary imagery, where ravening animals or monsters devour human bodies in an allegory of the triumph of death over life.
□ Stead 1985a, 40–2, pls I–III; Green 1986, 136; Megaw & Megaw 1989, 170–1.

Lir is an Irish SEA-GOD, one of the Tuatha Dé Danann who were driven underground after the invasion of Ireland by the Sons of Mil (the Gaels). The *Book of Invasions* tells of Lir's displeasure at not being chosen as king of the Tuatha Dé and of his withdrawal to live alone under a large hill in County Armagh. Bov, the chosen king, makes overtures to Lir, offering him the choice of his daughters in marriage. Lir selects Eve and has three children by her; when she dies, he marries her sister Eva. But she is jealous of the children, whom Lir adores. Eva uses magic to enchant the children, transforming them into SWANS for 900 years.

Lir is the father of the sea-deity MANANNÁN. Both Lir and Manannán may be identified as the Irish equivalents of the Welsh LLŶR and Manawydan.
□ Rolleston 1985, 113, 139; O'Fáolain 1954.

Lleu Llaw Gyffes The Welsh Lleu may have links with the Irish LUGH: both names have associations with light. Like Lugh, Lleu was a divine warrior. In the 'Story of Math', which forms the *Fourth Branch of the Mabinogi*, Lleu Llaw Gyffes ('The Bright One of the Skilful Hand') is the son of ARIANRHOD, who imposes three taboos at the time of his birth. The first is that he should not be named until his mother chooses to name him: the magician Gwydion tricks her into giving him the name of Lleu. The second taboo is that the child should not bear arms until and unless Arianrhod herself arms him. Again, Gwydion causes the oath to be nullified. Thirdly, Arianrhod swears that Lleu will never marry a human woman. To counteract this spell, Math and Gwydion, who both possess magical powers, contrive a woman out of flowers, her name BLODEUWEDD.

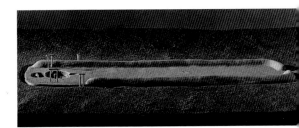

Model of the 3rd c. BC ritual enclosure at **Libeniče** in Czechoslovakia, showing the sunken area and standing posts.

A Celt suffering from infirmity or disease might offer a **votive limb/organ** to a Healer-god. This image of a blind girl was dedicated to Sequana, the curative spirit of the Seine at its spring source.

The bog-body found at **Lindow Moss** was that of a young man ritually murdered in the Iron Age.

But Blodeuwedd takes a lover, Gronw, and together they plot to do away with him. Lleu himself is almost impossible to kill. The only way that he can be slain is if one of his feet is on a goat's back and the other on the edge of a vat of water. Blodeuwedd manages to persuade Lleu to simulate the position in which he is vulnerable, and Gronw spears him in this position. As he is struck, Lleu gives a great scream, turns into an EAGLE and flies to a magic OAK tree. Here, Gwydion finds him, and he is transformed back into a man. Gronw is killed, and Blodeuwedd transformed into an owl.

There is so much magic and mythology surrounding Lleu that he may well be an ancient British god. His birth itself, to the virgin Arianrhod, is supernatural, and his ability to shape-change (see METAMORPHOSIS) is also a possible mark of divinity. His associations with light and with oak trees are appropriate to a Celtic god, perhaps a celestial deity. In Roman religion, the sky-god Jupiter's emblems included both oaks and eagles.
□ Jones & Jones 1976.

Llyn Cerrig Bach The sacred LAKE of Llyn Cerrig Bach on the island of Anglesey was a centre of ritual activity during the late Iron Age. The area of Llyn Cerrig is one which is full of rocky outcrops and small lakes, which would have been perceived as a numinous spot in prehistory. The finds at Llyn Cerrig come from the edge of a bog at the foot of an 11-foot-high sheer rock-cliff which provided an excellent vantage point for throwing in offerings. The metalwork, which was deliberately cast into the lake as votive gifts, has a date range between the 2nd c. BC and the 1st c. AD. The uncorroded condition of the objects indicates that they sank immediately into water. The deposition of the metal may be interpreted as a result of repeated offerings over a long time span or as an accumulation of material dedicated over centuries, which was then deposited as a single act of propitiation.

The offerings cast into the lake at Llyn Cerrig are nearly all prestige items associated with warfare and the aristocracy: these include weapons, chariots, harness fittings, trumpets, slave gang-chains, CAULDRONS and ironworkers' tools. Many of the objects were deliberately bent or broken to 'kill' them before consigning them to the realm of the gods (see RITUAL DAMAGE). The wealth of these divine gifts suggests that the site possessed more than local sanctity, and indeed some of the metalwork may have come from as far away as Somerset and beyond. In addition, the number of chariots represented implies a wider clientele than a local élite. It is possible, therefore, that Celtic chiefs may have travelled some distance to visit and do homage at a lake sanctuary which was perhaps sacred to all Britons.

Whilst it can be no more than speculation, it is tempting to associate this holy place with the sacred druidic stronghold on Anglesey alluded to by Tacitus (*Annals* XIV). In AD 60 the Roman governor, Suetonius Paulinus, was in process of smashing this centre of British nationalism when he was recalled by the rebellion of Boudica in the south-east. Tacitus mentions sacred groves and barbaric rites including human sacrifice and the draping of altars with the entrails of victims. It is possible that, when their sanctuary was threatened, the druids organized the deposition of a precious treasury of hoarded objects, in a desperate act of appeasement to their gods. *See also* DUCHCOV; LLYN FAWR.
□ Fox 1946; Lynch 1970, 249–77; Green 1986, 142–3.

Llyn Fawr In the mid 1st millennium BC, Llyn Fawr was the site of a sacred LAKE. In 1911 and 1912 a hoard of bronze and iron objects was found in a peat deposit which had been the bed of a natural lake. The metalwork included exotic Hallstatt material – harness, vehicle fittings, socketed axes and sickles – the whole cache being deposited in the lake in about 650–600 BC. The fine quality and method of manufacture of the ironwork indicates that these objects were made during the period of transition from bronze to iron technology.

Two of the bronze items were CAULDRONS made of thin plates riveted together to form a globular body; these would have been deposited as antiques, some centuries old when cast into the water. The deposit may have been an offering to the god of the lake, made perhaps from loot carried off from a rich settlement in the English lowlands: some of the bronzes belong to types which were probably made further east than South Wales. But the cauldrons were of local Welsh manufacture. *See also* DUCHCOV; LLYN CERRIG BACH.
□ Savory 1980, 58–9, nos 291–4.

Llŷr is the head of a great Welsh divine house. He is mentioned in the *Second Branch of the Mabinogi*, as the father of Branwen, Bendigeidfran and Manawydan. Llŷr is the Welsh equivalent of the Irish LIR.
☐ Jones & Jones 1976; Rolleston 1985, 348.

Loucetius *see* MARS LOUCETIUS

Luchta *see* GOIBHNIU

Lugh (Welsh equivalent Lleu) belongs to the Mythological Cycle and the Ulster Cycle. He is related by blood both to the Tuatha Dé Danann and to their enemies the Fomorians (he is the grandson of BALOR). Lugh's name means 'Shining One', and he may well have been a god of the sun or of light. The summer festival of LUGHNASAD on 1 August is associated with him: tradition has it that Lughnasad was established by Lugh in memory of his foster-mother. The word 'lugos' means 'RAVEN', and there is a tenuous link between Lugh and ravens; before the Second Battle of Magh Tuiredh, Lugh is warned by ravens of the coming of the Fomorians. Towns such as Luguvalium (Carlisle) and Lugdunum (LYON) are linked by scholars to Lugh, and at Lugdunum, coins depict images of ravens.

In the Irish tradition Lugh is portrayed as a shining god of light, but also as a warrior, sorcerer and master of crafts. He appears at Tara, the royal court of NUADU, king of the Tuatha Dé, presenting himself as the master of all crafts and skills. This has led to a link between Lugh and the Gaulish MERCURY, whom Caesar (*de Bello Gallico* VI, 17) refers to as 'inventor of all the arts'. Lugh appears at Nuadu's court to encourage him to stand up to the FOMORIANS. Nuadu surrenders the kingship to him, and Lugh then orchestrates the military campaign. He engages the three craftsman-gods, GOIBHNIU, Luchta and Creidhne, to forge magic weapons. He himself has a magic spear, but it is with a sling-shot that he kills his grandfather, the Fomorian king, Balor. Lugh's surname 'Lámhfhada' ('of the Long Arm') may refer either to spear-throwing or to his use of the sling. To help the Tuatha Dé against the Fomorians, Lugh brings with him such magic objects as 'Wavesweeper', the boat of MANANNÁN the seagod, and 'Answerer', a sword which will cut through anything. Lugh is himself a magician: he chants spells to encourage the army of

Merlin's Oak in Carmarthen, said to bring luck to the town. The Welsh **Lleu Llaw Gyffes** flew as an eagle into a sacred oak, after being dealt a mortal spear-blow by his wife's lover.

Detail of a bronze disc, decorated with a triskele, 1st c. BC, from **Llyn Cerrig Bach**, Anglesey.

the Tuatha Dé. After the latter are driven underground by the Invasion of the Gaels, the Daghda assigns to Lugh the sídh of Rodrubán.

In the Ulster Cycle, Lugh of the Long Arm is associated with Cú Chulainn. He is a kind of Otherworld father to the young hero, and when Cú Chulainn is wounded and exhausted by his battles against Connacht, Lugh appears to soothe his hurts and heals him by causing him to sleep for three days.

□ Macalister 1931; O'Fáolain 1954; Carey 1984, 1–22; Even 1956, 81–110; Ó'Riain 1978, 138–55; Anon. 1889, 238–43; Gricourt 1955, 63–78; van Tassel Graves 1965, 167–71; O'Rahilly 1946, 308–16; Berresford Ellis 1987, 153–4; Ross 1967a, 250–5; Loth 1914, 205ff; Mac Cana 1983, 24–5.

Lughnasad is one of the four major Celtic festivals of Ireland, which were linked to seasonal rites. All these festivals were based on the pastoral or agricultural year. Lughnasad took place on 1 August and seems to have been linked with the harvest. Traditionally, the festivities were of a month's duration, beginning on 15 July and ending on 15 August.

As its name suggests, Lughnasad is associated with the Celtic god LUGH, a warrior-deity but possessing also a light or solar function, as evinced by his name. At Lugdunum (the 'fort of Lug') at LYON, the emperor Augustus established the Imperial Cult in 12 BC, deliberately on 1 August, probably in recognition of the Gaulish festival. The fair of Lughnasad was apparently introduced by Lugh in Ireland either to commemorate his foster-mother Tailtu or to celebrate his marriage. The festival was held at various locations within Ireland: in Ulster it was celebrated at Emhain Macha; in Leinster at Carman. In addition, Lughnasad was held at Tara for the whole of Ireland.

□ de Vries 1963, 58, 163, 236; Rhŷs 1901, 312; Berresford Ellis 1987, 154; Ross 1967a, 226; 1986, 120; Stokes 1895, 50–1; Ó'Riain 1978, 138–55; van Tassel Graves 1965, 167–71; MacNeill 1962.

Luxovius The eponymous god of the settlement of Luxeuil (Haute-Saône), Luxovius was worshipped only at this site. The name implies a light symbolism, but we know that a divine couple (see COUPLE, DIVINE), Luxovius and BRICTA, presided over the thermal spring sanctuary at Luxeuil. The shrine produced evidence of the worship of other deities, including the sky-horseman who bears a solar wheel, and Sirona, another deity associated with healing springs. In the Celtic world, there was a strong link between water and light symbolism, and Luxovius himself would appear to combine the two concepts: he was a god of light and of curative spring water, and his companion deities reflect this same dual imagery.

□ Wuilleumier 1984, no. 403; Green 1989, 45–6; 1986, 153; Duval 1976, 117; Espérandieu 1917, 72–86.

Lydney The temple at Lydney Park is situated on a hill overlooking the River Severn in Gloucestershire. It was a large and important sanctuary, probably built in the 3rd c. AD and refurbished in the 4th c. The shrine was dedicated to the British healer-god NODENS; it consisted of a temple building, an inn or guest-house, baths and a long building, perhaps a dormitory or *abaton* for the pilgrims to sleep in and be cured after a visitation from the god.

The temple itself is a hybrid of architectural types: its basic plan is that of a Romano-Celtic shrine, with a central *cella* (inner sanctum) surrounded by an ambulatory or portico. But the rectangular shape is reminiscent of a Roman temple plan. The rear wall of the *cella* was divided into three, perhaps for a triad of cult statues. We know of a 4th c. priest called Titus Flavius Senilis, who dedicated a mosaic floor to the temple. The inscription on the mosaic refers to Senilis' occupation as superintendent of religious rites. The mosaic was paid for out of offerings.

Lydney was a wealthy, prosperous sanctuary: not many Romano-Celtic shrines were decorated with fine mosaic floors. Gilt bronze letters were for sale, so that pilgrims could nail up their own inscriptions onto a wooden board. Visitors brought as offerings to Nodens images of DOGS, perhaps reflective of the god's therapeutic powers. They made inscribed dedications to Nodens, either on his own or linked with Mars or Silvanus.

The healing function of the Lydney sanctuary is demonstrated by such votive offerings as a model bronze arm (*see* LIMB/ORGAN, VOTIVE), showing some signs of disease, and occulists' stamps. A stone figure of a Mother-goddess with a *cornucopia* may be indicative of a plea for fertility. Solar symbolism is present in the form of a bronze diadem

depicting the sun-god in a four-horse chariot,'
with tritons and anchors; and this marine
imagery is echoed on the *cella* mosaic. The
sanctuary at Lydney overlooks the great River
Severn and was perhaps deliberately so sited.
Nodens would thus have commanded the
impressive Severn Bore. So he may well have
been a god associated with water, like so
many of the great Celtic divine healers.
□ Wheeler & Wheeler 1932; Henig 1984,
51–6, 135, fig. 58; Green 1986, 140, 159–61;
Le Roux 1963, 425–54; R.I.B., 305–8.

The town of Lyon, which was associated with
the cult of **Lugh**.

Lyon On the opposite bank of the River
Rhône from the Roman *colonia* was the old
Celtic sacred site of Condate, which celebrated the cult of the confluence of the
rivers Rhône and Saône. The importance of
this native Gaulish cult was acknowledged
by the Romans who, on 1 August (the Celtic
festival of LUGHNASAD) 12 BC, established the
Imperial Cult of Rome and Augustus at
Condate. Here, a great altar was erected,
inscribed with the names of sixty Gaulish
tribes, and the place was the focus of the
annual Gallic Provincial Council. The ceremonies associated with the cult were presided over by a Celt, the chief priest of the
Aedui.

In the Romano-Celtic period, Lyon or
Lugdunum continued as a religious centre:
the Celtic cults of the Hammer-god and
the Mother-goddesses were particularly
important. The name 'Lugdunum' suggests
the presence of a cult associated with LUGH,
a god of light and war in the Irish vernacular
tradition. Lugh's zoomorphic emblem was
the RAVEN (*lugos* means raven), and it is
interesting that coins associated with ancient
Lugdunum bear images of ravens.
□ Green 1986, 140; 1989, 82–3; Drinkwater
1983, 111; Ross 1967a, 249–50.

 M

Mabon In the *Tale of Culhwch and Olwen*,
as told in the *Red Book of Hergest*, Mabon
is the son of MODRON. Indeed, the translation
of their two names is 'son' and 'mother'.
Mabon was stolen from his mother when
three nights old, and no trace of him was
found until he was sought and discovered in
prison at Gloucester by Culhwch and Arthur
(*see* CULHWCH AND OLWEN). The fortress

Bronze Hammer-god, decorated with crosses and
other symbols, from **Lyon**.

could be approached only by water; by the time Mabon was delivered from captivity, he was the oldest of all living creatures. In this Welsh mythological story, Mabon's role is that of a hunter: he pursues the magic boar TWRCH TRWYTH, and retrieves from between his ears the razor and comb required by Culhwch in fulfilment of his quest.

Several points concerning the nature of Mabon are of interest: firstly, his father is never mentioned; he is the 'son of mother', and Modron herself may well be an early Mother-goddess. Another feature is the possible link between stories: the stealing of Mabon as a three-day-old child parallels the theft of PRYDERI from Rhiannon, told in the *First Branch of the Mabinogi*. Are Mabon and Pryderi one and the same? It is also possible to relate the character of Mabon, the Divine Youth, to that of the Irish OENGHUS, son of Boann and the Daghda. The third point is that the Mabon of Welsh literature is almost certainly the same god as MAPONUS, who is known in North Britain and at Chamalières in Central Gaul.
□ Gruffydd 1912, 452–61; Bémont 1981, 65–88; Lambert 1979, 141–69; Mac Cana 1983, 31; Ross 1967a, 370.

Mac Da Thó was a king of Leinster at the time when Medb and Ailill ruled in Connacht. He appears in an Ulster Cycle story similar to that of the Feast of Bricriu. The main story of Mac Da Thó concerns his possession of a huge hound which is coveted by King Conchobar of Ulster and by the people of Connacht. The Leinster king promises the dog to both sides, and both the Ulstermen and the Connachtmen arrive to collect it. Mac Da Thó invites them to a feast at his great house, at which an enormous pig is killed. An inevitable quarrel breaks out as to whom should qualify for the champion's portion of pork. Fierce fighting ensues; Mac Da Thó releases his hound to see which side it favours; it chooses the Ulstermen and the men of Connacht are routed.

Mac Da Thó is in reality a god of the Otherworld. His 'bruidhen' or banqueting hall is the festive hall in his sídh, over which he presides as lord of the Otherworld feast. The symbolism is very clear: his hound and his pig are both supernaturally large. Indeed, the lord of the OTHERWORLD feast is often perceived or represented as a man carrying a pig.

□ O'Rahilly 1946, 120–2; Mac Cana 1983, 97; Even 1953, 7–9, 50–4.

Macha is one of the group of Irish goddesses who are concerned with war, fertility and the prosperity of Ireland (*see* WAR-GOD). Like her sister-goddesses, the Morrigán (plur. Morrigna) and the Badbh, Macha is sometimes perceived as one deity, sometimes as three. Macha has a number of zoomorphic associations: she is called 'Macha the CROW' by the 9th c. glossator Cormac. She is also linked with horses (see below). The goddess gave her name to EMHAIN MACHA, the capital and royal court of Ulster.

The first Macha is the wife of Nemedh, leader of the Third Invasion of Ireland. She prophesies the destruction wrought by the Táin Bó Cuailnge (when Connacht fought Ulster over the great Brown Bull of Cuailnge) and died of a broken heart. Macha number two ruled Ireland as a warrior and established Emhain Macha. The third story concerns Macha as a divine bride who marries a mortal man. It is this legend which associates Macha with horses. Macha marries the Ulster widower Crunnchu; she has a reputation for being a fast runner, and this leads to her downfall. At the great Ulster assembly, there is to be a horse race. Crunnchu boasts that Macha can outrun the king's horses; the king takes up the challenge, and Macha is forced to compete, even though she is heavily pregnant. Macha wins the race, but immediately gives birth to twins ('emhain' in Irish) and dies, leaving a curse of a kind of magical paralysis on the Ulstermen, so that in their times of greatest danger they will be as weak as a woman in childbirth, for five days and four nights. The curse materializes: when Connacht threatens Ulster, the only warrior exempt from Macha's curse is the hero CÚ CHULAINN. He himself has a famous horse, the 'Grey of Macha', named presumably for the speed of the goddess.

Thus Macha is a triple goddess, sometimes seen as one entity with three aspects: she is a prophet, a warrior and a matriarch. She represents the sovereignty and fertility of Ireland; she is concerned for its welfare, but vengeful when she is wronged by human beings.

□ Mac Cana 1983, 86–9; Ross 1967a, 95, 219–29; de Vries 1963, 136–7; Rolleston 1985, 178–80; Killeen 1974, 81–6; Hennessy 1870–2, 32–55.

magic *see* CURSE; METAMORPHOSIS; WITCH-
CRAFT

Manannán mac Lir was the son of the Irish
sea-god LIR. In early texts, Manannán is not
specifically listed as a member of the Tuatha
Dé Danann, but in later documents, he is
included. As a SEA-GOD, Manannán, is the
protector of Ireland, enclosing the island with
his own element which guards it. He is
associated with the sea journey to the happy
Otherworld: in the 7th c. *Voyage of Bran*,
Manannán rides the sea in a horse-drawn
chariot. The sea waves are perceived as his
horses, like those of the Greek god Poseidon.
Manannán wears a great cloak which catches
the light and can assume many colours, like
the sea itself.

Apart from being a sea-god, Manannán is
also a master of skills, wisdom, trickery,
illusion and magic. The divine warrior Lugh,
in helping Nuadu and the Tuatha Dé to
vanquish the Fomorians, obtains magical gifts
from Manannán: these are a boat which
obeys the thoughts of its sailor and requires
neither oar nor sail; a horse that can travel
with equal ease on land or sea; and a dreadful
sword named 'Fragarach' ('the Answerer')
which can penetrate any armour. Cú Chulainn has a visor as a present from Manannán.
The sea-god possesses magic pigs which are
killed and eaten on one day and are alive and
ready for the same fate on the next. Many
other tales of magic surround the character
of this god.

Manannán is traditionally associated with
the Isle of Man, of which he was the first
king. It is probable that he is the same deity
as the Welsh MANAWYDAN.
□ Wagner 1981, 1–12; Vendryes 1953–4,
239–54; O'Rahilly 1946, 120–2; Rolleston
1985, 113; Mac Cana 1983, 66–71.

Manawydan, son of Llŷr, may, in origin, be
the Welsh equivalent of the Irish MANANNÁN,
son of Lir, though, unlike Manannán, there
is no evidence that he is a sea-god. Manawydan is the brother of Bendigeidfran and
Branwen, the protagonists of the *Second
Branch of the Mabinogi*. The character of
Manawydan develops in the *Third Branch*,
which is named after him. Here, he appears
as a powerful wielder of magic, a superb
craftsman and a cultivator of wheat. There
are elements in the story that indicate Manawydan's mythico-divine status.

The Irish **Macha** may have had a similar role to
Epona, here represented on a Burgundian
carving.

Silver horse trappings
decorated with heads
and tri-legged symbols,
of the early Iron Age,
from Italy. The central
motif resembles the
symbol of the Isle of
Man, said to be
associated with the sea-
god **Manannán**.

In the *Third Branch of the Mabinogi*, Manawydan marries RHIANNON, the widow of Pwyll. After a court feast at Arberth (Narberth), Pryderi, his wife Cigfa, Rhiannon and Manawydan go to the Gorsedd Arberth, where a spell is woven over the area so that people, animals and settlements all disappear in a magic mist. The four travel to England, where Manawydan and Pryderi set up as craftsmen in various towns. But wherever they go, Manawydan's skills are so superior – whether at saddle-making, shoe-making or other skills – that they are driven off by local artisans. The four return to Dyfed, hunting to support themselves. But they encounter a magic boar, huge and shining white, who lures their hunting dogs into an old fort or caer. Pryderi goes after them despite Manawydan's warning, and he too is enchanted: he lays hands on a golden bowl in the caer, is stuck to it and loses the power of speech. Rhiannon follows Pryderi and incurs the same fate.

It is at this point that Manawydan turns to cultivating wheat. His crops grow well but are ruined by a mouse whom he captures and attempts to hang. But he is interrupted by a bishop who tries to redeem the mouse. Manawydan's terms are that Pryderi and Rhiannon be set free, that the seven cantrefs of Dyfed be released from their enchantment and that the true identity of the mouse be revealed. Manawydan's own power as a magician causes him to recognize the magic of others. All these demands are met: it turns out that the bishop is one Llwyd, who has himself cast the spells to avenge the old wrong done by Pwyll, Pryderi's father, to Gwawl, in robbing him of Rhiannon (a story told in the *First Branch*). The mouse is Llwyd's transformed wife, sent specially to damage Manawydan's corn. Manawydan then uses his own magical powers to restore the mouse to human form.
□ Jones & Jones 1976; Vendryes 1953–4, 239–54; Gruffydd 1912, 452–61; Wagner 1981, 1–28.

Maponus Equated with the Celtic Apollo, Maponus ('Divine Youth' or 'Divine Son') had a cult following in North Britain during the Roman period. At Chesterholm (Vindolanda), a unique crescent-shaped silver plaque was inscribed 'Deo Mapono'. On some dedications, the god's name is linked with that of Apollo, for instance at Corbridge. The *Ravenna Cosmography* mentions a 'locus Maponi' which may have been in Dumfries and Galloway. Dedications imply that Maponus was probably associated with music and poetry: on an altar from Hexham, he is conflated with Apollo the cithara player; but on a dedication at Ribchester, Maponus shares a stone with a hunter-goddess (*see* MODRON). Maponus may be convincingly linked with MABON, the Divine Youth of the *Tale of Culhwch and Olwen*, where he does have a hunting role.

Interestingly, Maponus was not confined to Britain: he was venerated at Bourbonne-les-Bains; and he also occurs at Chamalières (Puy-de-Dôme) where he was invoked on a lead *defixio* or curse tablet.
□ Green 1978, pl. 59; Birley 1973, 113, fig. 1; 1977; Richmond 1943, 206–10, figs 10, 11; Jones & Jones 1976; Bromwich 1961; Ross 1967a, 368–70; de Vries 1963, 84–6; Lambert 1979, 141–69; Bémont 1981, 65–88; R.I.B., 583, 1120–2; C.I.L. XIII, 5924.

Marne, River Rivers possessed a special sanctity for the Celts; they were considered as life sources, and each RIVER was perceived to have a divine spirit. The great River Marne, flowing through eastern Gaul, takes its name from the ancient word 'Matrona', meaning 'divine mother'. In the free Celtic and Roman periods, objects such as miniature bronze solar-wheel symbols were cast into the Marne, presumably as propitiatory offerings to the goddess.

Mars in the Celtic world was a complex deity. Caesar (*de Bello Gallico* VI, 17) mentions him as a popular WAR-GOD in Gaul. Indeed, there is plenty of evidence for warrior-cults in Celtic lands. But the character of Mars underwent a transformation: in a Celtic milieu, Mars was given a number of different native surnames or titles; his identity was adopted as a peaceful protector, a healer and a territorial or tribal god. Thus, MARS LENUS was the great curative god of the Treveri and Mars NODENS the healer of the sanctuary at Lydney on the Severn. Celtic surnames or epithets applied to Mars in Gaul and Britain do refer to him as a lord and fighter, but more often, such sobriquets betray a beneficent, guardianship role for the god named Mars. He was given the epithet 'Toutatis', for instance, at Barkway (Herts), a name which infers his protection of the tribe. One of the

Berne commentaries on Lucan's *Pharsalia* makes the same equation between Mars and TEUTATES. So in a Celtic context, the warlike nature of Mars appears to have been modified so that he was often perceived as using his fighting prowess in order to protect rather than to engage in combat for gain. This transformation is particularly interesting in that the original Italian Mars was also a peaceful guardian of fields and boundaries. It was only his later identification with the Greek Ares which gave the Roman god the combative function for which he is renowned. *See also* COCIDIUS; CONDATIS; RUDIANUS; SNAKE, RAM-HORNED.

□ Duval 1976, 71–3; Green 1986, 110–17; 1989, 111–16; de Vries 1963, 63–9; Thevenot 1955.

Mars Albiorix was venerated as a tribal guardian in southern Gaul. He was the topographical MOUNTAIN spirit of the little tribe of the Albici in Vaucluse. Whilst god name and tribe appear to have this close etymological association, some scholars have interpreted the name Albiorix as meaning 'king of the world'. *See also* MARS NABELCUS.

□ Duval 1976, 71; de Vries 1963, 65; Barruol 1963, 345–68; Green 1989, 111.

Mars Camulos Camulos appears to have been a war-god indigenous both to Britain and to Gaul, who was equated on occasions with the Roman MARS. The two divinities are linked on Continental dedications at Rindern, among the Remi in the region of Reims and in Dalmatia. Camulos may have been an important deity in Britain: the native town of Camulodunum at Colchester was called the 'Fort of Camulos', and the name recurs at Almondbury (Yorks). In lowland Scotland, the place-name 'Camulosessa' is suggested as meaning 'seat of Camulos', and at least one inscription, at Bar Hill on the Antonine Wall, reads 'to the god Mars Camulos'.

□ de Vries 1963, 65; Green 1989, 113; Ross 1967a, 180; R.I.B., 2166.

Mars Caturix 'Caturix' means 'master of fighting' or 'king of combat' and was one of the Celtic epithets given to MARS in Gaul. He may have been the tribal god of the Caturiges. He was venerated at Chougny near Geneva.

□ de Vries 1963, 65, 68; Vallentin 1879–80, 1–36.

Maponus was a hunter-god: this 3rd c. AD image of a hunter-deity comes from a Roman well at Southwark, London.

The River **Marne** derives its name from 'Matrona', meaning Mother. The Mother-goddess depicted here is from Alesia.

Sculpted head of **Mars**, from London.

Mars Corotiacus A local British version of the Celtic MARS from Martlesham in Suffolk, the god appears on a bronze statuette as a cavalryman, armed and riding a horse which tramples a prostrate enemy beneath its hooves. Beneath the figure is a base bearing a dedication to the god by an individual with the Celtic name of Simplicia. The cult of Mars as a HORSEMAN was especially popular among the tribes of eastern Britain, but the name Corotiacus is unique to Martlesham. The imagery is strongly reminiscent of certain 1st c. AD tombstones which depict soldiers riding down fallen foes; it also recalls the iconography of the Romano-Celtic sky-horseman carved at the summit of JUPITER-GIANT COLUMNS.
☐ Green 1976, 218; 1986, 115; R.I.B., 213.

Mars Lenus A great healer-god of the Treveri, Lenus presided over important curative spring sanctuaries at Trier and Pommern. The equation of the native Lenus with MARS is an example of Mars' Celtic function as a protector and guardian against disease.

At Trier, Lenus was coupled with a native goddess ANCAMNA, who elsewhere among the Treveri (at Möhn) was linked with SMERTRIUS. In the main cult centre of Lenus Mars at Trier the indigenous name, significantly, nearly always comes first on dedications, an indication that Lenus was the established god, with whom Mars was later equated. The sanctuary was situated in a small, steep and wooded valley at the bottom of which was a stream, on the left bank of the Moselle and opposite the Roman city of Trier. This spot was probably sacred to Lenus for some centuries before the Roman occupation: certainly, an early and relatively humble shrine preceded the main temple. In the mid 2nd c. AD, the great Romano-Celtic temple was erected, on a massive scale and exhibiting considerable Graeco-Roman architectural influence. There was a huge altar and what was probably a theatre for the enactment of ceremonies associated with the ritual of Lenus' cult. The spring above the precinct had a long-lasting reputation for curative properties (see SPRING, HEALING): its waters were canalized to supply a small set of baths for Lenus' pilgrims.

Lenus, at his Trier sanctuary, was sometimes invoked by the name 'IOVANTUCARUS', signifying that one of the god's special roles was as protector of the young. Many images offered to the deity have been found at the site, including children holding such gifts to the god as pet birds (see DOVE). Representations of divinities other than Lenus show that pilgrims prayed to their own personal patron-deity in addition to their invocations to Lenus himself.

Another major shrine built for Lenus was at Pommern in the Treveran countryside. The buildings were enclosed in a large precinct or *temenos*, and the shrine was equipped with an *abaton* or dormitory in which pilgrims slept, dreamed and hoped for a vision of the god who would visit and cure them in their sleep. That belief in the efficacy of Lenus was sometimes justified is demonstrated by an inscription thanking him for curing a devotee of a dreadful illness.

Interestingly, Lenus Mars was worshipped in Britain, at Caerwent in Gwent and probably also at Chedworth in Gloucestershire. On the base of a statue (which has been almost totally lost) at Caerwent is a dedication to Mars Lenus, otherwise known as Ocelus Vellaunus. Above the base are the feet of a god and a web-footed bird, probably a GOOSE (geese were considered sacred to war-gods because of their aggressive and alert nature). From the same Roman town comes another dedication, this time to Mars Ocelus, though the same deity is probably being alluded to on both stones. VELLAUNUS was known in Gaul, and OCELUS appears to have been a god local to South Wales, though he was also invoked at Carlisle. The other British dedication comes from the great villa complex at Chedworth (Glos). Some scholars argue that the whole site is a great healing sanctuary rather than a villa. Here, the name Lenus or Lenumius was scratched on a small altar on which is a crude incised figure of a warrior-god with a hammer and spear. If this image does represent Lenus, then the Dobunnic altar provides our only depiction of the god: its rough execution may imply that it belonged to the lower echelons of Romano-British society, perhaps the property of a servant or worker at the villa (if villa it was).

Both the Caerwent and the Chedworth evidence indicate that, though Lenus was a peaceful healer, artistically he could be envisaged as a warrior. He was a potent protector against disease, and he used his aggressive attributes to fend off evil and to guard his suppliants against illness and death.
☐ Wightman 1970, 208–17; Thevenot 1968,

60–73; Green 1986, 158ff; R.I.B., 126, 309, 310, 949; Duval 1976, 70; Ross 1967a, 173, pl. 60b; Goodburn 1972, pl. 10; Webster 1986a, 81.

Mars Loucetius On an altar at the great healing temple of Sulis Minerva at Bath is a dedication to a divine couple called Mars Loucetius and NEMETONA, which was set up by a citizen of Trier. Both Loucetius and Nemetona are recorded elsewhere in western Europe, for instance at Mainz. At Altripp in Germany an inscription to MARS and Nemetona may also refer to Loucetius. Elsewhere Loucetius is associated with the war-goddess Bellona (see COUPLE, DIVINE).

The epithet Loucetius is a term meaning 'light' or 'bright' and would seem to associate the Celtic Mars with sky or solar cults. In a Roman context, Loucetius is a title belonging to Jupiter. At Bath Mars Loucetius may have been venerated as a healer; the name of Sulis, the goddess of the sanctuary, is etymologically related to the sun, presumably as an instrument of healing. The name Loucetius could also refer to lightning, thus giving the god a more aggressive role; it is known that Mars was a storm-god in Italy. The Celtic Mars has other light associations: he is called BELA-TUCADRUS – 'bright' or 'shining' – in North Britain.
□ R.I.B., 140; C.I.L. XIII, 7253, 6221, 7241, 6131; Duval 1976, 89; Ogilvie 1969.

Mars Mullo The cult of the native god Mullo, linked with the Roman MARS, was popular in northern and north-western Gaul, particularly in Brittany and Normandy. The word 'Mullo' may denote an association with horses or mules; it is the Latin for 'mule'. Mars Mullo had a circular temple at Craôn in the Mayenne, situated on a hillock commanding a confluence of two rivers. An inscription at Nantes reflects the presence of a shrine there. An important cult centre must have existed at Rennes, the tribal capital of the Redones: here inscriptions refer to the onetime presence of statues and of the existence of an official, public cult. Town magistrates were instrumental in setting up urban sanctuaries to Mullo in the 2nd c. AD. Even more important is the evidence at ALLONNES (Sarthe), where a shrine was set up to Mars Mullo as a healer of eye afflictions. His high status is suggested by his link with Augustus on a dedicatory inscription. Pilgrims visiting

(Above left) The Celtic **Mars** on an altar from King's Stanley, Gloucestershire.
(Above right) Bronze **Mars**, holding two ram-headed snakes, from Southbroom, Wiltshire.

Altar to **Mars Loucetius** and Nemetona from Bath.

the shrine offered numerous Celtic coins to the presiding deity and votive images of themselves (*see* LIMB/ORGAN, VOTIVE), their eye problems clearly manifest.

☐ Térouanne 1960, 185–9; 1965, 209ff; Thevenot 1968, 65–6; Green 1989, 113.

Mars Nabelcus was a local spirit, equated with the protective cult of the native MARS in Provence. He was venerated in the mountains of Vaucluse, for example on Mount Ventoux near Vaison and at Moncieux. A bronze plaque dedicated to this MOUNTAIN divinity is recorded at Châteauneuf-Miraveil (Basses-Alpes); and Nabelcus was worshipped in other high places in the south of Gaul. *See also* MARS ALBIORIX.

☐ Barruol 1963, 345–68.

Mars Nodens *see* NODENS

Mars Olloudius *see* OLLOUDIUS

Mars Rigisamus 'Rigisamus' means 'Greatest King' or 'King of Kings', and the Celtic MARS was given this name or title at West Coker in Somerset, where a crudely made bronze figurine and inscribed plaque dedicated to the god were found in a field along with traces of a building, perhaps a shrine. The plaque is of ansate form (with 'handles'), with a punched inscription and a central perforation for attachment, probably to a wooden surface. The figurine depicts a standing naked male figure with a close-fitting helmet; his right hand once held a spear, and he probably also originally had a shield (both are lost). The figure has pointed plugs under his feet for placement within a wooden block.

The same title for a god is recorded from Bourges in Gaul. The use of such an epithet for Mars is interesting, since it implies an extremely high status for the god, over and above any warrior function.

☐ Collingwood 1931, figs 1, 2; Green 1976, 184; 1986, 112, 116; Duval 1976, 71.

Mars Rigonemetis was the 'King of the Sacred Grove', the name reflecting the Celtic word 'nemeton' ('grove'), in the same manner as, for example, 'Arnemetia' and 'Nemetona'. In 1961, a dedication to Rigonemetis and the Numen (spirit) of the Emperor inscribed on a stone was found at Nettleham (Lincs) together with pottery of a 2nd–4th c. AD date. The stone may have been part of the arch of a temple. Rigonemetis is known only at this site, and it seems as if he was a god belonging to the tribe of the Corieltauvi. His association with the emperor may imply high status.

☐ Green 1976, 203; Lewis 1966, 121.

Mars Segomo *see* SEGOMO

Mars Smertrius *see* SMERTRIUS

Mars Teutates *see* TEUTATES

Mars Thincsus may have been a German divinity. He was invoked at Housesteads on Hadrian's Wall, where his name is linked with two goddesses called the 'Alaisiagae'. These female deities are again linked with MARS on another Housesteads dedication. Anne Ross would associate Thincsus with a sculpture also from the fort which shows a god flanked by goddesses and accompanied by a GOOSE – a frequent companion of the war-gods (perhaps because of its aggressive, watchful nature). It should be recalled that Mars Lenus/Ocelus VELLAUNUS at Caerwent had a goose. In cases where Mars became a peaceful god of well-being, the goose was still relevant as a guardian against the evils of the world.

☐ R.I.B., 1593, 1594; Ross 1967a, 173, 272, pl. 58a.

Mars Visucius *see* VISUCIUS

Mars Vorocius was a Gaulish healer-god invoked at the curative spring shrine at VICHY (Allier) as a curer of eye afflictions. On images, the god is depicted as a Celtic warrior.

☐ Duval 1976, fig. 53; Green 1986, 158.

mask A hollow metal image of a head or face, sometimes life-size, formed part of the ceremonial regalia of Celtic and Romano-Celtic religion. Many small metal heads were also made for application to vessels or crowns, but genuine Celtic masks are quite rare. They may have been made to be held in front of a priest's face during a procession or religious ceremony, to adorn a wooden cult image or to be nailed up on the door of a shrine to represent a particular divinity. The best-known masks are the example from Tarbes in southern Gaul, which may be as early as the 3rd c. BC, and the pewter mask found in the culvert of the baths of Sulis' sanctuary at Bath. A recent East Anglian discovery is that

of a large gold mask which, like the Bath one, has perforations indicating its suspension from a pillar, door or shrine wall.
□ Green 1986, 23–4; Pobé & Roubier 1961, 52; Henig & Taylor 1984, 246; Ross 1967a, 97–9.

Math is the lord of Gwynedd, and he appears in the *Fourth Branch of the Mabinogi*, which is named after him. Math, the son of Mathonwy, has a curious quirk, in that he has to keep his feet in a virgin's lap. The reason for this is probably that he thus derives a constant source of vitality from the contact of this untapped womanhood. The first 'footholder' of whom we know is Goewin, who is seduced by Math's nephew Gilfaethwy, after Math is lured to war with Pryderi of South Wales, by the trickery of Gilfaethwy's brother GWYDION. Math is so angry when he returns that he turns the two young men into animals for three years. The next candidate for the office of footholder is ARIANRHOD: she has to pass a virginity test by stepping over Math's magic wand. Sadly, she fails, and at the crucial moment she gives birth to two baby boys. Later, Math and Gwydion use their power as magicians to conjure up a wife of flowers for Arianrhod's son, Lleu Llaw Gyffes. Elsewhere in the *Fourth Branch*, Math is involved with the myth of the introduction of pigs into Britain. Gwydion informs Math that Pryderi of Dyfed has pigs, which were gifts to his father Pwyll from Arawn, king of the underworld. Gwydion uses magic to obtain these creatures.

The most important characteristic of Math is his power of magic; this may mean that he acquires divine status. His magic is more powerful than Gwydion's in that he is able to curse his nephews and transform them into beasts. It may be significant that the animals involved in the METAMORPHOSIS change each year – from deer to pigs to wolves – and that in each instance the creatures into which Gwydion and his brother are changed are male and female respectively. This, together with the footholding magic, may mean that Math was particularly associated with fertility.
□ Mac Cana 1983, 72–6; Ross 1967a, 315; Jones & Jones 1976.

Matholwch appears in the *Second Branch of the Mabinogi*, which is called Branwen. BRANWEN is the sister of BENDIGEIDFRAN

The Housesteads Roman fort on Hadrian's Wall, where the Celto-Germanic **Mars Thincsus** was venerated.

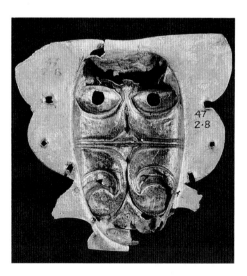

Bronze chariot-mount in the form of a **mask**, 1st c. AD, from the Brigantian stronghold of Stanwick, Yorkshire.

(Brân the Blessed), who gives her in marriage to Matholwch, king of Ireland. One of Branwen's brothers, on hearing of the betrothal between Branwen and Matholwch, is angry and mutilates Matholwch's horses. In revenge, Branwen is ill-treated in Ireland. The insults and humiliations done to her and her family cause a great war between the Britons and the Irish, in which Bendigeidfran and his followers seek revenge against Matholwch and his court. *See also* CAULDRON.
□ Jones & Jones 1976.

Matres, Matronae *see* MOTHER-GODDESS; TRIPLISM

Matres Comedovae This local version of the triple Mothers was worshipped at AIX-LES-BAINS; the Comedovae were associated specifically with healing and the curative properties of the thermal springs at Aix. The 'med' part of their surname may refer to health.
□ de Vries 1963, 130.

Matres Domesticae In Britain, the three Mothers could be worshipped with the epithet 'Domesticae', referring to their function as deities of the homeland. The Domesticae were venerated at Chichester, where a dedication to the goddesses was set up by a treasurer (*arcarius*) in the town. The Matres Domesticae were worshipped elsewhere in Britain, at York, Stanwix (Cumbria) and Burgh-by-Sands (Northd). But their cult may be associated with that of the MATRONAE AUFANIAE at Bonn, who were called 'Aufaniae Domesticae'. However, the term 'Domesticae' in Britain may equally be a general term associated specifically with British MOTHER-GODDESSES. The Chichester inscription is on fragments of a Purbeck marble pediment, which may have come from a shrine in which seated images of the goddesses were carved. The dedicant may have been a local government official, or he could have been attached to a local guild.
□ Barnard 1985, 237–43; Hassall & Tomlin 1979, 339–41, no. 1; Henig 1984, 49; C.I.L. XIII, 8021; R.I.B., 652, 2025, 2050.

Matres Griselicae were venerated at Gréoulx in southern Gaul, where they were associated with therapeutic springs. The topographical surname is linked to Gréoulx itself. *See also* MOTHER-GODDESS.
□ Clébert 1970, 254.

Matres Nemausicae *see* NEMAUSUS

Matronae Aufaniae were a triad of MOTHER-GODDESSES worshipped by the Celto-Germanic tribes of the Rhineland. Several stone monuments to the Aufaniae were set up in the area of Bonn during the 2nd c. AD. Images of the goddesses conform to the normal Germanic type, consisting of a young central goddess with long flowing hair seated between two older matrons with distinctive large circular bonnets. All three deities wear long robes and bear baskets of fruits. The side panels of their altars generally display carvings of foliage or scenes of sacrifice. A temple at Nettersheim near Bonn, dedicated to the Aufaniae, contained a number of monuments attesting their worship: on one, each goddess carries a box, and the central deity has a distaff, perhaps symbolic of the spinning of life's thread, in addition to the homely domestic ideas associated with such crafts (*see* FATES). On a relief from Bonn, the three divinities are accompanied by busts of three women, perhaps acolytes or novitiates: this stone was set up in AD 164 by a *quaestor* (a financial official) of Cologne. This high-ranking dedicant is typical of the kind of individual who was attracted to the cult of the Aufaniae, and the good lettering and high standard of carving on these monuments reflect the high status of the Aufaniae's devotees.

The imagery associated with the cult is interesting: often the goddesses are depicted in company with female suppliants who carry baskets of fruit to offer to the Mothers. A striking feature is the abundance of floral and faunal symbolism: trees, branches and flowers are represented on the stones; birds perch in branches, and snakes wind their bodies round the trunks of trees, probably to guard them. One stone, with a military dedication, bears no image of the goddesses, but on the rear surface are a tree, a snake twined round its trunk and a triple-bodied goat, replicating the TRIPLISM of the Mothers themselves.
□ Espérandieu, nos 6307, 6560, 6559, 7761, 7765, 7768, 7772, 7774; Wild 1968, pl. 1; Green 1989, fig. 85; von Petrikovits 1987.

Matronae Vacallinehae were a local variant of the Celto-Germanic MOTHER-GODDESSES who were venerated in the Rhineland. The Vacallinehae had a temple complex at PESCH, where there was a sacred precinct containing several shrines. Pilgrims visiting the sanctuary, mainly soldiers, dedicated more than 160 altars to the goddesses. Many images of the Mothers at Pesch show them with loaves of bread as their main attribute; bread was standard legionary fare, and the emblem may thus have been chosen as an appropriate symbol of bounty by the military devotees of the cult.

□ Lehner 1918–21, 74ff.

Mavilly (Côte-d'Or) is important for the presence there of a carved stone PILLAR on which Celtic divinities are represented. Mars is depicted on one surface, as a warrior with a lance and a hexagonal shield of late La Tène Iron Age type. He wears chain mail and is accompanied by a goddess and a ram-horned snake. On another surface of the pillar is a scene which must represent a divine healer of eyes: here a god appears seated, accompanied by a DOG and a RAVEN; behind him and to one side is a human figure with his hands over his eyes. Mavilly may have been a cult centre of Mars the healer, so important as Lenus Mars at Trier. Mars Mullo at Allonnes (Sarthe) was an eye healer, and the god at Mavilly may have performed a similar function. His appearance as an armed god of war may denote his role as a protector against disease; his raven may be present as a sharp-eyed symbol and his dog as a healing image. The ram-horned serpent is perhaps present at Mavilly as a symbol of regeneration and thus healing (*see* SNAKE, RAM-HORNED). The Mavilly pillar may once have been placed at the site of a healing spring shrine (*see* SPRING, HEALING).

□ Thevenot 1955; 1968, 67–8; Green 1989, fig. 25.

Medb is the great goddess-queen of Connacht. Her name means 'she who intoxicates' and is philologically related to the word 'mead'.

In the Ulster Cycle of tales, Medb appears as a queen, but it is clear that she is in fact a euhemerized goddess, having been endowed with a spurious historicity. There are many indications that Medb is a goddess of sovereignty, one of the group of Irish female deities of war, territory and sexuality (*see* TERRITORY, GOD OF; WAR-GOD). She is promiscuous, mating with at least nine mortal kings and refusing to allow any king to rule

Altar to the Germanic Mothers, the **Matronae Aufaniae**, from Bonn.

The Celtic Mars, a goddess and a ram-horned snake on a relief from **Mavilly**, Burgundy.

in Tara who has not first mated with her. One of her consorts is FERGHUS, a hero of extreme virility, who needs seven ordinary women (or Medb) to satisfy him. In all her unions, Medb is the dominant partner. Indeed, her role as goddess of sovereignty may be betrayed by her name, since liquor was involved in the sanctification of marriage between the territorial goddess and the king (*see* SACRAL KINGSHIP). Medb's very promiscuity marks her as a goddess, symbolic of the fertility of Ireland. She is the personification of the land itself and its prosperity. Other indications of her divinity include her ability to shape-shift between young girl and aged hag: in the story of Niall of the Nine Hostages, Medb appears to Niall as a crone guarding a well. She gives him water, and he agrees to mate with her; she is immediately transformed into a beautiful young woman, who grants him the kingship of Ireland. The goddess of sovereignty could also be a deity of death, and Medb possesses this characteristic also. She brings about the death of CÚ CHULAINN and of her own husband AILILL, infuriated (though hardly fairly) by his infidelity. She incites the former Ulster hero, CONALL CERNACH, to murder him on the Feast of Beltene. Medb has other supranormal traits: she has animal attributes, in the form of a bird and a squirrel who perch on her shoulder; she can run very fast; and she is able to deprive men of their strength simply by her presence.

The most important tradition concerning Medb is in the *Táin Bó Cuailnge* of the Ulster Cycle. Medb is queen of Connacht, who rules variously at Tara or at CRUACHAIN (County Roscommon). She is married to King Ailill, but she is the dominant partner. The war with Ulster comes about entirely through Medb's jealousy and scheming: because Ailill has a magnificent BULL, she covets the Ulster Brown Bull of Cuailnge, and the conflict revolves around her desire to acquire this creature. Medb appears as a warrior, inciting her armies to fight, sowing seeds of dissonance and driving around the battlefield in her chariot. Several times she pits her wits against the Ulster hero Cú Chulainn, endeavouring to bribe him with her daughter Finnebair. She fails, and finally brings about his death by magic. During the conflict, Medb is warned of Cú Chulainn's supremacy and of the ruin of Connacht by her female seer FEDELMA. The goddess-queen is also beset by druids, who force her to wait for a propitious day before joining battle.

Medb's death is described in an 11th c. text: she is killed by her nephew, Furbaidhe, whose mother, Clothra, has been murdered by Medb. Her death is somewhat bizarre: she is killed by a sling-shot with a lump of hard cheese.

□ Jubainville 1907, 17–42; O'Fáolain 1954; Lehmann 1989, 1–10; Bhreathnach 1982, 243–60; Thurneysen 1933, 352–3; O'Máille 1928, 129–46; O'Rahilly 1946, 176; Bray 1987, 209–15; Mac Cana 1958–9, 59–65; 1983, 84–6; Kinsella 1969; Jackson 1964; Hull 1938, 52–61; Ross 1967a, 223.

Mercury was perhaps the most popular god in Gaul and Britain. Caesar (*de Bello Gallico* VI, 17) makes this comment, and this is endorsed by the enormous number of inscriptions and depictions which represent the god in some form. Caesar states that Mercury was the inventor of all the arts; this has caused some scholars to link him with the Irish LUGH. Caesar also alludes to the money-making prowess of the god. The Celtic Mercury was given a number of native epithets or titles (see below). He was a deity of plenty and particularly of commercial success. That he was fully adopted into the Celtic pantheon is shown by some of his iconography and associations: he may be represented with three heads (*see* MERCURY, TRIPLE-FACED) or three phalluses (*see* MERCURY, TRIPLE-PHALLUSED), and his frequent companion is his indigenous consort ROSMERTA (*see* COUPLE, DIVINE). There were some important sanctuaries dedicated to the Celtic Mercury: in Gaul, the remote mountain shrine of LE DONON (Vosges) belonged to him; at Uley (Glos) there was a temple to Mercury, and here, one of his images shows the god with Celtic HORNS. *See also* COCKEREL; RAM; SNAKE, RAM-HORNED.

□ de Vries 1963, 48–63; Duval 1976, 69–71; Ellison 1977.

Mercury Artaios Some forty-five Gaulish surnames or epithets are known to have been attached to MERCURY on epigraphic dedications. One local name for the god was Artaios, a descriptive epithet referring to 'BEAR'. The god was invoked thus at Beaucroissant (Isère). In this instance, Mercury was probably venerated as a god of the hunt, guardian of hunters against bears but at the

same time a protector of the creature itself (*see* HUNTER-GOD). Mercury was not the only deity to be given a 'bear' name; a goddess at Muri near Berne was called ARTIO.
□ C.I.L. XII, 2199; Thevenot 1968, 157; Duval 1976, 51–2.

Mercury Arvernus Few of the many surnames for the Celtic MERCURY appear with any frequency, but one such is the epithet 'Arvernus', a topographical spirit who was invoked around the banks of the Rhine. His name suggests that he was the special deity of the Arverni, but his dedications do not occur in the territory of this tribe.
□ C.I.L. XIII, 6603, 7845, 8164, 8235, 8579, 8580, 8709; Duval 1976, 70.

Mercury Cissonius Dedications to Mercury Cissonius were made as far apart as Cologne and Saintes in Aquitania. Interestingly, Cissonius alone (without Mercury's name being present) was mentioned on a dedication at Metz. The widespread pattern of veneration suggests that Cissonius was not a local topographical spirit; the presence of his worship simply as Cissonius implies that he may have existed as an independent Celtic deity and that the name was not simply an epithet applied to MERCURY. Cissonius' cult was centred above all in Upper Germany. A goddess Cissonia is also recorded.
□ C.I.L. XIII, 3659, 5373, 6085, 6119, 4500, 3020, 6345, 7359, 8237, 4564, etc; de Vries 1963, 49; Duval 1976, 70.

Mercury Gebrinius At Bonn, an altar was set up in the 2nd c. AD to honour a local version of MERCURY. The stone depicts the god in full Roman guise, but it is nevertheless dedicated to 'Mercury Gebrinius', perhaps the name of the local divinity of the Ubii, whose cult was linked with that of the Roman god.
□ Green 1989, 108; Horn 1987, fig. 227.

Mercury Moccus This god may have been associated with hunting, like Mercury Artaios. 'Moccus' is a Gaulish word for 'pig' or 'hog', and Mercury Moccus may have been the protector of BOAR hunters among the tribe of the Lingones, where he was invoked at the tribal centre, Langres.
□ Mac Cana 1983, 51; Thevenot 1968, 157.

Mercury, triple-faced There was a recurrent link between the iconography of the Celtic

Schematized image of **Mercury**, with winged hat or horns, from a Romano-British well at Emberton, Buckinghamshire.

Altar to **Mercury Gebrinius**, a local god of the Ubian tribe, from Bonn.

MERCURY and triple-faced or triple-headed images (*see* HEAD, TRIPLE). On a relief from Paris, a triple-faced deity holds Mercury's purse in one hand and the head of a RAM (another common Mercury motif) in the other. Thus, on this stone, complete identification is made between Mercury and the Gaulish triple-faced image. On a stone at Malmaison, Mercury and his Celtic consort Rosmerta share a stone with a three-faced head. Many of the triple-visaged stone heads at Reims are surmounted by emblems traditionally associated with Mercury – ram's heads and cockerels; and at Soissons, a ram and a COCKEREL are carved beneath the triple head. Thus, in northern Gaul, three-faced images may be equated or identified with the Celtic Mercury. There is evidence that triple images (*see* TRIPLISM) are often associated with the veneration of Mercury, who was a Romano-Celtic divinity of prosperity, business success and general well-being.
☐ Espérandieu, nos 3137, 3756, 7700; Lambrechts 1942, fig. 11; Hatt 1984, 287–99.

Mercury, triple-phallused The cult of the Celtic MERCURY took many iconographic forms: on one occasion, on a bronze figurine from a cemetery at Tongeren (Tongres) in Belgium, the god is endowed with three phalli. The statuette is damaged, but when complete it possessed one PHALLUS in the normal position, one at the top of Mercury's head and a third replacing his nose. Thus the image combines the magic symbolism of 'three' (*see* TRIPLISM) with the intensification of the potent fertility and good-luck motif of the phallus. Polyphallic images are not confined to the Celtic world: an example of a multi-phallused statuette of Mercury is recorded at Naples.
☐ Deonna 1954, 420; Santrot 1986, 203–28.

Mercury Visucius *see* VISUCIUS

metamorphosis The lack of rigid boundaries between humans and animals in Celtic religion and mythology is demonstrated above all by shape-shifting or metamorphosis, the power of supernatural beings to change form. The world of the vernacular Welsh and Irish tradition is redolent with enchanted animals who were once in human form, and divinities who could transform themselves back and forth between human and animal shape. The Irish war-goddesses frequently indulged in shape-changing. Both the MORRI-GÁN and the BADBH appeared to warriors as crows or ravens. When the Morrigán encounters Cú Chulainn, she is in the form of a young noblewoman, but when he spurns her, she changes to an eel, a wolf and a hornless red heifer in quick succession. These Irish goddesses also habitually changed between the forms of young girl and old hag (*see* MEDB).

Other mythological beings were metamorphosed, frequently into birds or boars. Caer, beloved of OENGHUS, changed every alternate year to SWAN-form. Significantly, this transformation took place on the Feast of Samhain (when the barrier between the mundane and the supernatural was temporarily broken down). DIARMAID's foster-brother was an enchanted boar, destined to be the cause of the hero's death. Individuals could be transformed against their will, as punishment or in revenge. Thus, the Welsh TWRCH TRWYTH, in the *Tale of Culhwch and Olwen*, was changed from a king to a boar as punishment for his wickedness. In the *Fourth Branch of the Mabinogi*, GWYDION and his brother are punished by Math for their trickery: the two are changed into male and female of three different animals, each for a year. The children of Lir are metamorphosed into swans by their jealous step-mother. Ferghus proclaims that the two great Bulls of Ulster and Connacht, the protagonists of the *Táin*, are in fact transmogrified humans sent by the gods to be the cause of Ireland's ruin.

Any attempt to trace examples of this shape-shifting tradition in the archaeological record must be speculative. But there are instances of semi-zoomorphic, semi-human divine images: the horned gods and Cernunnos, the antlered deity, spring to mind as possible shape-shifters. Iron Age coins struck by Gaulish and British tribes, showing a huge raven perched on a horse, may reflect the Insular tradition of the raven-goddesses.
☐ Kinsella 1969; Hennessy 1870–2, 32–55; Bhreathnach 1982, 243–60; Müller 1876–8, 342–60; O'Fáolain 1954; Lloyd, Bergin & Schoepperle 1912, 41–57; Mac Cana 1983, 72; Allen 1980, no. 526; Duval 1987; Laing 1969, 164; Ross 1961, 59ff; Green 1989, 86–96.

Midhir In the Irish Mythological Cycle, Midhir is the lord of the sídh of Brí Léith (sídhe were the underground kingdoms of the gods, once they had been driven from the land of Ireland by the Milesians). The *Book of Invasions* tells of the invasion of Ireland by the Sons of Mil (or Milesians), who drove the divine Tuatha Dé Danann underground to become lords of the Otherworld beneath the hills. The most important story of Midhir concerns his wooing of ÉTAIN. He incurs the wrath of his wife Fuamnach by bringing home his new bride, and she uses magic to transform her young rival into a butterfly, buffeted about the world for many years. Midhir makes desperate attempts to find Étain and finally tracks her down, reborn more than 1,000 years after her initial birth, as a beautiful young girl. But the new Étain is married to Eochaidh, king of Ireland, and she is at first reluctant to return to Midhir, since she has forgotten him. By means of trickery, he manages to kiss Étain; she remembers and loves him, and the pair finally escape from the royal court at Tara in the form of two swans. They are pursued by the king, but Midhir magically conjures fifty women, all identical to Étain. By mistake, Eochaidh chooses not the real Étain but their daughter, and thus commits the horror of incest. *See also* OENGHUS.

Another story about Midhir also concerns his association with birds: the *Book of Leinster* has a tale in which Midhir possesses three hostile cranes, who discourage travellers from stopping at his dwelling, and who rob warriors of their courage (*see* CRANE).
□ Ross 1967a, 266; Mac Cana 1983, 90; Bergin & Best 1938, 137–96; Nutt 1906, 325–39; O'Fáolain 1954.

mistletoe The Roman writer Pliny in his *Natural History* (XVI, 95) chronicles a Celtic festival held on the sixth day of the moon, when the druids climbed a sacred oak tree, cut off a mistletoe bough using a 'golden' sickle (probably actually gilded bronze, since gold would be too soft) and caught it in a white cloak; they then presided over a rite in which two white bulls were sacrificed. The Celts considered mistletoe to be efficacious in curing barrenness when mixed in a drink, perhaps because of the property mistletoe has of flourishing in winter when its host oak is seemingly without life. The druids were responsible for FERTILITY ritual, hence the BULL sacrifice. It was their job to foretell by divination what were the most auspicious

The antlered god Cernunnos, on a stone at Vendoeuvres, Indre, reflects the Celtic tradition of **metamorphosis** or shape-changing.

Drawing of a British druid, accompanied by his oak tree with **mistletoe** growing from it, from William Stukeley's *Stonehenge*, 1740.

days for sowing and reaping, putting flocks
and herds out to pasture and slaughtering
beasts before the winter (*see* DRUID).

When the Iron Age bog body, Lindow
Man, was recovered from the Cheshire marsh
in 1984, his stomach contents were examined,
and he was found to have consumed a ritual
meal just prior to his death. The 'porridge'
or bread consisted of many different seeds
and fruits; but the discovery that he had
eaten mistletoe pollen as part of this meal
has led to speculation (and it can be no more
than that) that he may have been a druidic
sacrifice.

□ Cunliffe 1979, 106–10; Stead & Turner
1985, 25–9; Stead et al. 1986.

Moccus *see* MERCURY MOCCUS

model tool/weapon The tradition of manufacturing miniature replicas of weapons,
implements and other everyday objects was
widespread in antiquity and was not confined
to the Celtic world. Double-axe models (*see*
AXE, DOUBLE) occur in Minoan Crete by about
2000 BC, and the burial of model implements
in Egyptian tombs was commonplace.

But the use of miniature objects as votive
offerings seems to have been especially prevalent in Gaul and Britain during the free
Celtic and Romano-Celtic periods. They were
buried in Iron Age graves, for instance at the
Dürrnberg in Austria: here a young girl
suffering from stunted growth died and was
accompanied on her journey to the afterlife
by a model AXE and WHEEL. The appearance
of miniature items in temples lends credence
to their interpretation as sacred objects. At
such pre-Roman shrines as Frilford (Oxon),
Worth (Kent) and HARLOW (Essex) miniature
swords and shields were offered, perhaps to a
warrior-deity. Many Romano-Celtic temples,
too, have produced model objects: devotees
at Woodeaton (Oxon) offered six model
spears, three of which had been deliberately
bent as a religious act (*see* RITUAL DAMAGE).
The temples at Lamyatt Beacon (Somerset)
and Thistleton (Leics) also contained spear
models.

It is not always clear whether or not models
were dedicated to particular divinities. Some
Swiss axe models are inscribed with the
names of specific deities – Jupiter, Minerva
and the Mother-goddesses. Weapons, such
as swords, or defensive armour, like shields,
may have been offered to a WAR-GOD, or the

worshipper may himself have been a soldier.
Spears, especially in civilian areas of Roman
Britain, may have been offerings to hunter-
gods rather than war-deities. Wheel models
were probably votives associated with the
cult of the sun-god. But the largest group of
models consists of axes, and it is this category
which is difficult to ascribe to a specific cult.
It is sometimes suggested that axes possessed
a generalized good-luck symbolism.

The reasons for offering miniature objects
in shrines and their occurrence as grave goods
are complex. Factors of convenience and
economy may well have been important.
Indeed, some miniatures were worn as talismans, and they would of necessity be small.
A striking feature of many models is the
fact that care was taken to copy a genuine
prototype as accurately as possible. Thus, the
craftsman who made the axe model found at
Tiddington (Warks) took the trouble to cast
the shaft and the blade separately, in close
imitation of a real axe made of wood and
iron. It is quite possible that miniaturization
was a deliberate religious act; to make an
object purposely too small to be used in the
real world was perhaps to make it a suitable
gift for receipt by the supernatural powers.

□ Green 1975, 54–70; 1981b, 253–69; 1985,
238–41; 1986, 220–2; Pauli 1975, fig. 3; Kirk
1949, 32ff; Leech 1986, 259–328.

Modron In the Welsh *Tale of Culhwch and
Olwen*, Modron is alluded to as the mother
of MABON (the Divine Youth, or Divine Son),
who was taken away from his mother when
only three nights old. This allusion is interesting because of the indirect evidence it provides for descent through the female line:
only the mother of Mabon, not his father,
is mentioned. The name 'Modron' means
'Divine Mother', and she may be depicted
on a Romano-British stone at Ribchester in
North Britain, which is dedicated to MAPONUS
(Mabon), and which bears the figures of two
goddesses.

□ Ross 1967a, 215.

Mogons The name of this god means 'Great
One'; he was venerated in North Britain,
where he was especially popular in the area
of Hadrian's Wall. Mogons was invoked at
Netherby   (Cumbria)   and   Risingham
(Northd), Old Penrith and High Rochester.
Like VITIRIS, the name of the god was subject
to such variations as 'Mogunos', 'Mountus'

and 'Mogtus'. The god appears at High
Rochester as a multiple divinity, where an
altar was dedicated 'Dis Mountibus' – 'to the
gods Mountus/Mogons'. Interestingly, the
Netherby inscription is to Mogons Vitiris,
implying a confusion and conflation between
the two deities.

Mogons was not confined to Britain but is
known in Upper Germany and eastern Gaul:
a goddess, Moguntia, is recorded at Sablon
in Alsace, and APOLLO GRANNUS Mogounus
was invoked at Horburg. The various combi-
nations and associations of Mogons' name
suggests that the word is less a true name
than a title, which could be applied to a
number of different divine entities.
☐ Ross 1967a, 375; Jackson 1953; R.I.B., 971,
921, 922, 1225, 1226, 1269; C.I.L. XIII, 5315;
Bémont 1981, 65–88.

monster This term is used to describe the
hybrid, unnatural beings who occur in Celtic
iconography and in the vernacular literature.
A feature of Celtic perceptions of the supernatural was the lack of rigid boundaries
between human and animal forms, and the
deliberate departure from naturalistic representation. Thus, there were such sacred
images as the triple-horned bull (*see* BULL,
TRIPLE-HORNED), the ram-horned snake (*see*
SNAKE, RAM-HORNED), large-headed or three-
headed beings, horned gods and the semi-
human, the semi-serpent form of the giant of
the JUPITER-GIANT COLUMNS. Other monsters
occurring in the imagery include the 'Tarasque' of NOVES and the LINSDORF monster,
which are hybrid beasts of prey, devouring
human bodies in an allegory of the triumph
of death over life.

The vernacular mythology of Wales and
Ireland is full of monstrous, unnatural beings,
giants and hybrid forms. In the *Tale of
Culhwch and Olwen*, the father of Olwen is
a giant, named Ysbaddaden. In the Irish story
of Diarmaid and Gráinne, the fugitive lovers
come across a magic forest where a tree of
immortality is guarded by a giant, Sharvan
the Surly, who has long crooked tusks, a single
eye and who is virtually impossible to kill.
☐ Stead 1985a, 40–2; Green 1986, 135–6,
189–99; Jones & Jones 1976; O'Fáolain 1954.

moon Though the Celtic cults of sun and sky
are well-attested, there is, by contrast, little
evidence for the veneration of the moon. This
is curious, for it is the major nocturnal

The name of the Welsh goddess **Modron** means
Mother. This little Mother-goddess comes from
the Roman town of Caerwent, South Wales.

The 'Tarasque' of Noves, an Iron Age **monster**
from Provence, who is depicted devouring a
human limb, with his claws resting on human
heads, 3rd c. BC.

luminary and is visibly very prominent, in its changing form. Pliny (*Natural History* XVI, 95) alludes to a druidical rite concerned with bull sacrifice and MISTLETOE, which took place on the sixth day of the moon. He further states that the druids regarded the moon as a great healer. Caesar comments on Germanic religion, saying (*de Bello Gallico* V, 21) 'they count as gods ... sun, fire and moon'.

The Roman goddess DIANA was a moon-goddess, and because of its monthly cycle of waxing and waning, both Diana and the moon were associated with women, especially in childbirth. There is some evidence that this link between the moon and human fertility was maintained in the Celtic world: Rhineland Mother-goddesses appear in the iconography wearing lunar amulets; and a small clay figurine of a Mother-goddess with a dog at Cologne wears a moon pendant.

Moon symbolism was sometimes associated with that of the Celtic Sun-god: thus gold and silver solar pendants at, for instance, Dolaucothi (Dyfed) and Newstead in southern Scotland are found in company with lunar amulets. A 6th c. BC gold bowl at Zürich Altstetten is decorated with deer, suns and crescent moons (or alternatively with full and new moons). The little Romano-Celtic clay HORSE figurines at ASSCHE-KALKOVEN in Belgium, which wear moon-shaped pendants, may be associated with a solar cult: horses were constant companions of the Sun-god.
□ de Laet 1942, 41–54; Green 1981b, 253–69; 1989, 197, fig. 58.

Moritasgus *see* APOLLO MORITASGUS

Morrigán ('Phantom Queen') belongs to the group of Irish war-goddesses (*see* WAR-GOD). Others include Nemhain, the BADBH and Macha. They all share the characteristics of occurring in either single or triple form and in combining a sexual and a war role. These deities do not engage in battle themselves, but they affect armies psychologically, by means of their fearsome presence. To an extent, the different goddesses in the group are interchangeable. For example, both the Badbh and the Morrigán shape-change to RAVENS or CROWS in the field of battle.

The ability to metamorphose between different human forms and between human and animal form is common to several Irish goddesses (*see* METAMORPHOSIS): the traditions surrounding the Morrigán stress this aspect of her character: one story concerning Cú Chulainn exemplifies this characteristic. The Ulster hero encounters the Morrigán in the guise of a young and beautiful girl, and she professes her love for him. He spurns her, and in revenge she attacks him in the successive guises of an eel, a wolf and a hornless red heifer. Cú Chulainn overcomes her, and in his exhaustion, the Morrigán then appears to him as an old woman milking a cow. She gives him milk, he blesses her, and she is healed of the battle wounds inflicted on her by the hero. But it is in the form of a carrion bird, a raven or crow, that the Morrigán most frequently appears. In some traditions, it is her, not the Badbh, who alights on Cú Chulainn's shoulder at his death, thus signalling that it is safe to approach and behead him. It is in bird form that the Morrigán communicates with the Brown Bull of Cuailnge, warning him of his fate.

In addition to her war attributes, the Morrigán possesses powerful sexual and fertility symbolism. This is evident in her advances, as a young girl, towards Cú Chulainn. In another story, the Morrigán ritually mates with the father-god, the Daghda, astride a river with a foot on either bank. So here is the fertility-goddess mating with the tribal protector-god. The Morrigán's sexual/maternal role is additionally reflected in an Irish place-name, 'the paps of the Morrigán'. This combination of a war/sexual function is common to several of the Insular goddesses: it occurs in the character of the Macha, and the euhemerized queen/goddess Medb of Connacht also possesses this dual role.

A further aspect of the Morrigán's character concerns her role as a prophetess (*see* ORACLE). During the war between Connacht and Ulster, she warns the Brown Bull of Cuailnge of the fate which awaits him. After she mates with the Daghda, the Morrigán advises the god how to deal with the Fomorians, the enemies of the Tuatha Dé Danann. After the Tuatha Dé's victory, she then indulges in doom-filled prophecies. Like the Badbh, the Morrigán appears as the 'Washer at the Ford', the war-fury who foretells the deaths of warriors, washing their armour and weapons in a stream. The Daghda meets up with the Morrigán in this guise, on the Feast of Samhain, and this is the occasion of his ritual union with her.

Finally, the Morrigán is able to cast spells: she possesses a herd of magic cows and, as related in one legend, she enchants a mortal woman, Odras, turning her into a pool of water, because Odras' bull has mated with the Morrigán's cow. This punishment is perhaps because of the mixing of mortal and immortal, the earthly world with that of the supernatural.

☐ Hennessy 1870–2, 32–55; Olmsted 1982, 165–72; Kinsella 1969; Mac Cana 1983, 86, 92; Ross 1967a, 219, 244, 247; Stokes 1895, 65.

Mother-goddess The concept of the earth-mother, divine provider of FERTILITY and abundance, was dear to the Celts. The iconography and epigraphy of Romano-Celtic Europe attest the importance and popularity of the Mother-goddess cult in all echelons of society. Inscriptions frequently allude to the 'Deae Matres' or (especially in the Rhineland and Cisalpine Gaul) the 'Matronae'. The iconography supports these plural dedications, often depicting images of triple goddesses (*see* TRIPLISM). These Mothers are portrayed wearing long garments, sometimes with one breast bared, accompanied by various symbols of fertility: babies, older children, fruit, bread, corn or other motifs of plenty. Certain groups of images cluster in particular regions: thus, the Burgundian Mothers are often depicted with a baby, a napkin and bathing equipment, or with a child, napkin and a balance or spindle, thus displaying an affinity with the FATES. The 'Matronae' of the Rhineland are distinctive in that their iconography almost invariably shows a pattern of two mature goddesses wearing huge linen bonnets, flanking a younger girl with long flowing hair. In Britain, the triple Mothers cluster among the Gloucestershire Dobunni and in the area of Hadrian's Wall. The first group, perhaps with a cult centre at Cirencester (*see* CUDA), was venerated with images of the goddesses with babies, fruit or loaves; they are often portrayed in company with the Genii Cucullati (*see* GENIUS CUCULLATUS). Among the Santones of Aquitaine, a type of image consists of two Mothers, one older than the other.

Single images of Mothers are found all over the Celtic world. At Cirencester, a stone statue depicts a seated goddess with three apples in her lap, thus maintaining the imagery of triplism. At Caerwent, a stone Mother-goddess holds a palm branch or conifer, perhaps symbolic of victory or of fertility.

Figurine of a Mother-goddess, from a baby's grave at Arrington, Cambridgeshire. She wears a **moon** amulet at her neck.

Triple **Mother-goddess**, with baby, napkin and bathing equipment, from Vertault, Burgundy.

In the Rhineland, small figurines depict the goddess with a lap-dog. The 'DEA NUTRIX' or nursing-goddess is the name given to a particular group of clay figurines depicting a goddess seated in a chair, suckling one or two babies.

The context of the Celtic mothers is interesting: some of the Germanic Matronae – such as the MATRONAE VACALLINEHAE or the MATRONAE AUFANIAE – had large, important temple complexes. This prominence of the Rhineland Mothers is reflected by the sophistication of the cult, as demonstrated by the high quality of the carving and of the epigraphy and by the high and official status of some of the dedicants. Other images were the cult objects of humbler folk, belonging to small rural sanctuaries or domestic shrines. The Mothers were frequently venerated at curative spring shrines, as at Bath, where they were called the 'SULEVIAE', and at GLANUM, as the 'Glanicae'.

In the mythological traditions of Ireland, the Mother-goddess is again prominent. Here, the territorial goddess of sovereignty mates with the mortal king to promote the fertility of the land. The euhemerized goddess-queen MEDB is an example: she mated with nine successive Irish kings. The eponymous goddess of Ireland, ÉRIU, performed the same function (*see* SACRAL KINGSHIP). Triadism is associated with certain of the Irish female divinities, like MACHA and the MORRIGÁN, who combine the attributes of sexuality/maternity with war. *See also* COUPLE, DIVINE; DOG; IUNONES; MATRES COMEDOVAE; MATRES DOMESTICAE; MATRES GRISELICAE; NERTHUS; SIRONA; VAGDAVERCUSTIS.
□ Green 1986, 78–91; 1989, 24–39, 188–205; 1990b; Barnard 1985, 237–43; von Petrikovits 1987, 241–54; Haverfield 1892, 314–39.

mountain The animistic foundations of Celtic religion caused the existence of cults associated with such natural phenomena as rivers, springs and mountains. In the hilly regions of Gaul, a number of gods of high places were worshipped. VOSEGUS was the god of the Vosges mountains; Albiorix presided over the hills around Mount Ventoux in Vaucluse; and LATOBIUS belonged to Mount Koralpe in Austrian Carinthia. The great sanctuary of LE DONON was built in the high mountains of the Vosges and dedicated to the Celtic Mercury. In the Pyrenees a Celtic form of JUPITER was venerated: in small, remote mountain shrines, dedications to him were inscribed on small stone altars, which were decorated with the solar signs of the wheel and swastika. Other Pyrenean dedications were simply 'to mountain': this occurred, for instance, at Marignac. The Celtic Sky-god was particularly associated with mountains, because they reached high into his own element. JUPITER BRIXIANUS was associated with Brescia in North Italy; JUPITER LADICUS was the spirit of Mount Ladicus in northwest Spain; JUPITER POENINUS guarded the Alpine St Bernard Pass. These gods would have been linked with the weather and storms as well as the sky and mountains. Weather-deities of mountain summits are well-known outside the Celtic world, especially in the East: Dolichenus of Mount Doliche in Syria is an example; Hadad of Nabataea is another, similar, god.
□ Hatt 1964; Green 1986, 67–8; 1984, 257–60; Pascal 1964, 76–83; Toutain 1920, 143ff; de Vries 1963, 39; Alföldy 1974, 23; Leber 1967, 517–20.

Mšecké Žehrovice The Czechoslovakian site of Mšecké Žehrovice, not far from Prague, has produced a rare example of pre-Roman representational, religious art, in the form of a life-size ragstone head of a male deity, dating from the 3rd or 2nd c. BC. The head betrays classic Celtic stylization in the round staring eyes, striated hair, curling eyebrows and extravagant moustache. The neck is adorned with a torc with expanded terminals, and the head was broken off what may have been a complete male figure. The find-spot of the head may be significant: it was discovered in 1943 just outside the south-west corner of a VIERECKSCHANZE or ritual enclosure, in the vicinity of which were graves and pits containing animal sacrifices. *See also* LIBENICE.
□ Megaw 1970, 113, no. 171; Megaw & Megaw 1989, 124, fig. 178, pl. XVII.

Mullo *see* MARS MULLO

  N

Nabelcus *see* MARS NABELCUS

Nages was a Celtic *oppidum* near Nîmes in Provence. Here, there was a shrine, the lintel of which survives. Carved on the stone is a kind of frieze representing severed heads which alternate with images of galloping horses. In view of the abundant imagery from such nearby sites as ENTREMONT and ROQUEPERTUSE, the imagery of the lintel at Nages may reflect the predilection of the Celts of this area for HEAD-HUNTING. Classical writers allude to the Celtic practice of collecting the heads of slain enemies, hanging them from the saddles of their horses and offering them up in their shrines.

□ Green 1989, 111; Bémont 1984, no. 154.

Nantosuelta On a stone relief found near the Mithraeum at Sarrebourg, in the tribal region of the Mediomatrici, is a depiction of a divine couple (*see* COUPLE, DIVINE); they are named on an accompanying dedication 'Sucellus and Nantosuelta'. The god bears a pot and a long-shafted hammer; she has a *patera* from which she sacrifices onto an altar, and in her left hand a curious object in the form of a small house set on a long pole. Beneath the couple is the depiction of a raven. SUCELLUS' name means 'The Good Striker'; hers is generally interpreted as meaning 'Winding River' or 'Meandering Brook', a water name which would seem to group this goddess with the aquatic deities, though her imagery does not reflect such symbolism. An altar found with the first Sarrebourg stone which names Sucellus and Nantosuelta bears an image of the goddess alone, and it was dedicated by a Mediomatrician. Here, the goddess again has her house-on-pole in one hand whilst, in the other, she carries what could be the representation of a beehive on which a RAVEN perches. To her left are three objects piled on the ground which have been interpreted as honeycombs. Other depictions of a goddess carry essentially similar symbolism, making an identification with Nantosuelta likely: a lost portrayal at Speyer, in the territory of the Nemetes, also in eastern Gaul, represents a goddess with house-sceptre, fruit and a raven perched at her feet. At Teting in the land of the Treveri, a female divinity has a pot and house-symbol. Depictions of a goddess who may be Nantosuelta occur in the Luxembourg area, also in Treveran territory: here the imagery is that of a female deity seated in a house-like *aedicula* or miniature shrine, accompanied by a raven. On these images, the essential symbolism appears to be that of well-being, prosperity and abundance.

Stone head of a god, wearing a torc, from a *Viereckschanze* at **Mšecké Žehroviče**, Czechoslovakia, 3rd c. BC.

Lintel decorated alternately with galloping horses and severed human heads, from the pre-Roman Celtic *oppidum* of **Nages**, in Provence.

The house-shaped 'sceptre' and hive proclaim Nantosuelta as a homely spirit, guardian of hearth and house; the pot may be an emblem of regeneration, like the CAULDRON; but the raven, as a carrion bird, may introduce the more sombre element of death and the role of the goddess as protector of souls in the Otherworld.

On images in many other parts of Celtic Gaul and the Rhineland, a goddess accompanies a god who bears a long-shafted hammer as his principal attribute. It is possible, though by no means certain, that these partners are identifiable with the Sucellus and Nantosuelta named on the Sarrebourg stone. Such divine couples were common, particularly in Burgundy, in the tribal lands of the Aedui and Lingones. Here, the deities are associated with WINE and the grape harvest, and are frequently represented with large wine jars or barrels. Once again, the goddess' personal emblems of *cornucopia* and *patera* indicate her role as a divinity of nourishment, fertility and plenty.

Only one possible British depiction of Nantosuelta is recorded: a small stone from East Stoke (Notts) in the territory of the Corieltauvi, represents a couple. The elderly man holds his long-shafted hammer; the goddess is portrayed with bushy hair, a heavy Celtic torc or neckring and wearing a flounced skirt. She holds a bowl of apples in front of her, as if reflective of the bounty of the land. □ Espérandieu, nos 4566, 4568, 6000; C.I.L. XIII, 4542, 4543; Green 1989, 27, 42–3, 49, figs 18, 19; Wilhelm 1974; Linckenheld 1929, 40–92; Toynbee 1964, 176.

Naoise is one of the three sons of Uisnech. He appears in the Ulster Cycle as a man doomed to die because of his entanglement with the powerful DEIRDRE.

Before Deirdre is born, the druid Cathbadh foretells that she will be extremely beautiful but that she will cause ruin to the Ulstermen. King Conchobar fosters her and keeps her beauty hidden from the world, since he wishes to marry her himself. On one occasion, Deirdre sees Conchobar skinning a calf and a raven drinking its blood in the snow. She vows that the man she will love will possess that same combination of colours, black hair, white skin and red cheeks. Deirdre's companion comments that Naoise looks like this. Deirdre escapes from Conchobar's fosterage and makes advances to Naoise. Mindful of Cathbadh's prophecy, Naoise at first resists her, but she then challenges his honour and he elopes with her. Naoise's two brothers, Ainle and Ardan, go with them, and they flee first into southern Ireland and then to Scotland, where they offer service to the king. But the Scottish king desires Deirdre, so the fugitives prepare to flee once again. King Conchobar tracks them down and treacherously sends pardon to the sons of Uisnech, bidding them to return to Ulster and sending envoys and friends to persuade them to come home. Deirdre dreams of treachery and warns Naoise and his brothers. But they make the journey to Emhain Macha, their friend FERGHUS acting as a pledge of safe conduct. However, as they approach Emhain Macha, Ferghus is separated from the brothers by trickery. Conchobar lures Naoise and the brothers to lay down their arms, and they are killed all together by a single blow of a sword wielded by Eoghan, son of Duracht.

There are a number of significant points about this story: firstly, Naoise's two brothers have no separate identity or personality; they are ciphers and are present solely in order to add a triadic dimension to the character of Naoise himself. Secondly, Deirdre is an example of a powerful Irish heroine, having a much stronger personality than Naoise and being so beautiful that no man can resist her, even if his honour is at stake. The story belongs to a well-attested mythological theme, where a semi-divine heroine unites with one of a closely knit trio of brothers. □ O'Fáolain 1954; Cormier 1976–8, 303–15; Rolleston 1985, 201.

Nature, god of see HUNTER-GOD; SILVANUS; CERNUNNOS

Nechtan The *Dinnshenchas*, the *History of Places* which was compiled in the 12th c., contains a great deal of Irish topographical lore, some of which may relate to a much earlier period. Nechtan appears here as the husband of BOANN, the personification of the River BOYNE. Nechtan was an early water-deity who possessed a sacred well, the source of knowledge; only he and his three cup bearers were allowed near this well. But Boann disobeyed the taboo and visited the well of Nechtan: the waters rose in anger, flowed out in a great stream, chasing and engulfing Boann, and thus the River Boyne was created.

□ Stokes 1894, 315–16; Ross 1967a, 21; Mac Cana 1983, 32; Berresford Ellis 1987, 178; Gwynn 1913, 28ff.

Nehalennia was a Celtic goddess who was venerated at two shrines on the North Sea coast of the Netherlands, in the tribal area of the Morini. One sanctuary was on the Island of Walcheren at DOMBURG, the other on the estuary of the East Scheldt River, at COLIJNSPLAAT: both were drowned in antiquity by encroachment of the North Sea.

The sanctuaries were wealthy, patronized by prosperous dedicants, and many altars survive which give valuable information about the deity and her cult. Nehalennia was primarily a goddess of seafarers, devotees who prayed to her for safe passage across the sea and for success in business transactions (*see* SEA-GOD). Some of her suppliants were Roman citizens, many were Celts, and the names of some proclaim their Germanic origin. The dedications frequently record the professions of these worshippers – sea-captains, traders in wine, salt, fish sauce (*garum*) and pottery.

Nehalennia's name may mean 'Leader' or 'Steerswoman', and her iconography frequently echoes marine symbolism: sometimes the goddess appears standing on a ship's prow, with a steering oar or a boat rope. The goddess is sometimes associated with the imagery of sea creatures (*see* DOLPHIN) or the Roman water-god NEPTUNE.

The other two main features of Nehalennia's symbolism are FERTILITY and the imagery of the DOG. The deity herself is depicted as a youthful woman, often shown wearing distinctive clothes with a short shoulder-cape and a small round cap which may be local costume. She is frequently portrayed sitting in a chair, sometimes beneath a shell-shaped canopy, surrounded by her special symbols, a fruit basket on her lap, another near her on the ground and nearly always a large benign-looking hound-like dog at her side. *Cornucopiae* and trees (*see* TREE) frequently decorate the side surfaces of her altars, and the top surfaces of the stones often bear carvings of fruit, heaped up as though in imitation of an offering table.

Nehalennia is distinct from many Celtic female divinities in that she is accompanied by a dog on the vast majority of her images. The very close affinity between goddess and animal is demonstrated by the fact that the

The goddess **Nantosuelta**, with her house-sceptre, accompanied by Sucellus, from Sarrebourg near Metz, France.

The marine goddess **Nehalennia**, with her dog and fruit basket, from a sanctuary on the North Sea coast of Holland.

creature is often depicted gazing up at Nehalennia, and on an altar from Domburg, the animal sits so close that its nose touches her knee. The dog is large but clearly benevolent: this may indicate that in this context, it represents the dog's role as protector and peaceful guardian of both the goddess herself and her human suppliants. Some scholars see the creature as possessing an underworld symbolism, but if so, then it bears no relationship to Cerberus, the savage canine guardian of the Classical Hades. But Nehalennia's cult may have possessed many facets: her water imagery, overtly associated with the North Sea, may in addition reflect healing and regeneration, and the goddess may well have been concerned with the welfare of her devotees after death as well as in this life.

Nehalennia's cult is distinctive in its wealth and popularity, in the variety and yet homogeneity of the iconography and in the amount of information we are given about the dedicants themselves. In addition to her marine symbolism, the recurrence of vegetation motifs places Nehalennia within the large group of goddesses whose concerns were the florescence and abundance of earth and the prosperity of humans. The symbolism of the dog may serve as a link between all the different aspects of Nehalennia's role: it may have combined elements of guardianship with healing and rebirth after death. Nehalennia seems to have presided over a cult which was both powerful and multifaceted, with varying but related concerns.
□ Green 1989, 10–16; Hondius-Crone 1955; van Aartsen 1971.

Nemausus was the ancient name for the town of Nîmes in Provence: here, there was an important healing spring sanctuary which was dedicated to the personified spirit of the place, also named Nemausus, a Celto-Ligurian name (the Ligurians were a group of tribes living in the extreme south of Gaul and who were pre-Celtic). The shrine to Nemausus was established in some form at least as early as the Iron Age but was expanded and monumentalized after the Romans colonized the region in the late 2nd c. BC, when there was active Roman encouragement of the Celtic cult of Nemausus. Nîmes was extensively upgraded as a town in the Augustan period (30 BC – AD 14), and it may have been that pilgrims from a wide area were attracted to the spa waters and Nemausus' curative sanctuary.

Another set of local spirits worshipped at Nîmes were the Nemausicae, or Matres Nemausicae, who were female fertility and healing deities belonging to the spa sanctuary. There seems to have been a tradition in Provence of the worship of a single male spirit and multiple *numina* who share the same name. Thus at GLANUM, Glanis and the Glanicae were venerated.
□ Rivet 1988, 162; Clébert 1970, 253.

Nemetona As the name of this divinity suggests, she was a Celtic goddess of the sacred GROVE or 'nemeton'. Nemetona was venerated above all among the Celto-Germanic tribe of the Nemetes, the name of which shares the same root, and this may indicate her tribal status within the region.

Nemetona occurs in dedications on her own, for example at Klein-Winternheim near Mainz, where she is invoked on a bronze tablet by a member of the Roman imperial aristocracy. But the goddess is more usually paired with a Celtic version of the Roman Mars (*see* MARS RIGONEMETIS): she appears thus on a dedication at Altripp near Speyer in Germany; and Mars and Nemetona were propitiated also on an inscription at Grosskrotzenburg near Hanau. At Bath, a dedication set up by a citizen of Trier couples Nemetona with MARS LOUCETIUS. This god, a divinity of light, appears, for instance, in Gallia Lugdunensis. The Bath inscription reads 'Peregrinus son of Secundus, a Treveran, to Loucetius Mars and Nemetona willingly and deservedly fulfilled his vow'.

It is possible that Nemetona may herself originally have possessed a martial function, in that her name could be associated with that of NEMHAIN, a goddess of battle-frenzy who appears in Irish mythology.
□ de Vries 1963, 68; Cunliffe & Davenport 1985, 130; R.I.B., 140; C.I.L. XIII, 6131, 7412.

Nemhain The Celtic pantheon in Ireland contained a number of war-goddesses, all of whom were to a degree interchangeable with each other (*see* WAR-GOD). Three important ones were Nemhain, Macha and the Morrigán, though the Morrigán herself was sometimes three and so was Macha. These deities were like Furies: they harried armies and wreaked terror by their presence, though

they took no active part in battles. Nemhain's name means 'Frenzy', and it was her function to spread panic among warriors. In the war between Connacht and Ulster, Nemhain and her sister-goddesses stirred up fear among the Connacht men: at the last battle, she raised a howl of such horror over the armies of Ireland facing Cú Chulainn and his Ulstermen that a hundred Connacht soldiers fell dead from sheer fright.
☐ Kinsella 1969; Hennessy 1870–2, 32–55; Mac Cana 1983, 86.

Neptune The Roman water-god does not appear to have been generally adopted into the Celtic pantheon. But there is a small amount of evidence for some association between this deity and the indigenous cults of western Europe. There was a link between the imagery of the goddess of the North Sea, NEHALENNIA, in the Netherlands and that of Neptune. In Britain, a fragmentary inscription from Chesterholm in the area of Hadrian's Wall is variously interpreted as a dedication to Neptune alone or to Nodens Neptune. If the latter is correct, then Neptune is here equated with the Dobunnic god NODENS, who had a major sanctuary at Lydney on the Severn. Finally, the great temple pediment at the shrine of Sulis Minerva at Bath shows the face of a being who may be interpreted as a male Medusa, but whose waving hair and beard closely resemble the locks of a water-god, perhaps Neptune or a native equivalent.
☐ Hondius-Crone 1955; van Aartsen 1971; R.I.B., 1694; Ross 1967a, 178; Cunliffe & Fulford 1982, pl. 10.

Nerthus is a Germanic earth-goddess who is mentioned by the Roman historian Tacitus (*Germania*, 40) as riding in procession through her cities on a wagon. She thus has links both with the early Irish queen-goddess MEDB of Connacht, recorded in the Ulster Cycle, who drives round the battlefield in a chariot, and with certain Romano-Celtic representations of MOTHER-GODDESSES. A Burgundian sculptured group at Essey depicts two mothers seated together in a *biga* (a two-horse chariot). Tacitus' description of Nerthus also brings to mind the 7th c. BC cult wagon at STRETTWEG in Austria, where a goddess is carried on a wagon, surrounded by soldiers and animals. It is probable that images of Nerthus were borne on a cart around her

Part of the great sanctuary to the spring-god **Nemausus** at Nîmes.

A druid in his sacred grove at Stonehenge. **Nemetona** was the goddess of groves. From a drawing in the 18th c. *Antiquities of England and Wales* by Francis Grose.

The male Medusa from the temple pediment at Bath. He represents a Celtic version of **Neptune**, with his long flowing hair and his association with an important water shrine.

lands in order that the fields might be blessed and fruitful.

☐ Espérandieu, no. 2325.

Neuvy-en-Sullias On the left bank of the Loire, opposite the Celtic sanctuary of Fleury (Floriacum), a late Iron Age cache of bronze figurines was discovered, which were perhaps buried at the time of the Roman conquest of Gaul. These bronzes include males and females in the act of a sacred dance, and some superb statuettes of animals, three boars which are almost life-size, a horse and a stag. The horse bears an inscription 'sacred to the god RUDIOBUS'; the stag has antlers in velvet, indicative of seasonal spring imagery.

☐ Pobé & Roubier 1961, no. 54, pls 47–50; Megaw 1970, no. 238; Espérandieu, nos 2978, 2984; Green 1989, figs 55, 59, 63.

Niall *see* EMHAIN MACHA; MEBD

Nîmes *see* NEMAUSUS

Nodens A great healing sanctuary at Lydney Park in Gloucestershire, probably built during the 3rd c. AD, was dedicated to a British god named Nodens. His name is etymologically related to 'Nuadu Argat-lam', the Irish 'NUADU of the Silver Hand', who is one of the king-gods of the Tuatha Dé Danann. The name Nodens is sometimes interpreted as 'wealthy one' or 'cloud-maker'.

At LYDNEY, inscriptions alluding to Nodens are either dedications to him alone or equated with Mars or Silvanus; and Nodens may have had another shrine in the north of Britain, since the bases of two statuettes found near Lancaster are also dedicated to Mars Nodens.

That Nodens was a healing god is indicated not only by the Lydney temple itself, which contained a probable *abaton* or dormitory for the healing sleep, but also votive objects suggesting the presence of sick pilgrims (*see* LIMB/ORGAN, VOTIVE). A votive bronze arm shows evidence of disease, and oculists' stamps attest the presence of eye problems. In addition, there is an 'anatomically explicit' bone plaque of a woman from the site. One interesting feature of Nodens' sanctuary is that whilst no human representation of the god is present, there are no less than nine images of dogs; these include a handsome bronze deer-hound. It may be that the DOG symbolism comes from the reputed therapeutic properties in the lick of the creature.

The equation of Nodens with Mars and Silvanus deserves examination: the Celtic MARS possessed, above all, a protective or guardianship role, and he was frequently associated with healing cults in Continental Europe. Thus, it is no surprise to find the god linked to a great British healing cult at Lydney, as a combattant against ill health. The association with the Roman woodland god SILVANUS is more curious, but there does seem to have been a religious relationship between hunting and regeneration: the god Apollo was both hunter and healer. In any case, Silvanus was a deity of the flourishing forest, and thus would have embodied fertility and florescence – both appropriate to a curative cult. *See also* NEPTUNE.

☐ Wheeler & Wheeler 1932; Carey 1984, 1–22; R.I.B., 305–8, 616, 617; Henig 1984, 51–6; Green 1986, fig. 72.

Noves A curious Provençal sculpture from Noves (Bouches-du-Rhône) is the so-called 'Tarasque' of Noves. It consists of a ravening MONSTER, a lion or wolf, with a dismembered human limb hanging from its mouth. Its huge front paws, claws extended, rest heavily on two bearded severed human heads. Heads are often depicted in the pre-Roman religious art of this region (*see* ENTREMONT, ROQUEPERTUSE); and the imagery on the Noves carving may reflect the symbolism of the triumph of death over life. The image probably dates from the 4th–3rd c. BC and represents a subject almost identical to that of the LINSDORF monster from Alsace. These images owe much to Roman funerary art, where lions and other creatures devour human bodies, in an allegory of death's destructive powers. The term 'Tarasque' comes from a Provençal legend in which a monster periodically clambered out of the Rhône at Tarascon and devoured the inhabitants of the settlement. St Martha came from Les-Saintes-Maries-de-la-Mer and vanquished the beast with the sign of the cross, thereby saving the town.

☐ Megaw & Megaw 1989, 170; Bémont 1984, no. 162.

Nuadu was a king of the Irish race of gods, the Tuatha Dé Danann. In the First Battle of Magh Tuiredh, between the Tuatha Dé and the Fir Bholg, Nuadu loses his arm and thus has to relinquish the kingship, because he no longer meets the criterion of physical perfection which was a rule of sovereignty.

The divine smith/leech DIAN CÉCHT makes Nuadu an artificial arm of silver and thus makes it possible for him to resume his power. Henceforth, he is known as 'Nuadu argat lámh' (Nuadu of the Silver Hand). But during the subsequent wars with the Fomorians, Nuadu is daunted by the terrible power of the Fomorian leader BALOR of the Baleful Eye, and he again gives up his kingship to the hero LUGH. Lugh takes over the organization of the war and overcomes Balor himself.

Nuadu has various counterparts: in British archaeology, he may be identified with NODENS, the god of Lydney on the River Severn. Both names may mean 'cloud-maker'. In Welsh mythology, Nuadu may be identical with Nudd or Lludd, who was probably a sun-god. The loss of his arm gives Nuadu a resemblance to the Germanic Tyr whose right arm was bitten off by a wolf. After the Tuatha Dé Danann are driven underground by the next invaders of Ireland, the Milesians, Nuadu has a SÍDH or Otherworld mound called Almu, which is wrested from him by Finn. *See also* BRES.

□ Carey 1984, 1–22; Krappe 1932, 90–5; Le Roux 1963, 425–54; O'Rahilly 1946, 279; Rolleston 1985, 107–8, 346–7; Rhŷs 1901, 447; Mac Cana 1983, 58, 66; Macalister 1931; O'Fáolain 1954.

Dancer and stag, part of the hoard of bronze figurines from the 1st c. BC shrine near **Neuvy-en-Sullias**, Loiret, France.

number was an important religious concept. By far the most symbolic number was 'three': supernatural entities in the vernacular mythological tradition constantly occur in triplicate (*see* TRIPLISM); and in Celtic iconography, both male and female divinities appear as triads (*see esp.* MOTHER-GODDESS; GENIUS CUCULLATUS).

In the literary tradition of early Wales and Ireland, odd numbers generally were significant. Three and multiples of three – such as nine and twenty-seven – stand out. Five and seven also occur as symbolic numbers: five was associated with totality or wholeness – the four cardinal points plus the centre. But the number three appears to have possessed especial sanctity. Not only were whole images triplicated but certain gods may have three heads (*see* HEAD, TRIPLE; MERCURY TRIPLE-FACED) or three phalli (*see* MERCURY, TRIPLE-PHALLUSED); and the Celtic bull was frequently depicted triple-horned (*see* BULL, TRIPLE-HORNED). *See also* CÚ CHULAINN.

□ Rees & Rees 1961, 186–204; Green 1989, 169–205; 1990b.

The sanctity of **number** is reflected in this pot from Bavay, Nord, with its triple head.

oak There is a consistent thread of evidence for the sanctity of oak trees. Pliny (*Natural History* XVI, 95) makes mention of a festival on the sixth day of the moon, when the druids climbed a sacred oak, cut down a branch of mistletoe and sacrificed two white bulls, in a fertility rite. Indeed, the word 'druid' is sometimes perceived as deriving from the 'dru' root meaning 'oak'. Strabo (XII, 5, 1) speaks of the meeting of the three Galatian tribes (groups of Celts living in Asia Minor) at 'DRUNEMETON', the 'oak grove sanctuary', for the purposes of discussion on government matters. Maximus of Tyre, writing in the 2nd c. AD, comments that the Celts worshipped Zeus in the images of high oak trees (*Logoi* VIII, 8).

Oaks were the Classical dendromorphic attributes of the sky-god Jupiter, perhaps because of their size, majestic appearance and longevity. The Celtic Jupiter retained this association with oaks: at Séguret in Provence, a depiction of the Celtic Sun-god (equated with Jupiter) was accompanied by an oak tree.

Some of the Celtic JUPITER-GIANT COLUMNS demonstrate that they are representative of oak trees: the PILLAR at Hausen-an-der-Zaber near Stuttgart is decorated with oak leaves and acorns. Apart from the link with solar-sky cults, there is some archaeological evidence for the deliberate choice of oak for use in making images. The great majority of the wooden votives from the great spring sanctuary at *Fontes Sequanae* were made of oak heartwood: this was not strictly necessary, in practical terms, since there were plenty of other suitable trees available on the Châtillon Plateau.

Finally, the oak retained some significance in the mythology of Wales: an example of this is the mythical tale of Lleu Llaw Gyffes, which appears in the *Fourth Branch of the Mabinogi*. When Lleu receives a mortal spear blow from his wife's lover Gronw, he shrieks, is transformed into an eagle and alights in a magic oak tree. *See also* EMHAIN MACHA; TREE.

□ Bauchhenss 1976; Green 1984a, 179–81; 1986, 63; Espérandieu, no. 303; Deyts 1983; 1985; Ross 1967a, 274; Jones & Jones 1976.

Ocelus Three inscriptions from Roman Britain allude to the god Ocelus. He is twice invoked on dedications at Caerwent: one stone is the base of a statue of which only a pair of 'human' feet and a pair of goose feet survive. The invocation is to MARS LENUS or Ocelus Vellaunus and the '*numen*' (spirit) of the emperor, and it was dedicated on 23 August AD 152. The second Caerwent inscription dedicates an altar to Mars Ocelus. The god was venerated again at Carlisle, where he was once more equated with Mars and again linked to the Imperial cult. So Ocelus seems to have been a British, perhaps Silurian god, associated with the Roman Mars, probably in the latter's Celtic capacity as a protector. At Caerwent, he is linked with Lenus, a Treveran healing deity and with VELLAUNUS, who is recorded among the Gaulish Allobroges.

Oenghus of the Birds was an Irish god of love and a member of the Tuatha Dé Danann. In the early literature, he is presented as one who is himself in love, and he also helps other lovers in adversity. Oenghus was known as 'mac Óc', 'the Young Son', and this may be because of circumstances surrounding his birth. He was the product of an illicit union between the Dagdha and BOANN, who concealed Boann's pregnancy by causing the sun to stand still for nine months, so that Oenghus was conceived and born on the same day.

Three main stories surround the character of Oenghus: in two, he is presented as a helper of lovers. In the story of Midhir and ÉTAIN, Oenghus woos Étain on Midhir's behalf. Later, Oenghus is able partially to remove the butterfly spell cast on Étain by Midhir's jealous wife Fuamnach. She is thus restored to human form from dusk to dawn and is cherished in Oenghus' palace on the River Boyne. In the story of DIARMAID and GRÁINNE, Oenghus intervenes to help Gráinne and Diarmaid against Finn, who desires Gráinne. Oenghus is Diarmaid's fosterfather, and on one occasion, he takes on Diarmaid's form to lure away Finn's companions who are hunting him. Oenghus also spirits Gráinne away to safety on two occasions where her discovery is threatened by Finn.

In the *Dream of Oenghus*, it is the god of love himself who is smitten by passion. He dreams of a young girl whom he does not recognize, and falls desperately in love with her. He learns that the girl's name is Caer

Ibormeith ('Yew Berry'), and he finds her
with her companions on a lake. He also learns
that Caer is a shape-changer, and every other
year she transmogrifies from human form to
that of a SWAN. King Ailill of Connacht
intercedes with Caer's father Ethal Anbual
of Sídh Uamain on behalf of Oenghus, but to
no avail. The only way to win Caer is to take
her when she is in swan form. The shape-
change occurs on the Feast of Samhain on
1 November, and it is now that Oenghus
approaches Caer and flies off with her, having
transformed himself also into swan form. The
two fly three times round the lake, sending
everyone to sleep for three days and nights
by their magic song, and they then fly off to
Brugh na Bóinne, Oenghus' palace.

Oenghus is the archetypal 'young man' or
'divine youth'. As such, he may be identified
with the British MAPONUS and the Welsh
MABON.

□ O'Fáolain 1954; Nutt 1906, 325–39; Müller
1876–8, 342–60; Le Roux 1966, 132–50;
Guyonvarc'h 1966b, 117–31; Lambert 1979,
141–69; Bergin & Best 1938, 137–96; Ross
1967a, 237.

Drawing of a sacred **oak**, from Mary Roberts'
Ruins and Old Trees, 1880.

Ogmios We know of the god Ogmios from
the writings of Lucian of Samosata, a Greek
author who wrote during the 2nd c. AD.
Ogmios was apparently equated with the
Classical demo-god hero HERCULES. Lucian
describes a picture of Ogmios which he saw
in Gaul, when residing in Gallia Narbonensis,
perhaps around Marseille: he was depicted
with bow and the club normally associated
with Hercules, but instead of the powerful
god of Graeco-Roman mythology, Ogmios-
Hercules was portrayed as an old man, bald
and burnt by the sun. Curiously, the god in
Lucian's picture drew behind him a happy
band of men who were attached to him by
thin gold chains linking their ears to the tip
of his tongue. Lucian was informed by a
Gaulish acquaintance that the Celts associated eloquence with Hercules, because of
his strength. Apart from Lucian's testimony,
Ogmios is invoked on two lead *defixiones* or
curse tablets from Bregenz on Lake Const-
ance; on one of these, Ogmios is requested
to intervene and lay a curse on a barren
woman so that she would never marry.

Two features, apart from the name, may
identify the Romano-Celtic Ogmios with the
Irish god mentioned in the early literature,
known as Oghma. Not only was Oghma

Altar from Caerwent, South Wales, dedicated to
Mars **Ocelus**.

described as a 'strong man', like Hercules, but he was credited also with the invention of ogham, a system of writing which consisted of horizontal or slanting strokes and notches cut on stone or wood and branching out on either side of a vertical line or corner.
□ Mac Cana 1983, 35–6; Thevenot 1968, 123–4.

Oisin In the early Irish Fionn Cycle, Oisin is the son of the war leader, FINN. Oisin's mother is Sava, who first came to Finn's territory in the form of a fawn, having been enchanted by the Black Druid. Finn finds Oisin abandoned in the wilderness, when Sava is reclaimed by the druid. Oisin is brought up among the Fianna (Finn's war band) and becomes one of its bravest champions.

The most famous tale of Oisin concerns his sojourn in the Land of the Ever Young. He was bewitched by Niav of the Golden Hair, daughter of the king of TIR NA NOG, the Land of the Ever Young, and he marries her. But he often feels a yearning for his old life, and against Niav's will, he travels back to his land, only to find that 300 years have passed. Niav has warned Oisin that if he wishes to return to her, he must not set foot on his own land. By accident, Oisin falls from his horse and instantly dies as a withered old man of 300 years. *See also* STAG.
□ O'Fáolain 1954; Mac Cana 1983, 104.

Olloudius Locations as far apart as Custom Scrubs in Gloucestershire and Ollioules in southern Gaul attest the veneration of a god named Olloudius. The only image that exists depicts a male figure from the Cotswold site, rendered in native style, with a small head and a large, elongated body, carrying a *patera* or offering plate and a double *cornucopia*. The image is dedicated to 'Mars Olloudius', but the god carries no military attributes; and he wears a cap and cloak rather than armour. Mars Olloudius belongs to the important group of Celtic gods who adopted the name of MARS but who were peaceful protectors, healers and fertility spirits. The double horn of plenty stresses the prosperity function of Olloudius among the Dobunni of Gloucestershire. Custom Scrubs produced another image, quite clearly the work of the same craftsman, and on this second depiction, Mars is represented with shield, spear and sword, but again the *cornucopia* is present,

this time indicating the hybrid nature of the Celtic Mars: in this peaceful region, the warrior is not combative in the true sense but instead plays the role of guardian against disease, barrenness and other evils.
□ Clébert 1970, 252; Green 1986, fig. 14; Ross 1967a, 172.

oracle A feature of Celtic (as of Greek and Roman) religion was the desire to know the future and to judge the best time and method for certain activities. APOLLO brought his oracular powers to Gaul and Britain, and his association with healing springs may not only be curative, but also have taken place because the bubbling 'voice' of the spring was perceived as the speech of the oracle. At the great Celtic healing sanctuaries, professional interpreters of dreams were probably employed, to explain the visions of the sleeping pilgrims and to ascertain whether the god had visited and would cure them.

The Celtic druids and filidh (seers) were concerned with prognostication (*see* DRUID; FILI): they took the omens by means of DIVINATION, augury and other studies. Irish druids foretold events: CATHBADH could tell if a day were lucky for a boy to take up arms, and the youthful hero Cú Chulainn took advantage of this; Cathbadh also foretold the disaster to Ulster which the rearing of Deirdre would bring. The late Roman writer Vopiscus (*Aurelianus* XLIII 4, 5) alludes to the consultation of Gaulish druidesses by the Emperor Aurelian, who wished to know if his descendants would retain the Imperial throne.

Various Insular deities were particularly associated with oracular powers: one was BRIGIT, beloved of the filidh for her prognosticatory abilities; another was the raven battle-goddess, the MORRIGÁN, who advised the Daghda on the outcome of battles before they took place. Interestingly, ravens were closely bound up with prophecy, perhaps because of their distinctive 'voices'. Doves, too, with their rather human call, were traditionally associated with oracles. This may be why images of doves occur at Gaulish Apolline sanctuaries, like those at Beire-le-Châtel and Alesia in Burgundy. *See also* DOVE; RAVEN.
□ Ross 1986, 116, 121; Henig 1984, 154; Green 1989, 143.

Otherworld All types of evidence – that of the Classical writers, the vernacular mytho-

logy and archaeology – point to a strong Celtic
belief in an afterlife. The Gaulish druids
taught that the soul was immortal, and there
existed the concept of the TRANSMIGRATION
OF SOULS. The presence of Iron Age graves
filled with food, drink and other equipment
attests to the belief that the deceased would
have need of possessions in the next world.

The vernacular tradition of Wales and
Ireland fleshes out the Celtic perception of
the Otherworld. In Wales, it was called
ANNWN; in Ireland, there was a series of
'sídhe' (see SÍDH). This Otherworld was a
fluid, ambiguous place, which cut across spa-
tial boundaries: thus, it was perceived as
being located on an island or a group of
islands in the western sea, as in the *Voyage
of Bran*, beneath the ocean or under mounds.
The Irish sídhe were the dwelling places of
the divine Tuatha Dé Danann and were
beneath Ireland itself. Another Irish perception of the Otherworld was the hostel or
'bruidhen'. There are common characteristics
for the Otherworld: it is essentially a happy
place, the source of all wisdom, where there
is peace, harmony, but also fighting amongst
heroes. There is perpetual feasting, sport,
beautiful women, enchanted music; it is age-
less and without disease, in fact a magical,
idealized mirror image of the human world.
Each sídh or bruidhen had its own feast and
its inexhaustible CAULDRON, presided over
by a god: the smith-god GOIBHNIU is an
example. Pigs are killed, eaten and reborn
the next day, and the ruler of the Otherworld
feast is portrayed as a man with a pig slung
over his shoulder (*see* BOAR). The lords of the
sídhe were controllers of magic.

The literature is full of allusions to the
enticement of heroes to the Otherworld by
supernatural beings, who may appear in the
form of men, women or animals. A lady from
the sídh of Donn mac Midir is sent in the
shape of a fawn, to lure Finn to his domain.
Sometimes, as in the case of PWYLL and CÚ
CHULAINN, a mortal is asked by the ruler of
the Otherworld to fight battles on his behalf.
The idea here may be that a red-blooded
mortal hero is required to fight effectively in
the land of ghosts.

The Otherworld is a timeless land: if
humans sojourn there before death, they
remain young whilst there but age instantly
when they return. This happens to one of
BRAN's men in the *Voyage of Bran*, and
to Finn's son OISIN, when he leaves his

Stone images of Mars **Olloudius** and another
local Mars, from Custom Scrubs, Gloucestershire.

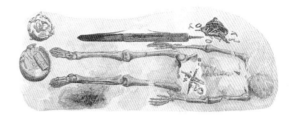

The grave of an early Iron Age warrior at
Selzen, Germany. He was buried with his
possessions, for his use in the **Otherworld**.

A 6th c. BC gold cup from a grave at Cannstatt,
Germany. The vessel would have held food or
wine for the **Otherworld** feast.

supernatural lover, Niav. This Otherworld can be reached by various means: Bran travels there by boat across the sea, but the entry can also be by means of a cave or lake. A famous gateway to the Otherworld was the Cave of Cruachain. It is at the feast of SAMHAIN on 1 November that the boundary between the earthly and the supernatural worlds is broken down; spirits and humans can move freely between the two lands, and the Otherworld dwellers can interfere in human affairs.

There is a dark as well as a happy aspect to the Otherworld. As a land of the dead, it can be a sombre place, and DONN, the Irish lord of the dead, is a stark character. Annwn is a 'Court of Intoxication', but it is also the setting for a catastrophic expedition by Arthur, who barely escapes with his life after going to Annwn to obtain the magic cauldron of plenty. The idea seems to be that if mortals go to the Otherworld of their own free will, they may encounter its dark side. Thus, Cú Chulainn describes his visit to the Otherworld, with its monsters, severed heads and other horrors. This sombre aspect is displayed, too, for instance, in the story of DA DERGA's Hostel, whither King Conaire travels, according to his destiny. The hostel is, in fact, the land of the dead; on his way there, Conaire encounters such harbingers of doom as the three red horsemen, messengers from the underworld. *See also* CLIODNA; DEATH; FEAST; MIDHIR; PIT; REBIRTH; TIR NA NOG.

□ Jackson 1961–7, 83–99; Mac Cana 1972, 102–42; 1975, 33–52; 1976, 95–115; 1983, 122–31; O'Rahilly, 1946, 106–22, 127, 318; Sims-Williams 1990, 57–81; Dyer 1990, 157–9.

ox *see* BULL

 P

Parthinus *see* JUPITER PARTHINUS

Partholón appears in the *Book of Invasions*, as the mythical leader of the first colonization of Ireland after the Flood. The story is that Partholón comes from Greece accompanied by three sons, four women and a large retinue. He also has three druids, Tath, Fiss and Fochmarc. Like all the early invaders of Ireland, Partholón had to do battle with the demonic race of Fomorians: their leader at this time was one Cicul.

Partholón is credited with bringing civilization to Ireland: he divided the country into four parts, introduced law, crafts, ale brewing and hospitality. He and his followers were finally wiped out by a plague. Partholón was probably originally a euhemerized god or demon: no races claimed descent from him. He survives in modern Irish folk-lore as a fertility demon.

□ Mac Cana 1983, 54; van Hamel 1933, 217–37; Even 1956, 81–110.

Paspardo CAMONICA VALLEY in North Italy is noteworthy for its religious rock art, which dates from the late Neolithic to the end of the Iron Age. One site within the Camonica Valley is Paspardo, where complicated symbolism, involving images of sun and STAG, is exhibited.

The Camunians' religion as a whole was greatly concerned with the veneration of both the sun and the stag, but at Paspardo the two symbols are conflated and a combination of antlers and solar rays forms a single composite image. The carvings here also include the figure of a man with a dagger and antlers, perhaps the stag-horned Celtic god CERNUNNOS; and a rock carved with five daggers, a stag and a stylized torc. All these images probably date from Camonica Period III, the proto-Celtic later Bronze Age phase of Camunian rock art.

□ Anati 1965, 100, 164–7, 213; Green 1991a.

peacock This BIRD, with its superb tail symbolizing the orb of the sky, was the attribute of the Roman goddess Juno, consort of the sky-god Jupiter. Images of peacocks were adopted by Celtic craftsmen to reflect the celestial element in the native cult of the solar-sky deities of the Celtic world. Thus, at Tongeren in Belgium, the Celtic Jupiter and Juno are depicted: she has her peacock and her partner his Roman eagle, but the indigenous character of the imagery is demonstrated by Juno's possession of a solar WHEEL. Likewise, on an altar at Vaison (Vaucluse), Jupiter as a sun-god appears with the Celtic Juno and her peacock. On a curious monument at Dôle (Jura) a peacock is depicted associated with a sun-wheel.

□ Vanvinckenroye 1975, 73; Green 1984a, 332, 343–4; Sautel 1926, no. 705.

Pesch This hill-top settlement in the lower Rhine frontier region of the Eifel near Zülpich was an important cult centre of Germanic Mother-goddesses known as the MATRONAE VACALLINEHAE, which grew to prominence in the 3rd c. AD. The sacred precinct had a TREE as a cult focus. The sanctuary possessed several shrines and assembly areas, attesting to public worship. More than 160 altars were dedicated to the Vacallinehae; suppliants appear to have been mainly soldiers belonging to Legion XXX Ulpia. Images of the Mothers display the goddesses in normal Germanic form, with large linen headdresses, and their usual attribute consists of bread, perhaps significant inasmuch as this would have been the staple diet for legionaries.
□ Lehner 1918–21, 74ff; Rheinisches Landesmuseum Bonn 1973, 74–5, fig. 65.

Pfalzfeld At Pfalzfeld, St Goar, in Germany was discovered a carved sandstone PILLAR stone, probably dating from the 5th or 4th c. BC. The sub-conical, four-sided stone is broken at the top and may once have been surmounted by a human HEAD. The pillar is covered with curvilinear Celtic foliate designs, but each facet of the stone bears the image of a stylized human head, with round eyes and with the characteristic Celtic double-leaf crown and lotus bud carved on the forehead. *See also* HEIDELBERG.
□ Megaw & Megaw 1989, 74, fig. 83, left; Megaw 1970, no. 75.

phallus The Celts' preoccupation with fecundity caused them, on occasions, to represent their male deities with the phallus over-emphasized. This stressed their virility and their ability to promote the FERTILITY of humankind, their flocks and herds and their crops. The Iron Age Celts in CAMONICA VALLEY in North Italy sometimes depicted ithyphallic divinities in their rock art. In North Britain, images of naked war-gods were represented with horns and huge, erect phalli. A bronze figurine of the Celtic Mercury at Tongeren is triple phallused (*see* MERCURY, TRIPLE-PHALLUSED). The hooded shape of the Genii Cucullati may be interpreted as phallic and, indeed, certain images of Cucullati in Germany possess hoods which can be removed to reveal phalli beneath (*see* GENIUS CUCULLATUS).

In addition to sexual potency and fertility, the phallus may be simply a symbol of male-

A 4th c. BC rock carving of Cernunnos, with antlers and torcs, from **Paspardo**, Camonica Valley.

Iron Age wooden figure with huge **phallus**, from **Broddenbjerg**, Jutland.

ness. Among the Romans, the motif of the plain or winged phallus was a general good-luck symbol, and it could have been emphasized on some images of Celtic deities as a similar motif of good fortune. *See also* SNAKE.

pig *see* BOAR; MATH

pillar All over the Celtic world, there is evidence for the erection of wooden or stone pillars as the focus for a sacred place or *locus consecratus*. The concept probably derives from the imitation of a sacred TREE. The ultimate prototype for the Romano-Celtic JUPITER-GIANT COLUMN was a growing tree, often an oak. The 5th–4th c. BC central European pillar stones, like that at PFALZFELD, may also derive from such an origin. This faceted stone bears floreate La Tène decoration on each of its four sides, together with the image of a leaf-crowned human head. The top of the pillar was once surmounted by another head. The pillar carved with heads at the pre-Roman shrine of ENTREMONT in Provence may also imitate a wooden post or tree hung with genuine human skulls.

There is substantial evidence for the erection of tall posts or pillars in sanctuaries. These would have acted as landmarks over wide areas. If they do ultimately derive from living trees, then their symbolism may be similar, the perception of a link between the upper and lower worlds. The great ritual enclosures at the GOLORING and the Goldberg in Germany, both dating from the 6th c. BC, each possessed a great central post; the same phenomenon was identified at the 3rd c. enclosure of Libeniče in Czechoslovakia. At the site of Emhain Macha (Navan Fort) in Northern Ireland, there is evidence for the presence of an enormous oak post, some 36 ft high, the focal point of a sanctuary built about 100 BC. The OAK used for this great pillar was already 200 years old when it was felled: it was perhaps a sacred tree or 'bile'. In Britain, pre-Roman Celtic shrines possessed sacred pillars: this can be seen at Ivy Chimneys in Essex where a large timber upright may have been the focus of the site. Similarly, at the early shrine at Hayling Island, pre-dating the more massive Roman temple, a central pit probably held a sacred post or stone. The tradition continued into the Romano-Celtic period: the great sanctuary of the Matronae Vacallinehae at Pesch in Germany had a post or tree as its focal point.

□ Powell 1958, 134–6; Green 1986, fig. 4; Ross 1986, 109; Lehner 1918–21, 74ff; von Petrikovits 1987, 242–8; Downey, King & Soffe 1980, 289–304; Piggott 1968, 71; Rybová & Soudský 1962.

pit The tradition of digging deep shafts or pits in the ground, with a primary religious function, can be traced back in Europe to at least as early as the middle Bronze Age. In the Mediterranean world, Greek *bothroi* and Italian *mundi* were sacred pits in which sacrifices were made and which were perceived to link the earth to the underworld. In Celtic and pre-Celtic Europe, there was a similar perception of pits as entrances to the Otherworld. Ritual shafts at Swanwick and Wilsford in southern England date from the later 2nd millennium BC: the Swanwick pit is of especial interest since in it was a wooden post with traces of what may be human blood and tissue adhering to it. This precisely parallels the occurrence much later at HOLZHAUSEN in Bavaria, a VIERECKSCHANZE probably dating from the end of the Iron Age.

The digging of pits, perhaps to appease the gods of the underworld, was especially important in Iron Age religious practices. At the DANEBURY hillfort, about a third of the grain-storage pits were associated with ritual behaviour, which probably took place when the pits were no longer in active use. Here, human bodies and parts of bodies, skulls, animals and inanimate objects were deliberately buried in pits in religious acts. On the Continent, particularly in Bavaria, the late Iron Age *Viereckschanzen* consisted of square enclosures built round deep shafts. Holzhausen produced its possible evidence for human sacrifice (*see* SACRIFICE, HUMAN); another example, at FELLBACH SCHMIDEN, contained wooden images of animals. In Aquitaine, deep pits dating from around 50 BC contained cremations and animal bones, including those of toads, often thought of as possessing magical properties. In the Vendée area, at St Bernard, a shaft contained a cypress trunk, antlers and a figurine of a goddess.

Most ritual pits in Britain occur in the late pre-Roman and Romano-Celtic period and group geographically in southern England, though many outliers are recorded. Too many of what are probably ordinary rubbish pits have been claimed as having a ritual function, but some undoubtedly do. Some contained images of deities, others special layers of complete pots and other material. Many pits had chambers constructed inside them; some contained complete animal skeletons, often in large numbers (*see* SACRIFICE, ANIMAL). At Muntham Court (Sussex) a pit 200 ft deep, associated with a temple, was filled with dog skeletons. At Cambridge, a group of shafts each contained a human burial accompanied by a dog. A pit at Goadby (Leics) contained two adult humans, buried face-down and covered with stones; similar occurrences were noted at Danebury, where some human bodies in pits were weighted down with stones, presumably to prevent their spirits from 'walking'. At the Iron Age hillfort of South Cadbury, a young man was buried in a pit dug into the rear of the rampart, perhaps to appease the gods on whose territory the stronghold was built, or to bless the installation.

The recent discovery of a pit at Deal in Kent provides what may be our only known evidence for an image of a chthonic divinity associated with a pit. At the bottom of the shaft, which was some 8 ft deep, was an oval chamber which contained a crude chalk figure, a featureless piece of dressed chalk, roughly formed into a human torso, with a head on a long slender neck. The face is in Celtic style, with a straight slit mouth, wedge-shaped nose and deep-set eyes under jutting brows. The figure may have once stood in a niche carved high up in one wall. The shaft had footholds down into the 'shrine', but this chamber was very small and it was probably meant mainly to house the deity rather than his devotees. Pottery associated with the shaft dates from the 1st or 2nd c. AD.

So all over the Celtic world, pits were dug, with the primary purpose of contacting and propitiating the gods of the underworld. Humans and animals – sometimes deliberately sacrificed – were buried in these pits, and the chthonic gods were offered other gifts – food, drink, metalwork and wooden votives.
□ Green 1986, 132–5; Ross 1968, 255–85, Ashbee 1963, 116–20; Megaw & Simpson 1979, 272; Cunliffe 1983, 156ff; Wait 1985; Parfitt & Green 1987.

Poeninus *see* JUPITER POENINUS

pool Water in all its forms was sacred to the Celts: rivers, lakes, springs, wells and pools

Celtic quadrangular **pillar** stone, decorated with foliage and human heads wearing leaf crowns, 5th–4th c. BC, from Pfalzfeld, Germany.

Chalk figurine, of 1st or 2nd c. AD date, from a ritual **pit** at Deal, Kent.

were all venerated, each perceived as possessing its own divine spirit. WATER was a life source, a cleanser, healer and destroyer. The calm surface of a pool or LAKE reflects not only light but also the image of those who look into it. All of these properties gave rise to water cults.

It is difficult to distinguish between cults associated with springs, lakes, bogs and ponds. Springs may create pools; shallow ponds or pools occur in marshes; and a small lake may equally be classified as a large pool. None the less, certain ritual activity seems specifically to have been associated with pools, naturally formed or artificially created. The reservoir of Sulis' spring sanctuary at Bath was a focus of votive offerings (see SPRING, HEALING); so was the pool at Coventina's Well, Carrawburgh (see COVENTINA). Springs and associated pools formed the centre of Sequana's cult at *Fontes Sequanae*. Lindow Man, the Iron Age bog body, was killed and thrust face-down into a small pool in the bog. A sacred pond or pool seems to have been associated with cult activity at the Harlow Celtic temple; and the religious site at Ivy Chimneys, Witham, also in Essex, had an artificial pond or pool as its focal point. Finally, we know of a Cumbrian divinity, LATIS, 'Goddess of the Pool', who was worshipped at Birdoswald and Fallsteads.
□ Turner 1982; Ross 1967a, 231; Green 1989, 155–64; Deyts 1985; Allason-Jones & McKay 1985; Cunliffe 1969; Cunliffe & Davenport 1985; Stead et al. 1986.

priest *see* BARD; DRUID; HEADDRESS; SCEPTRE

Pryderi is the son of Pwyll, lord of Dyfed, and the supernatural RHIANNON, whose tale is told in the *First Branch of the Mabinogi*. Pryderi himself is closely associated with the divine and the supernatural. His father has underworld connections, in that he has ruled as king of Annwn, the Otherworld, for a year in place of Arawn. Rhiannon is herself other than human, as is indicated by her horse, which cannot be caught up with by living men. Three nights after Pryderi is born, he disappears in mysterious circumstances, and turns up on the doorstep of a house belonging to one Teyrnon Twryf Liant, lord of Gwent Is-Coed. Before Pryderi arrives here, strange events have been happening at Teyrnon's house: every year, on the eve of 1 May, his mare, a superb creature, gives birth to a foal,

which immediately disappears. On the night of Pryderi's arrival, Teyrnon decides to keep watch over his mare; she casts her foal, and immediately it is seized by a huge claw which appears through the stable window. Teyrnon hacks off the arm and saves his foal, but at the same time, he hears a scream and a commotion outside. He investigates, and there is a three-day-old baby boy on his doorstep.

The child is large and very advanced for his age – a supernatural sign. When he is four, his foster-parents recognize his resemblance to Pwyll, lord of Dyfed, and realize that he must be his missing son. Teyrnon and his wife return Pryderi to Arberth amid much rejoicing, and they are handsomely rewarded for caring for the prince.

The mythology surrounding the early life of Pryderi is intense: he develops at superhuman speed; his birth is closely linked with that of a foal, just as Rhiannon, his mother, is associated with horse symbolism. And Teyrnon, his foster-father, may also be a divine figure: his name means 'Great' or 'Divine' lord. Pryderi himself is often identified with the Welsh god MABON ('Divine Youth'), son of Modron, who was also abducted when three nights old.

When Pwyll dies, Pryderi becomes lord of Dyfed, and Rhiannon marries the divine MANAWYDAN. Their story is chronicled in the *Third Branch of the Mabinogi*, which is largely concerned with the enchantment of Dyfed and the wanderings in England of Pryderi and Manawydan.
□ Jones & Jones 1976; Mac Cana 1983, 81–2; Gruffydd 1912, 452–61.

Pwyll appears in the *First Branch of the Mabinogi*, as lord of Dyfed with his palace at Llys Arberth (modern Narberth). He has a very close association with the supernatural: at the beginning of the tale, Pwyll encounters ARAWN, king of ANNWN, the Welsh Otherworld. Pwyll is out hunting in Dyfed when he sees a pack of strange hounds which pursue and overcome a stag. He drives off the dogs and sets his own pack to the body of the deer. At once, a horseman appears, announces himself as Arawn and pledges enmity to Pwyll for the insult he has done him. Pwyll asks how this hostility may be revoked; Arawn tells him that he must do him a favour. He and Pwyll must exchange physical forms and identities for a year.

Arawn will rule in Dyfed as Pwyll, while Pwyll must take Arawn's form, rule in Annwn for a year, and at the end of that time, he must meet and kill Hafgan, the other underworld king and Arawn's enemy. Arawn warns Pwyll that he must strike Hafgan only once; if he deals two blows, Hafgan will recover and fight with renewed vigour. Pwyll carries out the pledge and meets Arawn, as agreed, after the year has passed. Each returns to his own kingdom, good friends, and Arawn sends many gifts to Pwyll's palace. Pwyll is known as 'Lord of the Otherworld' because of his sojourn in Annwn.

Bronze pig from Ireland. Pigs are associated with the Welsh divine heroes **Pryderi** and **Pwyll**.

The other main story about Pwyll concerns his marriage to RHIANNON. Her supernatural status is indicated by the manner of their meeting. Pwyll sees a horsewoman passing him on the road, but neither he nor his men on their swiftest horses can catch up with her, even though the lady's own steed is apparently travelling quite slowly. When he challenges her, she stops, introduces herself as Rhiannon, and says that she has come to him because she wishes to marry him rather than her official suitor Gwawl. Pwyll wins Rhiannon from Gwawl by treachery; they marry and produce a son, PRYDERI, the future lord of Dyfed.
□ Jackson 1961–7, 83–99; Jones & Jones 1976.

R

rain Celestial phenomena, the rising and setting of the sun, the weather activities of lightning, THUNDER and rain must have been perceived as undeniable evidence of the existence of supernatural powers. There is little specific evidence for a Celtic rain-god; rain-deities are commoner in parts of the world where water is scarce and drought endemic. But there is no doubt that the Celtic SKY-GOD was also a weather-deity, who presided over storms. The thunder-god TARANIS must have been master of lightning and rain as well as of the noisy phenomenon of thunder itself.
□ Green 1982, 37–44; 1984a, 251–64.

Gold drinking-horn mounts with **ram**-head terminals, 5th c. BC, from Klein Aspergle, Germany.

ram In Classical imagery, Mercury was associated with either a goat or a ram, as a symbol of fertility. The Romano-Celtic version of Mercury was linked particularly with the ram. At Bath, Mercury and Rosmerta are accompanied by a ram; and the Remic triple-headed god was associated with Mercury's two zoomorphic emblems of ram and cockerel. The small figurines of rams found all over Britain and Gaul may belong to the native cult of Mercury.

Ram imagery may take a number of forms. Apart from the Mercury association, which stems from the Graeco-Roman world, the symbol may also be related to war cults, perhaps because of the sexual aggression exhibited by rams. Thus, some northern British warrior-gods are depicted with ram horns: a good example is the horned head at Netherby in Cumbria; and at Lower Slaughter (Glos) an altar depicts a crudely carved, naked WAR-GOD with a ram.

The other important aspect of ram symbolism concerns the image of the ram-horned or ram-headed snake (see SNAKE, RAM-HORNED). Here, a hybrid, monstrous creature exhibits the fertility imagery of the ram combined with the symbolism of regeneration which is evoked by the serpent. Interestingly, a sculpture from Blain near Nantes demonstrates the link between ram and snake in a different way: here a horned god is accompanied by both a ram and a snake.

Finally, it should not be forgotten that ram motifs are present on many examples of La Tène art, which may or may not have a religious function: thus, a flagon at Reinheim in Germany is decorated with ram heads which have human heads superimposed on them.
□ Ross 1967a, 155, 342–4, pl. 63a; Espérandieu, no. 3015; Green 1986, 98; 1978, 65, 76; 1976, 184, 210, 217; 1989, 173–4, fig. 77.

rat As a scavenger and carrion eater, burrower in dark places, the rat was a natural chthonic symbol in the ancient world. It is not common in Celtic imagery, but occurs very occasionally in association with known deities.

On a stone relief at Reims, a rat is carved on the pediment of a gabled niche which contains images of the Celtic antlered god Cernunnos, Apollo and Mercury. Its occurrence here may refer to an underworld aspect to the cult of Cernunnos; but it is possible that the rat owes its presence here to an association with Apollo, who was a god of plagues in the Classical world.
□ Espérandieu, no. 3653.

raven As a large, black carrion BIRD, consumer of dead things, the raven was a chthonic emblem, symbol of darkness and death; its sharp beak and reputed cruelty reinforce this image. But ravens were also prognostic birds, associated with oracles, perhaps because of their distinctive 'voices' (see ORACLE). Both these roles are reflected in the vernacular literary tradition and in the archaeological record.

In the Irish literature, prophecy and destruction are associated with ravens: magic ravens warn LUGH of the approach of the Fomorians; the Ulster hero Cú Chulainn is linked with magical ravens; and he destroys a large flock of Otherworld birds whose evil nature is stressed. Irish goddesses of war and destruction can change shape from human to raven form at will: an example is the BADBH who, as 'Badbh Catha' ('Battle Raven') confronts the Ulster armies on the battlefield as a terrifying harbinger of death, gloating over the bloodshed. Indeed, Iron Age coins minted by Breton tribes depict a large raven or crow perched on a horse, as if in reflection of this battle myth (see also MORRIGÁN). In the Welsh Mabinogi, ravens are beneficent Otherworld creatures associated with Rhiannon. In the Dream of Rhonabwy (dating from the 13th c. in its present form) Owein ap Urien has a raven army which is attacked by Arthur's men, but the ravens are restored to human form when Owein's standard is raised and turn on their persecutors.

Ravens accompany many deities in Celtic iconography: Lugh was traditionally linked both with ravens and with the founding of Lugdunum (Lyon), and coins show the 'Genius' of the Roman city accompanied by a raven. The goddess NANTOSUELTA is depicted with a raven, probably as an Otherworld symbol; and other goddesses, such as Epona and the Mother-goddesses, may be depicted with ravens. At Mavilly in Burgundy, a raven is the attribute of the presiding healer-god, perhaps because its bright eyes symbolically attested the eye cures for which the shrine was renowned. In Britain, at Felmingham Hall (Norfolk) and Willingham Fen (Cambs), the Celtic Sky-god appears accompanied by ravens, perhaps reflecting the underworld aspect of this dualistic cult. See also CROW.
□ Kinsella 1969; Jones & Jones 1976; Ross 1967a, 242–56; Green 1986, 187–8; 1989, 25–7, 64–5, 142–4, 186–7.

rebirth The theme of regeneration or resurrection after DEATH runs as a consistent thread through the Celtic mythological tradition. There is, quite naturally, a close association between the concept of rebirth and that of the OTHERWORLD, which was perceived as being essentially similar to life on earth.

Caesar (*de Bello Gallico* VI, 14) informs us that the Gaulish druids promoted the idea of the TRANSMIGRATION OF SOULS, in order to encourage warriors not to be afraid of death. The archaeology of pagan Celtic religion hints strongly at the belief in rebirth. Tombs may contain elaborate grave goods; the iconography implies that regeneration was seen as a function of the gods. The wine motifs associated with many divinities have been interpreted as symbolic of blood and resurrection. The Mother-goddesses seem to have been venerated as deities of life, death and rebirth. The habit of skin sloughing by snakes was perceived as an allegory of rebirth (*see* SNAKE). There existed much seasonal symbolism: the 'death' of winter followed by the rebirth of spring. Thus, deciduous trees were seen to 'die' and be 'reborn', as was the corn seed buried in the dark tomb of earth. Stags, too, with their autumnal shedding and spring regrowth of antlers, possessed a seasonal, cyclical symbolism.

Rebirth is a concept to which frequent allusion is made in the vernacular mythology: here, there is a persistent association with cauldrons, which possessed the ability to resurrect the dead. In the *Second Branch of the Mabinogi*, the Irish have a magic CAULDRON which brings dead warriors back to life, though they cannot speak. In the Irish Otherworld, each 'bruidhen' or hostel has its own inexhaustible cauldron of plenty. At the Otherworld feasts, pigs were killed, eaten and reborn the following day. The theme of warrior resurrection appears in the account of the great battle between the Tuatha Dé Danann and the Fomorians: the divine leech Dian Cécht resurrects dead soldiers by casting them into a well, presumably fulfilling the same function as a cauldron. So perhaps the idea of water is more important than the vessel itself. It is interesting that this kind of resurrection may be depicted on one of the plates of the Gundestrup Cauldron, where an army is accompanied by a god who dips one of their number into a vat of liquid.
□ Olmsted 1979, pl. 3E; Mac Cana 1983, 58, 127; Green 1986, 61; 1989, 45–73, 142.

Relief of a Healer-god, with **raven** and sick pilgrim, from Mavilly, Burgundy.

Skull and bones from the Neolithic chamber tomb at West Kennet, Wiltshire. The Celts and their remote ancestors believed in **rebirth** after death.

Reinheim In 1954, during sandpit operations, the rich burial of an Iron Age princess was discovered overlooking the River Blies at Reinheim. The burial was under a mound and was originally part of a group of barrows. Of these, one other mound has been investigated, which was found to contain the body of a middle-aged man. The princess was interred in an oak-lined chamber, together with personal objects and jewellery of gold, bronze, glass, amber and coral. Indeed, the lady appears to have been buried with the entire contents of her jewel-box, about 200 items. She had a mirror and vessels for food and drink in the afterlife. The funerary feast was attested particularly from the presence of a large, spouted wine jug. Some of the gold jewellery, a heavy gold bracelet, for instance, shows conflated images of human and animal form, perhaps reflective of divine shape-changing. One may imagine that the high-ranking lady buried at Reinheim may have attained almost divine status, similar to the euhemeristic Queen Medb of Connacht. Finds from the grave indicate that the Reinheim princess was buried during the 4th c. BC.
□ Megaw 1970, nos 73, 79–83; Megaw & Megaw 1989, 90–2.

Rhiannon Most of our knowledge about Rhiannon comes from the *Mabinogi*, where she appears as the traditional entity, the 'wronged wife'. Her name may derive from 'Rigantona', meaning 'Great' or 'Divine Queen'. Rhiannon was a goddess of Dyfed, whose image is closely linked with horses: this has led to her supposed association with the Celtic horse goddess Epona. Rhiannon's divine status is indicated by her first encounter with PWYLL, King of Dyfed: she appeared before him dressed in a golden robe, riding slowly past him on a large white horse. But however fast she was pursued by Pwyll or his followers, even on their swiftest mounts, she could not be overtaken. In desperation, Pwyll called to her, and Rhiannon stopped willingly to converse with him, admitting that she was seeking him anyway. Pwyll and Rhiannon married after Pwyll won her from Gwawl, her betrothed, by trickery. When the newly married Rhiannon arrived at the court of Arberth (Narberth), she gave precious gifts to all the nobles presented to her. Thus, her image was of a generous, bountiful queen-goddess.

The theme of the 'calumniated wife' comes in when Rhiannon's baby son, PRYDERI, born after many years of waiting for an heir, was spirited away on the eve of 1 May (the Feast of Beltene), and she was falsely accused of murdering him by the women on watch. For her penance, Rhiannon had to sit for seven years by the horseblock outside the gate, offering to carry visitors into the palace on her back. After some years, the boy Pryderi was restored to his parents by Teyrnon, a vassal of Pwyll, who had fostered the child in ignorance of who he was.

After the death of Pwyll, Rhiannon married MANAWYDAN, son of Llŷr. Soon after, both Dyfed and its ruling family were afflicted by various enchantments woven by one Llwyd, in vengeance for Pwyll's trickery against Gwawl. Manawydan forced Llwyd to undo the spell and restore Dyfed from desert to its former fertile state.

In the *Mabinogi* of 'Branwen', and in the *Tale of Culhwch and Olwen,* Rhiannon was endowed with Otherworld symbolism, by means of the 'three magic birds of Rhiannon', whose sweet singing, heard from over the sea, could wake the dead and lull the living to sleep.
□ Jones & Jones 1976; Gruffydd 1912, 452–61; Jackson 1961–7, 83–99.

Rigisamus *see* MARS RIGISAMUS

Rigonemetus *see* MARS RIGONEMETUS

Ritona or Pritona was venerated at Trier, where she was a goddess of fords and water crossings. Her name is indicative of a passage or passage way: routes and ways possessed a special sanctity in Celtic and in other religions, in that they formed a link which could be interpreted as connecting the earthly and the spirit world, the living and the dead. Over and above this, there would be the natural respect for a convenient river-crossing place, which facilitated communications, travel and trade.
□ Wightman 1970, 217; Green 1986, 85, 165; 1989, 40, 161.

ritual *see* BURIAL; DEATH; DECAPITATION; DIVINATION; DRUID; FEAST; HEAD-HUNTING; RITUAL DAMAGE; SACRIFICE

ritual damage The practice of deliberately bending, smashing or otherwise damaging an object before it was offered to the gods was a widespread phenomenon in antiquity. It occurred in the Classical world, where pots were broken in shrines, as for example at the sanctuary of Hera at Samos. In barbarian Europe, the custom of ritual breakage began during the Neolithic period, and there is plentiful evidence for the tradition by the early Iron Age. The idea seems to have been that by damaging an object and removing its function in the real world, the worshipper was consecrating it and rendering it appropriate as an offering to the powers of the supernatural.

The site of FLAG FEN in Cambridgeshire has produced abundant evidence for ritual breakage: there, from about 1200–200 BC, weapons and other votive offerings were cast into the water, many of which were 'killed' before being committed to the gods. More than 300 items of martial equipment have been recovered, including nine complete swords. The weapons had to 'die' before they were acceptable to the supernatural forces. A Hallstatt warrior grave at Ebberston (Yorks), dating from the 6th c. BC, contained two bodies, each with a sword which had been broken deliberately in four places. La Tène warriors' tombs in the Moselle were accompanied by ritually bent swords. The sacred lake at LLYN CERRIG BACH on Anglesey contained martial and prestige offerings dating from between the 2nd c. BC and 1st c. AD, which were in perfect condition except that they had been bent or snapped before being thrown into the water.

Many Iron Age and Romano-Celtic sanctuaries have produced evidence of ritual damage: at the Gaulish pre-Roman shrine of Gournay-sur-Aronde (Oise), hundreds of deliberately damaged weapons were consecrated to the divine powers. Very similar activity is recorded at the pre-Roman temple at Hayling Island in Hampshire; here, there was a small circular shrine, but the ritual activity was concentrated in the surrounding courtyard. Here again, martial equipment was ritually damaged before being offered to the gods of the temple. The late Iron Age sanctuary at Harlow, Essex, has very recently produced four miniature swords, of 1st c. AD date, all of iron and one in a bronze scabbard: two of these models had been snapped in two in antiquity (*see* MODEL TOOL/WEAPON). The practice of ritual damage continued into the Roman period: at the great healing shrine

Replica of a gilt-bronze flagon, earlier 4th c. BC, from the Celtic princess' grave at **Reinheim**, Germany.

The Welsh **Rhiannon** is the equivalent of the Gaulish Epona, seen here on a relief at Kastel, Germany.

of Sulis at Bath, many of the 16,000 coins found cast into the reservoir had been clipped to render them useless in the real world and suitable as votive offerings to the presiding goddess. Some of the miniature bronze spears at the Woodeaton Romano-Celtic temple site were deliberately bent in half. One very curious occurrence is the practice, in some Gaulish shrines, of collecting Neolithic axes, which were already 2,000 years old in the Romano-Celtic phase, and placing them in these temples as votives, having first smashed them. Was this to consecrate them or to defuse some of their ancient power?

The final feature to note about ritual breakage as a phenomenon is that, in barbarian Europe at least, the practice seems to have been concentrated above all on martial equipment. Perhaps weapons needed to be 'pacified' before being offered to the gods.
□ Pryor 1990, 386–90; Downey, King & Soffe 1980, 289–304; Adkins & Adkins 1985, 69–75; Brunaux 1986; Green 1986, fig. 52, 155; Cunliffe 1974, 287–99; Wightman 1970, 242–6; Fox 1946; Lynch 1970, 249–77.

river Celts and pre-Celtic peoples perceived rivers as cult foci for ritual practices. From the middle Bronze Age (the mid 2nd millennium BC), the peoples of barbarian Europe cast valuable metalwork into rivers as offerings to the supernatural powers. Such rivers as the THAMES received huge quantities of fine, prestige metal objects – weapons and body armour, for example – throughout the middle and later Bronze Age and the free Celtic Iron Age. In the later Iron Age, a group of worshippers threw into the Thames such high-status material as the Battersea Shield and the Waterloo Helmet. The spirit of the River Witham in Lincolnshire received a shield and a bronze boar-headed war-trumpet. Celtic coins and jewellery, too, were consigned to the riverine deities. Indeed, most Iron Age metalwork found in British contexts comes from rivers, where it was deliberately deposited.

In many religions of antiquity, rivers have been venerated as sources of life. They have been endowed with sanctity, and a divine spirit was perceived as dwelling in each. The many great rivers of Gaul – like the MARNE, SEINE and Saône (see SOUCONNA) possessed particular divinities: the name of the Marne was, significantly, 'Matrona' (mother). British river-goddesses, too, were venerated, like

VERBEIA of the River Wharfe and Sabrina, the spirit of the Severn. In Ireland, the goddess BOANN was the spirit of the river BOYNE.

Rivers at their sources and confluences possessed especial numinosity. SEQUANA was the goddess of the River Seine at its source, where there was an important therapeutic spring sanctuary (see FONTES SEQUANAE). The local river cult which existed at the confluence of the two great rivers Rhône and Saône outside Lugdunum was acknowledged in the introduction there at Condate ('confluence') of a great Roman cult centre (see LYON). Here, on 1 August 12 BC, the Imperial cult of Rome and Augustus was established. A great altar was set up, inscribed with the names of sixty Gaulish tribes. Interestingly, the ceremonies were presided over by a Celt, the chief priest of the Aedui, and the date itself was also significant: 1 August was the Celtic festival of Lughnasad.
□ Green 1986, 139–41; Merrifield 1983, 4–9, 15; Fitzpatrick 1984, 180–2; Cunliffe 1975, 89–108; Drinkwater 1983, 111.

Roquepertuse was the site of a pre-Roman Celtic cliff-top sanctuary in Provence, not far from Entremont. The shrine was entered by a portal or portico consisting of three stone pillars with lintels or cross-beams. The pillars were carved with niches in which were nailed the skulls of young adult men (see PILLAR). Sculptures from the temple include a frieze of horse heads in profile; a large free-standing GOOSE perched on a lintel; a pair of janiform heads held in the beak of a huge bird of prey; and statues of cross-legged warrior-gods. The iconography and the presence of the skulls closely resembles the material from the nearby sanctuary at ENTREMONT. The heads may be those of battle victims, offered to the gods of the shrine as trophies of victory (see HEAD-HUNTING). Diodorus Siculus (XIV, 115) and Strabo (IV 4, 5) attest to the Celtic custom of placing the heads of vanquished victims in shrines.

The deity or deities venerated at Roquepertuse may have been war-gods, represented by the statues of men seated cross-legged, wearing cuirasses and helmets. The janiform heads watched both ways and guarded the shrine (see HEAD, JANIFORM), as did the watchful goose on the lintel. The images of horses (see HORSE) accord with those at other Provençal sites, such as Entremont and

NAGES, where horses and human heads are represented in association, again reinforcing the remarks of Classical writers, that the Celts slung their head trophies from the saddles of their horses (Diodorus Siculus V 29, 4; Livy X, 26).

The mountain sanctuary of Roquepertuse may have been constructed as early as the 6th c. BC; and the sculptures may be of 4th c. date, the human skulls may have been collected in the 3rd c. The sanctuary fell at the time of the Roman conquest of the region towards the end of the 2nd c. BC.

□ Benoit 1955; Lambrechts 1954; Bémont 1984, nos 153, 160; Hodson & Rowlett 1973, 189; Pobé & Roubier 1961, no. 13; Megaw 1970, no. 236; Green 1989, 146–7, fig. 62.

rosette In Greek and Roman funerary symbolism, rosettes and roses were carved on tombstones, in recognition of spring and rebirth beyond the grave. Allusion was made to roses in funerary inscriptions, and they were painted on the walls and vaults of tombs.

There is evidence that rosettes played a part in Celtic symbolism. The chthonic significance is present, for instance, where rosettes appear on tombstones in Alsace. A relief of the Genii Cucullati from Lower Slaughter in Gloucestershire shows the triad accompanied by ravens and a rosette, perhaps all of them symbols of death. Several Celtic deities are associated with rosettes, either in reflection of a chthonic aspect to their cults or because of the sun-like shape of the rosette symbol. Images of Epona sometimes depict her with rosettes, and Classical writers allude to the goddess being offered roses by her devotees (Juvenal, *Satires* 8, 157; Apuleius, *Metamorphoses* 3, 27). Rosettes appear decorating clay figurines of the Celtic 'Venus' and on bronze statuettes of the Gaulish Hammergod. The association between rosettes and the cult of the Celtic solar god seems definitely to have occurred because of the resemblance between the rosette and the sun: thus, the mounted celestial god at Meaux (Seine-et-Marne) is depicted with his hand thrust through a rosette-like sun-wheel; and an altar at Tresques in southern Gaul bears a dedication to Jupiter, a wheel symbol and a rosette.

□ Green 1984a, 160–2; 1986, 157, fig. 71; Linckenheld 1929, 40–92; 1927; Toynbee 1971, 63; Magnen & Thevenot 1953, no. 181.

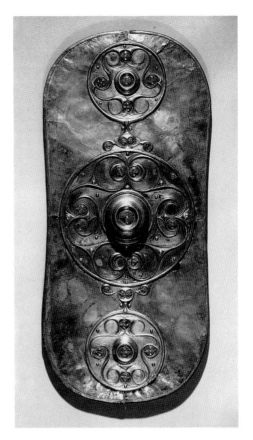

Ceremonial bronze shield, thrown into the **River Thames** at Battersea, London, as a votive offering in the 1st c. AD.

Stone janiform head from the pre-Roman Celtic shrine of **Roquepertuse**, southern France.

Rosmerta The name of this goddess means 'The Great Provider'. She was generally worshipped as part of a divine partnership, as the native consort of the Roman MERCURY. The divine couple were the focus of an important and popular cult, which pervaded much of Romano-Celtic Europe, being especially prominent in central and eastern parts of Gaul, along the rivers Rhône, Meuse, Moselle and both banks of the Rhine (*see* COUPLE, DIVINE). There is an outlying British cluster of monuments among the Dobunni of south-west England: at least one temple must have been established at the Roman *colonia* of Gloucester, where three sculptures of the couple have been discovered. The importance of the cult and its high status is reflected at a temple to Mercury and Rosmerta at Wasserburg in Alsace, where a dedicant in AD 232 was a freedman (ex-slave) of the Roman Imperial House and the *tabularium* (archivist) of the Emperor Severus Alexander.

The identification of Mercury and Rosmerta is possible because certain images of the couple are accompanied by dedications naming the pair: this occurs at, for instance, Eisenberg and Metz. As the partner of Mercury, Rosmerta has the role of a goddess of prosperity and plenty; this is demonstrated not only by her name but also by her images, where she often has a *cornucopia* and a *patera*. But her very close link with her consort is displayed by her frequent adoption of Mercury's attributes of purse and caduceus. At a temple to Mercury and Rosmerta at Baden in Germany, the couple are both depicted with purses and caducei; at Wiesbaden Rosmerta is portrayed in a relief, sitting on a throne receiving the contents of a purse offered to her by Mercury who stands before her. On a carving at Mannheim, it is Rosmerta alone who holds the purse of plenty, on which a snake rests its head as if deriving nourishment from it. Sometimes both deities hold only caducei: at Bierstadt the two sit in identical attitude, each holding a caduceus against the left shoulder; and this is similar to the couple's imagery at Bath.

The essentially Celtic character of the cult of Mercury and Rosmerta may sometimes be displayed by the presence of specifically Celtic images which share the same stone as the couple. In Britain, this is demonstrated on the relief at Bath, where Mercury and Rosmerta are accompanied by a small group of three Genii Cucullati who scurry along at the base of the plaque. At Trier, a stone was dedicated to Mercury in the 1st c. AD by a Mediomatrician called Indus, who may have been a shipper on the Rhine. On one surface of this monument are carved Mercury and Rosmerta; on another the Celtic divine woodcutter ESUS is depicted, with his willow, three cranes and a bull.

There are two striking features of Rosmerta's character, which contradict the notion, often argued, that she was merely a cipher, the feminine principle in the cult of Mercury. One concerns her imagery in Britain, where she possesses independent and distinctive attributes of her own. On the Bath relief, Rosmerta has a wooden, iron-bound bucket, and this symbolism is repeated at Gloucester, where the goddess is depicted with a sceptre and a ladle poised over a bucket. On another Gloucester relief, she is joined by FORTUNA: Rosmerta carries a torch reversed and Fortuna another facing upwards. The bucket may symbolize regeneration and rebirth, like the Celtic CAULDRON of renewal; the torches may reflect life and death. In Britain at least, it was Rosmerta's imagery which provided profundity of meaning, quite apart from the symbolism of earthly prosperity.

The second feature of Rosmerta's cult is associated with her presence among the tribe of the Aedui in Burgundy. The essential independence of the goddess is demonstrated at the site of Escolives-Sainte-Camille (Yonne), where Rosmerta was worshipped alone, without Mercury. She is depicted by herself in a niche with her *patera* and *cornucopia*, and on a dedication her high rank is indicated by her epigraphic association with the emperor. In the same tribal region, at Gissey-la-Vieil, Rosmerta once again appears alone, once more linked on a dedication with the emperor, but this time she appears as a goddess of a sacred spring. So Rosmerta was far from being, in all instances, a subservient and contrived partner to the dominant Mercury. Her independence and her special imagery indicates that she existed in her own right, quite possibly pre-dating the cult of the Celtic Mercury in Gaul and Britain.

□ C.I.L. XIII, 2831, 4208, 3656; Espérandieu, nos 6039, 4929; Espérandieu *Germ.*, nos 18, 39, 428; Hatt 1971, 187–276; Alfs 1940, 128–40; Cunliffe & Fulford 1982, no. 39; Wightman 1985, 178; Schindler 1977, 32, fig. 91; Green 1986, figs 47–8; 1989, 42–3, 52–61; Bémont 1969, 23–44.

Rudianus is a southern Gaulish WAR-GOD, equated with MARS. He was invoked at Saint-Andéol-en-Quint and Rochefort Sanson (Drôme), and at Saint-Michel-de-Valbonne (Var). The name 'Rudianus' means 'red', and this reflects the warlike nature of the god. The St Michel dedication is interesting because at the same place was found a prehistoric image of a mounted war-god, who could perhaps be Rudianus himself. The menhir-shaped stone depicts a roughly incised figure of a HORSE-MAN, with an enormous head, riding down five severed heads. The iconography here is evocative of the HEAD-HUNTING exploits of the Celts, who hung the heads of their battle victims from their saddles, as chronicled by Classical writers.
□ Espérandieu, no. 38; C.I.L. XII, 1566, 2204; Duval 1976, 71; Thevenot 1968, 56–7.

Rudiobus A group of superb bronze figurines comes from NEUVY-EN-SULLIAS (Loiret). These include a prancing horse, bearing an inscription 'sacred to the god Rudiobus'. So it is permissible to assume the presence of a Celtic deity to whom the HORSE was sacred. Indeed, it is known that horses were linked with many Gaulish and British deities, including the Sky-god and the Celtic version of Mars. The name 'Rudiobus' may refer to the colour red, perhaps indicative of a war (blood) symbolism, like that of RUDIANUS.
□ de Vries 1963, 118–19; Green 1989, 132, fig. 63, Espérandieu, no. 2978.

Stone plaque depicting Mercury and **Rosmerta**, with her double-axe sceptre, bucket and offering plate, from Gloucester.

S-symbol Double spirals or S-shaped symbols are associated with sky and solar cults in Romano-Celtic Europe (*see* SKY-GOD; SUN-GOD). A bronze figure of the solar wheel god at Le Châtelet (Haute-Marne) depicts a naked, bearded man with a thunderbolt in one hand and his wheel in the other (*see* THUNDER). Hanging from his shoulder are nine free-cast, S-shaped objects, slung from a ring. If one examines the god's thunderbolt closely, it can be seen that it is made up of individual spiral-shaped strands. It is thus possible that the nine S-symbols the god carries are lightning bolts. The association of sun WHEEL and S-symbol recurs on a pot at Silchester (Hants) which is decorated with alternating wheels and S-motifs. A bronze

Bronze horse, dedicated to **Rudiobus** in the 1st c. BC, from Neuvy-en-Sullias, Loiret, France.

wheel-model from Grand-Jailly (Côte-d'Or) had three S-symbols soldered onto its surface; and a sculpture of the Wheel-god at Nieder-würzbach in Germany depicts a wheel with curvilinear, S-shaped spokes. The close relationship between sun and S-symbols suggests that the latter does have a link with the solar cult. Its most likely significance is that of another light source, perhaps a light-ning flash.

☐ Green 1984a, 165–7.

sacral kingship There was a tradition in the Irish mythology that the king was fundament-ally bound up with the fortunes and pros-perity of the land. If the king's character was good, Ireland would flourish. But under the parsimonious King Bres, the land became infertile. Both tribal and universal kingship existed. TARA was the sacred site of kingship from very early. Here, the pre-Christian Feast of Tara legitimized the new king, and it was here that the ritual marriage took place between the king and the land. The concept of sacral kingship was intimately associated with sacred places and, in particular, sacred trees, which were present at the site of the king's inauguration, as symbols of wisdom, sovereignty and perhaps also representative of the land itself (*see* TREE).

Various rituals and tests were practised in choosing a king: the phallic Stone of Fál on the hill of Tara gave a loud cry when touched by the rightful king elect. The candidate himself underwent certain tests: if the royal chariot accepted him and if the royal mantle fitted him, he would be chosen. In addition, there was the 'TARBHFHESS' or 'bull-sleep', in which the flesh and broth of a sacrificed bull were consumed by an individual who then slept and dreamed of the rightful king. Like the priests of Roman religion, certain ritual bonds, taboos or GEISSI surrounded the sacral king, restricting and governing his behaviour. Such bonds are exemplified by the case of Nuadu, king of the Tuatha Dé Danann, who had to abdicate the kingship once he had lost his arm, because he no longer fulfilled the kingly requirement of physical perfection.

The tradition in Ireland was that the mortal king assumed true sovereignty by union with one of the goddesses of the land. An example of this is the marriage of ÉRIU, the eponymous goddess of Ireland, who sealed her union with her royal spouse by handing him a golden goblet full of red liquor. The queen-goddess MEDB cohabited with nine kings of Ireland; she would not allow any king in Tara who did not mate with her. Many of these goddesses underwent transformation once the union had taken place. This may take the form of a change from old hag to young girl or from wild and mad female to sane and beautiful woman. The third form of transfor-mation concerns the girl of royal birth brought up among peasants, who is restored, by union with the king, to her rightful status.

☐ Bhreathnach 1982, 243–60; Watson 1981, 165–80; Mac Cana 1955–6, 76–114, 356–413; 1958–9, 59–65; 1983, 114–21.

sacrifice, animal was endemic in antiquity, both in Europe and elsewhere. For a rural, subsistence community, the sacrifice of an animal represents a considerable economic loss and thus would take place only in response to a special event or crisis within that community. There were two categories of sacrifice: the first consisted of animals who were burned or buried whole; the second of creatures who were butchered and, at least partly, consumed. At the Iron Age temple of GOURNAY-SUR-ARONDE (Oise), both types of sacrifice were discovered; horses and cattle were interred entire; young pigs and lambs were butchered. The choice of pigs and sheep for ritual meals is found elsewhere, for instance at Hayling Island (Hants).

The variety of animals sacrificed is con-siderable. Of the wild beasts, boars were ubiquitous; whole BOAR skeletons were ritu-ally buried; and the 'champion's joint of pork' (it is not always possible to distinguish wild from domestic pigs) is attested in many Celtic graves. Stags, hares, birds and other wild creatures were sacrificed (*see* HARE; STAG). Of domestic animals, horses, cattle and dogs were sacrificed (*see* BULL; DOG; HORSE). Pliny (*Natural History* XVI, 95) alludes to the druidic sacrifice of bulls. At the King's Barrow in East Yorkshire, the horse team as well as the cart were interred with the dead chieftain (*see* CART/CHARIOT BURIAL). Dogs were some-times the subject of complex funerary ritual: at the late Romano-British cemetery at Winchester, dogs accompanied humans to the Otherworld. At Muntham Court in Sussex, numerous dogs were placed in a 200-foot-deep shaft near a 1st c. AD temple (*see* PIT).

A note of caution needs to be sounded in any analysis of animal sacrifice. It is some-times impossible to distinguish between animals which have died naturally and are subsequently subjected to ritual and beasts which were killed for specifically sacrificial purposes. For example, the horse mandibles found in storage pits at Iron Age DANEBURY (Hants) may have come from horses which did not die as the result of sacrificial acts but were rather representative of revered animals which died naturally or in battle.

☐ Green 1986, 167–89; 1989, 133; Wait 1985; Cunliffe 1983, 155–71; MacDonald 1979, 404–33; Brunaux 1986; Downey, King & Soffe 1980, 289–304.

sacrifice, human Most of our information concerning human sacrifice among the Celts comes to us from the writings of Mediterranean commentators. The main perpetrators of such practices were the DRUIDS, who studied the death throes and the entrails of their victims for divinatory purposes (*see* DIVINATION). Lucan (*Pharsalia* III, 399–452) refers to a sacred wood in the vicinity of Marseille, where altars were heaped with hideous offerings, and every tree was sprinkled with human blood. Diodorus Siculus (V, 31, 2–5) and Strabo (VII, 2, 3) refer to the druidical custom of stabbing victims and foretelling the future by observations of their struggles. Tacitus describes the sacred GROVE of the druids on Anglesey, with its altars drenched with blood and entrails (*Annals* XIV, 30). Strabo remarks that the Cimbri cut the throats of their sacrifices for divinatory purposes and examined the blood, which was collected in cauldrons. Evil-doers were imprisoned for five years and then killed by impaling. Victims could be burnt alive in huge wicker images of men, or shot with arrows. Caesar has an interesting comment on how the minds of the druids worked (*de Bello Gallico* VI, 16): he remarks that they believed that the supernatural powers could only be neutralized or controlled if one human life were exchanged for another. Thus, if the Gauls were threatened, for example, by battle, then the druids would organize human sacrifice: if criminals were unavailable, then the innocent would have to supply that life for a life.

Sometimes, human sacrifice was demonstrably associated with particular deities: Dio Cassius (LXII, 2) refers to the perpetration of human sacrifice in the woods sacred to the Icenian goddess of victory, ANDRASTE, initiated by the tribal ruler Boudica. Lucan

The 8th c. AD Ardagh Chalice. A chalice of wine was offered by the goddess of sovereignty to mortal kings in Irish rites associated with **sacral kingship**.

An 18th c. drawing of a druidical **animal sacrifice**, by William Stukeley, 1759.

(*Pharsalia* I, 444–6) describes three savage Celtic gods, TARANIS, ESUS and TEUTATES, all of whom were appeased by human blood. The later Berne scholiasts on Lucan elaborate on his statement: they elicit the information that Taranis was propitiated by burning, Teutates by drowning and Esus by means of suspending his victims from trees and ritually wounding them. The horror and distaste of Graeco-Roman writers for these 'barbarian' practices is very evident.

It would be surprising if all this literary evidence were not, at least partially, supported by archaeology. But there is, in fact, little hard-and-fast evidence for human sacrifice, though there are plenty of instances of abnormal burial. But it is important to distinguish between bodies who were demonstrably the victims of specific ritual murder and those who may have died naturally and were subsequently subjected to religious activity. The late Iron Age *Viereckschanze* at HOLZHAUSEN in Bavaria contained a ritual shaft with a post at the bottom: adhering to this stake were traces of human tissue and blood. This replicates, almost exactly, the contents of the Swanwick (Hants) ritual PIT, the date of which is almost a millennium earlier, about 1000 BC. Garton Slack (E. Yorks) in North Britain provides evidence for what looks very like an Iron Age punitive ritual killing: the bodies of a youth and a woman of about thirty were found huddled together, a wooden stake having been driven between them, pinning their arms together. Below the pelvis of the female was a foetus, which had been expelled from the womb when the mother was unconscious. The couple had probably been buried alive. A seemingly unequivocal human sacrifice was Lindow Man, the young male who was buried facedown in a bog pool in the 4th c. BC (*see* BOG-BURIAL; LINDOW MOSS). He had been poleaxed, garotted and his throat cut before being interred in the marsh. The strangulation closely resembled that of the TOLLUND bog body from Denmark, which perhaps dates from about 500 BC. An instance of what may have been 'suttee' occurred at Hoppstädten in Germany: here, a La Tène grave produced the bodies of what looks like an entire family. Caesar (VI, 19) alludes to the practice of 'suttee', which apparently went out of fashion not long before he was present in Gaul. He comments: 'not long ago, slaves and dependants known to have been their

master's favourites were buried with them at the end of the funeral'.

There is a mass of evidence for abnormal human burial which may or may not have been the result of sacrifice. The infants buried as foundation deposits at such shrines as Springhead (where they were decapitated) may have followed deliberate killing or natural death (*see* INFANT-BURIAL). Likewise, the bodies of young men found in pits at the DANEBURY (Hants) hillfort or behind the rampart at SOUTH CADBURY (Somerset) could well have been battle victims, subsequently buried as acts of appeasement to the gods rather than human sacrifices *per se*. There is no means of being sure. The human heads found on many Iron Age sites (*see* DECAPITATION; HEAD-HUNTING) could, in the same way, have come from individuals who were killed in warfare and their heads collected as trophies. Head collection is recorded by several Classical writers, but they do not make it clear as to whether these were always the heads of vanquished and slain warriors or whether in some instances, ritual killing by beheading took place.

There is little in the vernacular mythology which points specifically to human sacrifice. One Irish legend alludes to the ritual triple-killing of the king, by burning, wounding and drowning, on the 1 November Feast of Samhain. This probably relates to mythological ritual associated with sacral kingship. One piece of Celtic iconography may refer to human sacrifice: that is a plate of the Gundestrup Cauldron which shows the scene of a god apparently about to drown a human victim in a vat of liquid. It is tempting to relate this image to the literary reference to Teutates and his drowned sacrifices.

□ Olmsted 1979; Green 1986, 27–30, 131; Cunliffe 1974, 187–99; 1979, 92ff; Collis 1975, 101; Zwicker 1934–6, 50; Alcock 1972; Wait 1985; Wightman 1970, 242; Brewster 1976, 115; Mac Cana 1983, 27; Piggott 1963, 286–7.

salmon In both the Irish and Welsh mythological traditions, the salmon was a symbol of wisdom and knowledge. The most famous Insular tale is in the Fionn Cycle and concerns the hero FINN, who acquired wisdom and the gift of prophecy from contact with the Salmon of Knowledge. The story is that Finn comes across Finnegas the Bard, who lives on the bank of the River Boyne. Finnegas has been fishing for the Salmon in a pool for seven years. He catches it and gives it to Finn to cook. The hero burns his thumb on the grilling fish and puts it in his mouth: he instantly gains knowledge, and Finnegas then gives him the flesh of the salmon to eat, thereby endowing Finn with eternal wisdom. The salmon itself has acquired knowledge by eating the nuts of the nine hazel trees which grow beside a well at the bottom of the sea. Another Insular tale, this time part of the Ulster Cycle, concerns the mythical king of Munster, Cú Roi, whose soul is said to reside in a certain salmon.

In the Welsh *Tale of Culhwch and Olwen*, Culhwch consults a number of beasts who can communicate with humans, in his quest to find the divine hunter Mabon. One of these fabulous creatures is the Salmon of Llyn Llyw, one of the oldest animals on earth.

The mythical status of the salmon is difficult to explain. It may be due to its size, its beauty or its pink, human-like flesh. Alternatively, it may have been endowed with sanctity on account of its complicated life cycle, and its need for both the sea and fresh water.
☐ Jones & Jones 1976, 125; Ross 1967a, 351; O'Fáolain 1954; Best 1905, 18–35.

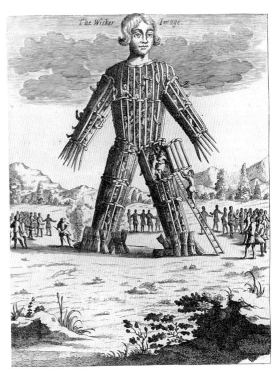

Human sacrifice by burning in a wicker man; from Aylett Sammes' *Britannia Antiqua Illustrata*, 1676.

Samhain was a Celtic seasonal festival which heralded the passing of summer and the beginning of winter and the New Year. It was a pastoral festival, which marked the time at which livestock were rounded up and brought in from the fields; some were chosen for slaughter, others kept for breeding purposes. Samhain was celebrated at the end of one pastoral year and the commencement of the next. In the Gaulish bronze tablet known as the Coligny Calendar, which dates from the 1st c. AD, Samhain is recorded as 'Samonios'. The great assemblies of the five Irish provinces at Tara took place at the feast of Samhain, the festival being marked by horse races, fairs, markets, pastoral assembly rites and political discussions. But there would be ritual mourning, too, at the death of summer.

Samhain was a strange time: the festival took place on 1 November and the night which preceded it. It was considered a time of great danger and vulnerability, for it stood at the boundary between two halves of the Celtic year. It was considered as outside or suspended from time, when the normal laws of the world were temporarily in abeyance.

The 'Drummer of Tedworth', from an engraving by Joseph Glanvill, 1700. Spirits like this escaped into the human world at the autumn festival of **Samhain**.

The barriers between the real world and the supernatural dissolved, and the OTHERWORLD spirits could move freely from the sídhe to the land of the living. This worked in reverse, too, in that mortals could penetrate the underworld. So Samhain marked a time of immense spiritual energy, when the gods of the Otherworld had to be accorded special rituals to control them, and when strange happenings occurred.

In Insular mythology, Samhain figures very prominently as a period when curious and supernatural events took place. It is at Samhain that the tribal god, the Daghda, ritually mated with the Morrigán, the raven-goddess of war and fertility, who had considerable oracular powers. Samhain was the time of the year that the Fomorians exacted their crippling tribute from the people of Ireland (two-thirds of their corn, milk and children). The triple killing of the Irish king (by wounding, burning and drowning) took place at Samhain. This is an image of sacral kingship, when the king died at the end of each year to make way for the new ruler and for springtime.

Samhain is involved with many of the Irish tales of the gods and the supernatural. The Ulster hero Cú Chulainn had encounters with Otherworld ladies at this time. It was during Samhain that the swan-girl Caer assumed her bird form and could be taken by OENGHUS, the god of love, who was in love with her. The festival of Samhain was the night on which the goblin Aillen annually burned down Tara, until he was killed by FINN. Aillen visited the stronghold, played his harp, lulled everyone to sleep and then set fire to the palace. The only way Finn could stay awake to kill Aillen was by means of an enchanted spear, made by Len, the swordmaker to the gods, which Finn kept pressed against his forehead.

So the feast of Samhain was a curious time, when gods visited men, supernatural beings changed shape and the year died and was reborn. It was both a sombre and a joyous occasion (just as New Year's Eve is today), but most of all it was a time of great numinosity, full of spirits and supernatural energy, when the worlds of life and death were inextricably intertwined. *See also* FIRE.

☐ Macalister 1931; O'Fáolain 1954; Le Roux 1961, 485–506; O'Hógáin 1990; Green 1986, 74; de Vries 1963, 237–8; Mac Cana 1983, 127–8; Ross 1967a, 237; 1986, 120–1.

Scáthach, daughter of Ardgamm, was a supernatural female warrior who ran a kind of academy in Ulster for training young heroes in the art of combat; Scáthach's name means 'The Shadowy One'. In the Ulster Cycle, Scáthach instructs the hero Cú Chulainn in war skills. This teaching takes place in Alba, the part of north-west Britain facing Ireland. It was from Scáthach that Cú Chulainn receives the 'Gae Bulga', his formidable barbed spear whose thrust was invariably fatal. Scáthach has the gift of prophecy, and she foretells Cú Chulainn's fate during the course of Queen Medb's onslaught against Ulster.
☐ Stokes 1908, 109–52; O'Fáolain 1954; Olmsted 1982, 165–72; Meyer 1907, 112ff; Kinsella 1969; O'Rahilly 1946, 61.

sceptre Items of priests' liturgical regalia found on temple sites include a category of objects which may be called sceptres, maces or wands of religious authority. Sometimes, these are plain or simply decorated; others, however, incorporate cult imagery which is of intrinsic interest. Two of the latter type, which have particular significance, come from British contexts. The hoard of religious bronzes from WILLINGHAM FEN (Cambs) contains many plain fragments of sceptres but, in addition, what may be the terminal of such a mace is also present. This bears elaborate iconography related to the cult of the Celtic sun/sky-god. The imagery consists of a figure of a naked, dancing god brandishing a thunderbolt and with his foot on the head of a chthonic being. He is accompanied by a solar wheel, an eagle, a triple-horned bull's head and a dolphin. The other object is from the temple at Farley Heath (Surrey). This is a sheet-bronze binding which was once curled round a wooden or iron core: punched in repoussé on the binding are schematized figures of deities and animals; the Sun-god, the Hammer-god and smiths' tools can be identified, together with ravens, a dog, a stag and other creatures.

Apart from objects which may properly be termed maces or sceptres are other processional items, sometimes called pole tips, like that from the hoard of cult bronzes at Felmingham Hall (Norfolk) and another from the shrine at Brigstock (Northants). These consist of tapering bronze terminals with holes and rings for the suspension, perhaps, of bells or jangles, which would make a noise when carried in ceremonies. Similar to these

is a curious object from Milton (Cambs) which consists of a long bronze shaft terminating in a flat oval with two perforations, again for the suspension of rattles or other pendants.
□ Green 1976, 210; 1986, 23; 1984a, no. C6; Henig 1984, fig. 62; Alföldi 1949, 19ff; Goodchild 1938, 391ff; 1947, 83ff; Gilbert 1978, 159–87.

schematism is a method of image making, where the representation of the human or animal form is reduced to absolute essentials, with no attempt at realism or naturalism. Celtic artists and devotees did not feel it necessary always to represent their gods as if they were true people or beasts. Instead, the idea only of the human or animal shape was sometimes depicted, with no attention to detail. The images thus presented seem almost like a kind of 'shorthand', a coded message which was understood by both deity and worshipper. This sort of image making was totally at variance with the mimesis or life copying which was chosen by the Mediterranean world for representation of their gods. Celtic schematic portrayal, which may take the form of very simply incised matchstick figures, has frequently been condemned by Classical art historians as inferior art. But this is to misunderstand the purpose of the artist. Schematic representation was a conscious, deliberate and highly successful form of divine image making. Rigid realism was considered unnecessary within the context of cult imagery. On the other hand, realistic representation was perhaps quite positively rejected as being inappropriate for depicting the supernatural. There is a great deal of power in such images as the three Genii Cucullati at Cirencester where only the essential characteristics of threeness and hoodedness are present, or the stylized figures of gods, pilgrims and animals at the sanctuary of FORÊT D'HALATTE near Senlis (Oise).

Celtic schematism may have existed in the Romano-Celtic artistic and religious tradition because of the roots from which it sprang. La Tène (free Celtic) art was more interested in abstract designs based on animal and vegetal motifs than in the depiction of the human or animal form *per se*. In the Romano-Celtic phase, Roman artistic traditions of figural representation stimulated Celtic artists to depict their gods in human form, but although realism was adopted to some extent, the earlier abstract traditions continued to act as

(Above left) Sheet-bronze **sceptre** binding from the Romano-Celtic temple at Farley Heath, Surrey.
(Above right) Bronze **sceptre** terminal depicting the Wheel-god, from a hoard of religious bronzes at Willingham Fen, Cambridgeshire.

Sheet-bronze plaque of a god, from the Woodeaton temple, Oxfordshire, displaying **schematism** in the 'matchstick-man' form of the figure.

an influence on image making. Celtic artists displayed a sophisticated brilliance in their ability to look at a model – perhaps a human figure – and reduce the representational essentials to a few minimal lines and shapes, enough for the code to be recognizable but no more. Economy of detail could make for a powerful image, capturing the essence of the figure with no distracting additions. For an image to be successful, it may have required no more than a mere scratched outline, so long as it retained the essential power of its prototype. The schematic imagery of Celtic religious art was consciously obscure, enigmatic and ambiguous, features which may have enhanced its religious efficacy.
□ Green 1986, 200–8, fig. 90; 1989, 214–16, fig. 89; Gombrich 1968, 93, 141; Boardman 1973.

Sea-god Sea-deities are known in the Celtic world but do not figure prominently in the archaeological or iconographic record. The Roman NEPTUNE seems not to have possessed a Celtic counterpart, though he does appear associated with one or two Celtic cults. NEHALENNIA was the Celtic goddess of the North Sea, who had two shrines on the coast of the Netherlands. She protected travellers on their hazardous marine journeys and blessed their business transactions.

In the Irish mythological tradition, LIR was the god of the sea. But his son MANANNÁN mac Lir was a far more prominent character. He rode a chariot across the ocean, and he possessed a huge cloak which was an allegory for the sea itself. In Ireland, the sea was regarded as one of the ways of approaching the Otherworld.
□ Ross 1967a, 39; Green 1989, 10–16; Mac Cana 1983, 66–71.

Segomo means 'Victorious'; as an epithet it was applied to Celtic versions of both Mars and HERCULES. The tribe of the Sequani worshipped Mars Segomo, and he was invoked, for example, at Lyon. It may have been to this deity that a bronze horse inscribed with the name Segomo was dedicated at the shrine of Bolards, Nuits-Saint-Georges, in Burgundy, where other representations of horses and horsemen are recorded. The Gaulish and British Mars was frequently venerated as a HORSEMAN. In Britain, at Silchester, a fragmentary dedication to 'Her

cules Saegon' may represent the same epithet – Segomo – in slightly different form. The application of the same descriptive name to two gods is not surprising, since the term is more of a title than a name *per se*.
□ C.I.L. XIII, 1675; R.I.B., 67; Thevenot 1955, Green 1986, 172–3.

Seine, River Like most of the great rivers of Gaul, the Seine had its own divine spirit. The Seine, at its source, was presided over by the goddess SEQUANA, who had an important curative temple at FONTES SEQUANAE, north-west of Dijon. Elsewhere, people habitually cast votive objects into the river in acts of private or public ritual. Among these deposits were numerous solar wheel amulets, dedicated to the Celtic Sun-god. This behaviour could relate to certain fire/water sun festivals, where a flaming wheel was rolled down a hill into a river to bless the fertility of the land. The *Acts of St Vincent* contain an account of such a custom in 4th c. AD Aquitaine.
□ Green 1984a, 311; 1986, 164; 1991a; Hatt 1951, 82–7; Zwicker 1934–6, 302–3.

Sequana was the female personified spirit of the River SEINE at its source in a valley in the Châtillon Plateau, to the north-west of Dijon in Burgundy. Here, a healing shrine to Sequana was established at FONTES SEQUANAE ('the Springs of Sequana') in the 2nd or 1st c. BC. The sanctuary was later monumentalized by the Romans, who built two temples, a colonnaded precinct and other related structures centred on the spring and pool.

It is known how Sequana's devotees perceived their goddess, in that there is a large bronze statuette of a young woman from the shrine. She appears as a draped divinity wearing a diadem to indicate her high status, and with her arms outstretched to welcome her suppliants. Sequana stands in a boat which is in the form of a DUCK, reflective of her riverine symbolism. Many dedications were made to the goddess at her temple, including a large pot inscribed with her name and filled with bronze and silver models of parts of human bodies to be cured by Sequana (*see* LIMB/ORGAN, VOTIVE). Wooden and stone images of limbs, internal organs, heads and complete bodies were offered to her in the hope of a reciprocal cure, as well as numerous coins and items of jewellery. The votives suggest that, amongst the many afflictions endured by the pilgrims, respiratory illnesses

and eye troubles were particular scourges:
some images of devotees exhibit blindness or
swollen eyes. Many of the depictions of
Sequana's suppliants show them in the heavy
outdoor woollen hooded cloak which reflects
the peasant livelihood of ordinary Celtic people – farming, hunting, trading or mule driving. The pilgrims are frequently portrayed
carrying offerings to the goddess; these consist of money, fruit or a favourite pet dog or
bird. *See also* RIVER.
☐ Deyts 1983; 1985; Green 1989, 40–1, fig.
16.

shape-changing *see* METAMORPHOSIS

Sharvan the Surly *see* DIARMAID; GRAÍNNE;
MONSTER

shrine For the Celts, foci of worship could be
either built sanctuaries or natural, sacred
places (*loci consecrati*), which could be a
TREE, GROVE, MOUNTAIN, SPRING, RIVER or
LAKE – any natural feature of the landscape
which was deemed to be numinous (i.e. to
possess a spirit).

If worship and ritual activity did take place
in a sacred structure, then until the Romano-
Celtic period such buildings were simple
circular or rectangular shrines without any
specifically religious architecture. The evidence for their holy purpose is thus indirect,
suggested either by their position beneath
unequivocally religious Romano-Celtic buildings or by the occurrence of material pertaining to ritual activity. Thus, the free Celtic
shrine at GOURNAY-SUR-ARONDE (Oise) was
associated with specific and idiosyncratic
ritual involving animals and weapon deposits. At HAYLING ISLAND (Hants) a massive
Roman-built shrine succeeded a late Iron Age
wooden round structure: the courtyard outside yielded abundant evidence for religious
activity, which involved the deliberate deposition of ritually damaged weapons and the
sacrifice of particular species of animal. At
Frilford (Oxon) two contiguous shrines of
Roman date (circular and of rectilinear Romano-Celtic type respectively) were preceded
by two earlier structures, one represented by
a penannular ditch, the other by a circular
pattern of post holes. Inside the penannular
gully were six pits (*see* PIT) associated with
the votive offerings of a ploughshare and
a miniature sword and shield (*see* MODEL
TOOL/WEAPON). Iron Age buildings of small

Stone and wooden images of pilgrims and human
heads, dedicated to the healing goddess **Sequana**
at *Fontes Sequanae*, Burgundy, 1st and 2nd c. AD.

A 1st c. BC wooden horse-
figure dedicated to Sequana,
goddess of the **Seine** at
Fontes Sequanae.

and simple design, normally interpreted as shrines, may be found in hillforts. They occur at DANEBURY, and at SOUTH CADBURY a simple porched building is associated with pits containing the bodies of young animals. The only evidence for a religious function for a late Iron Age circular building at Maiden Castle (Dorset) consists of an INFANT-BURIAL just outside the door and the presence of a Romano-Celtic temple nearby. Many continental temples of Roman date had Iron Age predecessors: St Germain-les-Rocheux (Côte-d'Or) is an example. In the Marne region, small Iron Age shrines were associated with Celtic cemeteries.

The Iron Age structure at Heathrow near London is an enigma. Though it appears to date from the 4th c. BC, its architectural plan, with square inner *cella* and surrounding portico, appears to anticipate the much later, 'mass-produced' Romano-Celtic shrine type.

In the Romano-Celtic period, both in Britain and Europe, the simple rectilinear and circular shrines continued to exist alongside a type of temple with a specific architectural style. This is the so-called Romano-Celtic temple, which may be circular, polygonal or rectilinear. All examples of this type share the distinctive characteristic of concentricity, possessing an inner sanctum or *cella* surrounded by an ambulatory of the same shape. There are variations within this basic type: there may be an annexe, a divided *cella* or other refinements. But the idea common to all temples of Romano-Celtic type seems to have been the presence of a secret inner chamber, to house the cult statue and other temple furniture, and an outer gallery, with openings in the walls through which pilgrims might view cult offerings. None of these shrines would have been for congregational worship. Indeed, there is evidence that much of the ritual activity took place in the sacred enclosure outside the temple itself. *See also* SACRIFICE, ANIMAL; SACRIFICE, HUMAN.

□ Lewis 1966; Rodwell (ed.) 1980; Brunaux 1986; Downey, King & Soffe 1980, 289–304, Cunliffe 1974, 287–99; 1983, 155–71; Harding 1974, 96–112; Alcock 1972; Piggott 1968, 56ff; Green 1986, 18–21.

sídh is the Irish word for a 'fairy mound', a dwelling-place for spirits. The word can also mean 'peace', perhaps deriving from the association with the OTHERWORLD. When the Sons of Mil (the Gaels) invaded Ireland,

according to mythological tradition, the divine race of the TUATHA DÉ DANANN were driven underground, to establish Otherworld kingdoms beneath the hills. The Daghda assigned each member of the Tuatha Dé one of these mounds, or 'sídhe'. Nuadu was lord of the sídh of Almu; Midhir of the sídh of Brí Léith, and so on. The war-goddess, the Morrígan, emerges from her sídh to destroy Cú Chulainn. Each sídh forms part of the Irish happy Otherworld, in which there is feasting, hunting and revelry, no pain, disease or old age, and where there is plentiful food and drink. The Daghda's sídh possesses three trees which perpetually bear fruit, a pig which is always alive and an inexhaustible supply of drink. The festival of SAMHAIN on 1 November was a time when the boundaries between the natural and the supernatural worlds were temporarily negated, and the spirits moved freely from their own sídhe. The burial mounds of the Neolithic and Bronze Ages were long believed to be the dwelling-places of the Irish gods.

□ Macalister 1931; Wagner 1981, 1–28; O'Rahilly 1946, 279; Rhŷs 1901, 677–8; Ross 1967a, 220.

Silvanus was the Roman god of wild nature and the woodland. He was associated with a number of Celtic cults which were concerned with vegetation, hunting, the forest and fertility. One of the main centres for the worship of the Celtic Silvanus was in Gallia Narbonensis, or Provence. Here, Silvanus was equated with the Celtic HAMMER-GOD: dedications to Silvanus may be accompanied by hammer symbols, as at St-Gilles. Sometimes the Hammer-god appears in the guise of a woodland deity: on bronze figurines, for instance at Glanum and Orpierre, the god with his hammer is dressed in a wolfskin cloak and a leafy crown, as if he is a god of beasts and the wild forest. He may be a protector of animals and hunters and a promoter of abundance (*see* HUNTER-GOD). The Hammer-god himself certainly had a role as a divinity of plenty and florescence. On a curious altar at Aigues-Mortes near Nîmes is a dedication to Jupiter and Silvanus: the Celtic sky-sun god is represented by his symbols of a wheel and thunderbolt; Silvanus is represented by a billhook, symbolizing the taming of wild nature, and his link with the Hammer-god is reflected in the motifs of hammer and pot.

In Britain, Silvanus was equated with various local deities. He was a hunter-god on Hadrian's Wall, where his name is coupled with that of COCIDIUS. Elsewhere in Britain, Silvanus is linked with NODENS at Lydney and is called SILVANUS CALLIRIUS ('Woodland King') at Colchester. *See also* VERNOSTONUS. □ Espérandieu 1924, 33, no. 121, pl. 6; Espérandieu, no. 497; Phillips 1977, no. 234, pl. 63; Green 1989, 79–83, 100, fig. 32.

Silvanus Callirius The Roman woodland deity SILVANUS was only rarely equated overtly with a native divinity. One example, occurring only at Colchester, is Silvanus Callirius, the surname being interpreted as 'Woodland King' or 'God of the Hazel Wood'. In a pit in the vicinity of a rectangular shrine at Colchester was found a bronze plaque with a punched dedication to Silvanus Callirius, offered to the god by a coppersmith. With the plaque was a small bronze figurine of a STAG. Callirius was thus the local spirit of the forest, invoked with the votive offering of an image of the king of woodland animals. He was perhaps the protector of stags but may also have been propitiated as a HUNTER's god. □ Ross 1967a, 37; Green 1976, 215–16; 1986, 183, figs 79, 80; R.I.B., 194.

Sirona was a Gaulish goddess who was associated particularly with healing shrines attached to thermal springs (*see* SPRING, HEALING). Her name is etymologically related to 'star', though there is no external evidence for a celestial role.

This goddess was most often linked with a consort, the Celtic APOLLO, frequently named as APOLLO GRANNUS. The divine couple were venerated above all among the Treveri, although they were known and worshipped over a wide area (*see* COUPLE, DIVINE). In Treveran territory, the couple were invoked at a shrine at Niedaltdorf, at the curative sanctuary of Bitburg and at Sainte-Fontaine near Freyming (Moselle). In the neighbouring tribal area of the Mediomatrici, Apollo and Sirona were worshipped at a water shrine built in the tribal capital at Metz.

The most well-documented and important shrine dedicated to Apollo and Sirona was at HOCHSCHEID, a Treveran sanctuary between ' Trier and Mainz. Coins found at the site suggest that the main temple was built in the 2nd c. AD, succeeding an earlier, free Celtic (pre-Roman) structure made of wood. The

The megalithic tomb of New Grange, Ireland, c. 2500 BC. The Celts believed that this was a **sídh** or fairy mound, lived in by the gods.

The Gaulish Hammer-god as **Silvanus**, with his hammer, pot and leaf crown, from Glanum, Provence.

temple was erected around a spring whose waters fed a small cistern. Here pilgrims came to be cured and offered coins, figurines and other votive objects. It seems to have been a relatively elaborate, wealthy and Romanized sanctuary, curious for such a remote region. It was perhaps endowed by a rich villa owner. Many clay figurines on the site represent a seated 'Mother-goddess' holding a small DOG on her lap or in her arms: the association of Sirona with dogs is probably due to the healing associations of that animal; many Celtic Mother-goddesses are associated with dogs.

The main cult statues of the presiding deities at Hochscheid support the notion of a sophisticated cult. Both Sirona and Apollo are represented: he closely resembles his Classical counterpart, being young, naked and with his attribute, the lyre, as befitted the divine patron of music. But the native Celtic Sirona is herself depicted with more interesting symbolism: she is portrayed wearing a diadem, indicative of her high status; she carries fertility emblems in the form of three eggs; and a SNAKE twines itself round her arm, its head towards the eggs. The presence of the serpent maybe reflects aquatic and regenerative imagery, supporting the goddess' role as a spring-deity and a healer.

Sirona appears at healing shrines outside Treveran territory, as at Wiesbaden and Luxeuil (Haute-Saône). That she was known over a very large area of the Celtic world is attested by her occurrence as far apart as Brittany and Hungary. Both these regions provide evidence for how Sirona's name could change: at Corseul in Brittany she is called 'Tsirona', and her high rank may be implied by the linking of her name with the 'numen' or spirit of the emperor. In Hungary, where there was a 3rd c. AD temple to Apollo Grannus and Sirona at Brigetio, the goddess was 'Sarana'.

The imagery of the goddess constantly reflects the same fertility/regenerative role which is apparent at Hochscheid. At Sainte-Fontaine, Sirona has corn and fruit; at Mainz and at Baumburg in Noricum, the goddess also has ears of corn, and at the latter site she also has grapes. A beautiful little bronze group found at Mâlain (Côte-d'Or) depicts Sirona and Apollo, who turn towards each other as if in intimate conversation. Here Sirona appears half-draped and with her snake curled round her right arm, whilst

Apollo has his lyre: on the base is a dedication to the pair.

Although Sirona appears most frequently in the company of Apollo, her independent status as a divinity in her own right is indicated by her occurrence alone at such sites as Baumburg in Noricum and Corseul in Brittany. She probably existed as a healing and fertility goddess long before the Romano-Celtic phase, and her marriage with the intrusive Apollo may have reflected the fusion of Celtic with Roman culture.

□ Green 1986, 152; 1989, 42–5, 61–3; de Vries 1963, 143, Musée Archéologique de Metz 1981; Marache 1979, 15; Schindler 1977, 33, fig. 92; Wightman 1970, 220–1, pl. 22; Dehn 1941, 104ff; Thevenot 1968, 103–4, 110; Szabó 1971, 66; Espérandieu, nos 4470, 5102.

Sky-god Much of the evidence pertaining to a celestial religion is related specifically to solar cults. However, sky symbolism and sky-deities did exist separately from those associated with the SUN.

The Roman Sky-god JUPITER was adopted into the Celtic pantheon and was endowed with indigenous epithets, titles or surnames, like Jupiter Poeninus or Jupiter Taranis. Some of these show him to have been perceived as a mountain-deity or a thunderer. In terms of iconography, the worship of the Romano-Celtic Sky-god (as distinct from that of a solar divinity) manifests itself above all in the iconography of the celestial HORSEMAN (*see* JUPITER-GIANT COLUMN). This imagery consists of depictions of the Sky-god as a warrior on horseback, fighting the forces of evil and darkness, personified as a semi-serpentine monster. Whilst the sky-horseman sometimes bears a solar wheel, as at Obernberg and Luxeuil, more commonly he brandishes a metal or stone thunderbolt as an offensive weapon. The sculptures are mounted high on columns, to raise the image of the Sky-god as close as possible to his celestial element. The entire monument at Merten near Metz was about 45ft high.

The Celtic Sky-god had power over all elements associated with the sky: the firmament, the sun, RAIN, storms and THUNDER. He was a weather-god, who commanded lightning, floods and drought. He was above all a champion of light, day and life who constantly opposed the forces of darkness, night and death, in a dualistic cult of interde-

pendent balance between good and evil. *See also* S-SYMBOL; TARANIS.
□ Bauchhenss 1976; Bauchhenss & Nölke 1981; Green 1986, 61–71.

Smertrius The name 'Smertrius' comes from the same root as 'Rosmerta', the 'smert' referring to the provision of abundance. 'Smertrius' may thus mean 'The Purveyor' or 'The Provider', a title rather than a true name.

Smertrius is one of the Gaulish gods to whom epigraphic allusion is made on the *Nautes Parisiacae* monument found in Paris in a series of blocks beneath Notre-Dame in 1711 (the other Celtic deities represented being Esus, Tarvostrigaranus and Cernunnos). The monument was dedicated by a corporation of Parisian sailors during the reign of Tiberius in the early 1st c. AD. On one block, the word 'smert' appears above a fragmentary representation of a well-muscled, bearded man confronting a snake which rears up in front of him. The god brandishes an object which has usually been interpreted as a club but which rather resembles a torch or firebrand.

The normal interpretation of the god's attribute as a club has led to the identification, by modern scholars, between Smertrius and the Graeco-Roman HERCULES. But there is other evidence which links Smertrius with the peaceful Celtic version of Mars (*see* MARS LENUS): at Möhn near Trier, there was a spring sanctuary dedicated to the divine couple Mars Smertrius and ANCAMNA. The shrine consisted of an enormous enclosure containing a spring near to which was the principal temple; this was of square plan, with a *cella* and colonnaded portico; its walls were decorated with red stucco. This structure was rebuilt and refurbished several times; coins found here indicate that there was a shrine here before the Roman period, in the free Celtic phase. Inside the *cella* was a dedication to Mars Smertrius and Ancamna. Another Treveran inscription links Mars with Smertrius; and Smertrius himself is known outside Gaul, for example on a fragmentary invocation at Grossbach in Austria.
□ C.I.L. XIII, 3026, 4119, 11975; Espérandieu, nos 3132, 3133; de Vries 1963, 67; Wightman 1970, 223–4.

Smith-god In the Celtic world the smith's craft was surrounded by a certain mystery,

The goddess **Sirona** with her snake, symbol of regeneration, accompanied by her consort Apollo, at Mâlain, Burgundy.

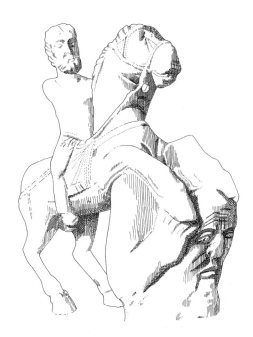

Stone image of the **Sky-god** and giant, from the top of a Jupiter-Giant column at Neschers, eastern France.

an air of supernatural competence, and great prestige attached to smithing. The ability to transform rough, rocky lumps of dull ore into gleaming edge-tools was something which was regarded with awe by warrior and peasant alike. Craftsmen were held in high esteem and had elevated rank within Celtic society.

Archaeological evidence provides certain information pertaining to a smith cult, particularly in Britain during the Roman period. The native god was probably assimilated with Vulcan, the Roman divine smith. A bronze image of a smith comes from Sunderland, closely paralleling an example from Lyon. But most interesting are a series of potsherds all in rough grey ware from North Britain, which are decorated with appliqué smiths' tools – hammers, tongs and anvils. Examples come from Chester-le-Street (Durham), Elmswell, Malton and Norton (N. Yorks) and Corbridge (Northd). This last site has also produced a complete figure of a Smith-god applied to a pottery vessel. He stands over his anvil with an ingot held in a pair of tongs in one hand and his hammer in the other. He is bearded, wearing a conical cap and a belted tunic, leaving his left shoulder bare. The sherd dates from the 2nd c. AD.

In southern Britain, there is less evidence of a smith cult, but a pot at Colchester is decorated with applied smithing equipment; and the sceptre binding at Farley Heath (Surrey) has smiths' tools as part of its iconographic repertoire (along with depictions of the Sun- and Hammer-gods and various cult animals). Vulcan himself is represented on silver plaques at Barkway (Herts) where he is depicted on two of the sheets, one of which bears an inscribed dedication to him.

The divine smith occupied a prominent position in the mythology of vernacular tradition. He was GOFANNON in Wales, GOIBHNIU in Ireland. Goibhniu was an important divinity, who fashioned magical weapons for the other gods, which were guaranteed to find their mark. Goibhniu had another function: he presided over the Otherworld feast, and all who partook of it became immortal.
□ Green 1976, 209; 1978, 55–72, pls 53, 56; Leach 1962, 35–47; Toynbee 1964, 328–30; Goodchild 1938; Mac Cana 1983, 34–5.

snake The physical characteristics of this creature have endowed it with multifarious symbolism. Its earthbound image and rippling movement link the snake to the underworld and to water. Its habit of sloughing its skin three or four times a year has been perceived as an allegory of death and regeneration (*see* REBIRTH). Fertility associations may derive from the multiple penis of the male and the prolific number of young produced by the female: the shape of the serpent also suggests phallicism (*see* PHALLUS). The venom and carnivoracity of the beast inspired awe and fear.

In Roman religion, snakes were considered as protective house-spirits: thus they were depicted in *lararia* (small domestic shrines set in house walls). The great Graeco-Roman healing god Asklepios/Aesculapius had a snake as a curative (regenerative) and chthonic emblem. In a Celtic milieu, the snake fulfilled the composite role of fertility, healing and underworld symbol. On the Romano-Celtic JUPITER-GIANT COLUMNS, the monster trampled by the Sky-god is shown to represent the chthonic, negative forces by means of his snake limbs. Many Celtic healers appear with snakes: Sirona's image at Hochscheid bears a bowl of eggs in one hand and a snake twines round her arm, its head towards the eggs. Sirona appears again with a serpent on a bronze figurine of the goddess accompanied by Apollo at Mâlain in Burgundy. Another healing-goddess, Damona, also has a snake as one of her attributes. The cult of the Three Mothers in the Rhineland was associated with snakes: on some reliefs, the image or dedication is accompanied by a snake curled round a TREE, as if it is protecting the sacred symbol of life embodied by the tree. Similar imagery occurs in southern Gaulish representations of the Sky- and Sun-god, for example at Séguret, where a serpent is curled round an oak tree. In the Nîmes area, the Gaulish Hammer-god is sometimes accompanied by a snake which twines itself round the hammer handle. Here the creature may be present as an emblem of fertility, healing and guardianship.

The rippling movement of the serpent has endowed it with water symbolism in Celtic iconography and mythology. A depiction of a goddess at Ilkley (Yorks) shows her with two snakes rippling down from her hands: she may be Verbeia, the spirit of the River Wharfe. At the spring sanctuary of Mavilly in Burgundy, a goddess has a snake which may also reflect water symbolism. Interestingly, this water connection is maintained in Irish mythology, for instance, in one of the tales about the heroic war-leader Finn: he is recorded as killing great water snakes. Many other mythological serpents occur in the vernacular literature. The Ulster hero CONALL CERNACH has an affinity with snakes: he overcomes a poisonous reptile which guards treasure in a fort which he attacks. The idea of a treasure-guarding snake appears again in Giraldus Cambrensis' story of a Pembrokeshire well which contains a torc, watched over by a snake who bites thieves. In an Irish myth, war and evil perceptions of snakes are illustrated by a story in which Meiche, son of the warrior-goddess Morrigán, was killed by Dian Cécht, and was found to have three snakes in his heart. It was believed that, had these serpents been left to grow inside Meiche's body, they would eventually have destroyed all animal life in Ireland. *See also* SNAKE, RAM-HORNED.

☐ Green 1986, 185–7; 1989, 53, 124–9, figs 17, 24; Schindler 1977, fig. 92; Dillon 1953, 19; von Petrikovits 1987; Tufi 1983, no. 31; Thevenot 1955; Ross 1967a, 153, 345–6.

Bronze **Smith-god** from Sunderland, north Britain.

snake, ram-horned A curious iconographic phenomenon in the Celtic world was the merging of symbols to produce a hybrid image, thereby intensifying its potency. An example of this is the ram-horned or ram-headed serpent, which appears especially in north-east Gaul. The idea seems to have been to link the fertility symbolism of the RAM with the composite imagery of the SNAKE: this latter creature represented both underworld (chthonic) concepts and those of renewal.

The ram-horned snake was frequently depicted as an associate of various anthropomorphic divinities. In most instances, the monster accompanies beneficent gods who themselves reflect fertility, abundance, protection and healing. Most commonly, the ram-horned snake accompanies the antlered deity CERNUNNOS, himself a lord of animals and presider over well-being and plenty. An interesting feature here is that the association between Cernunnos and the ram-horned snake occurs well before the Roman period: the two images appear together at Camonica Valley, at Gundestrup and elsewhere.

In the Romano-Celtic phase, the close affinity between the ram-horned snake and the antlered god continued. This is probably because the presence of the snake serves to intensify the symbolism already there in the concept of the god himself, namely fertility,

The Celtic Mercury with his purse and **ram-horned snake**, accompanied by a goddess, from Néris, Allier, France.

florescence and regeneration. Some iconography is indicative of a symbiotic relationship between god and monster: thus, on a bronze statuette at Étang-sur-Arroux near Autun, the stag-god sits entwined by two ram-horned snakes who eat from a heap of fruit on his lap; and a stone carving at Sommerécourt (Haute-Marne) shows virtually identical symbolism. In these instances, the mythical beast is nourished and protected by the gods of fertility, who in turn receive potency from its presence. Cernunnos appears with his horned serpents on one British image: at Cirencester, capital of the Dobunni, a small plaque depicts the god flanked by two snakes who rear up on either side of him, tongues protruding, facing two open purses of coins on each side of Cernunnos' head. The intimate relationship between the deity and his snakes is demonstrated in that the lower bodies of the reptiles form the legs of the god.

Other beneficent protector-deities could be accompanied by this hybrid creature: the Celtic Mars, in his peaceful guardianship role, is sometimes thus represented. The god keeps his overt warrior image, but within a Celtic context, he is a protector of health and well-being rather than a combattant. So, at the spring-site at Mavilly (Côte-d'Or) Mars, wearing chain-mail and carrying a lance and shield of late Iron Age type, is accompanied by a goddess and a ram-horned snake. Mars and his serpent appear, too, on a small bronze statuette from Southbroom (Wilts), where a god clad in tunic and helmet grasps two of the creatures by their necks. The association between the snakes and healing spring sanctuaries, noted at Mavilly, is appropriate, bearing in mind the rebirth symbolism of the reptile: thus, at the thermal site of Lantilly in Burgundy, there is the image of a naked, seated deity with a ram-horned snake. Another curative shrine, at Néris-les-Bains (Allier) produced a representation of the native Mercury with a consort in the guise of a spring nymph: the god himself sits with his purse in one hand and nursing a large ram-horned snake which is draped over his knee, rather in the manner of Cernunnos at Sommerécourt. Mercury and the snake appear again on a relief at Beauvais, where the god is represented in full Classical form, but where, on each side panel of the stone is a large ram-horned serpent. The final association to be mentioned is that which occurs on a small altar from Lypiatt Park (Glos). On the focus of this stone is a wheel in low relief, and twined round the altar is a ram-horned snake. This apparent link between the symbolism of the solar wheel and the snake is obscure, but the sun cult was closely involved with fertility, and the snake is probably present at Lypiatt to augment that symbolism. It is well known that ordinary snakes are frequent companions of the Romano-Celtic Sky-god.

□ Bober 1951, 13–51; Olmsted 1979, pl. 2A; Green 1986, 192–5; 1989, 92–3, figs 21, 35, 39; Autun 1985; Espérandieu, nos 4831, 2067, 2072, 2332, 1573; Deyts 1976, nos 284, 285; British Museum 1964, 54, pl. XVII; Drioux 1934, 67–72; Thevenot 1968, 72–89.

Souconna Most, if not all, rivers were sacred in the Celtic world; they gave life to all along their route, and seemingly had independent life. Many are known to have possessed divine, named spirits. One such was Souconna, the deity of the River Saône at Chalon-sur-Saône, to whom epigraphic invocation was made (Musée Denon, Chalon). *See also* RIVER.

South Cadbury Castle The Iron Age fortified town at South Cadbury (Somerset) was not only important as a centre for industry and trade; it was also a prominent focus for religious activity. The body of a young man was deliberately buried in the rear of the bank, perhaps in order to propitiate the gods of the territory on which the hillfort was built, or to render good fortune to the rampart: the man may have died in battle or he could have been a human sacrifice (*see* SACRIFICE, HUMAN). Other evidence includes the burial of horse and cattle skulls carefully deposited right way up in pits associated with a possible SHRINE. The most convincing example of a sanctuary is a rectangular building with a deep porch or verandah in the front, which dates from the late Iron Age and which pottery evidence suggests was abandoned around the time of the Roman Conquest in AD 43. In a well-defined and narrow band or avenue associated with the building were more than twenty burials of young domestic animals, mainly calves but including piglets and newborn lambs. These were presumably sacrifices (*see* SACRIFICE, ANIMAL), perhaps to a nature-deity for whom gifts of young creatures would be appropriate. Discrete from the animal interments were weapon

deposits, perhaps the offerings of warriors which were kept separate from those of farmers.
□ Alcock 1972.

sovereignty, goddess of *see* SACRAL KINGSHIP; ÉRIU; MEDB; MORRIGÁN

spring, healing All WATER had an aura of mystery and possessed a certain sanctity. Perhaps the most important Celtic water cults were those associated with springs, which were perceived to have properties of purity, heat and sometimes contained curative minerals. Springs well up, seemingly spontaneously, from deep below ground and were envisaged as being of supernatural origin.

Whilst the therapeutic qualities of Gaulish and British springs were recognized long before the Romano-Celtic period, the great curative spring sanctuaries were not developed until the very end of the 1st millennium BC. Thereafter, shrines (*see* SHRINE), dormitories, baths and hostels grew up around particular springs, each of which was presided over by a deity.

Of the many spring sanctuaries, a few stand out as being of particular importance. FONTES SEQUANAE near Dijon and CHAMALIÈRES south of Clermont-Ferrand are two examples of sanctuaries which were apparently first visited by pilgrims during the 1st c. BC, when devotees seeking a cure offered wooden votive models of themselves or the afflicted parts of their bodies to the resident divinity (*see* LIMB/ORGAN, VOTIVE). The spirit at *Fontes Sequanae* was Sequana, goddess of the River Seine at its spring-source. MARS LENUS presided over the great healing spring sanctuary at Trier; the Celtic Apollo was venerated at many sacred spring temples, such as Sainte-Sabine (Apollo Belenus) and ESSAROIS (Apollo Vindonnus) in Burgundy. At HOCHSCHEID in the Moselle Basin, Apollo was worshipped with his native consort Sirona. In Britain, the most important spring shrine was that of SULIS Minerva at BATH, where the hot water pumps out of the ground beside the River Avon at the rate of a quarter million gallons a day.

The developed spring shrines possessed many common features, most of which derive from Graeco-Roman traditions, though they were dedicated to Celtic divinities. One feature was the concept of reciprocity, the giving of votive models of diseased parts of the body

Altar encircled by a **ram-horned snake**, from Lypiatt Park, Gloucestershire.

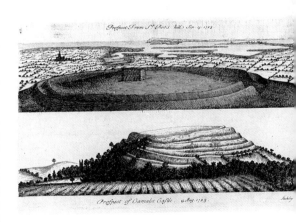

South Cadbury Castle, Somerset, from William Stukeley's *Itinerarium Curiosum*, 1775.

in order that the deity would reciprocate with a healthy arm, eye or other organ. Another was the healing sleep: pilgrims visiting the sanctuaries slept in special dormitories, where they hoped to see a vision of the god and be cured by his or her visitation. *See also* ARNEMETIA; COVENTINA; FONTAINES SALÉES; GLANUM; IANUARIA; ICOVELLAUNA; NEMAUSUS; ORACLE; POOL.

□ Green 1986, 150–5; Deyts 1983; 1985; Vatin 1969, 103–14; Cunliffe & Davenport 1985; Dehn 1941, 104ff; Thevenot 1968, 97–116.

stag The symbolism of the stag in Celtic religion and mythology was concerned with the particular qualities the animal was perceived to possess. Stags are fast, virile and aggressive during the rutting season. They are kings of the forest, their antlers symbolic of the spreading trees of the wood. The growth and shedding of their antlers in spring and autumn has endowed stags with seasonal imagery. All in all, the stag would appear to represent fertility, the abundance of the forest, speed and prestige.

The stag was depicted in multifarious iconography throughout the Celtic world, in both the pre-Roman and Romano-Celtic periods. In the Bronze Age and Iron Age phases at PASPARDO in Camonica Valley, stags formed a major part of the repertoire of the rock carvers. On the great Naquane rock, whose carvings date from the 7th c. BC, an ithyphallic hunter is accompanied by a creature that is half man, half stag. Stags were frequently shown as hunted beasts at Camonica, but the iconography displays reverence for the animal, as well. The stag is depicted enclosed within a circle of praying or dancing human figures. The beast is also concerned with the sun at Camonica, and sometimes antlers and rayed solar disc merge to form a composite symbol. A number of early Celtic images of stags are recorded: the 7th c. BC STRETTWEG bronze cult wagon depicts a goddess, soldiers and two small stags with enormous antlers, in what is probably a representation of a ritual hunt. On a 6th c. BC gold bowl at Zurich Altstetten, suns, moons and deer images are present. A bronze group dating from the 3rd c. BC at Balzars, Liechtenstein, depicts warriors, a boar and a stag, again with overemphasized antlers; and a bronze stag dating from around 100 BC comes from Saalfelden in Austria. Celtic coins depict stags: on a coin

from Maidstone in Kent a boar and a stag with huge antlers are depicted. This repeated stress on the antlers may have enhanced the virility and forest potency of the image. Certainly, seasonal imagery is present on the bronze stag from the late Iron Age hoard at Neuvy-en-Sullias, who is portrayed with his antlers in their spring velvet.

Many Romano-Celtic hunter-gods are depicted with stags (*see* HUNTER-GOD). These deities frequently have an ambiguous relationship with their quarry, in that they are projected as protectors of the inhabitants of the forest. Indeed, the divine hunt may well have symbolized renewal and immortality as well as destruction. A hunter with his weapons lays his hand in benediction on the antlers of a stag at the Le Donon sanctuary in the Vosges; at Treclun in Burgundy, a naked god is associated with a hunt scene with stags and hounds. Cocidius at Risingham in North Britain is accompanied by deer, including a stag; and the 3rd c. AD hunter image at London shows the god accompanied by his stag and hound. At Colchester, a pit associated with a shrine produced a bronze stag figurine and a bronze tablet inscribed with a dedication to SILVANUS CALLIRIUS ('Woodland King').

The Celtic god who is most closely linked with stags is CERNUNNOS ('the horned one'). He wears antlers on his head, showing his essential affinity with the animal, and he sometimes appears with the stag itself. The earliest such depiction is the image of Cernunnos with his stag beside him on one of the plates of the Danish Gundestrup Cauldron, which may date as early as the 2nd–1st c. BC. In Romano-Celtic imagery, Cernunnos and his stag appear together on a stele at Reims and on a relief at Nuits-Saint-Georges in Burgundy.

The stag featured in certain Celtic ritual activities: at St Bernard (Vendée) a ritual PIT contained a cypress tree, antlers and the figurines of a goddess; and an Iron Age pit burial at Villeneuve-Renneville consisted of the body of a Gaulish warrior accompanied by a domesticated stag, complete with bit. A ritual shaft at Ashill (Norfolk) contained boar tusks, antlers and more than 100 pots; and another pit at Mays Meadow (Worcs) contained antlers remaining from a complete skeleton. A pit deposit at Wasperton (Warks) shows evidence of a complex ritual: face-down in a shaft was a stone inscribed 'feliciter'; on the upper surface, below a layer of burnt material, were two sets of unburnt antlers with pieces of skull attached. These had been arranged to form a square within which a fire had been lit (*see* SACRIFICE, ANIMAL).

Magic or supernatural stags figure in the Insular and Welsh traditions: the Irish war-goddess, the Morrigán, could shape-change to stag form. Bulls were able to alter between human, bull and stag form. Many Irish tales allude to the enticement of humans to the Otherworld by stags. In the Fionn Cycle, the war-leader Finn hunts an enchanted stag, metamorphosed from the Irish god Donn. Finn's wife Sava is turned into a fawn by the Black Druid, and their son Oisin is sometimes considered as half deer, half child. Flidais is an Irish goddess of wild things, including deer. In the *First Branch of the Mabinogi*, Pwyll, lord of Dyfed, hunts a stag which is the quarry of Arawn, god of Annwn, the Welsh Otherworld. In the *Fourth Branch*, Math of Gwynedd turns his nephews Gwydion and Gilfaethwy into a stag and hind. In the *Tale of Culhwch and Olwen*, Culhwch is helped to hunt the enchanted boar Twrch Trwyth by a supernatural stag with whom he can communicate.

□ Olmsted 1979; Espérandieu, nos 3653, 7800, 7633; Planson & Pommeret 1986; Anati 1965; Pobé & Roubier 1961, no. 54; Hatt 1964, pls 150, 151; Phillips 1977, no. 234; Merrifield 1983, 188; Mohen, Duval & Eluère 1987, no. 27; Green 1986, 133–5, 182–4, fig. 54; 1989, fig. 38, 134–9; Anon. 1980, no. 76; Megaw 1970, no. 4; Ross 1968, 258; 1986, fig. 60; 1967a, 333–8; Stokes 1895, 274.

The great Roman bath at *Aquae Sulis* (Bath), the **healing spring** shrine of Sulis Minerva.

Strettweg in Austria is the find-spot of a unique bronze cult wagon model which dates from the 7th c. BC and thus belongs to the early Celtic or proto-Celtic Hallstatt Culture. The model consists of a four-wheeled platform on which stands a large central figure of a woman carrying a flat bowl above her head. This goddess (if goddess she is) is surrounded by statuettes of cavalrymen and infantry with spears and shields; at each end of the platform is an image of a STAG with huge antlers. It is possible that the entire scene represents a ritual hunt, with the goddess presiding over and blessing the proceedings: her bowl or cauldron may represent sacrifice – of wine or blood – or she may raise the vessel towards the sky in a fertility gesture

Bronze figurine of a **stag**, 1st millennium BC, from Germany.

to induce rain. The over-emphasis of the antlers may also be significant, in stressing the sexual aggression of the stags during the rutting season. *See also* NERTHUS.

☐ Megaw 1970, no. 38; Mohen, Duval & Eluère (eds) 1987, no. 27; Green 1986, 34, fig. 13.

Sucellus Near the Mithraeum at Sarrebourg near Metz, was found a relief of a Celtic divine couple (*see* COUPLE, DIVINE): the deities are depicted standing side by side in a niche. The male divinity is a mature, bearded man with curling beard and hair, carrying a small pot in his open right palm and a long-shafted hammer or mallet in his left hand. Beneath the couple is a raven. The relief bears a dedication to Sucellus and NANTOSUELTA. 'Sucellus' means 'the Good Striker' or 'He who strikes to good effect', and thus his name must refer directly to his hammer attribute. The iconography of the god at Sarrebourg is very similar to that of numerous unnamed images of a HAMMER-GOD, who appears either alone or with a consort, particularly in Burgundy, the Rhône Valley and Provence.

The name Sucellus occasionally occurs on other dedications: a silver finger-ring dedicated to the god comes from York. An appliqué ornament for a vessel in the Rhône Valley bears the name Sucellus, accompanied by an image of the god with his hammer and pot. The source of the River Arroux was presided over by 'Succelus'. Many other invocations to Sucellus, though without an image, come from Gaul and the Rhineland.

The symbolism of the hammer is not easy to interpret. The implement is a noisy, striking tool: it may be a weapon, a fencing mallet or a cooper's hammer. But it can also be perceived as an instrument of power – a wand of authority, like a sceptre. In view of the known affinity between Sucellus and fertility symbolism, especially the grape harvest (symbolized by the Hammer-god's pot and barrel), it could be that the hammer may reflect the striking of earth, awakening it after the death of winter. The hammer of Sucellus may also be a combative symbol, to ward off disease or famine. *See also* CAULDRON.

☐ Green 1986, 46; 1989, 46–54, 75–86; Duval 1976, 62, fig. 45; de Vries 1963, 99–100; Espérandieu, no. 4566; C.I.L. XIII, 4542; Linckenheld 1929, 40–92.

Suleviae The Suleviae were a triad of Mother-goddesses (*see* MOTHER-GODDESS) who are recorded in dedicatory inscriptions found in many parts of the Romano-Celtic world: in Hungary, Gaul, Germany, Britain and even in Rome. In Gaul, the goddesses were sometimes called 'Matres Suleviae' or 'Suleviae Iunones'. The IUNONES were a plural form of the spirit of Juno, the Roman goddess who looked after women in childbirth. It has been suggested that the XULSIGIAE were a version of Suleviae, because of the similarity between the two names.

In Britain, the Suleviae were worshipped at three sites: at Cirencester two dedications are recorded, one of which was found together with images of both single and triple Mother-goddesses in the ruins of a probable temple at Ashcroft. The Colchester altar comes from an apsidal shrine. A dedication at Bath is from the great sanctuary to Sulis Minerva. This and the name 'Suleviae' (so similar to that of Sulis) gives the goddesses a solar and healing dimension. Interestingly, a Celtic sculptor with another linked name – Sulinus – set up altars to the Suleviae at both Bath and Cirencester.

The fact that images of triple Mother-goddesses were found associated with the Suleviae at Cirencester and sharing the same shrine at Bath makes it possible that iconography and epigraphy may be associated, though no images are given the name of Suleviae. All the evidence points to these divinities being related to cults of fertility, maternity, healing and regeneration; their widespread veneration over so much of the Celtic world argues for the popularity and success of their worship.

☐ Szabó 1971, 65–6; Duval 1976, 87; Wightman 1970, 213ff; Green 1986, 80–1, figs 32, 33; R.I.B., 105, 106, 151, 192.

Sulis Beside the River Avon at Aquae Sulis (BATH) the hot springs pump out of the ground at the rate of a quarter of a million gallons a day. The place must have been sacred and visited by pilgrims long before the Romans arrived and converted the shrine to a massive religious complex. Roman engineers converted the spring into a great ornamental POOL, enclosing it in a huge building which was associated with an enormous bath suite and a temple constructed in a basically Classical architectural style. This temple may have been built as early as the time of Nero or early in the Flavian period (that is, between about AD 60–75).

The name of the goddess who presided over the spring was Sulis, perhaps one of the most important of the British water-deities. Her name is linked philologically with the sun, and this may have been because of the heat of the springs. She was a healing goddess, and in the Roman period she was equated or identified with an aspect of the Roman divinity Minerva, probably in her capacity as goddess of the craft of healing. The cult statue of Sulis Minerva depicted the deity in Classical guise; all that remains is a large gilded bronze head, once helmeted, which was at some time hacked from the body.

Numerous altars to Sulis were dedicated at the shrine, and worshipped here too were a number of Roman and Celtic divinities, the latter including the Celtic Mercury and Rosmerta, Mars Loucetius and Nemetona, the Mother-goddesses (including a triad called the SULEVIAE, who are found elsewhere in Britain and on the Continent) and the Genii Cucullati.

The 7th c. BC bronze cult wagon from **Strettweg**, Austria, depicting a ritual stag hunt presided over by a goddess.

Pilgrims who visited Minerva's shrine came to be healed of disease (*see* SPRING, HEALING), and many altars may have been set up in gratitude or hope. Visitors cast huge numbers of coins and other votives into the spring and the reservoir. The coins throw interesting light on religious beliefs and practices, in that there is evidence that certain coin types were specifically selected, and some were deliberately damaged (*see* RITUAL DAMAGE), perhaps to render them useless to would-be thieves, or as a ritual act to remove the offerings from the mundane world and make them suitable for acceptance into a super-natural milieu. One very interesting group of offerings is the huge number of lead *defixiones*, sometimes called CURSE tablets, though they may more properly be termed *nuncupationes* (or pleadings). These were thrown by devotees of Sulis into the water. The tablets are incised with crude, cursive writing and invoke the goddess' aid in revenge against ills done to the devotee. Some votive objects were specifically associated with healing: an example is the ivory model of a pair of breasts offered to Sulis in the hope that she would effect a cure, perhaps for milk deficiency. The breasts may have been hung round the neck of a woman during childbirth and, after the child was weaned, were perhaps dedicated to Sulis in thanks

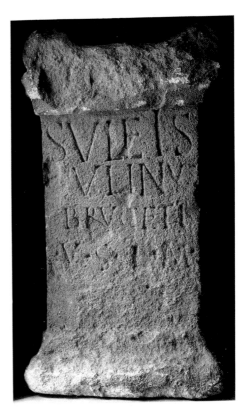

Altar to the **Suleviae** from Cirencester, Gloucestershire.

(see LIMB/ORGAN, VOTIVE). Milk failure would have represented a serious threat to the life of a young child.

The shrine of Sulis Minerva at Bath provides a superb example of the conflation and hybridization of Roman and Celtic religious beliefs and practices. On epigraphic dedications to the goddess where both Celtic and Roman names are mentioned, that of the indigenous goddess, Sulis, is always put first, thereby emphasizing that she was the patroness of the spring and that her cult was of long standing. Some of the iconography from the sanctuary endorses this fusion of cultural tradition: on the main temple pediment, for example, is a splendid carving of a Medusa head with staring, hypnotic eyes and snake hair, like the Gorgon of Classical myth. But Celtic influence manifests itself in that here, the female Medusa has been transformed into an aggressively male, bearded Celtic face. Classical artistic and mythological tradition has thus been used as a vehicle to portray a Celtic concept: the manner in which the hair and beard swirl around the head is evocative both of water and solar symbolism, each of which is relevant to the religion of Aquae Sulis: the presence of spring water was fundamental to the existence of the sanctuary, and the association between Sulis and the sun has been mentioned.

The importance of Sulis' shrine at Bath is indicated not only by the richness of the architectural, sculptural and votive material but also by the evidence of the temple's international status. One of the dedicants was a Treveran citizen who brought with him the cult of Mars Loucetius and Nemetona.
□ Cunliffe 1969; Cunliffe & Davenport 1985; Toynbee 1962, no. 25, pl. 20; Green 1986, 153–6.

sun/Sun-god The Celts perceived the presence of divine forces in all aspects of nature. One of the most important venerated natural phenomena was the sun, seen as a life-giver, promoter of fertility and healing. The archaeological evidence for sun cults manifests itself most clearly in the presence of the WHEEL as a solar symbol. In Bronze Age Europe, especially in Scandinavia, the cult of the sun predominated. Rock art consistently depicts solar images, and one of the most important finds of the North European Bronze Age is the Trundholm Chariot, a bronze model wagon pulled by a horse and bearing a gilded sun-disc: this dates from about 1300 BC.

In the Iron Age and Romano-Celtic period, people cast solar-wheel models into water, and placed them in shrines as offerings, as at Alesia and Lavoye, both in Gaul. They wore them as talismans and buried them with the dead, as at the Dürrnberg, Austria. The Iron Age people of Camonica Valley in North Italy carved images of the sun on the rocks of a valley which had been sacred since the later Neolithic. Celtic coins were struck with sun symbols associated with the HORSE, a solar creature in the Bronze Age and the Celtic period. In the Romano-Celtic phase, the sun cult was associated particularly with that of the Roman sky-god JUPITER. His images frequently depict him with the motif of the solar wheel. This occurs, for instance, on the bronze figurines at Le Châtelet and Landouzy-la-Ville. Sometimes, as at Luxeuil and Butterstadt, the god is a solar HORSEMAN, with a protective shield-wheel in one hand, riding down the dark forces represented by a monster with snake limbs. But in addition to his warrior role, the Romano-Celtic Sun-god was a healer, a life force and a companion to the dead. Curative spring sanctuaries such as Bourbonne-les-Bains (Haute-Marne) were visited by pilgrims who cast miniature sun-wheels into the water as offerings. The Sun-god was depicted holding the fertility symbol of a *cornucopia*, as at Netherby, Cumbria; and domestic goddesses may be portrayed accompanied by solar symbols, as on a clay figurine at Bro-en-Fégréac in Brittany. The association between the sun and death is evidenced by the burial of solar amulets with the dead, as at the cemetery in Basle, and by the carving of sun signs on tombstones in Alsace. The ceremonial mace head depicting a god with a wheel at WILLINGHAM FEN (Cambs) may have belonged to priests of the Romano-Celtic sun cult; and the large wooden wheel on a shaft recently found at the Romano-British site of Wavendon Gate (Bucks) may also have been regalia attached to a solar shrine. Officiants at sun ceremonies wore solar-decorated headdresses at the WANBOROUGH temple in Surrey, and wheel-pendants of gold and silver, found for instance at Dolaucothi (Dyfed) and Backworth (Tyne & Wear), may have been 'badges' of office.

There is little evidence for Sun-gods in the vernacular literature. The Irish LUGH ('Bright One') may be solar. An Insular goddess, ÉRIU, may be a Sun-goddess: in one legend, she is associated with a golden goblet which symbolizes the sun. *See also* EAGLE; HAMMER-GOD; OAK; ROSETTE; S-SYMBOL; SKY-GOD; SWASTIKA.

□ Green 1984a, 1984b, 25–33, 1986, 39–71; 1989, 116–23; 1991a; Anati 1965; Mac Cana 1955–6, 356–413.

swan Both archaeological and literary evidence attest the supernatural character of swans: in Urnfield and Hallstatt Europe, model wagons, often carrying vessels, are drawn by long-necked water-birds. An example of this is the wheeled cauldron at Orästie in eastern Europe, which dates from the 7th–6th c. BC. Swans occur very rarely in Romano-Celtic imagery, but at Alesia in Burgundy, a sculpture of the three Mother-goddesses with three children shows also another child seated in a boat and accompanied by a swan.

Irish literary sources abound in mythological stories associated with swans: all of these involve shape-changing between human and bird form, a habit particularly of females (*see* METAMORPHOSIS). The Ulster hero Cú Chulainn is repeatedly linked with magic swans: they appear as a flock of destructive and beautiful birds, ravaging the area round the royal palace of Emhain Macha, at the time of Cú Chulainn's conception. Again, when he is an adult, Cú Chulainn is associated with a flock of swans, at the 1 November festival of Samhain. The supernatural nature of these birds is demonstrated by the fact that they wear chains of gold and silver.

Swans, again wearing chains of precious metal, appear in other Irish tales: in the *Dream of Oenghus*, OENGHUS, son of the Dagdha, falls in love with a young girl, Caer Ibormeith (Yew Berry), whom he sees in a dream. When he visits the lake where Caer is to be found, he sees 150 young women, a silver chain between each pair. Caer is the tallest, and she wears a chain of gold. She and her followers take on swan form every alternate year and, interestingly, the shape-changing occurs on the feast of Samhain. Caer's father refuses to allow her to marry Oenghus, but he learns he must take her while she is in swan shape. He visits the lake at the correct time, calls Caer, who comes to him, and then he also assumes the form of a swan. The pair fly round the lake three times, casting a sleep-spell by singing as they go, before flying off to Oenghus' palace.

Altar to **Sulis** Minerva, dedicated by Sulinus, a Celt, from Bath.

The Celtic **Sun-god** had his origins in the Bronze Age. This is the 13th c. BC solar chariot with its gilded sun disc from Trundholm, Denmark.

The sea-god Lir is one of the Tuatha Dé Danann, the divine race of Ireland, driven underground at the coming of the Sons of Mil. Lir's children are turned into swans by their jealous stepmother Eva, who lures them to a lake and casts a spell on them with the aid of a magic druid's wand. The full curse is that they spend 300 years at each of three places; the enchantment will only be undone when a prince from the North marries a princess from the South, and when the swan-children hear the bell which is the 'voice' of Christianity in Ireland. These things finally come to pass, but when the children of Lir are restored to human form, they are extremely old people and die. They are buried by the Christian priest Kemoc, and a tombstone engraved in ogham is set up over their burial mound.

A final important swan myth concerns the Otherworld god MIDHIR; he and his lover Étain escape from her husband's fortress in the form of swans.

□ O'Fáolain 1954; Shaw 1934; Ross 1967a, 237–8; Coles & Harding 1979, 367–8; Espérandieu, no. 7107; Deyts 1976, no. 5; Green 1986, 147.

swastika This was a ubiquitous symbol of good luck and of the sun in many ancient cultures: in Europe, the Near East and as far east as India, where it is still a Hindu symbol of the sun. It was a widely used decorative motif in the Greek and Roman world. In Celtic Europe, the swastika was adopted above all as a solar symbol, similar in meaning to the spoked WHEEL, but stressing the element of rotary movement.

There is a group of small, roughly made altars from mountain sanctuaries in the French Pyrenees which were dedicated to the Celtic sky-sun god. Some of the stones bear inscriptions to Jupiter, and they sometimes have a wheel or swastika (or both) incised on the surface. The swastika and wheel frequently occur together on the same stone; invariably the solar wheel occupies the main front surface, the swastika is on the base. Some of these altars depict a swastika and a conifer: an altar from a Pyrenean shrine at Valentine bears a tree, a palm and a swastika on one surface and a wheel on the other side. The combination of sun-wheel, swastika and dedications to Jupiter make it reasonably certain that here, at any rate, the swastika is associated with solar and celestial symbolism. It may be that the wheel represents the sun itself, the swastika its movement across the sky. In addition to the presence of altars from sanctuaries, pots with swastikas scratched on them are also found in Pyrenean contexts.

Swastikas appear fairly rarely on other stonework, but a curious stele from Robernier (Var) further east in Provence, bears motifs in the form of a HORSE and a swastika. Horses and swastikas recur on the Roman quarry face at Bad Dürkheim in Germany, where in the 1st c. AD petroglyphs were carved, perhaps by Celtic workers, consisting of wheels, horses and swastikas. It is well known that horses were closely associated with the Celtic solar cult.

Small objects, too, bear the swastika symbol: a bronze figurine of the Gaulish Hammer-god at Viège (Switzerland) has crosses and swastikas decorating his tunic (*see* CROSS). Statuettes of this god frequently bear celestial symbols. A swastika was incised on a miniature axe from the Romano-Celtic temple at Woodeaton (Oxon); there is some evidence that axes could be emblems of the sun cult. Finally, there is a group of swastika-shaped brooches, mainly from the German frontier region, for example from Cologne, Zügmantel and Mainz, some of which carry decoration in the form of crosses and concentric circles.

Like the spoked wheel, the swastika seems primarily to have been a solar motif. But it may, again like the wheel, sometimes have taken on a more generalized symbolism of good fortune and well-being. It was certainly a beneficent motif, one which enhanced the power of the Sun-god by emphasizing the behaviour of the sun in the sky, and it perhaps brought good luck to people who wore it as an amulet.

□ Grapinat 1970, 54–6; Courcelle-Seneuil 1910, 70; Deonna 1916, 193–202; Bertrand 1897, 145ff; Green 1984a, 55ff, 158–9; 1991a; Spräter 1935, 32–9; Fouet & Soutou 1963, 275–95.

Tara in County Meath was a sacred site in Irish mythology, the royal seat of kings and the place in which were enacted the rites of initiation for SACRAL KINGSHIP. Tara is mentioned in the *Dinnshenchas* (the *History of Places*), and the vernacular literature of Ireland is full of allusions to the royal court. God-kings of the Tuatha Dé Danann, such as Bres and Nuadu, reigned here, and the goddess-queen Medb is chronicled as stating that no king could rule in Tara unless he first mated with her. It was at Tara that the 'TARBHFHESS' or 'bull-sleep' took place, to choose the rightful king-elect; and it was the site of the ritual union between the goddess of sovereignty and the king. The high kings of Ireland were also frequently called 'king of Tara'. The sacred stronghold is situated in the middle of the five provinces of Ireland. Here, a great assembly for all the provinces was held on the Feast of Samhain, when there were fairs, markets, horse races and agricultural rites.

The site of Tara was perhaps sacred from late Neolithic times: here, the 'Mound of the Hostages', a Neolithic passage-grave, was erected around 2000 BC. During the Iron Age, the hilltop of Tara (which commands a spectacular view over the plain to the west) was fortified. Inside this 'Rath na Ríogh' (the Fort of the Kings) are two conjoined ring-forts, in one of which is a 6 ft high standing stone. This is quite possibly the Stone of Fál, mentioned in the literature as being a magic stone which cried aloud when touched by the rightful king. There are many other earthworks at Tara, including the 'Banqueting Hall' and the 'Rath of the Synods', not all necessarily of the same date. Tara was a multi-period site, which may have been holy for more than two millennia. *See also* FINN.
□ Macalister 1931; O'Fáolain 1954; Mac Cana 1958–9, 59–65; 1983, 114–19; O'Rahilly 1946, 234; Berresford Ellis 1987, 217–18; Harbison 1988, 58, 187–91.

Taranis The word 'Taranis' comes from the Celtic root 'taran' and means 'thunderer'. Taranis was the Celtic Thunder-god. The Roman poet Lucan wrote in the 1st c. AD of events which took place in the mid 1st c. BC. In his poem, *The Pharsalia* (I, 444–6), which is an account of the civil war between Pompey and Caesar, Lucan mentions three great Celtic divinities encountered by Caesar's army in Gaul. One of these gods he calls Taranis, and describes his cult as being 'more cruel than that of Scythian Diana' (*see* SACRIFICE, HUMAN). This is the only literary evidence for a Celtic Thunder-god. A later Berne

Iron Age bronze flesh hook decorated with **swan** symbols, from Dunaverney, County Antrim, Northern Ireland.

(Above) The 8th c. AD **Tara** Brooch, from Bettystown, County Meath.
(Below) Aerial view of the Hill of **Tara**, with its ancient earthworks.

scholiast or commentator, probably writing in the 9th c. AD, equated or linked Taranis with Jupiter, and described him as *praeses bellorum*, or master of war.

Only seven altars to Taranis survive: these were set up by worshippers during the Roman occupation of Celtic lands; they all bear inscribed dedications to the god. The altars from Böckingen in the Rhineland and Chester in north-west Britain provide the most detailed evidence for the worshippers of Taranis: the Rhineland dedication reads: 'deo Taranucno: Veratius Primus ex iussu . . .' ('to the god, Thunderer, Veratius Primus by order . . .'). The Chester altar is almost completely weathered away, and for its reading we have to rely on earlier transcriptions. The reading is generally accepted as: 'To Jupiter Best and Greatest Tanarus, Lucius Bruttius Praesens, of the Galerian Voting Tribe, from Clunia (Spain), princeps of Legion XX Valeria Victrix, willingly and deservedly fulfilled his vow, in the consulships of Commodus and Lateranus' (i.e. AD 154).

The seven altars to Taranis come from Chester in Britain; Böckingen and Godramstein in Germany; Orgon, Thauron and Tours in France; and Scardona in Yugoslavia. The dedications fall into two groups, each of three, the remaining one being too fragmentary to classify. The stones from the Rhineland each bear an invocation to 'deus Taranucnus'; at Scardona, the inscription reads 'to Jupiter Taranucus'. If we set aside, for the present, the Jupiter part of the Dalmatian dedication, all three inscriptions refer to a thunderer, an adjectival, descriptive title, 'one who thunders'. By contrast, the dedications of the second group, at Chester, Tours (Indre-et-Loire) and Orgon (Bouches-du-Rhône), refer to 'Thunder', as if here the elemental force of THUNDER itself was personified and invoked as a deity. On three dedications, at Scardona, Thauron (Creuse) and Chester, the Celtic name of Thunderer or Thunder appears as a surname or epithet of the Roman Jupiter. This means that the Roman SKY-GOD was being conflated with the Celtic god of thunder, in a form of *interpretatio celtica*. This is interesting, especially in the case of the altar at Chester, since it was dedicated by a Roman legionary officer: here is a good example of the extent of Celtic influence on Roman religion. But we should remember that, as some of the dedications demonstrate, Taranis did exist in his own right; he was not simply an adjunct or aspect of Jupiter in a Celtic milieu.

Though Lucan and his later scholiasts imply that Taranis was an important and powerful Celtic god, this is not supported by the archaeological evidence, which amounts to just seven monuments throughout the entire Celtic world. As a counter-argument, it can be pointed out that these few altars are widely distributed, suggesting that Taranis was at least known over a number of provinces ranging from Britain, through Gaul and Germany to Dalmatia. It may be that Lucan exaggerated the importance of Taranis because of ignorance or poetic licence: he did not travel in Gaul himself, as far as we know, and he could have obtained his information second-hand, perhaps thus confusing his data. It could be that since only a few Celtic god names were recorded by Mediterranean observers, the known ones, like Taranis and Esus, assumed greater significance than was the reality.

Taranis is one of a large group of Celtic divinities who were personifications of natural phenomena. His name 'Thunderer' implies his veneration as a noisy, rumbling god, perhaps associated with lightning and storms. He was sometimes linked with Jupiter because the Roman Sky-god was traditionally represented brandishing a thunderbolt. But JUPITER was a complex god with a wide range of functions, as all-powerful over the sky, all its bodies and emanations and the immensity of the luminous atmosphere. Taranis embodies only the thunder aspect of this celestial role; the noisy image projected by his name may suggest a power struggle in the sky resulting in weather and storms, implying battle and perhaps a fertility role as a rain-god (*see* RAIN). Allusion should be made to one misconception about Taranis. Scholars frequently equate him with the Celtic solar Wheel-god who was also, on occasions, conflated with Jupiter. But there is no direct evidence for a true identification between the sun and thunder gods, except that because Jupiter's celestial function was so wide-ranging, it was natural for both Celtic thunder and solar forces to be linked with the omnipotent Roman Sky-god.

Before the Romans came to the Celtic world, bringing with them traditions of written dedications and naturalistic anthropomorphic imagery to represent divine beings, Taranis may well have existed as an elemental supernatural force, like the sun. Under subsequent Roman influence, inscribed altars mentioned his name in writing for the first time. But we have no representations – no statues or figurines – which may definitely be identified with the Thunder-god. The most likely candidate for such an image is the small bronze statuette of a god from Strasbourg, wearing a Gaulish *sagum*, or heavy woollen coat, bearing a large thunderbolt in his hand but with no other attribute or emblem. *See also* DISPATER; FIRE.

☐ Green 1982, 37–44; 1984a, 251–7; 1986, 66–7.

Altar dedicated to 'Taranucnus', a derivative of **Taranis**, the Thunder-god, from Böckingen, Germany.

Tarbhfhess This was a method of king selection in Insular tradition, associated particularly with the rulership of TARA. The term means 'bull-sleep' or 'bull-feast': in the ritual, a BULL was slain and a man feasted on the flesh, also drinking the broth in which the animal was cooked. He then lay down to sleep, was chanted over by four druids (*see* DRUID), and a vision of the next king was revealed to the sleeper in his dreams. *See also* SACRAL KINGSHIP.

☐ Mac Cana 1983, 117.

Tarvostrigaranus Two stone sculptures, from Paris and Trier respectively, portray an image of a BULL associated with three wading or marsh birds with long legs and long beaks – cranes or egrets (*see* CRANE). The Paris stone is part of the monument erected to Jupiter and dedicated by a guild of Parisian sailors during the reign of Tiberius. Here two panels of the monument are relevant: on one a god in the form of a woodcutter, named 'ESUS' ('Lord') hacks at the branch of a willow tree with an axe or chopper; on another, a bull is depicted with two cranes perched on his back and a third between his horns. The inscription above the image is 'Tarvostrigaranus' ('The Bull with Three Cranes').

The stone from Trier displays imagery which is virtually identical: it was dedicated to Mercury in the 1st c. AD by a Mediomatrician tribesman called Indus, who was perhaps a shipper on the Rhine. On one surface of the stone is a representation of Mercury and Rosmerta, while on another a woodcutter chops at a willow in which are the head of a bull accompanied by three marsh birds. Although 'Esus' and 'Tarvos' are not mentioned on the Treveran stone, the repeated symbolism of woodcutter, willow, cranes and

Tarvostrigaranus, the 'Bull with three Cranes', on the *Nautes Parisiacae* monument, Paris, early 1st c. AD.

bull must identify this imagery with that of the Paris monument.

The iconography of these sculptures is interesting and enigmatic: if the birds are egrets, then their link both with bulls and willow trees is appropriate; these birds are fond of willows (both egrets and willows have an affinity with water). Egrets also enjoy a symbiotic relationship with cattle (removing parasites from their hides). The other elements in this imagery are triplism and the destruction of the tree by the woodcutter. The association of water, tree and birds may imply the presence of cyclical imagery: the TREE of life may be depicted, the birds representing spirits which are released when the tree is chopped down; but trees are reborn after the 'death' of winter, and this seasonal myth may be enacted on these monuments. The bull reflects potency, sexual vigour and strength, which would enhance the fertility symbolism of the tree. The three cranes may have a further significance: in Irish vernacular tradition, cranes may represent women, and both early Welsh and Irish mythology possess tales of magic birds grouped in threes.

One other piece of Romano-Celtic iconography may be significant in the context of Tarvostrigaranus: in the mid 4th c. AD shrine within the Iron Age defences at Maiden Castle (Dorset) was found a silvered bronze figurine of a bull, originally triple-horned (see BULL, TRIPLE-HORNED), with three female 'human' figures perched on his back. It may be that, in keeping with Celtic literary tradition, the imagery reflects the transmogrification of women into cranes and vice versa. Certainly, the Maiden Castle statuette makes little sense if regarded in isolation, but viewed within the context of the iconography from Paris and Trier, it is possible to see that a specific myth may be illustrated.

□ C.I.L. XIII, 3026, 3656; Espérandieu, nos 3132–7; 4929; Duval 1961, 197–9, 264; 1976, 53; Wightman 1985, 178; Schindler 1977, 32, fig. 91; Mac Cana 1983, 87; Ross 1967a, 279; Green 1986, 191, fig. 85; 1989, 182; Toynbee 1962, 145, no. 40, pl. 45; Wheeler 1943, 75–6, pl. 31b.

Telo The goddess Telo was the eponymous spirit of Toulon in the Dordogne. She was the deity of the sacred spring around which the ancient settlement grew up. A series of dedications to Telo come from Périgueux nearby; on three of these, Telo is invoked with another goddess named Stanna.

□ Clébert 1970, 253; Aebischer 1930, 427–41.

temple see SHRINE

territory, god of The essentially animistic belief systems of the Celts caused them to perceive spirits as being present in all the natural features of the landscape. Thus, many of their gods were topographical in origin, as is the case with many ancient and modern pre-industrial societies. Epigraphic dedications refer to hundreds of local godlings, tied to specific localities, whose names betray this close association with place. Thus, the god ARAUSIO presided over the settlement of Arausio (Orange); NEMAUSUS and the female Nemausicae were worshipped only at Nemausus (Nîmes). The same pattern of topographical veneration may be seen, for instance, with some of the river and spring-deities. Thus, SEQUANA was the name of the goddess of the Seine at its source. Some of the triple Mother-goddesses had epithets which were tied to specific localities, especially in the Rhineland (see MATRES; MATRONAE).

The association of deities with the land and with territory has its counterpart in the Irish mythology. Here, the goddesses were frequently divinities, linked to the land of Ireland or to part of it. These deities, really personifications of the land itself, formed unions with mortal kings in order to promote the fertility of the earth (see SACRAL KINGSHIP). Thus ÉRIU, the eponymous goddess of Ireland, mated with the king, sanctifying the union by a gift to her consort of a golden goblet of wine. See also ARDUINNA; ARNEMETIA; GLANIS; MEDB; RIVER; TELO; VASIO.

□ Mac Cana 1983, 92–3; Green 1986, 22.

Teutates The Roman poet Lucan, writing in the 1st c. AD, alludes in his poem the *Pharsalia* to three major Celtic divinities whom Caesar's army encountered in Gaul (I, 444–6). These gods were Taranis, Esus and Teutates, and Lucan mentions that each was propitiated by human sacrifice (see SACRIFICE, HUMAN). Commentaries on Lucan's poem from Berne, dating from about the 9th c., elaborate on Lucan's statement: here Teutates is equated variously with Mars and Mercury and, furthermore, we are told that

Teutates was appeased by the drowning of his victims.

The term 'Teutates' is a title rather than a name; it refers to the tribe, and thus Teutates may be considered as a tribal chief and protector. A number of dedications to Teutates, or a variant on the name, are recorded from Gaul and Britain, and here, he is normally equated with MARS. Mars Teutates was invoked on a silver plaque at Barkway (Herts); Mars Toutates Cocidius was venerated at Old Carlisle. At York, a silver ring was inscribed 'TOT', which stands for 'Totates' or 'Teutates'. Part of a pot found at the site of Kelvedon in Essex bears a graffito 'Toutatis'. This is interesting since other sherds from the site have stamped decoration in the form of Celtic horsemen and infantry, bearing hexagonal native shields. The possible significance of this imagery and the dedication at Kelvedon lies in the iconography of one of the plates of the Gundestrup Cauldron, which depicts a god thrusting a human victim into a vat of water, accompanied by processions of cavalry and footsoldiers. In view of the drowning sacrifices alluded to in the commentary on Lucan, it is possible that Teutates is portrayed on this Gundestrup plate. Certainly, most of the archaeological evidence we have points to Teutates being connected with warfare, perhaps in guarding the tribe or 'tuath', which is probably philologically associated with his name. But though one of Lucan's commentators does equate him with Mars, the other links him with Mercury; and there is a dedication to Apollo Toutiorix at Wiesbaden. Perhaps the title of tribal protector could be granted to a number of different deities.
□ Zwicker 1934–6, 50; Toynbee 1978, 129–48, no. 26; Olmsted 1979; Rodwell 1973, 265–67; Hassall & Tomlin 1978, 478; Duval 1976, 29–31; de Vries 1963, 53–8; C.I.L. XIII, 7564; RCHM 1962, 133; Ross 1967a, 171–2.

Thames, River During the middle and later Bronze Age and the Iron Age in Europe, people used water, particularly rivers, as foci of cult activity and as places for communication with supernatural powers (*see* RIVER). Among other offerings, worshippers cast into the water prestigious metalwork, mainly in the form of martial equipment. The reason for such a tradition may have been the desire to propitiate the water-gods by committing to them gifts which represented power, prestige,

A *genius loci*, or **god of territory**, from Carlisle.

Detail of a plate on the Gundestrup Cauldron, showing a god, sometimes interpreted as **Teutates**, drowning a sacrificial victim in a bucket.

wealth and security. Two important Celtic élite offerings from the Thames are the Battersea Shield and the Waterloo Helmet. The shield may date from the 1st c. AD; it must have been either a ceremonial shield or have been made specially as a votive offering, since it is too thin ever to have withstood actual combat. It is a beautiful object, covered in sheet bronze and decorated with red glass. The Waterloo Helmet is horned, and was perhaps again a ceremonial item. It dates from the 1st c. BC. Diodorus Siculus (V, 30) alludes to the presence of horns on some Celtic helmets.

Many rivers in the Celtic world attracted large numbers of religious offerings. Rivers were a life source, representing a powerful, moving force and possessing particular divine spirits. It is possible that the repeated deposition of metalwork in the Thames over a long period of time may represent votive offerings to a River-god whose cult focus was at regular crossing places.
□ Fitzpatrick 1984; Hodder 1982; Merrifield 1983, 4–9, 15.

Thincsus *see* MARS THINCSUS

thunder The Celts venerated all natural phenomena, acknowledging the behaviour of the weather and storms as evidence of the supernatural power of the gods. They possessed a thunder-god, TARANIS, but they also absorbed the Roman cult of Jupiter, adapting his mythology and imagery to their own perceptions. The Romano-Celtic SKY-GOD retained much of his original Graeco-Roman symbolism, but the Celtic motif of the solar WHEEL was added to his imagery, and Jupiter's thunderbolt attained particular prominence.

On stone monuments to the Sky-god in Gaul, the sun-wheel and the thunderbolt occur together repeatedly, perhaps in acknowledgment of the god's power over all celestial activities. At Lansargues (Hérault), an altar dedicated to Jupiter is decorated with a wheel between two thunderbolts; the same combination of images occurs on an anepigraphic altar from Castelas de Vauvert, Nîmes. A stele at Montmirat in the same area of the lower Rhône Valley bears two wheel-symbols together with part of an inscription referring to the burial of a thunderbolt. This stone, therefore, combines evidence for Celtic solar worship with the Roman custom

whereby the ground hit by a thunderbolt was thereafter held sacred. The bronze figurine of the Celtic Sky-god at Le Châtelet (Haute-Marne) holds a wheel in one hand and a large thunderbolt in the other. The mounted Sky-god of the JUPITER-GIANT COLUMNS often carried a metal thunderbolt, presumably so that it would catch the sunlight.

The association of the wheel and the thunderbolt may mean more than a combination of solar and storm imagery. As well as a straightforward sun symbol, the wheel may represent the chariot of the solar god rumbling across the sky and inducing the noise of thunder. The sound element may also be an aspect of the symbolism of the Hammer-god's implement, striking the ground and inducing RAIN. *See also* S-SYMBOL.
□ Green 1984a, 183–4 & *passim*; Espérandieu, nos 517, 6843; Espérandieu 1924, no. 106.

Tir na Nog is the Land of the Forever Young. It is one of the descriptions of the Happy OTHERWORLD of Irish mythological tradition. This is the underground kingdom established by the displaced TUATHA DÉ DANANN, as a land where pain, age, decay and ugliness are unknown. Tir na Nog is the land in which OISIN, son of Finn, lives with Niav, daughter of the king of the Land of the Forever Young. It is the land which is visited by Bran in the *Voyage of Bran*. The divine Midhir, a member of the Tuatha De, invites his love, Étain, to Tir na Nog, his Otherworld SÍDH under the earth.
□ Mac Cana 1976, 95–115; 1983, 122–31; O'Rahilly 1946, 119–22; O'Fáolain 1954.

Tollund (Man) Many Iron Age bog bodies have been discovered in the peat marshes of Denmark; some of them show distinct signs of human sacrifice (*see* SACRIFICE, HUMAN). It is possible that these depositions represent the activities of the Teutonic Cimbri, who may have come from this region. The most famous of these bodies is Tollund Man, who was found in May 1950. He had consumed a ritual meal of some kind of porridge before being killed and placed in the BOG in about 500 BC (*see* BOG-BURIAL). He was garotted with a sinew rope and deposited in the marsh wearing nothing but a leather cap and girdle. This sacrifice bears a striking resemblance to that of Lindow Man, a British Iron Age body from a Cheshire peat bog which probably

dates from the 4th c. BC (*see* LINDOW MOSS).
Here, the individual was garotted in precisely
similar manner to Tollund Man, and placed
in the bog wearing only a fur armlet. The
similarity between these two depositions
suggests that Celts and Germanic tribes were
closely related and shared some ritual traditions.
□ Glob 1969, 18–37.

torc Torcs are Celtic neck-rings: they were
indicative of high status when worn by individuals; and they are frequently depicted
around the necks of Celtic divinities. It is
possible that the torc possessed intrinsic
magical and religious significance.

The Celtic Sun-god, with his
wheel, lightning flashes and
thunder symbol, from Le
Châtelet, Haute Marne, France.

People of high rank living in Hallstatt
Europe were buried with torcs. The late
Hallstatt prince at Hochdorf wore such an
ornament; and the princess at Vix in Burgundy was interred with a gold ring which is
usually interpreted as a diadem but which is
now thought to have been a torc. Hoards
containing gold torcs and coins occur in the
1st c. BC. They may have been treasure
dedicated to the gods: at Tayac in the Gironde
region of Gaul a heavy torc, deliberately
snapped in three, was buried with 500 coins
(*see* RITUAL DAMAGE). The weight of the
necklet is 1.65 lb, and it must, like the Crown
Jewels, have only been worn very occasionally, if at all. At Mailly in Champagne, a torc
has been found with an inscription in Greek
letters which alludes to its being part of a
large offering of treasure dedicated to the
gods by the tribe of the Nitrobriges of south-
west Gaul.

Classical writers mention the wearing of
torcs by the Celts: Strabo (IV 4, 5) speaks of
the Gaulish custom of wearing ornaments of
gold and torcs on their necks. Dio Cassius
(LXII 2, 1–4) writes that the Icenian queen
Boudica always wore a great twisted golden
necklace. This is of particular interest since
a huge electrum torc has been found in her
territory, at Snettisham in Norfolk, along with
many other lesser neck-rings.

There are many depictions of humans and
gods wearing torcs: the Roman marble statue
of the 'Dying Gaul', copied from a bronze
original at a sanctuary of Athene at Pergamon
in Asia Minor, shows a naked Celtic warrior
with a torc. Celtic coins show torcs being
worn; and pre-Roman statues, like the 3rd c.
BC image at Mšecké Žehrovice in Czechoslovakia, show the neck-ring. More significantly,

Tollund Man, a human sacrifice who was
strangled and deposited in a Danish peat bog in
the 5th c. BC.

Celtic and Romano-Celtic divinities are frequently depicted wearing this badge of high office. The Celtic Mercury with his consort Rosmerta wears a torc on a stone at Trier; Hercules adopts the neck-ring on an altar at Castlesteads in Northumberland; and a bronze figurine of Venus at Augst in Switzerland wears a torc.

However, it is the truly indigenous divinities who most often wear this ornament. The great Gundestrup Cauldron, possibly manufactured as early as the 2nd–1st c. BC, shows images of gods wearing torcs. This is paralleled on the bronze cauldron at Rynkeby, also in Denmark, where a bronze mask of a god is depicted wearing a large neck-ring. The stone image of a boar-god at Euffigneix (Haute-Marne), probably of 1st c. BC date, is simply fashioned, but there is a heavy torc at its neck. The pre-Roman warrior-gods of Provence wear neck-rings; and the northern British god Antenociticus at Benwell was venerated with a statue wearing a torc. Many of the Celtic Mother-goddesses wear heavy neck ornaments: examples occur, for instance, at Naix (Meuse) and at Winchester (Hants). The female consort of the Celtic Hammer-god at East Stoke (Notts) is portrayed wearing a neck-ring.

Greatest of all the divine torc wearers was Cernunnos, the stag-antlered god. He appears on the Gundestrup Cauldron wearing one torc and carrying a second: this pattern of two neck-rings is repeated on a number of monuments. A 4th c. BC rock carving at Camonica Valley in North Italy depicts Cernunnos with two torcs slung from his arms. The 1st c. AD monument at Paris shows the antlered god with a torc hung over each antler. In Romano-Celtic Gaul, Cernunnos again appears with two torcs, for instance on the bronze figurine at Étang-sur-Arroux. The cross-legged god at Bouray (Seine-et-Oise) wears nothing but a torc.

Torcs are infrequently mentioned in the vernacular mythology of Wales and Ireland. The *Tale of Culhwch and Olwen* describes Olwen as wearing a large gold neck-ring. Giraldus Cambrensis mentions a well in Pembrokeshire which contained a gold torc guarded by a serpent who bit anyone attempting to steal it.
□ Jones & Jones 1976; Megaw & Megaw 1989, 124, 182, 215–17; Ross 1967a, 164, 348, fig. 207; Espérandieu, nos 3133, 4929; Jones 1954, 134, Green 1989, *passim*.

transmigration of souls The richness of some Iron Age tombs, with attention paid to sumptuous grave goods, leads to the supposition that the Celts believed in an afterlife which was not so very different from life on earth. Caesar (VI, 19) remarks on this tradition, commenting that though Gaul was not wealthy, funerals were splendid and costly. Caesar also alludes to druidic lore (VI, 14) which relates directly to transmigration of souls: 'The druids attach particular importance to the belief that the soul does not perish but passes after death from one body to another …' Lucan (*Pharsalia* I, 446ff) remarks that the Celts regarded DEATH merely as an interruption in a long life, as a bridge between one life and another. According to him, the Celts believed that human souls remained in control of their bodies in another world after death. Diodorus Siculus (V, 28, 6) comments that the Celts perceived the souls of men to be immortal and that after a definite number of years, people lived another life, when their souls inhabited another body. This belief bears a strong resemblance to the ideas on the afterlife propounded by Virgil (*Aeneid* VI) in his great epic poem on the founding of the Roman race.

In the vernacular literature, life after death in the happy Otherworld, rebirth and regeneration are important belief systems which run as a strong thread through the mythology. Manannán was associated with rebirth; and there is frequently confusion as to which events belong to the world of earth and which to the supernatural Otherworld. Whether transmigration of souls itself was believed in is unclear from the Insular and Welsh mythology, but REBIRTH in some form and an existence in an OTHERWORLD which is better than, but essentially similar to earthly life are dominant features in the literature.
□ Green 1986, 121–2; Wiseman & Wiseman 1980, 121.

tree Forests, groves and single trees possessed a particular sanctity for the Celts. Individual species and trees in general evoked life and longevity, and in the case of deciduous trees, there was the added seasonal symbolism of 'death' in winter and spring resurrection with the new leaf growth. Trees also reflected a link between the upper and lower worlds; with their roots spreading deep underground and branches apparently touching the sky, they were an inevitable symbol of bridges between the chthonic and celestial powers.

Classical authors allude to the existence of the sacred GROVE or 'nemeton' (a Celtic word). DRUNEMETON was the site of a sacred oak grove in Galatia (Asia Minor) (Strabo XII, 5, 1); Tacitus describes in graphic detail the grisly druidical rites in the sacred groves on Anglesey (*Annals* XIV, 30); Dio speaks of the grove of the British goddess Andraste in East Anglia (LXII, 2). Certain Gaulish tribal names reflect a veneration for trees: the Eburones were the yew tribe; the Lemovices the people of the elm.

In old and middle Irish, the word for a sacred tree is 'bile'; and a place-name BILIOMAGUS 'the plain of the sacred tree' is recorded. For the Insular Celts, the sanctity of a tree depended in part upon its age. Oak, yew and ash are important in the literature, and the hazel is associated with the sacred wisdom of druids and filidh. In the 12th c. *Dinnshenchas* (the *History of Places*), trees are mentioned as sources of sacred wisdom. In Ireland, the sacred tree is closely interconnected with the concept of SACRAL KINGSHIP. Each tribe or confederation of tribes may have possessed its own sacred tree which stood at the site where the king was to be inaugurated, a symbol of continuity, wisdom and sovereignty.

Archaeological evidence confirms the veneration of trees on Celtic sites: the two 6th c. BC sacred enclosures at the Goldberg and Goloring in Germany each contained a huge central post, probably imitative of a growing tree, acting as the cult focus (*see* PILLAR). The same occurrence is recorded at the 3rd c. BC Czech sanctuary of Libeniče. At the La Tène site at Bliesbrück (Moselle), more than 100 ritual pits, filled with votive objects, were planted with tree trunks or living trees.

Iconography too is redolent with tree symbolism: on one of the plates of the pre-Roman Gundestrup Cauldron is a scene depicting a military procession which involves the carrying of a sacred tree. Trees were especially associated with nature cults of vegetation and hunting. The stag, with its spreading antlers, was perceived to have a close affinity with the wide-branched trees of the forest; the symbolism was enhanced by the spring growth and autumn shedding of antlers, which so closely resembles the seasonal leaf fall and regrowth in deciduous trees. Trees were associated with cults of fertility and

Image of a god wearing a **torc**, a symbol of high status and divinity, from Alesia, Burgundy.

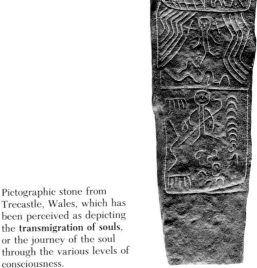

Pictographic stone from Trecastle, Wales, which has been perceived as depicting the **transmigration of souls**, or the journey of the soul through the various levels of consciousness.

regeneration: thus, they appear as images on altars of the Germanic Mother-goddesses, sometimes with a protecting serpent curled round them (*see* SNAKE). Trees appear, too, on altars of Nehalennia's cult. Here, they probably represent the Tree of Life, and this concept may well be reflected also in the presence of the willow tree on the altars of TARVOSTRIGARANUS at Paris and Trier. Here is depicted the imagery of a virile bull with three cranes or egrets on his back, associated with a willow which is attacked by a woodcutter. It is possible that the tree is 'killed' and reborn in an allegory of life, death and the seasons. The birds may represent the soul of the tree in flight, the bull the life force.

Tree imagery was especially important in the French Pyrenees, where altars were dedicated to 'FAGUS' ('Beech tree') or the 'God six trees'. In high mountain shrines in this region, conifers were symbols associated with a local Jupiter cult (*see* CONIFER). The Classical Sky-god was closely linked with the OAK tree; in a Romano-Celtic context, huge columns were set up to the Celtic Jupiter, which were copies of trees. Some, like the JUPITER-GIANT COLUMN at Hausen near Stuttgart, are decorated with oak leaves and acorns. In the imagery of the Celtic Sky-god, the column/tree seems to have been a symbol of a dualistic cult, where the forces of sky and underworld, day and night, life and death, were interdependent and mutually supportive. *See also* GRÁINNE; MISTLETOE; PESCH; VERNOSTONUS.

□ Watson 1981, 165–80; Maugard 1959, 427–33; Mac Cana 1983, 48–9; de Vries 1963, 195–9; Piggott 1968, 71; von Petrikovits 1987; Green 1989, 151–5, 103–6; Olmsted 1979; Hondius-Crone 1955.

triplism Number played an important role in Celtic symbolism. Most sacred or magical of all was the number 'three'. The idea of threeness is, indeed, a very common feature of Indo-European tradition, as it is in other families of cultures. Indo-European society itself was structured according to a tripartite classification: priests, warriors and cultivators. In Wales and Ireland, the triad was a literary formula used for traditional learning, which combined three concepts. In the vernacular literature, constant reference is made to triadic groups and triplication: the Morrigna were a triad of Irish war-goddesses, but really only one existed as a genuine entity;

she was sometimes presented singly, sometimes as three divinities, but there was only one identity, one character, one personality. The same is true of the three Machas (*see* MACHA). In Irish legend, there are three sons of Uisnech but only one, Naoise, the lover of Deirdre, has any real identity. The triple Brigit is slightly different in that her three different aspects were worshipped by poets, smiths and doctors respectively. Significantly, as a triple goddess, she was propitiated by the sacrifice of a fowl buried alive at the meeting of three waters. Triadic groups with different names form part of the Irish Celtic pantheon: there were three craftsmen gods, GOIBHNIU, Luchta and Creidhne; and three female personifications of Ireland, Ériu, Fódla and Banbha. There was a tradition of a threefold killing of the king, by wounding, burning and drowning. The hero Cú Chulainn had triple-braided hair and killed warriors in groups of three. In the *Mabinogi*, Branwen is described as one of three matriarchs.

In the vernacular literature, the repetition of NUMBER had the dual effect of exaggeration and intensification (*see* EMPHASIS), but this is in addition to the symbolism encapsulated within 'threeness' itself. Three was sacred and magical, and multiplication was often constrained by this sanctity. Three may have symbolized totality: in time, past, present and future may be reflected; in space, behind, before and here, or sky, earth and underworld.

Triplism is extremely prominent in the pagan Celtic religious iconography of western Europe. That triplication preceded the Romano-Celtic period is demonstrated, for example, by the deposition of three horse skulls together in Iron Age settlements, such as that of Winklebury Camp in southern Britain. But Celtic triplication manifested itself most prominently in the imagery of Germany, Gaul and Britain within the period of Roman influence. Two main types of triplism occur: where part of the human or animal form is multiplied, and where the whole form of a deity is repeated three times. One of the most distinctive of the first category is the triple-faced or triple-headed image (*see* HEAD, TRIPLE). It is a commonplace that the human head possessed special significance for the Celts, so it is no surprise that this element of the human body should have been singled out for triplism. Thus, among the Remi of north-east Gaul, their most important god was represented just as a stone block with a triple male face: sometimes youth and old age are presented on these triadic forms. What is interesting about the Remi is that this tradition did not begin in the Roman period; their Iron Age coins depict the same triple-headed imagery. Triple heads or faces are recorded from Britain, though generally without datable context. Such heads are known from, for example, Corleck, County Cavan, and from Sutherland in Scotland. But a secure context exists for the triple head from the Roman town of Wroxeter in Shropshire. In Burgundy, there are several male images of deities with single bodies but three faces. Where there is evidence, it appears that the three-faced type belonged to the large group of benevolent Celtic gods whose main concern was the blessings of abundance and prosperity. Certainly, a three-faced image is a recognition of potency: the image is unreal and thus supranatural; it can gaze in three directions at once; and its image enhances to the factor of three the power already residing in the human head. It is worth mentioning here that occasionally it may be the phallus rather than the head which is triplicated; this occurs on a figurine of the Celtic Mercury at Tongeren in Belgium (*see* MERCURY, TRIPLE-PHALLUSED), and on the image of a horse on an Iron Age coin from Bratislava in Czechoslovakia.

Triplism in animal imagery usually takes the form of a third horn added to the representation of a bull. About forty triple-horned bulls are recorded from Gaul and about six from British contexts (*see* BULL, TRIPLE-HORNED). These bull images are unequivocally sacred in character: they come from shrines and graves or may be accompanied by religious dedications. Here, we have a potent symbol of fertility and aggression multiplied as if to augment the symbolic source of power, but the horns are never more than three; the need to increase the visual symbolism of horns was constrained by the equally magical or sacred power of three.

Of the deities whose entire beings were triplicated, the most distinctive male image is the GENIUS CUCULLATUS, the 'Hooded Spirit', who appears in continental and British contexts, but only in Britain in triadic form. Like the triple-faced images, the Cuculati are concerned with fecundity and well-being; they appear at healing spring shrines and in company with Mother-goddesses. In Britain,

The Celtic **Tree** of Life, with its roots and branches forming a continuous symbol of eternity, an original design by Jen Delyth.

Three-headed god from Reims, France, symbolic of Celtic **triplism**.

there are two distribution clusters which are similar to those of the Mothers, the Dobunni of the Cotswolds and the region of Hadrian's Wall.

Female deities are often represented in triple form in Celtic iconography, just as they frequently appear as triads in the vernacular tradition. In the imagery it was the MOTHER-GODDESSES who were constantly envisaged as triads. These ubiquitous divinities appear all over the Romano-Celtic world. Sometimes, as in Burgundy, it is human fertility that is emphasized; but often it is the symbols of the earth's plenty, fruit, animals, bread and wine which are the emblems and attributes of the Mothers. Often the triadic images are accompanied by inscribed dedications to the 'deae matres' or 'matronae'. As with the Remic triple-faced images, the Mothers frequently demonstrate the representation of youth and maturity. In the Rhineland, there is a distinctive form of triadic Mother-goddess, where two middle-aged matrons wearing huge linen headdresses flank a young girl with free-flowing hair. In many cases, in fact, the three Mothers are not identical triplets, but have slightly different hair-styles, clothes or varying attributes. So whilst intensity of symbolism may be one factor in triplism, the idea of three entities in one may also be present: we may have three goddesses, or one Mother with three facets. In triplism, as in many other features of Celtic cult expression, fluidity and ambiguity in religious symbolism play a part, and the imagery does not lend itself to any one rigid interpretation.

So in many aspects of Celtic imagery and mythology, 'threeness' played a dominant role. Plurality and intensity in an image increased the amount of honour paid to the deity and the potency of the god itself. Repetition was important but so was triplication, presumably for magical or sacred reasons. What is important is that it was the Celtic deities who were concerned with the fates and fortunes of humans, their well-being and florescence, who were consistently represented in triadic form. *See also* FATES; MERCURY, TRIPLE-FACED.
□ Green 1986, 208–11, 1989, 169–205; 1990b.

Tuatha Dé Danann The Irish *Book of Invasions*, compiled in the 12th c. from earlier traditions, alludes to a number of successive mythical invasions of Ireland. The fifth of these groups of invaders was the Tuatha Dé Danann, the 'People of the Goddess DANU'. The Tuatha Dé were a race of divine beings, said to have inhabited Ireland before the occupation of the GAELS or Celts (the Sons of Mil). When the Tuatha Dé arrived in Ireland, they fought two great battles: the First Battle of Magh Tuiredh against the previous invaders, the FIR BHOLG; and the Second Battle of Magh Tuiredh against the FOMORIANS (Fomhoire). When they came to Ireland, the Tuatha Dé brought with them four powerful talismans to aid them in establishing themselves: the Stone of Fál (which cried out under a lawful king), the Spear of LUGH (which guaranteed victory), the Sword of NUADU (from which none could escape) and the Cauldron of the DAGHDA (from which none went unsatisfied).

The Tuatha Dé were skilled in magic and in druid lore. Many of their chiefs were powerful gods, often with specific functions. Thus, the DAGHDA (the 'Good God') specialized in druidic magic; Oghma in war craft; LUGH in arts and crafts; DIAN CÉCHT in medicine; GOIBHNIU in smithing; and there were many others. After the coming of the Gaels, the Tuatha Dé relinquished their possession of the upper world and created a kingdom underground in the Otherworld, a mirror image of life on earth. When they had been defeated by the Sons of Mil, they were still able to bargain, by depriving the Gaels of corn and milk. Under mutually agreed terms, Ireland was divided into two parts, the upper half for the Milesians, the lower half for the Tuatha Dé Danann, who then dwelled in their Otherworld sídhe (*see* SÍDH) or 'fairy' mounds in TIR NA NOG. This Otherworld was conceived of as a magical equivalent of the upper world, with rulers, hierarchies, loves and quarrels. But there was immortality there, agelessness and beauty, and the Tuatha Dé continued to practise their powers of magic and control over the supernatural.
□ Macalister 1931; Even 1956, 81–110; Carey 1984, 1–22; Krappe 1932, 90–5; Hull 1930, 73–89; Lehmacher 1921, 360–4; Kinsella 1969; O'Rahilly 1946, 141; Mac Cana 1983, 54–71.

Twrch Trwyth appears in the Welsh story of *Culhwch and Olwen*, as a king who has been transformed into a gigantic and destructive BOAR. Arthur asks him why he and his followers have been turned into swine, and Twrch Trwyth replies that when he was a king he

did such evil that God punished him for his
wickedness by changing him into the shape
of a pig. Before Culhwch can marry Olwen,
her father Ysbaddaden demands that he perform various tasks, of which one is that he
obtain the comb and razor (or scissors) that
repose between Twrch Trwyth's ears. In
order that the quest may be fulfilled, other
tasks have first to be accomplished, including
the release of Mabon, the divine hunter, from
his incarceration at Gloucester. Accompanied
by Mabon and Arthur, Culhwch hunts Twrch
Trwyth over Ireland, South Wales and
Cornwall and finally overcomes him.
□ Strachan 1937; Ross 1967a, 316; Rolleston
1985, 391; Hamp 1986, 257–8; Jones & Jones
1976.

Dun Connor, Inishmaan, Aran Islands. The
ancient fortifications were believed to belong to
the divine **Tuatha Dé Danann**.

Ucuetis was venerated with his female consort BERGUSIA at Alesia in Burgundy, where
they are named on inscriptions of the Romano-Celtic period. An image of a divine couple
(*see* COUPLE, DIVINE) has been found on the
same site, perhaps identifiable as Ucuetis
and Bergusia: he bears a hammer, and she
appears as a goddess of prosperity. That
Ucuetis may be a divine patron of craftsmen
is suggested by the context of an epigraphic
dedication to the couple. In 1908, a large
bronze vase bearing the names of Ucuetis
and Bergusia was discovered in the cellar of
a huge building; the rubbish found in this
underground room was made up entirely of
scraps of bronze and iron and appears to have
been part of the stock of metalsmiths. It is
possible that the crypt was a sanctuary to
the local craft-deities of ALESIA, and the
superstructure may have been a craft hall for
metallurgists.
□ Thevenot 1968, 125; Espérandieu, no.
7127.

Uffington (White Horse) There are about
fourteen hill figures of white horses in Wessex, of which only one, the Uffington White
Horse, has sufficient claim to antiquity to be
included here. This chalk figure was carved
high up on the escarpment immediately
below the Iron Age hillfort of Uffington
Castle. The horse is abstract in design (*see*
SCHEMATISM), with a long sinuous body, dis-
jointed legs and a bird-like, beaked face. Its

The white horse (upper left) carved in the chalk
below **Uffington** Castle, Oxfordshire, in about 50
BC. It was probably a tribal symbol of the local
Atrebates.

style has led to its interpretation as a Celtic beast, perhaps the tribal emblem of the Atrebates. The same treatment of the horse may have been seen on many Celtic coins, and there is a bronze model horse from Silchester, the Atrebatian capital, which closely resembles the Uffington figure. The HORSE may have been associated and coeval with the Iron Age hillfort of Uffington Castle. The animal itself has a long historical pedigree: White Horse Hill is mentioned in 1084, and there is another early reference to it in 1190. An interesting local tradition has it that the horse climbed the hill to its present position: this story may have come about because of the action of the eroding hill deposits, which actually have served to shift the position of the figure.

Numerous scourings or cleanings of the horse have been recorded, from about 1650 to 1900. These scourings were accompanied by ceremonies and festivals. Thomas Hughes, author of *Tom Brown's Schooldays*, wrote a treatise on the scouring of the White Horse in 1858, a graphic account of the last great scouring in the previous year. A late fertility festival, in which cheese rolling took place down the steep slope into the field below, is also recorded.

Dating the horse is difficult except on stylistic grounds. It is usually suggested as being carved perhaps around 50 BC. Recent investigations by the Oxford Archaeological Unit have gone some way to proving that the horse was always of its present schematic form and that this is not the result of erosion or recarving. Research by the Unit has also uncovered four successive recarvings of the horse's 'beak', and it is hoped that a new optical dating technique will be able to date the silt deposits interstratified with the horse, thus providing strong evidence for its chronology and origins.

Horses were powerful religious symbols for the Celts. They reflected prestige, speed, skill in warfare, fertility and power. Many Celtic horse-deities are known (*see* EPONA, HORSEMAN). If the Uffington horse belongs to the free Celtic period, then it may have been a tribal symbol of the Atrebates, carved on the hillside for all to see, as a potent guardian and protector of the tribe and its territory. The White Horse may be seen as both a sacred image and a sanctuary; subsequent rituals and festivities associated with the figure may well hark back to original cult

rites which took place to honour the tribe and its protective deities. *See also* CERNE ABBAS.
□ Woolner 1965, 27–44; Petrie 1926; Grinsell 1958, 149–50, pl. VIII; Palmer 1990, 28–32.

underworld *see* OTHERWORLD

Uxellinus *see* JUPITER UXELLINUS

  V

Vacallinehae *see* MATRONAE VACALLINEHAE

Vagdavercustis This goddess was a topographical spirit occurring in the Rhineland and to whom only one dedication is recorded. Her name is Germanic, and she was probably one of the Celto-Germanic Mother-goddesses whose worship was so popular on the German frontier during the Roman occupation (*see* MOTHER-GODDESS). The altar to Vagdavercustis comes from Cologne; there is no image of the goddess, but the presence of trees carved on the side panels of the stone may indicate a vegetation symbolism.
□ C.I.L. XIII, no. 12057; Green 1989, 40.

Vasio is an example of the numerous divinities in the Celtic world who were personified spirits of natural places or TERRITORY on which settlements grew up. Vasio was the native spirit presiding over the Roman town of Vaison-la-Romaine in the lower Rhône Valley. We know little about him, except that he was presumably perceived as the protector or guardian of the land, the town and its inhabitants. He would have been propitiated in order to secure the prosperity of the settlement.
□ Clébert 1970, 253.

Vellaunus Found during the excavation of a house at Caerwent in 1904 was a statue base recording the dedication of a statue 'to the god MARS LENUS, otherwise known as Ocelus Vellaunus, and to the Imperial *numen*'. Above this base a pair of human feet and those of a goose are all that survive of the statue. The dedication was set up in AD 152 by one Marcus Nonius Romanus. Vellaunus is known elsewhere from only one inscription, in the territory of the Allobroges in southern Gaul, where he was identified with Mercury. Mars Lenus was a Treveran god with great

cult centres at Trier and Pommern; OCELUS was a local British deity to whom another stone was inscribed at Caerwent, and who was venerated also at Carlisle. Mars Lenus was clearly equated in Britain with other, localized Celtic divinities. The association of the GOOSE with Mars Lenus is interesting: this creature had an affinity with the Roman Mars because of its qualities of guardianship and aggression.
□ Brewer 1986, no. 13, pl. 5; R.I.B., 309, 310, 949; C.I.L. XII, 2373.

Verbeia Many great Gaulish rivers are known to have been personified as female divine spirits, because of their life-giving properties (*see* RIVER). By contrast, we know of only a few of their British counterparts. One of these was Verbeia, goddess of the River Wharfe in Wharfedale (Teesdale). At Ilkley in North Yorkshire, an altar was set up to the goddess Verbeia; the same place produced an image of a woman who may represent this deity: she is depicted with an overlarge head and schematic features; she wears a long, pleated robe and she has two large snakes (*see* SNAKE), represented as geometric zig-zags, which she grasps, one in each hand.
□ Ross 1967a, pl. 68a; Tufi 1983, nos 30, 31, pl. 9.

The only known altar dedicated to the Celto-Germanic goddess **Vagdavercustis**, from Cologne, Germany.

Vernostonus The Celtic war-god Cocidius was worshipped in the region of Hadrian's Wall: in one dedication from the vicinity of Ebchester, Cocidius is linked or equated with a local god, Vernostonus, the personification of the alder tree. This occurrence serves to reinforce the link between Cocidius and the Romano-Celtic Silvanus, god of the woodland, with whom Cocidius is frequently identified in North Britain.
□ Fairless 1984, 224–42; Green 1986, 112.

Vichy was a healing spring sanctuary in the Allier region of France; it may have replaced the nearby shrine at Chamalières, which was only patronized until the 1st c. AD. Eye troubles particularly afflicted the pilgrims who visited the shrine, but a bronze statuette of a man holding a drinking cup from the site displays an appalling spinal deformity. The image suggests that an individual suffering in this manner sought a cure by imbibing the medicinal waters (*see* SPRING, HEALING).
    More than one deity was worshipped at Vichy: the Hammer-god is depicted with his

Statue base dedicated to Mars Lenus Ocelus **Vellaunus**, from Caerwent, South Wales.

pot, barrel and amphora, emphasizing the liquid symbolism of the cult. The Celtic 'Venus' too was invoked here, as attested by a pipe-clay figurine. Most important was a version of Mars, MARS VOROCIUS, who appears as a clay figure. *See also* BORVO.

☐ Thevenot 1955; 1968, 213–15; Espérandieu, no. 2750; Green 1989, 114–15.

Viereckschanze A distinct type of late Iron Age ritual site, occurring especially in Germany, is known as a *Viereckschanze. Viereckschanzen* consist of square earthen enclosures containing deep pits or shafts which were apparently centres of ritual activity (*see* PIT). An example is HOLZHAUSEN in Bavaria, where a large single enclosure contained three shafts, one of which had an upright pole with organic remains adhering to it. These remains are very possibly human (*see* SACRIFICE, HUMAN). Another important *Viereckschanze* is at FELLBACH SCHMIDEN, near Stuttgart, where a shaft contained wooden images of animals.

☐ Piggott 1968, 80–2; Green 1986, 133; Megaw & Megaw 1989, 162–3.

Vindonnus *see* APOLLO VINDONNUS

Virotutis *see* APOLLO VIROTUTIS

Visucius was invoked in dedications above all in Upper Germany (that is, the southern frontier area of the Gaul-Germany border), with an outlier at Bordeaux in Aquitaine. Interestingly, the Celtic Visucius was identified not only with an aspect of MERCURY (the usual equation for the native god) but also occasionally with MARS: a divine couple (*see* COUPLE, DIVINE), Mars Visucius and Visucia, recorded from Gaul.

☐ de Vries 1963, 150; Duval 1976, 88; C.I.L. XIII, 3660, 4257, 4478, 5591, 6118, 6347, 6384, 6404, 3665, 577.

Vitiris was a British god whose dedications cluster in North Britain among the confederation of the Brigantes. His name appears variously in inscriptions as 'Vetus', 'Vitiris', 'Vitris' or 'Hvitiris'. There was possibly a cult centre at Carvoran on Hadrian's Wall, where several dedications are recorded, but other evidence comes from Yorkshire and Durham. The dedicants were usually private individuals and were exclusively male, suggesting a masculine cult. During the 3rd c. AD the cult was particularly popular among the ordinary ranks of the Roman army.

Vitiris' name was never linked with that of a god of Classical origin, but he was invoked with another local god, MOGONS, at Netherby. Forty altars to this god are recorded altogether, some alluding to Vitiris as a single entity, others to a multiple version, perhaps a triad. Little is known about the specific function or character of the god, though the name appears to derive from the Latin word for 'old' and may therefore imply a god of great age and wisdom. Occasionally, there is iconography associated with Vitiris: for example, an altar to the god(s) from Carvoran is decorated with images of a boar and snake, the boar indicative of hunting or war and the snake healing or death.

☐ R.I.B., 971, 1793–805; Ross 1967a, 374, fig. 179; Haverfield 1918, 22–43.

Vix In the 6th c. BC a Celtic princess, about thirty-five years old, died and was buried in a barrow at Vix, below the stronghold of Mont Lassois near Châtillon-sur-Seine in Burgundy. The lady was interred in a plank-built mortuary chamber, which contained a dismantled funerary wagon (*see* CART/CHARIOT-BURIAL). The high status of the Vix princess is clearly demonstrated by the rich grave goods buried with her. Not only were the objects of intrinsic value, but they show evidence of wide trading contacts between Burgundy, Italy and Greece. The Etruscan objects include a bronze jug. An enormous Greek *krater* or wine-mixing vessel came from southern Italy or Corinth; and a pottery bowl was brought from Attica. Rich textiles adorned the funerary chamber; and the lady was wearing a heavy gold diadem or TORC, which may be of Italian origin.

The presence of very rich female burials, such as those at Vix and at REINHEIM, attest the high rank attainable by women in early Celtic society. It is evidence like this which makes the importance of Celtic female deities clearly explicable.

☐ Megaw & Megaw 1989, 46–7; Joffroy 1954.

Vorocius *see* MARS VOROCIUS

Vosegus This deity was the personified spirit of the Vosges mountains in eastern Gaul. There was a local nature-god to whom images were set up in this region, and who may well be Vosegus. A relief at Reichshoffen near

Strasbourg depicts a god wearing a heavy
Gallic cloak or *sagum*, carrying a piglet under
his arm. The same god was worshipped at
the high Vosges sanctuary at LE DONON, to
whom a dedication is recorded. This shrine
was situated on the boundary of three neighbouring tribes, the Triboci, Leuci and Mediomatrici; it was dedicated to the Celtic Mercury, but two identical stone images represent
a nature deity who may be identified with
Vosegus. They each depict a god with a
spear, hunting knife and chopper; he wears a
wolfskin over his shoulders and is accompanied by a stag. He carries the fruits of the
forest – including nuts, acorns and a pine-
cone – in a kind of open bag or haversack.
His boots are decorated with small animal
heads. He is the god of the Vosges Forest, a
HUNTER and protector of the inhabitants of
the woodland: he carries weapons for the
destruction of wild beasts, but he rests his
hand on his stag's antlers in an attitude of
benediction.
□ Hatt n.d., 42, pl. 23; 1964, 65–7, pls. 150,
151; Espérandieu, no. 7800; Linckenheld
1947; Duval 1976, 52.

The great wine-mixing bowl or *krater* from the
Hallstatt princess' burial of the late 6th c. BC at
Vix, Burgundy.

Walbrook The little stream known as the
Walbrook in London was apparently the focus
of aquatic ritual during the Iron Age. Large
quantities of ironwork and coins were offered
to the spirit of the WATER. During the Roman
period, the association of the Walbrook with
cult activity continued: the clay figurine of
the Celtic Venus found in the stream was
perhaps related to a healing, water cult
associated with renewal and rebirth.
Human skulls, perhaps of Roman date, have
been found here too, which may also have
been the result of ritual concerned with the
human head.
□ Green 1986, 165–6; 1976, 225; Merrifield
1969, 66–9; Fitzpatrick 1984, 180–2;
Manning 1972, 224–50.

Wanborough is a Romano-Celtic temple in
Surrey. It has two main features of interest:
firstly, large quantities of Celtic coins have
been found beneath the Roman levels, attesting that the site was sacred in the free Celtic
period. In the second place, the temple itself
has produced no less than three bronze chain

Pipe-clay statuette of the
Celtic Venus. A figurine like
this was found in the
Walbrook stream, London.

headdresses (*see* HEADDRESS). These must have been worn by clergy officiating at temple ceremonies. Of the greatest importance, however, is that two of the headdresses are surmounted by miniature bronze wheels (*see* WHEEL). The presence of these solar symbols may suggest that they belonged to priests of the sun cult (*see* SUN-GOD). It is worth noting that on a Celtic silver coin allegedly from Petersfield, Hampshire, the antlered god Cernunnos is depicted apparently wearing a wheel-topped headdress, which bears a close resemblance to the Wanborough regalia.
□ Green 1989, 165; 1991a; Surrey Archaeological Society 1988; Boon 1982, 276–82.

war/war-god Both the Classical and the vernacular literary sources describe a heroic Celtic society based on a warrior élite, where display of combative prowess and individual feats of bravery were an important feature of life. The Celtic tribe was protected by a tribal deity who guarded boundaries and warded off attackers.

From as early as the Bronze Age, it is possible to trace a form of ritual activity in which people deposited valuable items of metalwork, mainly martial equipment, into lakes, rivers and bogs. These offerings were not necessarily aimed specifically at a war-god, but were rather items of prestige. Weapons, some deliberately damaged (*see* RITUAL DAMAGE), were cast into the water at LLYN CERRIG BACH on Anglesey from the 2nd c. BC to the 1st c. AD. Earlier, in about 600 BC, arms and other high-status equipment were deposited in the lake at LLYN FAWR in mid-Glamorgan. The River THAMES received weapons and armour of Bronze and Iron Age date: spectacular 'free' Celtic examples include the Battersea Shield and the Waterloo Helmet, both deposited towards the end of the Iron Age. Celtic shrines, too, contained weapon offerings: at GOURNAY-SUR-ARONDE (Oise) numerous swords and spears were broken and given to the presiding god; virtually identical ritual took place at HAYLING ISLAND (Hants). At SOUTH CADBURY, a small Iron Age shrine was associated with weapon offerings. The presence of such votives is all the more interesting since allusion is made to ritual weapon deposits by Caesar (*de Bello Gallico* VI, 17) who comments on the Gaulish practice of piling weapons on the ground, dedicated to the god of the winning side in inter-tribal warfare.

Miniature arms, too, were offered to the gods in pre-Roman Celtic shrines (*see* MODEL TOOL/WEAPON): this occurs, for instance, at Frilford (Oxon) where a model sword and shield were found, and at Worth (Kent) which produced three model shields. The late Iron Age shrine beneath the Romano-Celtic temple at Harlow has recently produced four iron sword models, one with a sheet-bronze scabbard. This practice of miniature weapon deposition continued into the Romano-Celtic period, with examples of spears at, for instance, Lamyatt Beacon (Somerset) and Woodeaton (Oxon). But spears, of course, could be associated with hunting rather than warfare – perhaps more comprehensible in the context of peaceful, Romanized southern Britain.

Iron Age images of warriors perhaps sometimes represented gods: on Celtic coins, male and female soldiers, including horsemen and charioteers, are common iconographic themes. Southern Gaulish shrines, such as that at ENTREMONT, have produced lifesize sculptures of warrior-gods wearing armour; and other images of soldiers from Provence may also be divine. The 6th c. BC Hirschlanden armed stone figure may be interpreted as a dead hero or a god. In Britain, the group of wooden figures bearing round shields and set in a boat at Roos Carr (Humberside) belong to the Iron Age or may be even earlier in date. Little chalk figurines of warriors come from the Iron Age sites of Garton Slack and Wetwang Slack in East Yorkshire.

Caesar (VI, 17) comments on the popularity of MARS among the Gauls. So the Roman general must have encountered local war-gods whom he equated with the Roman Mars. But in the Romano-Celtic world, Mars was more important as a peaceful guardian, healer and protector against evil than as a combative warrior-god. Nevertheless, Celtic surnames to Mars on inscriptions show that the god retained a war role in the Celtic world: Mars 'Caturix' was 'Master of Fighting'; 'Segomo' was 'Victorious'. Mars Cocidius in North Britain has a surname which may mean 'red' and therefore blood. At Bewcastle in Cumbria, two silver plaques dedicated to COCIDIUS depict a stylized warrior with a spear and shield.

In Britain, especially in the North, simple, schematized war-gods were depicted iconographically in the Romano-Celtic period. These may often be naked, ithyphallic images bearing spears and shields, and frequently they are horned (*see* HORNS; PHALLUS). Thus, these deities combine characteristics of aggression and sexuality. At Yardhope (Northd), a remote rock face near a Roman marching camp was carved with the figure of a nude, native warrior with a small round shield and a spear. This reminds us of the remarks of Classical writers, who comment that the Celts often fought naked. A god at Caernarfon is portrayed with a spear and an odd trilobed helmet. Even in rural Gloucestershire, among the peaceful Dobunni, warrior-gods were depicted: a simple image comes from Stow-on-the-Wold; and a unique triple warrior-god was found with other sculptures in a well at Lower Slaughter.

In the heroic society of Ireland, as portrayed in the mythological tradition, most of the prominent war-deities were female: thus we have the MORRIGÁN, MACHA, NEMHAIN, the BADBH and MEDB, all of whom combined the attributes of fertility/sexuality and pugnacity. Here also are the tribal protectors, like the DAGHDA, who again had a sexual aspect, and who bore both a club of destruction and a cauldron of plenty and rebirth. *See also* HORSEMAN; RAM; RUDIANUS.

□ Megaw 1970, no. 12; Green 1975, 54–70; 1976, 176, 194; 1986, 103–20; 1990a; Burgess 1974, 209–11; Fitzpatrick 1984, 182–6; Alcock 1972, 163; Downey, King & Soffe 1980, 289–304; Leech 1986; Olmsted 1979; Allen 1980, 76, 92; Duval 1977, 136–7; Pobé & Roubier 1961, no. 45; Brewster 1976, 113; Fairless 1984, 224–42; Thevenot 1955; Charlton & Mitcheson 1983, 143–53; Mac Cana 1983, 86ff.

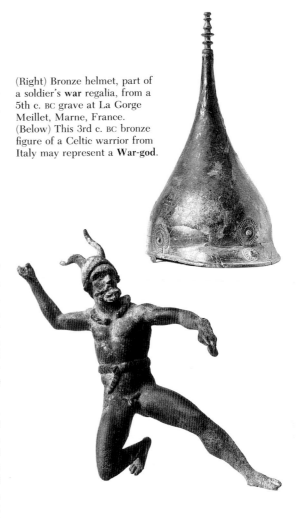

(Right) Bronze helmet, part of a soldier's **war** regalia, from a 5th c. BC grave at La Gorge Meillet, Marne, France. (Below) This 3rd c. BC bronze figure of a Celtic warrior from Italy may represent a **War-god**.

water held a fascination for the Celtic peoples. It was correctly perceived as essential to life and fertility, but capable of destroying as well as creating. The properties of spontaneous movement seen in rivers, springs and the sea must have given rise to the belief in the supernatural power of water. In addition, water has the ability to reflect light and appears to capture the sun on its surface. For the Celts, water may have signified a link with the underworld. Certainly, this seems to have been true of wells and springs, where water was seen to have emanated from deep within the earth. From the middle Bronze Age and right through the Celtic period in Europe, offerings of weapons, prestige goods, cauldrons, jewellery, coins, human and

Three nymphs or **Water**-goddesses, from the Roman fort of High Rochester, Northumberland.

animal sacrifices were cast into water as deliberate acts of veneration and ritual.

During the late pre-Roman and Romano-Celtic period, great healing shrines grew up around natural springs, which were sometimes hot and contained medicinal minerals, but were often simply sources of fresh, clear water (see SPRING, HEALING). Therapeutic spring sanctuaries, such as BATH in Britain and FONTES SEQUANAE in Gaul, were visited by pilgrims for hundreds of years. Many Celtic water-gods were worshipped, some local, like SEQUANA at *Fontes Sequanae*, some more generally venerated, like APOLLO GRANNUS. *See also* BOG; LAKE; NEHALENNIA; NEPTUNE; POOL; RIVER; SNAKE; WALBROOK; WELL.

□ Green 1986, 138–50; Coles & Harding 1979, 367–8; Fitzpatrick 1984, 180–2; Cunliffe 1975, 89–108.

weapon *see* GOIBHNIU; MODEL TOOL/WEAPON; RITUAL DAMAGE; WAR-GOD

well Two aspects of wells caused them to be endowed with sanctity: one involves underground forces, whereby wells were perceived as a means of communicating with the underworld, as a link between the upper and lower worlds. The second concerns WATER symbolism. Thus, wells represent similar symbolism to that of pits but with the additional dimension of water.

Most wells associated with ritual activity belong to the late pre-Roman Iron Age or Romano-Celtic period. It must be stressed that it is very difficult to distinguish between a ritual PIT and a dry well. But sometimes the evidence points to a specific religious activity associated with wells. On occasions, cult objects were deposited in wells: this occurred at Montbuoy near Orléans, where a well contained an Iron Age wooden figurine. The well at Kelvedon (Essex), possibly also of pre-Roman date, contained a ritual deposit of a chalk figurine.

The Romano-Celtic goddess COVENTINA had a shrine centred on a well at Carrawburgh into which coins, jewellery and cult objects were cast. One of the wells at Caerwent, near the temple, contained a small stone image of a Mother-goddess; in another five dogs had been interred (see SACRIFICE, ANIMAL). The 200 foot well associated with a round shrine at Muntham Court (Sussex) contained large numbers of dogs. A well at the Romano-British site at Goadby (Leics) was found to contain the bodies of two people buried head-down and covered with stones (see SACRIFICE, HUMAN). A cult well which exhibits signs of very deliberate ritual was that associated with a Romano-Celtic temple at Jordan Hill, Weymouth: at the base of the shaft were a stone cist, pots and ironwork; above were ashes, charcoal and sixteen pairs of tiles, each containing a skeleton of a crow and a coin. The layers of tiles were interrupted half way up the well by a cist deposit identical to that at the bottom. Underworld symbolism is suggested here by the presence of black carrion birds.

Wells are associated with the mythological traditions of Wales and Ireland. Insular stories link wells with hazel trees, sacred salmon and the underworld. In a legend of the Irish hero Finn, he acquires wisdom from an Otherworld well. Wells were still regarded as holy in Christian times and, indeed, were foci in such churches as St Mungo's Cathedral, Glasgow, and Exeter Cathedral. Human heads were traditionally associated with wells in Ireland: one story in the *Dinnshenchas* records the decapitation of one Gam, whose head was thrown into a well. The placing of heads in wells affected the water (for good or evil). In Christian times, the heads of saints were linked with wells: one such was St Melor of Cornwall and Brittany who had a holy healing well which depended for its power on the saint's severed head. The Irish St Brigit had many wells named after her. In Welsh tradition, snakes were associated with sacred wells: Giraldus Cambrensis speaks of a Pembrokeshire well whose golden treasure was guarded by a serpent.

□ Piggott 1968, 85; Goodburn 1979, 311; Allason-Jones & McKay 1985; Brewer 1986, no. 14, pl. 6; Green 1976, 183, 220; 1986, 153–7; Ross 1967a, 19–33, 107–9, 361; 1968, 255–85; Jones 1954, 134; O'Rahilly 1946, 318ff.

Welwyn The group of rich late Iron Age cremation burials from this area of southeastern England have been termed 'Welwyn' type graves. They are distinctive in that they are sumptuously furnished, often containing drinking vessels and amphorae (wine jars) imported from Gaul or Italy. Their importance here lies in the evidence they provide for the Otherworld Banquet or FEAST. Apart from wine, the tombs were furnished with

joints of pork and other food. The graves were
sunk into the ground in pits and contained
mortuary chambers. In one tomb, at Welwyn
itself, drinking equipment and the presence
of twin firedogs (for spit-roasting or for containing fires) suggest the provision of a feast
not simply for the dead chief but also for a
guest. In a grave at Welwyn Garden City, a
young man was committed to the earth clad
in a bearskin and placed in a grave PIT
together with five wine jars, Italian silver and
bronze vessels and a set of glass gaming-
pieces. This individual expected both to drink
and to be entertained in the afterlife.
□ Green 1986, 129; Collis 1984, 163–72;
Megaw 1970, 141; Dyer 1990, 155–7, pl. 58.

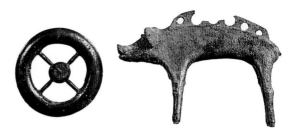

Miniature **wheel** and boar, found in a field at
Hounslow, outside London, 1st c. BC.

wheel/Wheel-god From about 1500 BC, the
symbol of the spoked wheel was a religious
motif in non-Mediterranean Europe. During
the pre-Roman Iron Age and the Romano-
Celtic period, the wheel was specifically
adopted as a symbol of the SUN, and became
associated with images of solar divinities. The
wheel bears a physical resemblance to the
radiate sun and embodies also the element
of movement, reflecting the sun's journey
across the sky.

Part of the hoard of religious bronzes, including a
solar **wheel**, from Felmingham Hall, Norfolk.

In the Celtic Iron Age, people buried
bronze model wheels with the dead, perhaps
to illuminate the dark places of the underworld. This occurred, for instance, at the
fortified town of the Dürrnberg near Hallein
in Austria. Devotees cast miniature wheel
images (*see* MODEL TOOL/WEAPON) into such
rivers as the Seine and Oise, to propitiate the
supernatural powers. Celtic shrines, such as
that at Alesia in Burgundy, which contain
numerous wheel models, may have been
dedicated to the Sun-god. Warriors wore solar
amulets as protection in battle: a warrior
image at Fox Amphoux in southern Gaul
wears a pectoral wheel pendant; and on the
arch at Orange, Celtic helmets are carved
with wheel-shaped talismans. Celtic coins
depict horses with wheel-shaped solar signs
above them. One of the plates of the Gundestrup Cauldron depicts a god with a wheel.

The solar nature of the Celtic wheel motif
is demonstrated above all in the Romano-
Celtic period. In Gaul, the Rhineland and
Britain, there is evidence that an indigenous
solar god, whose symbol was the spoked
wheel, was identified with the Roman SKY-
GOD Jupiter. Images of this deity show a
Jupiter-like being with his thunderbolt and a

Clay mould
depicting the Celtic
Wheel-god, from
the Roman military
supply base at
Corbridge,
Northumberland.

wheel: a bronze figurine at Le Châtelet (Haute-Marne) depicts a naked, bearded god with wheel, thunderbolt and S-shaped lightning flashes (see S-SYMBOL; THUNDER). A mace at Willingham Fen (Cambs) portrays a god with his wheel and thunderbolt. A statuette at Landouzy-la-Ville (Aisne) shows a god with a wheel and, beneath, a dedication to JUPITER. In North Britain, at Castlesteads and Maryport, and in the Rhineland, military altars dedicated to Jupiter were sometimes carved with the solar symbol. In civilian Provence, especially in the lower Rhône Valley, altars with or without dedications to Jupiter were carved with wheel symbols. Further west, in the Pyrenees (as at Le-Mont-Saçon), small, crudely made altars were decorated with wheels and swastikas (see SWASTIKA). Some of the JUPITER-GIANT COLUMN sculptures depicting the Sky-god as a horseman show him with a wheel as a shield. Examples include groups at Butterstadt (Germany) and Meaux (Seine-et-Marne). The carving of the sun motif on tombstones in Alsace reflects the continued association between the solar force and the underworld.

Model wheels continued to be dedicated to the Sun-god in the Romano-Celtic period: a hoard at Felmingham Hall (Norfolk) contained a number of religious bronzes including a head of the Sky-god and a twelve-spoked wheel model. At Plessis-Barbuise (Aube), a lead miniature wheel encases an image of the Sky-god with his sceptre. Wheel signs were scratched on or applied to pottery and clay tiles, as apotropaic symbols: a group of the latter has been found at the Roman legionary fortress at Caerleon (Gwent). Ritual headdresses at the WANBOROUGH temple in Surrey are decorated with wheels, perhaps the property of priests of the sun-cult. At Wavendon Gate (Bucks), a wooden wheel may have been a ceremonial object related to solar ritual. See also CROSS; FORTUNA; ROSETTE; SNAKE, RAM-HORNED.

□ Green 1984a; 1984c, 251–8; 1986, 39–61; 1991a.

Willingham Fen (Cambs) is the findspot of a hoard of Romano-Celtic religious bronzes which had been hidden in a wooden box and deliberately buried, presumably for safekeeping at a time of trouble. The cache may have been the property of priests and could have originally formed part of the temple furniture of a SHRINE. There is some recently discovered evidence for such a sanctuary in the peat fens 2.5 miles from where the hoard was found, a site which was apparently sacred ground as early as the Bronze Age.

In the hoard were a number of religious pieces, including figurines of a horseman, an owl, a raven, a bull's head, small human heads and a bust of Mars or Minerva. Ritual regalia is represented by 'pole tips' which may have been *sistra* or ceremonial rattles and part of an elaborate bronze SCEPTRE.

It is the sceptre or mace which is the most significant item in the Willingham hoard: it displays an iconography far more complex than is generally present on British cult objects. The imagery is of a young, naked god bearing a thunderbolt or club, accompanied by an eagle perched above a wheel, a dolphin and the head of a triple-horned bull. The god rests his foot on the head of a dolorous-looking individual who is crushed into the earth. So the sceptre depicts the symbolism of the Celtic solar-sky god, evidenced particularly by the emblems of solar wheel and eagle. He shows his dominion over the earth and underworld by his action in trampling the head of his chthonic companion. This imagery is identical in content to such iconography as occurs in Gaul, where small pipe-clay figurines of the Sky-god rest heavy hands on the heads of small snake-legged creatures. This in turn relates directly to the imagery of the JUPITER-GIANT COLUMNS, where the mounted Sky-god tramples the chthonic giant beneath his horse's hooves. On the Willingham sceptre, the presence of the dolphin and the three-horned bull represent the specific aspects of the Sky-god cult. The dolphin probably reflects death and the subsequent sea journey of the human soul to the Otherworld; this is what the creature frequently symbolizes in Classical funerary iconography. The triple-horned bull is probably a combined celestial and fertility motif: bulls were traditionally associated with the Graeco-Roman Sky-god; the presence of the triple-horned version adds a Celtic dimension to the depiction and may also reflect the fertility role of the celestial god, by the stressing of the horns. In addition, there is the deliberate presence of the potent symbol of three.

The sceptre or mace from Willingham Fen is a powerful piece of religious iconography and must have been a treasured and important item of cult regalia, perhaps carried

in processions at ceremonies in honour of the
Celtic Sun-god.
☐ Green 1976, 210; 1984a, 350, no. C6, pl.
LXXXI; 1986, 53–4, fig. 21; 1989, 129; Alföldi
1949, 19ff.

wine Many Celtic gods and goddesses, whose
images appear in Gaul and Britain, possess
attributes which are indicative of their
involvement with wine and the grape harvest.
These deities occur especially in the great
wine-growing regions of Burgundy and the
lower Rhône Valley. The HAMMER-GOD's imagery frequently includes barrels (*see* BARREL),
amphorae, large jars or wine goblets: at
Cussy-le-Châtel, he appears definitely the
worse for wine, with his foot on a wine barrel;
the Hammer-god and his consort at Alesia
have three wine barrels; at Vertault, a divine
couple have grapes and what may be a
vinegrower's billhook. One of the Hammer-
god's most frequent attributes is a small pot
or goblet. Many goddesses, too, are associated
with wine: a female deity at Entrains
(Nièvre) has the combined symbols of bread
and wine; this is repeated on a representation
of a male divinity at St-Aubin-des-Chaumes
in Burgundy. Bread and wine symbolism
occurs together with the triple Mothers at
London and in Scotland, where the goddesses
hold loaves and grapes. Rosmerta is associated with a vat in Britain, at Bath and
Gloucester; and similar images are recorded
at Carlisle and Corbridge.

Wine, especially red wine, may symbolize
not only plenty and the success of the grape
yield, but also blood, death and perhaps
resurrection (*see* REBIRTH). *See also* WELWYN.
☐ Thevenot 1953, 293–304; 1968, 133–42;
Green 1989, *passim*; Webster 1986b, 57–64;
Merrifield 1983, 167–70; Keppie & Arnold
1984, no. 61, pl. 19; Espérandieu, nos 2269,
3384; Musée Archéologique de Dijon 1973,
no. 117, pl. XLVIII.

witchcraft In early modern parlance, witchcraft is a term used to describe the control of
supernatural forces by means of black or
white magic. Malevolent sorcery or witchcraft was particularly prevalent, at any rate
in Britain, from the 15th to the 17th c. But
sorcery probably flourished in pre-Roman
and Romano-Celtic Europe: witchcraft is not
directly concerned with the gods but with the
powers of the occult. Magic was essentially
destructive, and steps were certainly taken

Early 4th c. BC bronze
wine flagon from Basse
Yutz, Lorraine.

Woodcut representing witches and **witchcraft**,
from Molitor's late 15th c. *Tractatus von den
bösen Weibern.*

to guard against it in the Roman world. Magic, witchcraft and sorcery must be regarded as a kind of sub-system of beliefs which existed below the stratum of religion and the perception of the gods.

Evidence of ancient witchcraft, by its very nature, does not often survive. One possible attestation of its presence exists in late Roman Britain, in Dorset, where a number of elderly women were buried in the later 3rd and 4th c. AD, decapitated and with the lower jaw removed. Each burial was accompanied by a spindle-whorl. Another example of such practice is at Kimmeridge, where two females were interred together. The rite of DECAPIT-ATION and, more significantly, the removal of the lower mandible may indicate the need to ensure that these ladies stayed dead and could no longer chant spells or incantations.

There is abundant evidence for magic and the casting of spells in the literature of Ireland and Wales. Many superhuman beings, for instance, have the power to metamorphose themselves and others by means of magic (see METAMORPHOSIS). Witchcraft itself is more difficult to distinguish in the context of the literature.

□ Merrifield 1987, 159–83; Henig 1984, 165–6; Green 1986, 131.

Xulsigiae Divinities called by the curious name of the Xulsigiae were invoked at Trier; they were possibly a triad of local Mother-goddesses associated with a sacred spring site. They were worshipped in a small chapel linked with one of the precincts dedicated to the great Treveran healing-god MARS LENUS. Their name may be related etymologically with the SULEVIAE, another triad of Mothers associated with the spring cult of Sulis at Bath and who occur elsewhere in Britain, at Cirencester, as well as on the continent of Europe.

At the Trier shrine to the Xulsigiae was found a clay GENIUS CUCULLATUS: these hooded spirits were frequently found associated with the Mothers and were probably themselves fertility gods.

□ Wightman 1970, 213ff; Green 1986, 84.

Bibliography

Abbreviations in textual references

C.I.L., *Corpus Inscriptionum Latinarum*, 1863–1986, vols I–XVII, Berlin

Espérandieu, Espérandieu, E., 1907–66, *Recueil général des bas-reliefs de la Gaule romaine et pré-romaine*, Paris; *Germ.* = *Recueil général des bas-reliefs, statues et bustes de la Germanie romaine*, 1931, Paris and Brussels

R.I.B., Collingwood, R.G. and Wright, R.P., 1965, *The Roman Inscriptions of Britain*, Oxford

Aartsen, J. van, 1971, *Deae Nehalenniae*, Middelburg, Rijksmuseum van Oudheden

Adkins, L. and Adkins, R., 1985, 'Neolithic axes from Roman sites in Britain', *Oxford Journal of Archaeology*, 4, no. 1, 69–75

Aebischer, P., 1930, 'La divinité aquatique Telo et l'hydronomie de la Gaule', *Revue celtique*, 47, 427–41

Aebischer, P., 1934, 'Témoignages du culte de l'Apollon gaulois dans l'Helvétie romaine', *Revue celtique*, 51, 34–45

Alcock, L., 1971, *Arthur's Britain*, Harmondsworth

Alcock, L., 1972, '*By South Cadbury, is that Camelot...*' *Excavations at Cadbury Castle 1966–70*, London

Alföldi, A., 1949, 'The Bronze Mace from Willingham Fen, Cambridgeshire', *Journal of Roman Studies*, 39, 19ff.

Alföldy, G., 1974, *Noricum*, London

Alfs, J., 1940, 'A Gallo-Roman temple near Bretten (Baden)', *Germania*, 24, 128–40

Allason-Jones, L., 1989, *Women in Roman Britain*, London, British Museum

Allason-Jones, L. and McKay, B., 1985, *Coventina's Well*, Chesters, Northumb., Chesters Museum

Allen, D.F., 1976, 'Some contrasts in Gaulish and British coins', in P.-M. Duval and C.F.C. Hawkes (eds), *Celtic Art in Ancient Europe: Five Protohistoric Centuries*, London, New York and San Francisco, Seminar Press, 265–82

Allen, D.F., 1980, *The Coins of the Ancient Celts*, Edinburgh

Ambrose, T. and Henig, M., 1980, 'A new Roman rider-relief from Stragglethorpe, Lincolnshire', *Britannia*, 11, 135–8

Anati, E., 1965, *Camonica Valley*, London

Anon., 1889, 'Le dieu irlandais Lug et le thème gaulois Lugu-', *Revue celtique*, 10, 238–43

Anon., 1978, 'The Cambridge Shrine', *Current Archaeology*, no. 61, 57–60

Anon., 1980, *Die Kelten in Mitteleuropa*, Salzburg, Keltenmuseum Hallein

Arsdell, R.D. van, 1989, *Celtic Coinage of Britain*, London, Spink

Ashbee, P., 1963, 'The Wilsford Shaft', *Antiquity*, 37, 116–20

Ashe, G., 1968, *The Quest for Arthur's Britain*, London

Ashe, G., 1990, *The Mythology of the British Isles*, London

Autun, 1985, *Autun Augustodunum, capitale des Éduens. Guide de l'exposition*, Autun

Bailey, J.P., 1915, 'Catalogue of Roman inscribed and sculptured stones ... at Maryport, and preserved at Netherhall', *Transactions of the Cumberland and Westmorland Antiquarian and Archaeological Society*, 15, 135–72

Barnard, S., 1985, 'The *Matres* of Roman Britain', *Archaeological Journal*, 142, 237–43

Barruol, G., 1963, 'Mars Nabelcus et Mars Albiorix', *Ogam*, 15, 345–68

Baswell, C. and Sharpe, W. (eds), 1988, *The Passing of Arthur: New Essays in Arthurian Tradition*, New York and London

Bauchhenss, G., 1976, *Jupitergigantensäulen*, Stuttgart, Württembergisches Landesmuseums

Bauchhenss, G. and Nölke, P., 1981, *Die Iupitersäulen in den germanischen Provinzen*, Cologne and Bonn

Baudiš, J., 1914, 'Cu-Roi and Cúchulinn', *Ériu*, 7, 200–9

Baudiš, J., 1921–3, 'On Tochmarc Emere', *Ériu*, 9, 98–108

Beard, M. and North, J., 1990, *Pagan Priests: Religion and Power in the Ancient World*, London, Duckworth

Bémont, C., 1960–1, 'Ro-Smerta', *Etudes celtiques*, 9, 29–43

Bémont, C., 1969, 'A propos d'un nouveau monument de Rosmerta', *Gallia*, 27, 23–44

Bémont, C., 1981, 'Observations sur quelques divinités gallo-romaines: les rapports entre la Bretagne et le Continent', *Etudes celtiques*, 18, 65–88

Bémont, C., 1984, *L'art celtique en Gaule 1983–1984*, Paris

Benoit, F., 1953, 'L'Ogmios de Lucien, la "tête coupée" et le cycle mythologique irlandais et gallois', *Ogam*, 5, 33–43

Benoit, F., 1955, *L'art primitif Méditerranéen dans la Vallée du Rhône*, Aix-en-Provence

Benoit, F., 1981, *Entremont*, Paris

Bergin, O. and Best, R.I., 1938, 'Tochmarc Étaíne', *Ériu*, 12, 137–96

Bergquist, A. and Taylor, T., 1987, 'The origin of the Gundestrup Cauldron', *Antiquity*, 61, 10–24

Berresford Ellis, P., 1987, *A Dictionary of Irish Mythology*, London

Bertrand, A., 1897, *La religion des Gaulois*, Paris

Best, R.I., 1905, 'The tragic death of Cúrói mac Dári', *Ériu*, 2, 18–35

Best, R.I., 1911, 'Cuchulainn's shield', *Ériu*, 5, 72

Bhreathnach, M., 1982, 'The Sovereignty Goddess as Goddess of Death', *Zeitschrift für celtische Philologie*, 39, 243–60

Binchy, D.A., 1958, 'The Fair of Tailtu and the Feast of Tara', *Ériu*, 18, 113–38

Birley, E., 1932, 'History of Roman Brougham', *Transactions of the Cumberland and Westmorland Antiquarian and Archaeological Society*, 32, 124–39

Birley, R., 1973, 'Vindolanda – Chesterholm 1969–1972', *Archaeologia Aeliana* (5th series), 1, 111–23

Birley, R., 1977, *Vindolanda*, London

Boardman, J., 1973, *Greek Art*, London

Bober, J.J., 1951, 'Cernunnos: origin and transformation of a Celtic divinity', *American Journal of Archaeology*, 55, 13–51

Boon, G.C., 1976, 'The Shrine of the Head, Caerwent', in G.C. Boon and J.M. Lewis (eds), *Welsh Antiquity*, Cardiff, National Museum of Wales, 163–75

Boon, G.C., 1982, 'A coin with the head of the Cernunnos', *Seeby Coin and Medal Bulletin*, no. 769, 276–82

Boucher, S., 1976, *Recherches sur les bronzes figurés de Gaule pré-romaine et romaine*, Paris and Rome

Bray, D.A., 1987, 'The image of Saint Brigit in the early Irish church', *Etudes celtiques*, 24, 209–15

Brewer, R.J., 1986, *Corpus Signorum Imperii Romani. Great Britain*, vol. 1, fasc. 5, *Wales*, London and Oxford

Brewster, T.C.M., 1976, 'Garton Slack', *Current Archaeology*, 5, no. 51, 104–16

British Museum, 1964, *Guide to the Antiquities of Roman Britain*, London

Brogan, O., 1973, 'The coming of Rome and the establishment of Roman Gaul', in S. Piggott, G. Daniel and C. McBurney (eds),

France before the Romans, London, 192–219

Bromwich, R., 1961, *Trioedd Ynys Prydein: The Welsh Triads*, Cardiff

Brunaux, J.L., 1986, *Les Gaulois; sanctuaires et rites*, Paris

Burgess, C., 1974, 'The Bronze Age', in C. Renfrew (ed), *British Prehistory: a New Outline*, London, 165–232

Burgess, C., 1980, 'The Bronze Age in Wales', in J. Taylor (ed), *Culture and Environment in Prehistoric Wales*, Oxford, British Archaeological Reports (British Series), no. 76, 243–86

Campbell, J.F., 1870–2, 'Fionn's enchantment', *Revue celtique*, 1, 193–202

Carey, J., 1984, 'Nodons in Britain and Ireland', *Zeitschrift für celtische Philologie*, 40, 1–22

Cavendish, R., 1978, *King Arthur and the Grail*, London

Chabouillet, A., 1880–1, 'Notice sur des inscriptions et des antiquités provenant de Bourbonne-les-Bains', *Revue archéologique*, 15ff.

Champion, T.C., et al., 1984, *Prehistoric Europe*, London, Academic Press

Charlton, D.B. and Mitcheson, M.M., 1983, 'Yardhope, a shrine to Cocidius?', *Britannia*, 14, 143–53

Charrière, G., 1966, 'Le taureau aux trois grues et le bestiaire du héros celtique', *Revue d'histoire des religions*, 69, 155ff

Clébert, J.-P., 1970, *Provence antique*, vol. 2, *L'époque gallo-romaine*, Paris

Coles, B. and J., 1989, *People of the Wetlands: Bogs, Bodies and Lake Dwellers*, London

Coles, J.M. and Harding, A.F., 1979, *The Bronze Age in Europe*, London

Collingwood, R.G., 1931, 'Mars Rigisamus', *Somerset Archaeology and Natural History Society*, 77, 112–14

Collingwood, R.G. and Wright, R.P., 1965, *The Roman Inscriptions of Britain*, vol. I: *Inscriptions on Stone*, Oxford

Collis, J., 1975, *Defended Sites of the Late La Tène*, Oxford, British Archaeological Reports (Supplementary Series), no. 2

Collis, J., 1984, *The European Iron Age*, London

Colombet, A. and Lebel, P., 1953, 'Mythologie gallo-romaine', *Revue archéologique de l'Est et du Centre-Est*, 4, no. 2, 108–30

Cook, A.B., 1925, *Zeus: A Study in Ancient Religion*, vol. II, Cambridge

Cormier, R., 1976–8, 'Remarks on the Tale of Deirdriu and Noisiu and the Tristan Legend', *Etudes celtiques*, 15, 303–15

Courcelle-Seneuil, J.L., 1910, *Les dieux gaulois d'après les monuments figurés*, Paris

Čremošnik, I., 1959, 'Totenmatildarstellungen auf römischen Denkmälern in Jugoslawien', *Jahrshefte des Österreichischen Archäologischen Instituts*, 44, 207ff

Cunliffe, B.W., 1969, *Roman Bath*, Oxford, Society of Antiquaries of London

Cunliffe, B.W., 1974, *Iron Age Communities in Britain*, London

Cunliffe, B.W., 1975, *Rome and the Barbarians*, London

Cunliffe, B.W., 1979, *The Celtic World*, London

Cunliffe, B.W., 1983, *Danebury: Anatomy of an Iron Age Hillfort*, London

Cunliffe, B.W. and Davenport, P., 1985, *The Temple of Sulis Minerva at Bath*, vol. I: *The Site*, Oxford University Committee for Archaeology, Monograph no. 7

Cunliffe, B.W. and Fulford, M.G., 1982, *Corpus Signorum Imperii Romani. Great Britain*, vol. I. fasc. 2, *Bath and the Rest of Wessex*, London and Oxford

Dayet, M., 1963, 'Le Borvo Hercule d'Aix-les-Bains', *Revue archéologique*, 167–78

Déchelette, J., 1910, *L'âge du bronze; Manuel d'archéologie II, Archéologie celtique ou protohistorique, pt. 2*, Paris

Dehn, W., 1941, 'Ein Quelheiligtum des Apollo und der Sirona bei Hochscheid', *Germania*, 25, 104ff

Delaney, F., 1989, *Legends of the Celts*, London

Dent, J., 1985, 'Three Cart Burials from Wetwang, Yorkshire', *Antiquity*, 59, 85–92

Deonna, W., 1916, 'Encore le dieu de Viège', *Revue des études anciennes*, 18, 193–202

Deonna, W., 1954, 'Trois, superlatif absolu: à propos du taureau tricornu et de Mercure triphallique', *L'antiquité classique*, 23, 403–28

Devauges, J.-B., 1974, 'Circonscription de Bourgogne', *Gallia*, 32, 434

Deyts, S., 1976, *Dijon, Musée Archéologique: sculptures gallo-romaines mythologiques et religieuses*, Paris

Deyts, S., 1983, *Les bois sculptés des Sources de la Seine*, Paris, XLIIe supplément à *Gallia*

Deyts, S., 1985, *Le sanctuaire des Sources de la Seine*, Dijon, Musée Archéologique

Dillon, M., 1933, *Táin Bó Fráich*, Dublin

Dillon, M., 1953, *Serglige Con Culainn*, Dublin

Downey, R., King, A. and Soffe, G., 1980, 'The Hayling Island Temple and religious connections across the Channel', in W. Rodwell (ed.), *Temples, Churches and Religion in Roman Britain*, Oxford, British Archaeological Reports (British Series), no. 77, 289–304

Drinkwater, J., 1983, *Roman Gaul*, London

Drioux, G., 1934, *Cultes indigènes des Lingons*, Paris and Langres

Dunn, J., 1914, *Táin Bó Cuálgne*, Dublin

Duval, P.-M., 1961, *Paris antique*, Paris

Duval, P.-M., 1976, *Les dieux de la Gaule*, Paris

Duval, P.-M., 1977, *Les celtes*, Paris

Duval, P.-M., 1987, *Monnaies gauloises et mythes celtiques*, Paris

Duval, P.-M., et al., 1962, *L'Arc d'Orange*, Paris, XVe supplément à *Gallia*

Dyer, J., 1990, *Ancient Britain*, London

Egger, R., 1932, 'Genius Cucullatus', *Wiener Praehistorische Zeitschrift*, 19, 311–23

Ellison, A., 1977, *Excavations at West Uley: 1977. The Romano-British Temple*, Bristol, CRAAGS Occasional Paper, no. 3

Espérandieu, E., 1907–66, *Recueil général des bas-reliefs de la Gaule romaine et pré-romaine*, Paris

Espérandieu, E., 1917, 'Le Dieu Cavalier du Luxeuil', *Revue archéologique*, 70, 72–86

Espérandieu, E., 1924, *Le Musée Lapidaire de Nîmes. Guide sommaire*, Nîmes

Even, A., 1953, 'Histoire du Cochon de Mac Datho', *Ogam*, 5, 7–9, 50–4

Even, A., 1956, 'Notes sur le Mercure celtique III: Le dieu celtique Lugus', *Ogam*, 8, 81–110

Fairless, K.J., 1984, 'Three religious cults from the northern frontier region', in R. Miket and C. Burgess (eds), *Between the Walls*, Edinburgh, 224–42

Farrar, R.A.H., 1953, 'A decorated bronze fragment from a Roman well near Winterbourne Kingston, Dorset', *Antiquaries Journal*, 33, 74–5

Filip, J., 1960, *Celtic Civilization and Heritage*, Prague

Fitzpatrick, A.P., 1984, 'The deposition of La Tène Iron Age metalwork in watery contexts in southern England', in B.W. Cunliffe and D. Miles (eds), *Aspects of the Iron Age in Central Southern England*, Oxford University Committee for Archaeology, Monograph no. 2, 178–90

Forrer, R., 1948, *Die Helvetischen und Helveto-Römischen Votivbeilchen der Schweiz*, Basel

Foster, J., 1977, *Bronze Boar Figurines in Iron Age and Roman Britain*, Oxford, British Archaeological Reports (British Series), no. 39

Fouet, G. and Soutou, A., 1963, 'Une cime pyrénéenne consacrée à Jupiter: Le Mont Saçon (Hautes Pyrénées)', *Gallia*, 21, 75–295

Fox, A., et al., 1948–52, 'Report on the excavations at Milber Down', *Proceedings of the Devon Archaeological Exploration Society*, 4, 27ff.

Fox, C., 1946, *A Find of the Early Iron Age from Llyn Cerrig Bach, Anglesey*, Cardiff, National Museum of Wales

France, N.E. and Gobel, B.M., 1985, *The Romano-British Temple at Harlow, Essex: A record of the excavations carried out by members of the West Essex Archaeological Group and the Harlow Antiquarian Society between 1962 and 1971*, Harlow, West Essex Archaeological Group

Frazer, J.G., 1922, *The Golden Bough*, London (abridged)

Gelling, P. and Davidson, H.E., 1969, *The Chariot of the Sun: and other Rites and Symbols of the Northern Bronze Age*, London

Gerloff, S., 1986, 'Bronze Age Class A cauldrons. Typology, origins and chronology', *Journal of the Royal Society of Antiquaries of Ireland*, 116, 84–115

Gilbert, H., 1978, 'The Felmingham Hall Hoard', *Bulletin of the Board of Celtic Studies*, 28, part 1, 159–87

Gimbutas, M., 1965, *Bronze Age Cultures in Central and Eastern Europe*, The Hague

Glob, P.V., 1969, *The Bog People*, London

Glob, P.V., 1974, *The Mound People*, London

Glück, W., 1965, *Deities and Dolphins*, New York

Gombrich, E.H., 1968, *Art and Illusion*, London

Goodburn, R., 1972, *The Roman Villa, Chedworth*, London, National Trust

Goodburn, R., 1976, 'Roman Britain in 1975', *Britannia*, 7, 291–377

Goodburn, R., 1978, 'Roman Britain in 1977', *Britannia*, 9, 404–72

Goodburn, R., 1979, 'Roman Britain in 1978', *Britannia*, 10, 267–338

Goodchild, R.G., 1938, 'A priest's sceptre from the Romano-Celtic temple at Farley Heath, Surrey', *Antiquaries Journal*, 18, 391ff.

Goodchild, R.G., 1947, 'The Farley Heath Sceptre binding', *Antiquaries Journal*, 27, 83ff.

Gourvest, J., 1954, 'Le culte de Belenos en Provence occidentale et en Gaule', *Ogam*, 6, 257–62

Grapinat, R., 1970, 'Les avatars d'un culte solaire', *Forum: Revue du Groupe archéologique antique*, 1, 54–6

Green, H.J.M., 1986, 'Religious Cults at Roman Godmanchester', in M. Henig and A. King (eds), *Pagan Gods and Shrines of the Roman Empire*, Oxford University Committee for Archaeology, Monograph no. 8, 29–55

Green, M.J., 1975, 'Non-ceramic model objects in south-east Britain', *Archaeological Journal*, 132, 54–70

Green, M.J., 1976, *A Corpus of Religious Material from the Civilian Areas of Roman Britain*, Oxford, British Archaeological Reports (British Series), no. 24

Green, M.J., 1978, *Small Cult-Objects from Military Areas of Roman Britain*, Oxford, British Archaeological Reports (British Series), no. 52

Green, M.J., 1981a, 'Wheel-god and ram-horned snake in Roman Gloucestershire', *Transactions of the Bristol and Gloucestershire Archaeological Society*, 99, 109–15

Green, M.J., 1981b, 'Model objects from military areas of Roman Britain', *Britannia*, 12, 253–69

Green, M.J., 1982, 'Tanarus, Taranis and the Chester Altar', *Journal of the Chester Archaeological Society*, 65, 37–44

Green, M.J., 1984a, *The Wheel as a Cult-Symbol in the Romano-Celtic World*, Brussels

Green, M.J., 1984b, 'Mother and sun in Romano-Celtic religion', *Antiquaries Journal*, 64, part 1, 25–33

Green, M.J., 1984c, 'Celtic symbolism at Roman Caerleon', *Bulletin of the Board of Celtic Studies*, 31, 251–8

Green, M.J., 1985, 'A miniature bronze axe from Tiddington', *Britannia*, 16, 238–41

Green, M.J., 1986, *The Gods of the Celts*, Gloucester and New Jersey

Green, M.J., 1989, *Symbol and Image in Celtic Religious Art*, London and New York

Green, M.J., 1990a, 'The iconography of Celtic coins', *Eleventh Oxford Symposium on Coinage and Monetary History*

Green, M.J., 1990b, 'Triplism and plurality: Intensity and symbolism in Celtic religious expression', *Sacred and Profane*, Oxford

Green, M.J., 1991a, *The Sun-Gods of Ancient Europe*, London

Green, M.J., 1991b, 'The Thistleton Roman Temple: The Finds', *English Heritage Monograph*

Green, M.J., 1991c, 'The early Celts', in G. Price (ed.), *The Celtic Connection*, Gerrards Cross, Bucks., Colin Smythe (Princess Grace of Monaco Series)

Green, M.J., et al., 1985, 'Two bronze animal figurines of probable Roman date recently found in Scotland', *Transactions of the Dumfriesshire and Galloway Natural History and Antiquarian Society*, 60, 43–50

Greenfield, E., 1963, 'The Romano-British shrines at Brigstock, Northants', *Antiquaries Journal*, 43, 228ff

Gricourt, J., 1955, 'Prolégomènes à une étude du dieu Lug. Oronyme "Soleille-Boeuf", les Cultes Solaires et le soleil patron des cordonniers', *Ogam*, 7, 63–78

Grinsell, L.V., 1958, *The Archaeology of Wessex*, London

Gros, P., 1986, 'Une hypothèse sur l'Arc d'Orange', *Gallia*, 44, fasc. 2, 192–201

Gruffydd, W.-J., 1912, 'Mabon ab Modron', *Revue celtique*, 33, 452–61

Guyonvarc'h, C.J., 1966a, 'Notes d'étymologie et de lexicographie gauloises et celtiques XXIV', *Ogam*, 18, 311–22

Guyonvarc'h, C.J., 1966b, 'Le rêve d'Oengus', *Ogam*, 18, 117–31

Gwynn, E., 1913, *The Metrical Dindschenchas*, Dublin

Hamel, A.G. van, 1933, 'Partholón', *Revue celtique*, 50, 217–37

Hamp, E.P., 1986, 'Culhwch, the Swine', *Zeitschrift für celtische Philologie*, 41, 257f.

Harbison, P., 1988, *Pre-Christian Ireland*, London

Harding, D.W., 1974, *The Iron Age in Lowland Britain*, London

Harding, D.W., 1978, *Prehistoric Europe*, London

Hassall, M.W.C. and Tomlin, R.S.O., 1979, 'Roman Britain in 1978. II Inscriptions', *Britannia*, 10, 339–56

Hassall, M.W.C. and Tomlin, R.S.O., 1980, 'Roman Britain in 1979', *Britannia*, 11, 403–17

Hatt, J.J., n.d., *Catalogue*, Strasbourg, Musée Archéologique

Hatt, J.J., 1945, *Les monuments funéraires gallo-romains du Comminges et du Couserans*, Toulouse

Hatt, J.J., 1951, '"Rota Flammis Circumsepta". A propos du symbole de la roue dans la région gauloise', *Revue archéologique de l'Est et du Centre-Est*, 2, 82–7

Hatt, J.J., 1964, *Sculptures antiques régionales Strasbourg*, Paris, Musée Archéologique de Strasbourg

Hatt, J.J., 1971, 'Les dieux gaulois en Alsace', *Revue archéologique de l'Est et du Centre-Est*, 22, 187–276

Hatt, J.J., 1984, 'De la Champagne à la Bourgogne: remarques sur l'origine et la signification du tricéphale', *Revue archéologique de l'Est et du Centre-Est*, 35, 287–99

Haverfield, F., 1892, 'The Mother-Goddesses', *Archaeologia Aeliana* (2nd series), 15, 314ff.

Haverfield, F., 1918, 'Early Northumbrian Christianity and the altars to the Di Veteres', *Archaeologia Aeliana* (3rd series), 15, 22–43

Heichelheim, F.M., 1935, 'Genii Cucullati', *Archaeologia Aeliana* (4th series), 12, 187–94

Henig, M., 1984, *Religion in Roman Britain*, London

Henig, M. and Taylor, J.W., 1984, 'A gold votive plaque', *Britannia*, 15, 246

Hennessy, W.M., 1870–2, 'The ancient Irish goddess of war', *Revue celtique*, 1, 32–55

Hodder, I. (ed.), 1982, *Symbolic and Structural Archaeology*, Cambridge

Hodson, F.R. and Rowlett, R.M., 1973, 'From 600 BC to the Roman Conquest', in S. Piggott, G. Daniel and C. McBurney (eds), *France Before the Romans*, London, 157–91

Hole, C., 1940, *English Folklore*, London

Hondius-Crone, A., 1955, *The Temple of Nehalennia at Domburg*, Amsterdam

Horn, H.G., 1987, *Die Römer in Nordrhein-Westfalen*, Stuttgart

Horne, P. and King, A., 1980, 'Romano-Celtic temples in continental Europe. A gazetteer of those with known plans', in W. Rodwell (ed.), *Temples, Churches and Religion in Roman Britain*, Oxford, British Archaeological Reports (British Series), no. 77, 369–556

Hull, V., 1930, 'The four jewels of the Tuatha Dé Danann', *Zeitschrift für celtische Philologie*, 18, 73–89

Hull, V., 1938, 'Aided Meidbe: The violent death of Medb', *Speculum*, 13, 52–61

Hull, V., 1956, 'How Conchobar gained the kingship', *Zeitschrift für celtische Philologie*, 25, 243–5

Jackson, K.H., 1953, *Language and History in Early Britain*, Edinburgh

Jackson, K.H., 1961–7, 'Some popular motifs in early Welsh tradition', *Études celtiques*, 11, 83–99

Jackson, K.H., 1964, *The Oldest Irish Tradition; A Window on the Iron Age?*, Cambridge

Jenkins, F., 1956, 'Nameless or Nehalennia', *Archaeologia Cantiana*, 70, 192–200

Jenkins, F., 1957a, 'The role of the dog in Romano-Gaulish religion', *Collection Latomus*, 16, 60–76

Jenkins, F., 1957b, 'The cult of the Dea Nutrix in Kent', *Archaeologia Cantiana*, 71, 38–46

Jenkins, F., 1978, 'Some interesting types of clay statuettes of the Roman period found in London', in J. Bird et al. (eds), *Collectanea Londinensia*, London and Middlesex Archaeological Society, 149–62

Joffroy, R., 1954, *Le trésor de Vix (Côte d'Or)*, Paris

Joffroy, R., 1979, *Musée des Antiquités Nationales Saint-Germain-en-Laye*, Paris

Johns, C.M., 1971–2, 'A Roman bronze statuette of Epona', *British Museum Quarterly*, 36, nos 1–2, 37–41

Jones, F., 1954, *The Holy Wells of Wales*, Cardiff

Jones, G. and Jones, T., 1976, *The Mabinogion*, London

Jubainville, H. d'Arbois de, 1893, 'Le Dieu Maponus près de Lyon', *Revue celtique*, 14, 152

Jubainville, H. d'Arbois de, 1907, 'Étude sur le Táin Bó Cuálnge', *Revue celtique*, 28, 17–42

Kellner, H.J., 1971, *Die Römer in Bayern*, Munich

Kent Hill, D., 1953, 'Le "Dieu au Maillet" de Vienne à la Walters Art Gallery de Baltimore', *Gallia*, 11, 205–24

Keppie, L.J.F. and Arnold, B.J., 1984, *Corpus Signorum Imperii Romani. Great Britain*, vol. 1, fasc. 4, *Scotland*, London and Oxford

Killeen, J.F., 1974, 'The debility of the Ulstermen – a suggestion', *Zeitschrift für celtische Philologie*, 33, 81–6

Kinsella, T., 1969, *The Táin*, Dublin, Dolmen Editions IX

Kirk, J.R., 1949, 'Bronzes from Woodeaton', *Oxoniensia*, 14, 32ff.

Knott, E., 1936, *Togail Bruidne Da Derga*, Dublin

Krappe, A.H., 1927, *Balor with the Evil Eye*, New York, Columbia University Press

Krappe, A.H., 1932, 'Nuadu á la main d'argent', *Revue celtique*, 49, 90–5

Kromer, K., 1959, *Das Gräberfeld von Hallstatt*, Florence

Laet, S.J. de, 1942, 'Figurines en terre cuite de l'époque romaine trouvées à Assche-Kalkoven', *L'Antiquité classique*, 10, 41–54

Laing, L.R., 1969, *Coins and Archaeology*, London

Lambert, P.-Y., 1979, 'La tablette gauloise de Chamalières', *Études celtiques*, 16, 141–69

Lambrechts, P., 1942, *Contributions à l'étude des divinités celtiques*, Bruges

Lambrechts, P., 1954, *L'Exaltation de la tête dans la pensée et dans l'art des Celtes*, Bruges

Layard, N.F., 1925, 'Bronze crowns and a bronze headdress from a Roman site at Cavenham Heath, Suffolk', *Antiquaries Journal*, 5, 258ff.

Leach, J., 1962, 'The Smith-God of Roman Britain', *Archaeologia Aeliana* (4th Series), 40, 35–47

Lebel P. and Boucher, S., 1975, *Bronzes figurés antiques, Musée Rolin*, Paris

Leber, P., 1965, 'Fund eines votiv-Altars auf der Koralpe', *Pro Austria Romana*, 15, 25f.

Leber, P., 1967, 'Ein Altar des Mars Latobius auf der Koralpe', *Carinthia*, 1, 517–20

Leech, R., 1986, 'The excavation of a Romano-Celtic temple and a later cemetery on Lamyatt Beacon, Somerset', *Britannia*, 17, 259–328

Le Gall, J., 1963, *Alésia, archéologie et histoire*, Paris

Le Gall, J., 1985, *Alésia*, Paris

Lehmacher, G., 1921, 'Tuatha Dé Danann', *Zeitschrift für celtische Philologie*, 13, 360–4

Lehmann, R.P.M., 1989, 'Death and vengeance in the Ulster Cycle', *Zeitschrift für celtische Philologie*, 43, 1–10

Lehner, H., 1918–21, 'Der Tempelbezirk der Matronae Vacallinehae bei Pesch', *Bonner Jahrbücher*, 125–6, 74ff.

Le Roux, F., 1961, 'Études sur le festiaire celtique: Samain', *Ogam*, 13, 485–506

Le Roux, F., 1963, 'Le dieu-roi Nodons-Nuada', *Celticum*, 6, 425–54

Le Roux, F., 1966, 'Le rêve d'Oengus', *Ogam*, 18, 132–50

Le Roux, F. and Guyonvarc'h, C.J., 1978, *Les druides*, Rennes

Lewis, M.J., 1966, *Temples in Roman Britain*, Cambridge

Linckenheld, E., 1927, *Les stèles funéraires en forme de maison chez les Médiomatriques et en Gaule*, Paris

Linckenheld, E., 1929, 'Sucellus et Nantosuelta', *Revue de l'histoire des religions*, 99, 40–92

Linckenheld, E., 1947, 'Le Sanctuaire de Donon', *Cahiers d'archéologie et d'histoire d'Alsace*, 38, 67–110

Linduff, K., 1979, 'Epona: a Celt among the Romans', *Collection Latomus*, 38, fasc. 4, 817–37

Lloyd, J.H., Bergin, O.J. and Schoepperle, G., 1912, 'The reproach of Diarmaid', *Revue celtique*, 33, 41–57

Loeschke, S., 1919, *Lampen aus Vindonissa*, Zürich

Loth, J., 1914, 'Le dieu Lug, la Terre Mère et les Lugoves', *Revue archéologique*, 23, 205ff.

Louibie, B., 1965, 'Statuette d'un dieu gallo-romain au bouc et au serpent cornu trouvée à Yzeures-sur-Creuse (Indre et Loire)', *Gallia*, 23, 279–84

Luttrell, C., 1974, *The Creation of the First Arthurian Romance. A Quest*, London

Lynch, F., 1970, *Prehistoric Anglesey*, Anglesey

Macalister, R.A.S., 1931, *Tara. A Pagan Sanctuary of Ancient Ireland*, London

Mac Cana, P., 1955–6, 'Aspects of the theme of king and goddess in Irish literature', *Études celtiques*, 7, 76–114; 356–413

Mac Cana, P., 1958–9, 'Aspects of the theme of king and goddess', *Études celtiques*, 8, 59–65

Mac Cana, P., 1972, 'Mongán mac Fiachna and "Immram Brain"', *Ériu*, 23, 102–42

Mac Cana, P., 1975, 'On the prehistory of Immram Brain', *Ériu*, 26, 33–52

Mac Cana, P., 1976, 'The sinless otherworld of Immram Brain', *Ériu*, 27, 95–115

Mac Cana, P., 1983, *Celtic Mythology*, London

MacDonald, J.L., 1979, 'Religion', in G. Clarke, *The Roman Cemetery at Lankhills*, Oxford, Winchester Studies 3. Pre-Roman and Roman Winchester, 404–33

MacNeill, M., 1962, *The Festival of Lughnasa*, Oxford

Magnen, R. and Thevenot, E., 1953, *Epona*, Bordeaux

Mallory, J.P., 1989, *In Search of the Indo-Europeans*, London

Manning, W.H., 1972, 'Ironwork hoards in Iron Age and Roman Britain', *Britannia*, 3, 224–50

Marache, R., 1979, *Les Romains en Bretagne*, Rennes

Maugard, G., 1959, 'Tarvos Trigaranus. Du taureau primordial et de l'arbre de vie', *Ogam*, 11, 427–33

Megaw, J.V.S., 1970, *Art of the European Iron Age*, New York

Megaw, J.V.S. and Simpson, D.D.A., 1979, *Introduction to British Prehistory*, Leicester

Megaw, R. and Megaw, J.V.S., 1986, *Early Celtic Art*, Princes Risborough

Megaw, R. and Megaw, J.V.S., 1989, *Celtic Art*, London

Merrifield, R., 1969, 'Folklore in London Archaeology Part 1. The Roman Period', *London Archaeologist*, 1, no. 3, 66–9

Merrifield, R., 1983, *London, City of the Romans*, London

Merrifield, R., 1987, *The Archaeology of Ritual and Magic*, London

Meyer, K., 1893, 'Two tales about Finn', *Revue celtique*, 14, 241–7

Meyer, K., 1897a, 'The death of Finn MacCunall', *Zeitschrift für celtische Philologie*, 1, 462–5

Meyer, K., 1987b, 'Finn and Gráinne', *Zeitschrift für celtische Philologie*, 1, 458–62

Meyer, K., 1907, 'The death of Conla', *Ériu*, 1, 112ff.

Miles, H., 1970, 'The Cosgrove Roman Villa', *Wolverton Historical Journal*, 9

Mohen, J.P., Duval, A. and Eluère, C. (eds), 1987, *Trésors des princes celtes*, Paris

Müller, E., 1876–8, 'Two Irish tales', *Revue celtique*, 3, 342–60

Musée Archéologique de Dijon, 1973, *L'Art de la Bourgogne romaine: découvertes récentes*, Dijon

Musée Archéologique de Metz, 1981, *La civilisation gallo-romaine dans la cité des Médiomatriques*, Metz

Musée Archéologique de Saintes, 1984, *Saintes à la recherche de ses dieux*, Saintes

Nash, D., 1976, ' "Reconstructing Posidonius". Celtic ethnography: some considerations', *Britannia*, 7, 111–26

Nash-Williams, V.E., 1950, *The Early Christian Monuments of Wales*, Cardiff

Nutt, A., 1906, 'Tochmarc Étaine', *Revue celtique*, 27, 325–39

Oaks, L.S., 1986, 'The goddess Epona: Concepts of sovereignty in a changing landscape', in M. Henig and A. King (eds), *Pagan Gods and Shrines of the Roman Empire*, Oxford Committee for Archaeology, Monograph no. 8, 77–84

Ó'Cúiv, B., 1954, 'Lugh Lámhfhada and the death of Balar Ua Néid', *Celtica*, 2, 64–6

O'Fáolain, E., 1954, *Irish Sagas and Folk-Tales*, Oxford

Ogilvie, R.M., 1969, *The Romans and their Gods in the Age of Augustus*, London

O'Hógáin, D., 1990, *The Encyclopaedia of Irish Folklore, Legend and Romance*, London

O'Leary, P., 1987, 'The honour of women in early Irish literature', *Ériu*, 38, 27–44

Olmsted, G.S., 1979, *The Gundestrup Cauldron*, Brussels

Olmsted, G.S., 1982, 'Morrigan's warning to Donn Cuailnge', *Études celtiques*, 19, 165–72

O'Máille, T., 1928, 'Medb Chruachna', *Zeitschrift für celtische Philologie*, 17, 129–46

O'Rahilly, T.F., 1946, *Early Irish History and Mythology*, Dublin

Ó'Riain, P., 1978, 'Traces of Lug in early Irish hagiographical tradition', *Zeitschrift für celtische Philologie*, 36, 138–55

Palmer, S., 1990, 'Uffington: White Horse Hill Project', *Archaeological News: The Quarterly Newsletter of the Oxford Archaeological Unit*, 18, no. 2, 28–32

Parfitt, K. and Green, M., 1987, 'A chalk figurine from Upper Deal, Kent', *Britannia*, 18, 295–8

Pascal, C.B., 1964, *The Cults of Cisalpine Gaul*, Brussels

Pauli, L., 1975, *Keltischer Volksglaube: Amulette und Sonderbestaltungen am Dürrnberg bei Hallein und im Eisenzeitliche Mitteleuropa*, Munich

Penn, W.S., 1960, 'Springhead: Temples III & IV', *Archaeologia Cantiana*, 74, 113ff.

Petrie, W.M.F., 1926, *The Hill Figures of England*, London

Petrikovits, H. von, 1987, 'Matronen und verwandte Gottheiten', *Ergebnisse eines Kolloquiums veranstaltet von der Göttinger Akademiekommission für die Altertumskunde Mittel- und Nordeuropas*, Cologne and Bonn

Phillips, E.J., 1976, 'A Roman figured capital at Cirencester', *Journal of the British Archaeological Association*, 129, 35–41

Phillips, E.J., 1977, *Corpus Signorum Imperii Romani. Great Britain*, Vol. 1, Fasc. 1, *Corbridge and Hadrian's Wall East of the North Tyne*, London and Oxford

Piggott, S., 1938, 'The Cerne Abbas Giant', *Antiquity*, 12, 323–31

Piggott, S., 1963, 'The Bronze Age pit at

Swanwick, Hants: A postscript', *Antiquaries Journal*, 63, 286–7

Piggott, S., 1965, *Ancient Europe*, Edinburgh

Piggott, S., 1968, *The Druids*, London

Piggott, S. and Daniel, G.E., 1951, *A Picture Book of Ancient British Art*, Cambridge

Planck, D., 1982, 'Eine neuentdeckte keltische Viereckschanze in Fellbach Schmiden, Remsmurr-Kreis', *Germania*, 60, 105–72

Planck, D., 1985, 'Der Keltenfürst von Hochdorf', *Katalog zur Ausstellung Stuttgart*, Stuttgart, 341–53

Planson, E. and Pommeret, C., 1986, *Les Bolards*, Paris

Pobé, M. and Roubier, J., 1961, *The Art of Roman Gaul*, London

Pokorny, J., 1925, 'Der Name Ériu', *Zeitschrift für celtische Philologie*, 15, 197–202

Powell, T.G.E., 1958, *The Celts*, London

Powell, T.G.E., 1966, *Prehistoric European Art*, London

Pryor, F., 1990, 'Flag Fen', *Current Archaeology*, 119, March, 386–90

Rees, A. and Rees, B., 1961, *Celtic Heritage*, London

Reinach, S., 1894, *Description raisonnée du Musée de Saint-Germain-en-Laye. Bronzes figurés de la Gaule romaine*, Paris

Reinach, S., 1917, *Catalogue illustré du Musée des Antiquités Nationales au Château de Saint-Germain-en-Laye*, I, Paris

Renfrew, C., 1987, *Archaeology and Language: The Puzzle of Indo-European Origins*, London

Reynolds, P.J., 1979, *Iron Age Farm: The Butser Experiment*, London

Rheinisches Landesmuseum Bonn, 1973, *Wir entdecken die Römer*, Bonn

Rhodes, J.F. and Toynbee, J.M.C., 1964, *Catalogue of the Romano-British Sculptures in the Gloucester City Museum*, Gloucester

Rhŷs, J., 1901, *Celtic Folklore. Welsh and Manx*, Oxford

Richmond, I.A., 1943, 'Roman legionaries at Corbridge, their supply-base, temples and religious cults', *Archaeologia Aeliana* (4th Series), 21, 127–224

Richmond, I.A., 1956, 'Two Celtic heads in stone from Corbridge, Northumberland', in D.B. Harden (ed.), *Dark Age Britain: Studies Presented to E.T. Leeds*, London, Methuen, 11–15

Richmond, I.A. et al., 1937, 'A new altar to Cocidius and "Rob of Risingham" ', *Archaeologia Aeliana* (4th Series), 14, 102–9

Richmond, I.A. and Crawford, O.G.S., 1949, 'The British Section of the Ravenna Cosmography', *Archaeologia*, 93, 1–50

Ristow, G., 1975, *Religionen und ihre Denkmäler in Köln*, Cologne

Rivet, A.L.F., 1988, *Gallia Narbonensis*, London

Roberts, B.F., 1982, 'Introduction', *Pedair Cainc y Mabinogi*, Gwasg y Dref Wen, 5–9

Roberts, B.F., 1988, 'Oral tradition and Welsh literature. A description and survey', *Oral Tradition*, 3, nos 1–2, 61–87

Rodwell, R., 1973, 'An unusual pottery bowl from Kelvedon, Essex', *Britannia*, 4, 265–7

Rodwell, W. (ed.), 1980, *Temples, Churches and Religion in Roman Britain*, Oxford, British Archaeological Reports (British Series), no. 77

Rolland, H., 1944, 'Inscriptions antiques de Glanum', *Gallia*, 3, 167–223

Rolleston, T.W., 1985, *Myths and Legends of the Celtic Race*, London

Ross, A., 1959, 'The human head in Insular pagan Celtic religion', *Proceedings of the Society of Antiquaries of Scotland*, 91, 10–43

Ross, A., 1961, 'The horned god of the Brigantes', *Archaeologia Aeliana* (4th Series), 39, 59ff.

Ross, A., 1967a, *Pagan Celtic Britain*, London

Ross, A., 1967b, 'A Celtic three-faced head from Wiltshire', *Antiquity*, 41, 53–6

Ross, A., 1968, 'Shafts, pits, wells – Sanctuaries of the Belgic Britons?', in J.M. Coles and D.D.A. Simpson (eds), *Studies in Ancient Europe*, Leicester, 255–85

Ross, A., 1986, *The Pagan Celts*, London

Ross, A. and Feacham, R., 1976, 'Ritual rubbish: the Newstead pits', in J.V.S. Megaw (ed.), *To Illustrate the Monuments*, London, 230–7

Ross, A. and Feacham, R., 1984, 'Heads baleful and benign', in R. Miket and C. Burgess (eds), *Between and Beyond the Walls*, Edinburgh, 338–52

Rouvier-Jeanlin, M., 1972, *Les figurines gallo-romaines en terre cuite au Musée des Antiquités Nationales*, XXIVe supplément à *Gallia*

Royal Commission on Historical Monuments, 1962, *Roman York*, London

Rybová, A. and Soudský, B., 1962, *Keltská Svatyně ve Středních Cechách: Sanctuaire celtique en Bohême centrale*, Prague

Salviat, F., 1979, *Glanum*, Paris

Sandars, N.K., 1957, *Bronze Age Cultures in France*, Cambridge

Santrot, J., 1986, 'Le Mercure phallique du Mas-Agenais et un dieu stylite inédit', *Gallia*, 44, fasc. 2, 203–28

Sautel, J., 1926, *Vaison dans l'Antiquité*, Avignon and Lyon

Sauter, M.R., 1976, *Switzerland*, London

Savory, H.N., 1976, *Guide Catalogue of the Early Iron Age Collections*, Cardiff,

National Museum of Wales

Savory, H.N., 1980, *Guide Catalogue of the Bronze Age Collections*, Cardiff, National Museum of Wales

Schindler, R., 1977, *Führer durch des Landesmuseum Trier*, Trier

Schwarz, K., 1962, 'Zum Stand der Ausgrabungen in der Spätkeltischen Viereckschanze von Holzhausen', *Jahresbericht Bayer. Bodendenkmalpflege*, 22–77

Shaw, F., 1934, *Aislinge Oenguso*, Dublin

Simco, A., 1984, *The Roman Period*, Bedford, Bedfordshire County Council (Survey of Bedfordshire)

Sims-Williams, P., 1990, 'Some Celtic otherworld terms', in A.T.E. Matonis and D.F. Melia (eds), *Celtic Language, Celtic Culture. A Festschrift for Eric P. Hamp*, Van Nuys, CA, 57–81

Sjoestedt, M.-L., 1936, 'Légendes épiques irlandais et monnaies gauloises; recherches sur la constitution de la légende de Cuchullin', *Études celtiques*, 1, 1–77

Sjoestedt, M.-L., 1949, *Dieux et héros des celtes*, Paris

Speidel, M., 1978, *The Religion of Juppiter Dolichenus in the Roman Army*, Leiden

Spräter, F., 1935, 'Der Brunholdistuhl bei Bad Dürkheim', *Mainz Zeitschrift*, 30, 32–9

Sprockhoff, E., 1955, 'Central European Urnfield Culture and Celtic La Tène: an outline', *Proceedings of the Prehistoric Society*, 21, 257–81

Stähelin, F., 1931, *Der Schweiz in römische Zeit*, Basle

Stead, I.M., 1979, *The Arras Culture*, York, Yorkshire Philosophical Society

Stead, I.M., 1985a, 'The Linsdorf Monster', *Antiquity*, 59, 40–2

Stead, I.M., 1985b, *Celtic Art*, London, British Museum

Stead, I.M. and Turner, R.C., 1985, 'Lindow Man', *Antiquity*, 59, 25–9

Stead, I.M., Bowke, J.B. and Brothwell, D., 1986, *Lindow Man. The Body in the Bog*, London, British Museum

Stebbins, E.B., 1929, *The Dolphin in the Literature and Art of Greece and Rome*, Menasha, WI

Sterckx, C., 1985, 'Survivances de la mythologie celtique dans quelques légendes bretonnes', *Études celtiques*, 22, 295–306

Stokes, W., 1862, *Sanas Cormaic*, Calcutta

Stokes, W., 1876–8, 'Cúchulainn's Death, abridged from the Book of Leinster', *Revue celtique*, 3, 175–85

Stokes, W., 1887, 'The Siege of Howth', *Revue celtique*, 8, 47–64

Stokes, W., 1894, 'The prose tales in the Rennes Dindshenchas', *Revue celtique*, 15, 272–336, 418–84

Stokes, W., 1895, 'The Rennes Dindshenchas', *Revue celtique*, 16, 31–83; 274

Stokes, W., 1900, 'Bruiden Da Choca', *Revue celtique*, 21, 149–65

Stokes, W., 1901, 'The destruction of Dá Derga's hostel', *Revue celtique*, 22, 9, 165, 282, 390

Stokes, W., 1908, 'The training of Cúchulainn', *Revue celtique*, 29, 109–52

Strachan, J., 1937, *An Introduction to Early Welsh*, Manchester

Surrey Archaeological Society, 1988, *Roman Temple, Wanborough*, Guildford

Szabó, M., 1971, *The Celtic Heritage in Hungary*, Budapest

Tassel Graves, E. van, 1965, 'Lugus, the commercial traveller', *Ogam*, 17, 167–71

Térouanne, P., 1960, 'Dédicaces à Mars Mullo découvertes à Allonnes (Sarthe)', *Gallia*, 18, 185–9

Thevenot, E., 1951, 'Le cheval sacré dans la Gaule de l'Est', *Revue archéologique de l'Est et du Centre-Est*, 2, 129–41

Thevenot, E., 1952, 'Un temple d'Apollon-Belenus à la source de l'Aigue à Beaune', *Revue archéologique de l'Est et du Centre-Est*, 3, 244–9

Thevenot, E., 1953, 'Deux figurations nouvelles du Dieu au Maillet accompagnie de tonneau ou amphore', *Gallia*, 11, 293–304

Thevenot, E., 1955, *Sur les traces des Mars Celtiques*, Bruges

Thevenot, E., 1968, *Divinités et sanctuaires de la Gaule*, Paris

Thill, G., 1978, *Les époques gallo-romaine et mérovingienne au Musée d'Histoire et d'Art, Luxembourg*, Luxembourg

Thurneysen, R., 1933, 'Zur Göttin Medb', *Zeitschrift für celtische Philologie*, 19, 352–3

Tierney, J.J., 1959–60, 'The Celtic ethnography of Posidonius', *Proceedings of the Royal Irish Academy*, 60, 189–275

Tomlin, R.S.O., 1985, 'Religious beliefs and practice: The evidence of inscriptions', in *The Roman Inscriptions of Britain*, paper given at Oxford Conference, April 1985

Toussaint, M., 1948, *Metz à l'époque gallo-romaine*, Metz

Toutain, J., 1920, *Les cultes päiens dans l'Empire Romaine*, Paris

Toynbee, J.M.C., 1962, *Art in Roman Britain*, London

Toynbee, J.M.C., 1964, *Art in Britain under the Romans*, Oxford

Toynbee, J.M.C., 1971, *Death and Burial in the Roman World*, London

Toynbee, J.M.C., 1978, 'A Londinium votive leaf or feather and its fellows', in J. Bird et al. (eds), *Collectanea Londinensia*, London and Middlesex Archaeological Society, 129–48

Tufi, S.R., 1983, *Corpus Signorum Imperii Romani. Great Britain*, Vol. 1, Fasc. 3, *Yorkshire*, London and Oxford

Turner, R.C., 1982, *Ivy Chimneys: an Interim Report*, Essex County Council Occasional Paper, no. 2

Vallentin, F., 1879–80, 'Les dieux de la cité des Allobroges, d'après les monuments épigraphiques', *Revue celtique*, 4, 1–36

Vanvinckenroye, W., 1975, *Tongeren Romeinse Stad*, Tongeren

Vatin, C., 1969, 'Ex-voto de bois gallo-romain à Chamalières', *Revue archéologique*, 103–14

Vendryes, J., 1924, 'Imbolc', *Revue celtique*, 41, 241–4

Vendryes, J., 1953–4, 'Manannan mac Lir', *Études celtiques*, 6, 239–54

Vesly, L. de, 1909, *Les Fana ou petits Temples gallo-romains de la région Normande*, Rouen

Vouga, A., 1923, *La Tène*, Leipzig

Vries, J. de, 1963, *La religion des Celtes*, Paris

Wagner, H., 1981, 'Origins of pagan Irish religion', *Zeitschrift für celtische Philologie*, 38, 1–28

Wait, G.A., 1985, *Ritual and Religion in Iron Age Britain*, Oxford, British Archaeological Reports (British Series), no. 149

Watson, A., 1981, 'The king, the poet and the sacred tree', *Études celtiques*, 18, 165–80

Webster, G., 1986a, *The British Celts and their Gods under Rome*, London

Webster, G., 1986b, 'What the Britons required from the gods as seen through the pairing of Roman and Celtic deities and the character of votive offerings', in M. Henig and A. King (eds), *Pagan Gods and Shrines of the Roman Empire*, Oxford University Committee for Archaeology, Monograph no. 8, 57–64

Wedlake, W.J., 1982, *The Excavation of the Shrine of Apollo at Nettleton, Wiltshire 1956–1971*, Society of Antiquaries of London

Wheeler, R.E.M., 1928, 'Romano-Celtic temple at Harlow …', *Antiquaries Journal*, 8, 300–27

Wheeler, R.E.M., 1943, *Maiden Castle, Dorset*, Society of Antiquaries of London

Wheeler, R.E.M. and Wheeler, T.V., 1932, *Report on the Excavations … in Lydney Park, Gloucestershire*, Society of Antiquaries of London

Whimster, R., 1981, *Burial Practices in Iron Age Britain*, Oxford, British Archaeological Reports (British Series), no. 90

Wightman, E.M., 1970, *Roman Trier and the Treveri*, London

Wightman, E.M., 1985, *Gallia Belgica*, London

Wild, J.-P., 1968, 'Die Frauentracht der Uber', *Germania*, 46, 67–73

Wilhelm, E., 1974, *Pierres sculptés et inscriptions de l'époque romaine*, Luxembourg, Musée d'Histoire et d'Art

Wilkes, J.J., 1969, *Dalmatia*, London

Williams, I., 1930, *Pedair Keinc y Mabinogi*, Cardiff

Wilson, D.R., 1975, 'Roman Britain in 1974', *Britannia*, 6, 220–83

Wiseman, A. and Wiseman, T.P., 1980, *The Battle for Gaul*, London

Woolner, S., 1965, 'The White Horse, Uffington', *Transactions of the Newbury and District Field Club*, 11, no. 3, 27–44

Wright, R.P. and Phillips, E.J., 1975, *Roman Inscribed and Sculptured Stones in Carlisle Museum*, Carlisle, Tullie House Museum

Wuilleumier, P., 1984, *Inscriptions latines des trois Gaules*, Paris, XVIIe supplément à *Gallia*

Zwicker, J., 1934–6, *Fontes Historiae Religionis Celticae*, Berlin

Sources of the Illustrations

References are to page numbers
a = above, b = below, c = centre, l = left,
r = right

Aerofilms Ltd 59a, Archeologický Ústav
Csav 133a. Autun, Musée Rolin 39b (photo
Miranda Green). Avignon, Musée Calvet
153b. Aylesbury, Buckinghamshire County
Museum 149a. Bartesago, Avignon 105b.
Bath, Roman Baths Museum 41a (photo Betty
Naggar), 75a (photo Bath Museums Service),
127c (photo Bath Museums Service), 143b,
161b, 199a (photo Bath City Council), 203a
(photo Betty Naggar). Beaune, Musée des
Beaux-Arts 67c (photo Miranda Green),
127a (photo Miranda Green), 139a (photo
Miranda Green). Berlin, Staatliche Museen
223c. Berne, Bibliothèque Nationale Suisse
131a; Historisches Museum (drawn by Paul
Jenkins) 35b. Bonn, Rheinisches Landesmuseum 95b, 115cl, 115cr, 131bl, 147a, 149b,
171a, 177b (photo Miranda Green). Brescia,
Museo Civico 139b. Bristol Museum and Art
Gallery 33a. British Lion Films 101a. British
Tourist Authority 135a. Budapest, Hungarian
National Museum 107b. Cambridge University Collection of Air Photographs 89b, 99b,
205b, 217b; Cambridge University Museum
of Archaeology and Anthropology 187ar.
Cambridgeshire County Council 155a. Cardiff, National Museum of Wales 53a, 53c,
135b. Carlisle Museum and Art Gallery 63a,
209a. Châtillon-sur-Seine, Musée Archéologique 155b (photo Jean Roubier), 221a. Chesters Museum of Roman Antiquities 121c
(photo Miranda Green). Peter Chèze-Brown
49b. Cirencester, Corinium Museum 73a
(photo Betty Naggar), 201b. Colchester and
Essex Museum 73b. Cologne, Römisch-Germanisches Museum 83a, 119b (photo Rheinisches Bildarchiv), 219a (photo Miranda
Green). Cim Combier, Macon 75b. Copen-
hagen, Danish National Museum 15 (drawn
by Margaret Scott), 29c, 85a, 111a, 169b,
203b, 209b, 211b. Danebury Archaeological
Trust (photo Mike Rouillard) 77a. Original
designs © Jen Delyth frontispiece, 45a, 215a.
John Dent, Humberside County Council
Archaeological Unit (photo Bill Marsden) 35a.
Dijon, Musée Archéologique 43a (photo
Miranda Green), 133c (photo Miranda Green),
189al (photo Miranda Green), 189ac (drawn by
Paul Jenkins), 189ar (drawn by Paul Jenkins),
189b (photo R. Rémy, Dijon), 193a (photo
Miranda Green), 213a (photo Miranda
Green). Dorchester, Dorset County Museum
115a (photo Miranda Green). Dublin, Com-
missioners of Public Works 17br, 109c, 173a
183a, 191a; National Museum of Ireland
47a, 61b, 173a (photo Miranda Green), 205c
(photo Irish Tourist Board). Edinburgh,
National Museums of Scotland 39a, 57b;
Edinburgh University, Department of Prehistoric Archaeology 175b. Epinal Museum 193b
(drawn by Paul Jenkins). Drawn by Rhiannon
S. Evans 31a, 69a. Gloucester City Museums
103b (photo Betty Naggar), 167a (photo Betty
Naggar), 181a. Graz, Landesmuseum Joan-
neum 201a. Hanover, Kestner Museum 31b.
Peter Harbison 109a. Harlow Museum 113b.
Højbjerg, Forhistorisk Museum, Moesgaard
(photo Danish National Museum, Copen-
hagen) 43b. Irish Tourist Board 65b (photo
J. Allan Cash), 71, 217a. P. Jacobsthal 131c.
Drawn by Paul Jenkins 91a. Karlsruhe,
Landesmuseum 119a (photo J.V.S. Megaw).
Leiden, Rijksmuseum van Oudheden 65a,
159b. Leningrad, Hermitage 29b. London,
British Library 185b; British Museum 17bl,
37b, 69b, 97a, 99a, 117a, 121a, 121b, 123c,
133b, 143ar, 145b (photo J.V.S. Megaw),
179a, 187al, 205a, 213b, 225a, 225c, 227a;
English Heritage 57c, 105a, 145a, 225b;
Museum of London 85b, 141b, 221b; Wor-
shipful Company of Goldsmiths 81a. Luxembourg, Musée d'Etat 93a (photo Miranda
Green). Lyon, Bibliothèque de la Ville 137a;
Musée de la Civilisation Gallo-Romaine 63b.
Mainz, Römisch-Germanisches Zentralmu-
seum 8, 117a. Manchester City Art Galleries
20. Marseille, Musée Borély 79a, 117b, 123a
(photo Miranda Green). 179b. Metz, Musée
Archéologique 159a (photo Miranda Green).
Néris-les-Bains Museum 195b (after E. Thevenot, *Divinités et sanctuaires de la Gaule*,
1968, drawn by Paul Jenkins). Newcastle-
upon-Tyne, Museum of Antiquities of the
University and Society of Antiquaries 31c
(photo University of London, Warburg Institute), 67b (photo University of London,

Warburg Institute), 127b, 223b. Newport Museum (photos National Museum of Wales, Cardiff) 153a, 165b, 219b. Nîmes, Musée Archéologique 157b (photo Miranda Green). Nuremberg, Germanisches Nationalmuseum 199b. Orléans, Musée Historique et Archéologique d'Orléanais 45b (photo Jean Roubier), 163c (photo Bulloz), 181b (photo Bulloz). Oxford, Ashmolean Museum 69c (photo Betty Naggar), 89c, 187b (photo Betty Naggar); Bodleian Library 107a, 183b. Keith Parfitt, Dover Archaeological Group (photo Ben Stocker) 171b. Paris, Cabinet des Médailles, Bibliothèque Nationale 63c, 163b (drawn by Paul Jenkins); Musée de Cluny 61a (photo Giraudon), 93b (photo Réunion des Musées Nationaux), 207b (photo Réunion des Musées Nationaux). Peterborough City Museum 123b; Fenland Archaeological Trust 101b. Prague, National Museum 157a. Private collection 83. Reims, Musée Saint-Remi 59b (photo Giraudon), 215b (photo Miranda Green). Jean Roubier 91b, 163a. Saint Germain-en-Laye, Musée des Antiquités Nationales 33b (photo Miranda Green), 49a (drawn by Paul Jenkins), 57a (photo Lauros-Giraudon), 77b (photo Miranda Green), 95a (photo Réunion des Musées Nationaux), 95c, 111b, 113a (drawn by Paul Jenkins), 129b, 137b (photo Miranda Green), 211a (photo Miranda Green), 223a. Saint-Rémy-de-Provence, Musée des Alpilles (photos Miranda Green) 53b, 67a, 191b. Sainte Reine, Musée d'Alise 141c (photo Miranda Green). Schleswig, Schleswig-Holsteinisches Landesmuseum für Vor- und Frühgeschichte 47b. Drawn by Margaret Scott 37c, 129al. Sémur-en-Auxois, Société de Science 27b. Senlis, Musée d'Art et d'Archéologie (photos Miranda Green) 103a, 103c. Sheffield Museum 41b. Shrewsbury, Rowley's House Museum 115b (photo Miranda Green). Edwin Smith 27a, 81b, 125b. Southwark and Lambeth Archaeological Excavation Committee 141a. Strasbourg, Musée Archéologique 131br. Stroud District Museum 143al, 197a. Stuttgart, Württembergisches Landesmuseum 61c (photo Landesbildstelle Württemberg), 97b, 129ar, 167b, 173b, 207a. Sunderland Museum and Art Gallery 195a. Torquay Museum (drawn by P.J. Lopeman) 89a. Vaduz, Liechtenstein Landesmuseum 125a (drawn by Paul Jenkins). Valcamonica, Centro Comuno di Studi Preistorici, Capo di Ponte 55a, 169a. Vendoeuvres, Musée de Châteauroux 151a (after E. Thevenot, Divinités et sanctuaires de la Gaule, 1968, drawn by Paul Jenkins). Vienna, Naturhistorisches Museum 37a, 51b (drawn by Paul Jenkins). Zürich, Schweizerisches Landesmuseum 17a, 55c.

After F. Benoit, Entremont (1981) 79b. Joseph Glanvill, Saduciones Triumphatus (1700) 185b. Francis Grose, Antiquities of England and Wales Volume IV (1773–87) 161c. After Lindenschmidt 167c. U. Molitor, Tractatus von den bösen Weibern (1495) 227b. Elias Schedius, De Dis Germanis (1648) 87b. William Stukeley, Itinerarium Curiosum (1725) 109b, 197b; William Stukeley, Stonehenge (1740) 151b. After E. Thevenot, Divinités et sanctuaires de la Gaule (1968) drawn by Paul Jenkins 147b, 175a.